READING ISRAEL IN ROMANS

ROMANS THROUGH HISTORY AND CULTURES
Receptions and Critical Interpretations

CRISTINA GRENHOLM AND DANIEL PATTE, SERIES EDITORS

Romans through History and Cultures includes a wealth of information regarding the receptions of Romans throughout the history of the church and today, in the "first" and the "two-thirds" world. It explores the past and present impact of Romans upon theology, and upon cultural, political, social, and ecclesial life, and gender relations.

In each volume the authors contribute to an integrated practice, "scriptural criticism," which takes into account: with contemporary biblical scholars, that different readings can be grounded in the same text by different critical methods; with church historians and practical theologians, that the believers' readings interrelate biblical text and concrete life; and with theologians, that believers read Romans as Scripture.

The cover art skillfully represents that any interpretation of a scriptural text is framed in three ways: (1) by an *analytical frame* that reflects each reader's autonomous choice of a textual dimension as most significant — see the individual studying the text; (2) by a *contextual/pragmatic frame* shaped by a certain relational network of life in society and community — see the people joining hands; and (3) by a *hermeneutical frame* inspired by a certain religious perception of life — see the bread and chalice and the face-to-face encounter.

By elucidating the threefold choices reflected in various interpretations of Romans through the centuries and present-day cultures, the volumes in the series — which emerge from a three-year SBL consultation and an ongoing SBL seminar — raise a fundamental critical question: Why did I/we choose this interpretation rather than another one?

READING ISRAEL IN ROMANS

Legitimacy and Plausibility of Divergent Interpretations

Edited by

**Cristina Grenholm
and Daniel Patte**

Trinity Press International
Harrisburg, Pennsylvania

Receptions, Critical Interpretations, and Scriptural Criticism

Cristina Grenholm and Daniel Patte

———— ◆ ————

Fruits from a Collective Interpretive Practice

The Origin of This Volume

The book series Romans through History and Cultures explores and highlights the relationship between receptions of Romans in different historical and cultural contexts and critical interpretations of this text. Instead of ignoring or dismissing each other, church historians, theologians, specialists of present-day receptions of Romans, and New Testament scholars enter into dialogue.[1]

Theologians and church historians bring to the table questions about theological issues that concern them or that they encounter in history. How are these issues dealt with in critical interpretations of Romans? And if they are not dealt with, why not? New Testament scholars respond and bring their own questions for theologians and church historians. New ways of addressing theological issues raised by Romans are envisioned. New topics are opened to critical investigation.

Soon this dialogue between two kinds of scholars becomes a three-way conversation. "Ordinary believers" are participants also. In most instances, receptions of Romans through the centuries have been interpretations by Christian believers who strove to live by the teaching of this scriptural text. So is the case today. Most contemporary receptions of Romans are interpretations by Christians who read this text as Scripture. As we consider these scriptural readings, we bring past and contemporary believers to the table, entering into dialogue with them. In the process, we, the coeditors of this volume and several of our colleagues, find that our own scriptural readings as Christians cannot be separated from our scholarly endeavors and need to be made explicit — of course, we are also ordinary believers.

Contributions of This Collective Interpretive Practice and Questions It Raises

Scriptural readings, whether by Augustine, by Celia Enriquez, or by Günter Wasserberg[2] or any other of the Christian contributors to this volume, raise the very question that feminists and other advocacy scholars insist theologians and biblical scholars must address: How does a given interpretation affect believers and people around them in daily life? In this volume we ask, How does each given interpretation affect the way we Christian believers relate to Jewish people? How do we "read Israel in Romans"? After Auschwitz, these questions cannot but weigh heavily on our interpretive practice.

Christian believers identify a great variety of teachings of Romans as the "Word of God" they should live by. How was this choice made? In each instance, what led believers to the conclusion that this is the teaching for them? What is the role of pragmatic and contextual factors in such choices? What is the role of believers' faith and experience in such choices?

By raising such issues, the multitude of believers and their diverse individual or communal scriptural readings call theologians and biblical scholars to assess their own choices of one interpretation or another as "the best." Focusing on a specific theological and/or critical issue has pragmatic implications. Interpretation of the Bible always matters. Could it be that choosing a particular focus for one's individual or communal interpretation reflects an implicit effort to address certain pragmatic concerns in a given life-context? And/or that it reflects convictions arising from a certain religious perception of life? To what extent was this theological or textual focus, chosen by an ordinary believer (or nonbeliever), hidden in the scholarship?

Naming a Collective Practice: Scriptural Criticism

Sitting around the table with the rest of us, believers call us to remember the importance in interpretation of faith, value judgments, and ethical responsibility. In turn, we academicians begin to recognize that critical biblical study is best understood as a joint endeavor among church historians, theologians, specialists of receptions, and biblical scholars.

A collective interpretive practice progressively began to develop. Respecting other scholars' approaches as we wanted them to respect ours led us to the realization that scholarly integrity in any interpretation requires integrating a plurality of approaches. Studying receptions of Romans through history and in diverse cultures helped us to recognize that each given interpretation of a scriptural text has been framed by the choice of certain textual features as most significant, by specific pragmatic concerns arising from a life-context, as well as by a hermeneutical engagement with the text about certain theological and/or ideological issues. Then, to our surprise, we, the editors of this volume, discovered that the integrated interpretive practice that emerges from the collective work of scholars of different disciplines has strong affinities with the practice that conscientious preachers strive to implement and that theological education programs call for when they are de-centered in an effort to come to grips with the needs of future pastors and priests in contemporary situations.

It is this broadened view of the task of critical biblical studies that we call *scriptural criticism*. We adopt this designation with some apprehension but also with determination. We fear that, for many, the term "scriptural criticism" will evoke a legalistic and authoritarian view of Scripture often associated with its designations as Canon and as inerrant Word of God. Without denying this view of Scripture, we, together with Burgess (1998, 1–37), deliberately resist its proponents' claim that it is the only view of Scripture.

Scriptural criticism is an integrated interpretive practice for the study of existing interpretations of biblical texts as scripture. It accounts for the fact that (1) believers trust that they can trace a religious dimension in these texts; (2) believers are powerfully affected in their concrete life-situations by the teachings of scriptural texts; and (3) at times, believers encounter divine mystery through the mediation of Scripture. This three-fold interpretive process is further mediated by authoritative traditions and church communities. In sum, for us the term "scriptural criticism" designates an interpretive practice that acknowledges that critical analytical biblical studies are part of a broader investigation that encompasses both the religious and critical dimensions of biblical interpretation.[3] Without denying the value and insightfulness of nonreligious readings, this approach is deliberately focused upon individual and communal interpretations of biblical texts by *believers,* because these interpretations have been neglected for too long by biblical studies.[4]

The Three Goals of This Overture

As coauthors of this overture, our role is threefold: (1) to help interpreters to recognize that scriptural criticism is an interpretive practice that explicates how existing modes of interpretation are interrelated; (2) to formulate procedures for this integrated interpretive practice; and (3) to provide tools for scriptural critical readings of Romans 4 and 9–11 by pastors, priests, seminarians, and their teachers.

Our first role is maieutic. Like midwives (see Plato's view of education as maieutic), we seek to bring forth the integrated interpretive practice, scriptural criticism, that, in our view, emerged after much gestation in the collective work of the Romans through History and Cultures project. This involves describing the practice we saw implemented by our colleagues in the following essays, but also, beyond them, in our collective work during the sessions at the 1997 and 1998 meetings of the Society of Biblical Literature and in preparation for future sessions.

During the first year, 1997, the dialogue between Thomas D. Parker and Robert L. Brawley comparing Karl Barth's theological interpretation with critical analytical studies, Joseph Sievers's review of the receptions of Rom. 11:29 and their pragmatic implications for Jewish-Christian relationships, as well as the spirited discussion led by Eugene A. TeSelle and Laurence L. Welborn already showed the necessarily interdisciplinary character of our project and its potentials. Through our collective effort we strove to envision the relationship among the theological, analytical, and contextual-pragmatic interpretive approaches, beyond the models we, the coauthors of this overture, proposed in our preliminary methodological responses at this session.

The second-year sessions made even more apparent that the relationship between analytical studies of Romans, theology, and receptions needed to be clarified. Günter Wasserberg's personal reception of Romans 9–11, William S. Campbell's critical analytical study of these chapters, and Mark D. Nanos's heartfelt and critical response were followed by a passionate discussion in which the title of this volume, *Reading Israel in Romans,* emerged. Dealing with receptions of Romans as we did in these papers (included in the present volume) meant that we had to account for the role both of the readers in construing the text and of the text in construing the readers' present reality.

Still another dimension came to the fore in Florinel T. Cimpean's and Revelation Enriquez Velunta's papers: the role of religious experience in biblical interpretation. These papers about contemporary receptions of Romans, respectively by Pentecostal and Orthodox Romanian communities and by Protestant Filipino communities, as well as Abraham Smith's and Robert Jewett's responses strongly underscored the role of religious experiences and perceptions of life — including communal religious experiences and perceptions — and of socio-cultural factors in receptions and in critical studies.

Studies on the receptions of Romans by Clement of Alexandria, discussed among Michael J. Brown, Laurence L. Welborn, and Kathy L. Gaca, and by Augustine, discussed among John K. Riches, Eugene TeSelle, Thomas Frank Martin, and Krister Stendahl, opened a dialogue among church historians and biblical critics that, as expected, groped once again for the relationship between the theological, analytical, and contextual-pragmatic approaches, but this time from a historical perspective. Yet, unexpectedly, the quest for the role of the interpreters' religious experiences and perceptions begun in preceding sessions reemerged in a fascinating discussion between John Riches and Krister Stendahl, who disclosed the clash of their personal faith in specific European contexts with what their respective churches taught about Romans and its message.

The very fact of discussions among all of these and many others who participated from the audience and/or who prepare future sessions shows that as a group we presuppose a relationship among our diverse approaches. Therefore, we, the coauthors of this overture, in this maieutic part of our task, seek to show how this collective practice weaves together three basic modes of interpretation through its study of receptions of Romans. This threefold collective interpretive practice is needed because the believers' receptions reflect a tripolar interpretive process. Here our goal is to provide a map of scriptural criticism that will help pastors, priests, seminarians, and their teachers to recognize that their own interpretive practice already includes most of the features of scriptural criticism.

Our second role is to contribute to the paideia, *or educational training, of pastors, priests, seminarians, and other Christian believers.* We hope to do so by helping them to discipline their own interpretations (Farley 1983, 138) through a deliberate practice of scriptural criticism. For this, they need to recognize that they have framed their interpretations in particular ways as they chose an interpretation, for instance, in preparation for preaching. Assuming responsibility for one's interpretive choices requires comparing them with several others. Thus, our second goal is to formulate procedures for such comparisons and for the assessment of the relative value of one's interpretation.

Our third role is to be facilitators. A scriptural critical interpretation of Romans requires comparing the receptions of Romans through history and cultures with its receptions in one's own context, and also with analytical studies of Romans by biblical scholars. In this volume our colleagues engage in such comparisons by presenting receptions of Romans 4 and 9–11 and comparing them with analytical studies of these chapters. Our third goal is, then, to facilitate these comparisons. For this, in the overture as well as in our individual essays and in marginal notations throughout this book, we underscore and classify different ways in which receptions of Romans are framed.

Mapping Out Scriptural Criticism

Overture to an Interpretive Practice Called Forth by Receptions of Romans

In this section we seek to elucidate the main characteristics of the integrated interpretive practice called forth by our collective study of the relationship between receptions and critical studies of Romans.

By saying that we "seek" to elucidate this interpretive practice, we, the coeditors of this volume, signal that our goal is not to offer a definitive formulation. This is an overture, a working document aimed at opening further discussions. We hope that our colleagues in the Romans through History and Cultures project will want to develop, complement, modify, or totally transform our preliminary formulation of this integrated interpretive practice, scriptural criticism. Yet, we can say that in its present form it proved to be a very helpful and fruitful heuristic tool in our respective endeavors in feminist theology (Grenholm's ongoing project)[5] and in the study of Christian Scriptures (Patte 1999).

Furthermore, by saying that we "elucidate" this interpretive practice, we want to underscore that scriptural criticism does not originate with us, the coeditors of this volume. Many people already practice it. We refer not only to our colleagues in the Romans project but also to Christian believers — including pastors and priests — who strive to be responsible when they discern and formulate the teaching of Scripture for believers today.

Our original intention was simply to develop an approach that would allow us and our scholarly colleagues to study the relationship between receptions and critical studies of Romans. We envisioned this project as a straightforward prolongation of our respective quests for a way to account for the relationship between theological and critical commentaries (Grenholm 1990; 1996, 233–80) or for the relationship between believers' scriptural readings and critical interpretations (Patte 1975, 73–112). Yet the collective work of our group progressively led us to envision a critical interpretive practice that integrates readings of the Bible as Scripture by believers and theologians.

Our Role in Formulating and Naming Scriptural Criticism

Even as we acknowledge that scriptural criticism does not originate with us, we also want to say that we are the ones who formulate what this interpretive practice entails following two criteria.[6] We looked for an interpretive practice that (1) accounts for the teaching of the text as Scripture for believers without neglecting the results of critical studies, and (2) is responsible.

The choice of this particular combination of criteria is not self-evident. As we studied receptions of biblical texts by believers and theologians, neither the theologian (Cristina Grenholm) nor the biblical critic (Daniel Patte) could afford to ignore that believers read these texts *as Scripture* on the basis of their faith and religious experience. Then, for both of us, it was all the more important to emphasize that practicing scriptural criticism must include being responsible as scholars for the rigor of the interpretation and assuming moral responsibility for the effects of the interpretation upon people (believers or not) in concrete life-situations.

We readily agreed to adopt these two criteria because they were long operative for both the theologian (Grenholm; see also Schüssler

Fiorenza 1988) and the biblical critic with ethical concerns (see Patte 1995). Furthermore, despite quite distinct points of departure and other differences, our respective theological outlooks overlap at central points.

Responsibility in Interpretation and Receptions of Romans

For both of us, responsibility in interpretation is both a scholarly and an ethical issue, because claiming a single criterion of truth is a scandalous suppression of the truth about our humanity and its limitations.[7] Well-intentioned univocal interpretations become oppressive and destructive. The feminist theologian evokes patriarchal and sexist interpretations. The post-Holocaust and postcolonial biblical critic evokes triumphalist interpretations that are often both anti-Jewish — indeed, anti-Semitic — and colonialist. Responsibility in interpretation involves keeping in mind that, whatever perspective and criterion we might adopt, our truth-claim about a text or an interpretation remains narrowly framed by one or another aspect of our human condition, and thus "we know only in part," seeing "in a mirror, dimly." It follows that in order to be responsible interpreters we must be open to other interpretations, with the expectation that they are at least as good as our own. The respectful attitude toward receptions of Romans by our colleagues exemplifies such a responsibility in interpretation. From this, we concluded that a sustained and respectful investigation of diverse receptions of Romans is a powerful heuristic way of promoting responsibility in interpretation, and a reminder that critical readings are themselves receptions.

Receptions of Romans and the Roles of the Reader-Believers

As we study receptions of Romans, we have in mind interpreters who come to the text as persons playing at least three different roles: they are members of society; they are readers; they are believers. Furthermore, we need to take into account that, in these different roles, interpreters use different criteria and make different truth-claims. Jeffner's analysis of "Criteria of Truth in Theology" (1987, 32–37)[8] is most helpful at this point.

Since, according to Jeffner, theological truth-claims always concern assertions about "what is the case in the real world," we can anticipate that the truth-claims of scriptural readings concern, among other things, assertions about actual life-contexts. In our terminology, interpreters use certain *contextual-pragmatic* criteria when they make truth-claims in their social roles in life as responsible members of a given society and culture — and, in the academic world, as practical theologians and activists. They use certain *analytical* criteria in their roles as responsible readers of biblical texts — and, in the academic world, as biblical scholars. Finally, they use certain *hermeneutical* criteria in their roles as responsible believers — and, in the academic world, as systematic theologians.

The diverse truth-claims that interpreters make in their interpretations are, of course, not easy to reconcile. Nevertheless, if a sermon on a biblical text — and by extension, a scriptural reading — does not integrate these different criteria and truth-claims, it cannot ring true for the church members as hearers, because they themselves have to play these different roles. Thus, conscientious preachers integrate these different criteria and truth-claims. And so do many believers in their receptions of Romans.

Since this essential integration cannot be done by giving primacy to one or another criterion of truth, it needs to be done on the basis of "value judgments" (as Jeffner [1987, 7] also suggests).[9] For believers and their receptions of Romans, these value judgments are based on their "religious perceptions." They do not hesitate to say that their scriptural readings reflect their religious experience and that they value (choose) them because they support their particular religious perceptions.

In sum, as receptions of Romans show, through their practice of scriptural reading, believers integrate the contextual-pragmatic, the analytical, and the hermeneutical dimensions of the interpretation by means of value judgments arising out of their religious perception.

Believers' Integrated Scriptural Reading and Academicians' Fragmented Approaches

As we examine receptions of Romans through history and cultures, most of which are scriptural readings, the question becomes, How are the contextual-pragmatic, the analytical, and the hermeneutical dimensions of the interpretive process integrated through the interpreter-believers' religious perception?

We academicians find it difficult to bring together the theological-hermeneutical, pragmatic, and analytical approaches that we use independently from each other in our research as theologians, church historians, specialists of receptions (including "practical theologians"), and biblical critics. By contrast, believers integrate all these approaches in their scriptural readings through their religious perception, and seem to do so quite spontaneously, in the same way as they strive to conform the different modes of their existence to their religious perception. Though this integration of the believers' existence is always in process — and thus is the pursuit of an ideal never truly reached — believers spontaneously give priority to their religious perception and to the experience upon which that perception rests.

As academicians, we have been taught to bracket out of our work our "religious perceptions," and thus we have a hard time envisioning it as the integrating factor for our interpretive practice. We might have less of an allergic reaction to terms such as "theology," which, of course, the theologian readily uses, or "ideology," which the post-Holocaust, post-colonial biblical critic had learned to use. Why are we more comfortable with terms like these? Apparently because they do not clearly suggest that this perception arises directly out of some kind of religious experience. But, as coauthors of this overture, we became convinced that we cannot critically assess scriptural readings as long as we do not account for the interpreter-believers' religious experience as well as our own.

Giving a Role to Religious Experience and Perception in Critical Practice

Part of our allergic reaction to giving any role in a critical interpretive practice to religious perceptions and especially to religious experiences stems from our narrow conceptions of these. In the present Western cultural and academic context, because of our secular perspective, we tend to take a monolithic view of religious experience as a remote and strange corner of the believer's individual existence. Thus we do not recognize that even for the most secularized of believers, their "religious" experience becomes the mode of existence that integrates the other modes of existence.

For the feminist theologian and the biblical critic alike, this integrating role of religious experience and religious perception became clear when, revisiting an important issue in feminist critical debates, we explored the relationship between *heteronomy,* as one basic mode of existence that corresponds to religious experience, and *autonomy* and *relationality,* the two other basic modes of existence.[10]

We quickly found that referring to "heteronomous experience" instead of "religious experience" does not dilute the religious connotation of the latter.[11] Heteronomous experiences include the religious experiences of the believers' encounter with the holy, in the mystery of whom they dare to abandon themselves. These are experiences of the *mysterium tremendum* in which they lose themselves in the Other and, in the process, give up control over their own selves and over their lives in relation with others, and thus lose control of their autonomy and of their relationality. Yet, we want to underscore that such heteronomous experiences should not be conceived of as limited to mystical or other traditional religious experiences. They also happen in the encounter with "a God who is not squeamish about disclosing the divine self in a thoroughly secular world and in the midst of ordinary daily existence, speaking to us through the noise of our hopeless routines and willing to touch us in our carnal places" (Weems 1999, 51); or in the midst of the silence and absence of God as one cries, "My God, my God, why have you forsaken me?" (Ps. 22:1); or again, in true heteronomous relationship with another whom we encounter as Other in the mystery of her or his otherness (see Lévinas 1985).

Within this broad range of possibilities ranging from traditional religious views to quite secular and skeptic ones, both the feminist theologian

and the biblical critic, as Christians living in Western cultures, acknowledged the importance of such heteronomous religious experiences.
Heteronomy is one of our modes of existence, alongside autonomy and
relationality. And for believers, such heteronomous religious experience
is very much a part of the interpretive process.

Taking the Believers' Scriptural Readings as Models

The question is, Do we want to take as a model for integrating our
interpretive practice the believers' scriptural readings and their receptions
of Romans?

In other words, do we want to allow heteronomy and religious experience to dominate our sense of autonomous identity and purpose —
including our identity as scholars with a mission? And to dominate our
relational existence with others in the web of the power games of daily
life — including our relations with our students and colleagues as we
teach and present our research? Do we want to allow heteronomy and
the religious perception it gives us to shape the analytical studies of the
text that we carry out as autonomous scholars who strive to respect
the integrity of the text and of our analytical skills and reason? Do we
want to allow heteronomy and our religious perception to shape the
way we teach and present our research to others in the relational web
of life, giving up on shaping it either on the basis of our autonomous
scholarly skills[12] or on the basis of ethical considerations concerning our
relationships with others?[13]

The biblical critic could not, at first, imagine answering any of these
questions positively, until the feminist theologian suggested it by repeatedly underscoring the importance of religious perceptions — expressed
in theological and hermeneutical categories — and by cautiously affirming heteronomy as a positive mode of existence (see Grenholm 1999b).
Could it be that what prevents us from conceiving of an integrated interpretive practice of scriptural texts is that we fail to acknowledge the
role of religious perceptions that arises out of heteronomous religious
experiences? Out of spiritual experiences? Could it be that we overlook
that experiences of heteronomy are conceptualized in views of life, which
need not be religious? That, for example, the views of the universe as a
machine or a fantastic organism or as divine creation are perceptions of
life that conceptualize heteronomous experiences?

Learning from believers throughout history and in many cultures,
we note that each reception of Romans as scriptural reading reflects
some kind of religious perception. We also note that this religious perception is an interpretation and thus a conceptualization of a religious
heteronomous experience, which in tragic situations or in secular contexts might be negative. Learning from these believers, both the feminist
theologian and the biblical critic progressively felt compelled to acknowl-

edge the role of heteronomous religious experiences in the choice of each interpretation.

We do so with fear and trembling, fully aware that all such experiences have the potential of becoming demonic — and unfortunately often do.[14] Yet, with Coakley (1995, 82–111), we want to affirm cautiously the positive value of heteronomy. In her well-balanced essay, Coakley takes contemplative prayer as a model of heteronomy, a mode of existence that should not be confused either with autonomy or with relationships governed by power/authority structures — a characteristic of relationality (although she does not use this concept). As such, Coakley deliberately rejects the many negative connotations that heteronomy appropriately has when it is conceived of as the bipolar opposite of autonomy, as Hampson (1996, 1–16) does, following a strong feminist tradition.[15]

Thus, by cautiously warding off our phobia for heteronomy and religious experiences, we can recognize their roles for both the believers' life and scriptural readings. In life, believers integrate the autonomous and relational modes of their existence in terms of their heteronomous religious experiences and perceptions. Similarly, in their scriptural readings, believers integrate the analytical and contextual-pragmatic modes of interpretations in terms of the hermeneutical mode of interpretation that is based on heteronomous experiences and religious perceptions.

Yet this statement, with its acknowledgment of the role of religious perceptions, has a critical edge. It is not an automatic endorsement of religious perceptions and of their role in scriptural readings. For both the feminist theologian and the biblical critic, there are many scriptural readings that, in our view, are both ethically and academically irresponsible, because the religious perceptions and the particular heteronomous experiences out of which they arise construct the relationship among the analytical/autonomous, the pragmatic/relational, and the hermeneutical/heteronomous in ways that we strongly feel are unacceptable both ethically and academically. Nevertheless, for both of us there are many scriptural readings that are both ethically and academically responsible.

Why this conclusion? What is the ground for this value judgment?

Our Theological Outlook and Its Role in Our Conception of Scriptural Criticism

Of course, in order to assess which scriptural readings are or are not ethically and academically responsible, we make use of our own theological views, that is, of our own religious perceptions. And these arise out of our particular heteronomous experiences as Christians.

To begin with, with Coakley, we reject Hampson's negative conception of heteronomy and religious experience, because this view "remove[s] the backbone that structures the central mystery of Christian salvation" (Coakley 1985, 84). This is why we acknowledge that heteronomous experiences may have a positive role as one of the foundations for the value judgment that integrates scriptural readings.

With Coakley, we readily affirm the positive value of certain types of heteronomous experiences and the negative value of certain other types. As Christians, we find that in accordance with God's incarnation in Jesus of Nazareth (Grenholm 1999a) and with Christic manifestations in human experience (Patte 1983, 122–231) it is appropriate to stress God's involvement in life, God with us. This means that, for us as Christians, encounters with the divine in genuine heteronomous religious experiences do not deny the value of either the believers' autonomy or the relationality of the believers' daily life — as is the case when the divine is conceived of as the elevated "King-God-Almighty-Father-All-Powerful-Protector" (Schüssler Fiorenza 1995, 106, quoting Wren 1990, 119). From both of our particular Christian perspectives, a "religious perception" is authentic when, and only when, it is a religious perception of the believers' relation to the concrete reality of their ordinary lives.[16] Consequently, for us, the teaching of a biblical text as Scripture cannot but be related to the believers as autonomous individuals and to their relational lives in concrete situations.[17]

This particular Christian theological perspective that we share plays an important role in our assessment of what constitutes genuine scriptural reading and scriptural criticism. We identify as exemplary those interpretative practices that are truly integrated. These are the practices that account for the teaching of the text as Scripture for believers in terms of their religious perceptions, and also conceive of the scriptural text and the believers' religious heteronomous experiences in all their mystery, because they are viewed as encompassing both the strength and the frailty of the individual autonomous existence and the richness and the messiness of relational life with others.

Scriptural Criticism and the Interpretive Practice of Certain Conscientious Preachers

Assuming responsibility for one's scriptural reading is part of practicing *scriptural criticism*. As we began mapping out some of the broad characteristics of scriptural readings found in receptions of Romans, we noted that these interpretive practices integrate basic modes of interpretation in the same way that believers strive to integrate the different modes of their existence. Thus, we can already say that scriptural criticism requires the interpreter-believers to assume responsibility for the ways in which they interrelate in their specific scriptural readings the three modes of existence (autonomy, relationality, and heteronomy) and the three corresponding basic modes of interpretation (analytical, contextual-pragmatic, and hermeneutical).

How does one proceed to a critical, and thus self-conscious, practice of scriptural reading? As we began pondering this question, we noted that certain pastors and priests were already practicing scriptural criticism.[18] The integrated nature of this interpretive practice became much clearer for us as we observed the way in which these conscientious preachers prepare their sermons. This preparation involves three interwoven moments.

- Conscientious preachers closely read and *analyze the biblical text.*

They consult or review critical studies of the text — including commentaries, monographs, articles, and biblical dictionaries — and quite a few make the effort to consult the text in its Greek or Hebrew original. They want to be sure that their interpretation is properly grounded in the text. This is an analytical interpretive moment, in which they deal with the biblical text as an autonomous object that can and must be respected and thus carefully analyzed.

Why do they feel an obligation to go beyond a casual reading? In brief, because their conclusions will have actual implications for life — for their own lives, those of their parishioners, and potentially those of many others. Yet, their careful, critical study of the text is not enough. A sermon cannot simply be a lecture about the text and what it says; it needs to proclaim a teaching that this text offers for believers today.

- In order to develop their sermons, pastors and priests seek to *discern how this scriptural text engages the members of their congregations* by addressing actual needs they have in their daily lives.

They ponder the life situations of their congregations — both the broader social and political contexts and their parishioners' private individual lives. Their careful analysis of this life situation is necessary to insure that the "teaching" of the text be a true teaching for believers today by bringing to them new insights for or about their lives, and thus by addressing their actual needs or problems. This is a contextual-pragmatic interpretive moment, concerned with the relationality of daily life.

- Furthermore, in order to conceptualize the teaching of the text and their sermon, conscientious preachers seek to *identify theological categories* that account for the way in which the text relates to the religious experiences of Christian believers.

Experiences of the presence or absence[19] of the divine transform the perception believers have of their relation to the conditions of their life. As a dialogue between the text and the believer's religious perceptions, the preachers' theological reflection might originate with the text and the theological issues it raises — for instance, through its representations of God, of sinful life, of Christ's presence among us. But this dialogue might also find its starting point in observations and questions arising from present-day believers' difficulties with traditional images of God, from their struggle with heart-wrenching personal or social tragedies brought about by human sinfulness, or from their awe-inspiring experience of the divine in the midst of the messiness of their lives. This is a hermeneutical interpretive moment that accounts for the perceptions of life arising out of heteronomous experiences.

For conscientious preachers, these three interpretive moments are necessarily closely interwoven because they intrinsically belong together in the process of reading the Bible as Scripture.[20] Scriptural reading is the primary mode of reading the Bible for pastors and priests, together with all other Christian believers. Yet, in view of the many possible readings of any biblical text as Scripture, conscientious preachers need to assume responsibility for their choice of a particular interpretation, so as to be in a position to preach it and say, either as individuals or as spokesperson of the church (in their ecclesial role), "*I* believe, *credo,* this is truly the Word of God for us, today" (Patte 1999, 7–13, 47–69, 190–210). It is always a struggle to determine whether or not the particular teaching one discerns with the help of a text is indeed a teaching that believers truly need in a given context. And any preacher knows how easy it is to preach a message that is everything but the Word of God for today. Thus, conscientious preachers strive to be as self-conscious as they can about their interpretive choices. Then, whether this Word is an exhortation, a theological view of life, an encouragement, or an agonizing questioning of God ("Why do you sleep, O Lord? Awake, do not cast us off forever! Why do you hide your face? Why do you forget our affliction and oppression?" [Ps. 44:23–24]), they can proclaim it with more integrity — although they might still delude themselves. For them, scriptural reading becomes a self-conscious process — scriptural criticism — in which both the distinctiveness of each of the three interpretive moments and their interrelatedness are made explicit.

Christian Believers Reading the Bible as Scripture, a Tripolar Interpretive Process

Our description of the way in which certain preachers prepare themselves to preach suggests that, for us, a scriptural reading can be more specifically envisioned as an interpretive process that interrelates three poles: (1) a scriptural text, (2) the believers' life, and (3) the believers' religious perception of life. The third pole includes interpretive traditions of all kinds that shape our preunderstandings of the biblical texts and reflect the religious experience of the presence or absence of the divine through which believers perceive their relation to the conditions of their life.[21] The three poles represent three loci where interpretation takes place, as well as three loci where revelation occurs for believers.

Scripture is a theological concept that clarifies how to think about scriptural texts as participating in the self-communication of God directed to human beings. As such, Scripture is revelatory and authoritative for believers. Yet, both revelation and authority are constructed in very different ways in various interpretations of biblical texts as Scripture (Grenholm 1996, 121–56). The differences among these various views of revelation and of authority can be understood as different ways of interrelating the three poles of the interpretive process.

Ways of Constructing Revelation. Concerning revelation, we can ask, Where is revelation located? Is it primarily in the believers' experience (be it in an ordinary life-context or in religious experience) or in the text? If it is in the believers' experience, is it primarily a revelation of God understood first and foremost as the hidden one *(Deus absconditus)* or as the revealed one *(Deus revelatus)?* In either case, is this revelation primarily located in common life and its complex network of relations, what we call relationality? Or is it primarily located in believers' religious experience of an encounter with the holy? Then, what is the relationship between revelation in religious experience and revelation in common life? If revelation is located in the scriptural text, does God communicate through the text itself? In that case, revelation is located in the text. Or did God communicate in the life of the people who wrote the texts? Revelation is then located behind the text; the text bears witness to revelation. Or does God communicate with human beings as they do something with the text? In that case revelation is located in front of the text, possibly in the believers' experience. (See Grenholm 1996, 121–22.)

As the circularity of these questions suggests, any given view of revelation of Scripture necessarily involves the three poles. Two illustrations clarify this observation. First, consider believers who hold a particularly strong view of revelation as located predominantly *in the text,* for instance, a *propositional* view of revelation as contained in the propositions of the scriptural text — usually associated with a view that revelation was concluded in the past.[22] Despite this emphasis, for such believers revelation is also manifested in their common life — at minimum, the implementation of God's will in daily life reveals it to the people who witness these good works (as Matt. 5:16 might suggest) — and in their religious experience, where the devotional reading (or reciting) of Scripture puts believers in the presence of the divine. Now consider other believers who hold a particularly strong view of revelation as located predominantly *in the common life* of the believers, including in the parts of life where one experiences God as absent or silent.[23] In such a case, believers do not deny that revelation was also located in the common life experience of the people to whom the scriptural text refers — revelation in and behind the text — and that revelation is also located in the believers' contemplative religious experience, although this is a contemplation of God in common life experience.

Ways of Constructing Scriptural Authority. Similarly, the authority of Scripture can be construed in very different ways, as Grenholm (1996, 137–56) illustrates. For instance, as "Word of God" Scripture can have the effect of silencing us to attentive listening or of challenging us to intense debates. In both cases, the authority of Scripture is affirmed. But the first leads the interpreter to "tune in on" the biblical texts, aiming for some kind of harmony through submission or obedience. The second establishes a mutual relationship between the text and its interpreter as dialogue partners. Thus, the construction of the authority of Scripture includes in each case several factors concerning the relationship between biblical text and believers, the basis of the text's authority (Word of God, words about God, text with an authoritative function for a community), and who or what confers this authority to the text (for non-hierarchical views of scriptural authority, see Grenholm 1996, 153–56; Patte 1999, 190–210).

Scriptural Reading as Tripolar. As we combine these features of the construction of authority with the different possible ways of constructing revelation, we find that a scriptural reading is an interpretive process that interrelates the three poles: text, life, and religious perception of life. Thus, we contrast scriptural readings with bipolar readings.

In the Western world, bipolar readings are common. These include pragmatic readings that limit themselves to the relationship between text and life and that Griffiths (1999, 40–54) calls "consumerist" readings by contrast with religious readings. The reading of a technical manual through which we learn how to put together a machine or a piece of furniture is an example of such pragmatic readings. Aesthetic readings belong to another type of bipolar readings that, this time, limit themselves to the relationship between text and a heteronomous aesthetic experience through which individuals gain a new vision of life or are lost in the pleasure of reading — for instance, the reading of poetry or of a thriller.

Unlike bipolar readings, a scriptural reading is a tripolar interpretive process that interrelates scriptural text, life, and religious perceptions of life. It includes both contextual-pragmatic interpretive dimensions (the text/relational life relationships) and aesthetic interpretive dimensions (the text/heteronomous experience relationships).

Terms such as "Holy Scripture" represent the aesthetic interaction between scriptural text and the believers' heteronomous religious experience, which results in a certain "religious perception of the believers' relation to life."[24] This aesthetic interaction might strongly emphasize the scriptural text as revelatory — so much so that the believers' heteronomous experience of the divine presence is centered on the text as sacrament (see Schneiders 1991, 40–43; Burgess 1998, 38–57). Then, reading Scripture is, in and of itself, a religious experience; it is holy time and space when the reader-believers encounter God, hear God's Word, are moved and transported by it. At the other extreme, this aesthetic interaction might be a mystical experience in terms of which the text is read; then the text as Scripture is an allegorical representation of the mystical experience, offering a language to speak what is beyond words.[25] And, in between, one finds all kinds of aesthetic interactions in which the text contributes to the believers' heteronomous experience of the divine by orienting their contemplative gaze toward certain aspects of common life — certain individuals, communities, events, joys, or sufferings — where believers can expect to encounter the divine, experience the holy, and thus be lost in awe.

Similarly, a scriptural reading is an interpretive process that includes a contextual-pragmatic dimension regarding the interaction between text and the believers' life. Here the functional roles of Scripture are emphasized, that is, the various ways in which the scriptural text affects believers in their particular contexts and conversely how they find a teaching for life and about life in the scriptural text. Once again, this relation can be constructed in all kinds of ways (as suggested in Patte 1999, 60–61). This pragmatic interaction between text and life might strongly emphasize the function of the scriptural text as containing a Word of God that believers should implement in their lives — for instance, when the scriptural text is read as a "lamp to my feet" (see Ps. 119:105) or as a "canon" providing guidance for individual or community life. To the other extreme, this pragmatic interaction between text and life might strongly emphasize revelation events in the believers' life, so much so that the scriptural text merely points toward these revelatory occurrences — for instance, when the scriptural text is read typologically as "corrective glasses" or as "empowering word."[26] And in between these two extremes one finds several kinds of functional views of Scripture — for instance, Scripture as "good news" or "family album" — which interrelate text and life by showing the import of a past revelation for the believers' life today in less spectacular or revolutionary ways.

Scriptural Criticism as an Interpretive Practice through Which the Three Poles Are Interpreted

The recognition that, by definition, a believers' scriptural reading is a tripolar interpretive process[27] shows that scriptural criticism needs to make explicit that, as certain preachers illustrate, this practice integrates three discrete interpretive moments. In order to apprehend their relationship it is helpful to recognize that the three scriptural poles — text, life, and believers' religious perception of life — are also three loci where interpretation takes place.

What is being interpreted? For the biblical critic, the answer to this question was so self-evident that, at first, he did not see the point of raising it. What is being interpreted? The text, of course! But as soon as the feminist theologian raised this issue, it became clear that this self-evident answer was simplistic, even misleading.[28] Of course, in their scriptural critical practice, preachers interpret the biblical text. Yet, they also inter-

pret the believers' concrete life situations, and their religious perceptions
of life. Furthermore, they interpret text, life, and religious perceptions of
life in terms of each other. This is why scriptural reading and (when it
becomes self-conscious) scriptural criticism is an integrated tripolar interpretive process. Interpretation occurs through the ongoing interaction
between text, life, and religious perceptions of life.

What are the three poles of the interpretive process? Once again, it is
not as self-evident as it seems at first. The list "text, life, and religious
perceptions of life" is deceptively clear, because it might be taken as
referring to three discrete entities. In fact, each of these poles is defined
through its interaction with the others.

What is the "text" when it is viewed as one of the three poles of
a scriptural reading? To begin with, it is a "scriptural text." The term
refers to a text that for the reader-believers is in a special relationship
with their life and religious perception. For Christian believers, such a
scriptural text is, in most instances, taken from the books of the Bible;
but other texts (e.g., traditions) often function in the same way for them.

The actual biblical text that is interpreted varies even in the case of
preachers who prepare a sermon on a given lectionary lesson. It might
be a single phrase (e.g., an exhortation), a single symbol, a few verses,
the entire passage read in and of itself, as well as this passage as part
of an entire biblical book, and very often this passage as part of a series
of other biblical texts dealing with similar themes. These variations of
the text as interpretive pole result from the fact that the biblical passage
is read *as Scripture.* Its interpretation cannot be divorced either from
the believers' (and the preachers') view of Scripture or from their life in
a specific context for which, hopefully, the biblical text will have some
teaching.

The heteronomous religious experiences represented by the scriptural
text and those of believers, whether they are congruent or in tension with
each other, necessarily inform each other. The specific *perception* of these
experiences, whether they are punctual or diffuse, defines the scope of the
text as a pole that participates in the interpretive process.[29] Similarly, the
scope of the text as an interpretive pole varies with the concrete issues of
life in the relational web of actual life-situations in the original context
and those of the believers' contexts.

What are the poles of the scriptural reading we called "the believers' life" and "their religious perception of life"? In each instance, these
poles are neither the entire life nor the entire religious perceptions of the
believers, but those broader or narrower features of life and religious
perception that are pertinent to the interpretive process.

It remains that each of the three moments of the preachers' interpretive practice is often devoted primarily to the interpretation of one of
these three poles: (1) a critical study of the *text,* (2) an analysis of the

believers' *life* situation, or (3) an elucidation of the theological issues involved in their *religious perceptions of life*. But by thoroughly integrating them into a single interpretive process, the preachers we took as models challenge the conception of these basic modes of interpretation found in the traditional academic disciplines in which they trained in seminary.

These preachers integrate in their practice of scriptural criticism the three basic modes of interpretation because of their commitment to their ministry and out of a sense of responsibility for their parishioners. We, the editors of this volume, believe that we and our colleagues in the Romans through History and Cultures project moved toward a similar practice of scriptural criticism. We recognize these preachers as models for us because of our sense of responsibility toward our students in theological education and because of our commitment to maintain the integrity of our academic disciplines — an integrity that, we increasingly recognized, cannot be maintained in isolation from the other disciplines.

Toward a Practice of Scriptural Criticism: Critical Interpretations, Theologies, and Contextual Receptions

Our reflections on believers' receptions of Romans studied by our colleagues in the Romans through History and Cultures project and on the interpretive practices of certain preachers made us aware that a scriptural reading is an integrated tripolar interpretive practice that involves many choices. The role of a scriptural criticism appears: making explicit these interpretive choices. The goal is to help the practitioners of scriptural readings — Christian believers, among whom are pastors, priests, seminarians, and many of their teachers — to assume responsibility for their choices of particular interpretations. This critical stance is essential since these believers live by the teaching they identify through their scriptural readings of biblical texts, and since, as a tripolar interpretive process, each scriptural reading is always new, surprising the believers with unexpected teachings and challenges.

What kind of critical practice will help the practitioners of scriptural readings to assume responsibility for their interpretations? We already suggested a tripolar critical practice. But how can we envision it?

Biblical critics, theologians, church historians, and specialists of receptions and of practical theology have different hurdles to clear. Biblical critics, when left on their own, are still lured by unipolar practices. Theologians (and church historians) as well as those biblical critics with whom they are in conversation are often content with bipolar practices. The growing number of colleagues — among whom are feminists, liberationists, and postcolonial critics, as well as practical theologians — whose primary concern is with receptions of biblical text and thus with the way interpretations affect people in life-situations have a very different problem. They are calling for integrated tripolar interpretive practices, but cannot implement them as long as their colleagues in biblical criticism, theology, and church history have unipolar or bipolar practices. Successively reviewing these three situations will allow us to envision a tripolar critical practice.

The Unipolar Practice of Biblical Critics— Benefits and Problems

Biblical critics have traditionally presupposed that critical biblical studies will allow any reader to assume responsibility for their interpretations *of the text* as the only thing that is interpreted. They found it most difficult to recognize that in a scriptural reading the three poles — scriptural text, life, believers' religious perceptions — are interpreted in terms of each other. Of course, biblical critics have long recognized that the most rigorous analytical interpretation cannot be unipolar, that is, that it cannot be a positivistic, objective analysis of the text. They are fully aware that, with Bultmann (1960, 289–96), one must answer negatively the question, Is exegesis without presuppositions possible? Interpretations of scriptural texts are necessarily caught in a hermeneutical circle. Thus two poles are involved in the interpretation: the text and the interpreters' theological or ideological presuppositions. Furthermore, with many others, the biblical critic in our team has acknowledged the importance of the contextual-pragmatic dimensions of interpretation (how people are affected by the interpretation in their lives), which appears when the issues of ethics of interpretation are considered (Fewell and Phillips 1997; Patte 1995, 1997). But, in his interpretive *practice,* despite his theoretical and methodological stances, this biblical critic catches himself having the knee-jerk reaction to ask unipolar questions, as if the only thing a critical study needs to account for is the interpretation of a single pole, the scriptural text.

How difficult it is for biblical critics, and also for many practitioners of scriptural readings (believers, including preachers, seminarians, and their teachers) to acknowledge that in the process of reading a text as Scripture a threefold interpretation is taking place! Dispelling the illusions of positivistic interpretations is an important step. But recognizing the roles of presuppositions and preunderstandings does not free us from a unipolar practice of interpretation. Of course, believers read the scriptural text from the perspective of their religious perceptions and from the perspective of their contextual life-situations. Yet, these observations still presuppose that only one thing is interpreted, the scriptural text. Moving beyond a unipolar interpretive practice involves acknowledging that *the biblical text also reads and interprets the believers and their religious perceptions, as well as their contextual life-situations.*

We acknowledge the covert but powerful claim that the unipolar practice of interpretation has upon biblical critics and theologians today, as throughout the history of critical scholarship. These scholars strive toward objective certitudes through their interpretations because, whether or not they make it explicit, they deeply feel that much is at stake in biblical interpretation. This is an appropriate concern, as we noted regarding conscientious preachers who want their interpretations to be solidly grounded in textual evidence because together with other believers they will live by them. Thus, rigorous analytical studies *of the text* are important. But reducing the interpretive practice simply to analytical studies *of the text* is academically irresponsible, as the many arguments against the positivistic views of biblical interpretation have shown. There is no need to repeat them here (see, e.g., Harvey 1966). It is enough to mention that what has been said about positivistic methodologies[30] also applies to other forms of unipolar interpretive practice. In addition to being academically irresponsible, these practices are ethically irresponsible, because of the inappropriate claims of universalism and neutrality made by the way these interpretations are presented. Feminists and cultural critics have readily exposed the problematic character of these claims by showing the androcentrism and Eurocentrism of many of these interpretations.[31]

The Bipolar Practice of Biblical Critics and Theologians — Contributions and Problems

Throughout the history of scholarship, the interpretive process has been commonly understood as bipolar. The interpretive work is understood as critical and theological. It includes both the analytical study *of the scriptural text* (one pole) and the hermeneutical implications for *the perception of life* (another pole).

As we seek to envision a tripolar critical practice that will help the practitioners of scriptural readings to assume responsibility for their interpretations, we have to reject unipolar practices as irresponsible and as antithetical to a tripolar practice. By contrast, we want to affirm that this bipolar analytical/hermeneutical practice is to be preserved, indeed sustained, and enhanced. This is one of the three bipolar interpretive processes that a tripolar practice should include. A tripolar practice should ideally include the bipolar interpretations of (1) the scriptural text and religious perceptions, (2) the scriptural text and life-situations, and (3) religious perceptions and life-situations.

Thus, we will *not* argue against a bipolar analytical/hermeneutical or critical/theological interpretive practice. On the contrary, we affirm it as an integral part of a responsible interpretive practice. Our concern is that too many times the bipolarity of this practice is betrayed, and that in effect its practitioners revert to a unipolar interpretation. In order to progress toward a responsible critical practice — a tripolar practice — we take note of the contributions that a critical/theological interpretive practice makes and/or promises to make; we seek to understand why too often it does not fulfill its promises, and why it betrays its bipolarity by subordinating one pole to the other; and we seek to identify some of the conditions that must be met in order to have a sustained bipolar process. It is essential to address these issues, because when the bipolarity of these practices is not respected their contributions, which are often significant, end up hindering rather than nourishing the theology and preaching of the churches (as Stendahl [1962, 422] warns).

Contributions and Problems of Critical/Theological Bipolar Practices. The bipolar interpretive practice, found throughout the history of scholarship, underscores the distance between critical and theological or hermeneutical interpretations. As most present-day preachers and scholars spontaneously view their task, they first analyze the text and then try to apply it. But they did not invent this practice. It is part of a powerful heritage since Gabler's day. This is the understanding of the interpretive process generally presupposed in the biblical commentaries preachers turn to when preparing their sermons.

Ideally for the writers of critical commentaries, theological issues should be left aside. It is not uncommon to find that the exegete explicitly hands over his (more rarely, her) work to the systematic theologian. Thus Morgan and Barton write, "It is for theologians to decide how to use the Bible; biblical scholars simply say what it means. That at least is a commonly held view" (1988, 16).

An early exponent of this view was Johann Philipp Gabler. In his famous inaugural address of 1787, "On the Proper Discrimination between Biblical and Dogmatic Theology and the Specific Objective of Each," he focused on the distinction between the historically oriented study of biblical texts and their theological usage. This bipolar view of the relation between critical and theological interpretations can thus be called "Gabler's gap" (Grenholm 1996, 265–68), a term that signals that the ultimate goal of the interpretive process is to bridge this gap. Krister Stendahl, in his well-known article on biblical theology (1962), also indicates the importance of making the distinction between "what a text meant" and "what a text means."

As Stendahl underscores, the interpretive practice based on this distinction has demonstrated that it can be fruitful for the theology as well as for the preaching of our churches, but at the condition of remaining truly bipolar. It needs to keep in tension "what it meant" and "what it means" by stressing the distance between the then and the now so that the relationships between the two poles might be fully assessed by means of hermeneutical principles. Thus, ideally this task requires the collaboration of biblical critics, who through their descriptive analyses establish what the text meant, and of theologians, who with hermeneutical tools proceed to address the question of the meaning for here and now (Stendahl 1962, 422).

The difficulty is that this delicate balance rarely is maintained. Thus, after critically reviewing the work of Karl Barth, Rudolf Bultmann, and Oscar Cullmann, Stendahl concludes,

> It thus appears that the tension between "what it meant" and "what it means" is of a competitive nature, and that when the biblical theologian becomes primarily concerned with the present meaning, he implicitly (Barth) or explicitly (Bultmann) loses his enthusiasm or his ultimate respect for the descriptive task. (1962, 421)

For all intents and purposes, the bipolar interpretive practice has collapsed into a unipolar practice. For Barth and Bultmann, the descriptive task of "what it meant" vanished; the hermeneutical interpretation of "what it means" completely took over. Conversely, as Stendahl also underscored, Cullmann, through his focus on the theological meaning of time and history, in effect dispenses himself from dealing with hermeneutical issues: "His work is basically confined to the descriptive task" (Stendahl 1962, 421). In this case, the hermeneutical task regarding "what it means" vanishes.

Neither Stendahl nor we, the coauthors of this overture, want to deny the immense contributions of scholars such as Barth, Bultmann, and Cullmann, and of many other biblical critics and theologians who emphasized one of the two poles so much that the other vanishes. With Stendahl, our concern is for the overall effect on theological education of this lack of respect for the tension between the two poles. When the distinction is not kept between "what it meant" and "what it means," and they are "carelessly intermingled," biblical critics and theologians fail to fulfill their role as theological educators: "The theology as well as the preaching of our churches becomes a mixed or even an inarticulate language" (Stendahl 1962, 422).

The problem is that this interpretive practice has great difficulty holding its two poles in tension; Gabler's gap is constantly in the process of being "filled up," rather than bridged, because the implicit goal of the practice is to resolve the tension, to overcome the distance between "what is meant" and "what it means," and thus, to transform the bipolar practice into a unipolar practice.

Seeking to Identify the Source of the Problem with Such Bipolar Practices and Envisioning Solutions for It. Beyond Stendahl's 1962 essay, we want to underscore, on the basis of the collective work in the Romans through History and Cultures project, that this bipolar practice quickly and inevitably collapses into a sterile unipolar practice when the relationship between the two poles is viewed as hierarchical, and thus as unidirectional. This hierarchal view is built in the image of Gabler's gap, which suggests that the role of biblical critics is to hand over exegetical results to the theologians. Critical biblical studies is often viewed as the handmaid of systematic theology. Then, as is the case for Barth and Bultmann, the description of "what the text meant" vanishes in the background in order to make room for the only worthy task, that is, the theological task (though it has benefited from the rigor of the historical studies, especially for Bultmann). When the hierarchical relationship between the two poles is reversed, as in the case of Cullmann, the effect is similar. Actually, critical biblical studies often claim veto power over systematic theology: in order to be legitimate, a theological development of "what the text means" must conform with the exegetical results that describe "what the text meant." In each case, we find once again a unipolar interpretive practice, with the problematic consequences noted by Stendahl.

Yet, there is a way out of this dilemma, as the collective work in the Romans project demonstrates. The tension between the two poles can be maintained to the benefit of theological education of responsible scriptural readers, including pastors, priests, seminarians, and their teachers, by making sure that a few basic conditions are met. Stendahl (1962, 421) spells out a first condition by calling for a cooperation between biblical critics and theologians. We, the coauthors of this overture, learned from our own work together that another and essential condition is that the biblical critic listen to the theologian with the expectation that he has much to learn from her about the practice of critical biblical studies, *and vice versa,* that the theologian listen to the biblical critic with the expectation she has much to learn from him about the practice of systematic theology. The analytical study of "what the text meant" has significant implications for the hermeneutical study of "what it means," and vice versa, the hermeneutical study of "what the text means" has significant implications for the analytical study of "what the text meant." We have also learned that another condition for sustaining this reciprocal interaction between biblical critics and theologians and this creative tension between the poles is that a third group of interpreters be involved in the interpretive practice, namely, specialists of the believers' receptions of biblical texts, including practical theologians, and that the interpretation become tripolar.

Illustrating the Contributions of and the Endemic Problems with Bipolar Interpretations. We acknowledge that many insights have been gained from keeping readings of the Bible initially free from any kind of dogmatic bindings.[32] Yet the very effort to keep critical studies free from theological influence, valuable as it is, has the effect of making it impossible for theology to contribute anything to critical biblical studies. This is the reverse of the problem that Stendahl noted regarding Barth and Bultmann. Two examples will make this double point.

Biblical critic James Barr offers profound insights regarding the role of certain theological categories in the standard interpretations of Genesis 3 (1992, 1–20). Christian theologians commonly read this text as telling the story of how human beings lost their immortality by an act of disobedience or sin. Barr shows that such an interpretation is possible only if one accepts Paul's interpretation of the text in Romans 5. Taken by itself, Genesis 3 does not say that Adam was immortal. Furthermore, neither sin nor guilt is mentioned. No other text of the Hebrew Bible refers to Genesis 3 as an explanation for sin and evil in the world, and so forth.

How could Paul interpret Genesis 3 as referring to human beings fallen in sin, bereft of immortality? The wisdom tradition contained the idea of the loss of immortality because of sin. Paul did not invent it. But Paul interpreted Genesis 3 in terms of these theological categories. For instance, Barr writes this concerning the motivation that Adam and Eve, particularly Eve, had for committing the original sin:

> Especially in the West, and since St Augustine, and increasingly so, if anything, in Protestant theology, if that were possible, the explanation given is *pride, superbia,* the will to be more than human, the desire to transcend the limitations of humanity and be like God, above and outside the world. This may well be an important imaginative insight and might, indeed, have much truth in it as a theology of human nature. But it is ill based in the story of Adam and Eve. (1992, 13)

In sum, we must acknowledge that such an interpretation of Genesis 3 as the story of the fall is a Christian interpretation dependent upon the wisdom tradition and Paul. The story needs to be framed in a certain way for Christian theologians to be able to give their standard interpretation. By keeping dogmatics out of the way of biblical interpretation, Barr as a biblical critic teaches a valuable lesson to the systematic theologians.

The theologian of our team looks for further teaching from Barr regarding her field. What conclusions are theologians prepared to draw from the critical interpretation put forth by James Barr? He says that Genesis 3 is "a story of how human immortality was almost gained, but in fact was lost" (1992, 4), and that this happened almost by mischance (14). Without going into the rest of his argument, let us simply ask, What are the theological implications of such an interpretation? According to the traditional Christian theological interpretation, God made blessedness dependent on obedience to a command that hardly makes any sense — unless it is allegorized, as often happens. Do Christian theologians really want to promote such a God? What are the ethical standards of a God who connects fundamental choices in life with eating or not eating a particular kind of fruit? With arbitrary commands? In sum, the critical interpretation apart from dogmatics brings relief to theologians. They are freed from this doubtful image of God, although they can still insist on the evil of a life profoundly cut off from God's will.

No doubt Barr would be pleased to have made this additional contribution to systematic theology. This is how it should be in a bipolar interpretive process: theologians learn about systematic theology from critical biblical studies.

But despite his deep concern for hermeneutical and theological issues (see, e.g., Barr 1980), in practice Barr does not seem to envision a reciprocal exchange. The bipolar interpretation is not really bipolar. The only true interpretation is that of the biblical critics. They tell the right understanding of the text to the theologians, who then have to correct their interpretations because they are inappropriately framed by theological categories foreign to the text. "Historical reading, without claiming to be the sole possible mode of reading, has actually increased the possibility for our understanding scripture in its proper theological function" (Barr 1980, 50). But what did the biblical critic learn from the theologians?

Biblical critics should learn from theologians that the interpretations of biblical critics are framed by theological categories that they brought to the text. The value neutrality that critical exegesis has been aiming for may turn out neither neutral nor harmless. Positively, they should learn about the role that theological, cultural, and value judgments played in focusing their critical interpretations upon certain features of the text that had been overlooked because their significance was not clear without such a focus. But the biblical critic of our team had a hard time envisioning all this until challenged to take into account a third pole by assessing the contextual implications of the interpretation. It takes a confrontation with feminist and other advocacy scholars to discover the androcentrism and Eurocentrism of one's interpretation; when one acknowledges that one's interpretation is subtly framed by specific cultural categories that one brings to the text, it becomes possible to envision that our own theological or ideological categories had a similar role in the interpretive process.

Another brief example. Biblical critic Peter Stuhlmacher, when interpreting Rom. 3:21–26, rejects "the dogmatic distinction which arose in the history of the church between a justification which is first only reckoned legally (forensic-imputed) and a justification which is creatively at work (effective)" as "an unbiblical abstraction" (1994, 63–64). By this comment Stuhlmacher provides a legitimate critique of traditional Lutheran theology. Yet he does so by implicitly claiming, as a biblical critic, a veto power upon theological interpretation. This sounds threatening, and clearly expresses the hierarchical relationship between critical biblical studies and systematic theology. But because he does not engage in any real dialogue with the theological perspective that he challenges, the critique first is very narrowly limited, and second lacks any assessment of whether or not the dogmatic distinction between forensic justification and sanctification is important or fruitful for contemporary theology. Consequently this critique is ineffective.

Bringing fundamental theological issues and theological points of view into dialogue with the analytical observations of the biblical critic could turn Stuhlmacher's brief comment into an interesting critique of a common understanding of the Lutheran doctrine of justification. Are there other understandings of the distinction between justification and sanctification that should not be regarded as unbiblical abstractions? What made the distinction so powerful, if it is not present in the text? Such questions could go on. The reader could have been given some guidance or at least been called to draw her or his own conclusions. But the way Stuhlmacher puts it, this distinction is off limits. No discussion of the theological views of the reader is allowed. The reader must go against the commentary to dare to explore the "unbiblical abstraction" of her or his theology! The veto power used by the biblical critic has absolutized the artificial border between the disciplines, and as a consequence the believers and their interpretations for life in specific contexts have been excluded.

Revitalizing Bipolar Practices by Introducing Life-Situations as a Third Pole

The two preceding examples are enough to illustrate how a critical/ theological, or in our vocabulary, analytical/hermeneutical, bipolar interpretive practice ends up subordinating one field to the other, failing to benefit from a truly reciprocal relationship between the two fields, and thus, despite valuable contributions, further isolating (rather than integrating) the disciplines and their interpretive practices and alienating (rather than helping) other interpreters of the biblical texts. As we reflected on the source of this problem we suggested that the introduction of the third pole, the believers in their life-situations, could contribute to restoring and sustaining a reciprocal and fruitful relationship between analytical/critical and hermeneutical/theological modes of interpretations.

Consider how the dynamics between these modes of interpretation are transformed when one introduces a contextual-pragmatic mode of interpretation focused on the believers' life situation — in this case, a feminist mode of interpretation with its concern for the implications of an interpretation for women in their life-contexts. Two examples will illustrate this transformation.

Reading Together Three Critical Biblical Interpretations. Our first example deliberately focuses on the interpretation of a narrative, because the issues are clearer in such cases. When we compare the interpretation of Genesis 16 and 21 given by mainstream critical scholar Gerhard von Rad with those of feminist scholar Phyllis Trible and Jewish scholar Jon Levenson, at the outset von Rad's interpretation seems insensitive to the slave woman who is sent into the desert to die and told by God to go back to her master and mistress.

The difference becomes very clear if we focus on Hagar. Von Rad reads the story as a suspension of the main narrative about the promise given to Abraham and Sarah (1987, 196, 234). He does not show much sensitivity for the tragic fate of the slave woman. Levenson is more aware of her (1993, 93). He understands the command of the angel to Hagar to return to Sarah as a shocking indication that, generally, God cannot be said to be on the side of the oppressed. Levenson even states,

> The reader aware of the larger Pentateuchal narrative will recognize in Genesis 16 a remarkable inversion of the story of Exodus: the Mother of *Israel* is abusing an *Egyptian* slave, and the God who reveals himself to the runaway bondswoman in the desert gives her there not a charter of freedom, but an order to return to the mistress of her oppression. (1993, 95)

Still, a difference remains between Levenson's interpretation and that of Trible. Like von Rad, Levenson takes seriously the promise given to Hagar to give birth to a son, the firstborn of a new people. They also conclude that this promise is fulfilled. Although Ishmael is not part of the covenant, he is not forgotten by God, according to both von Rad (1987, 196–97) and Levenson (1993, 93–98).

Trible draws on the inverted parallel between Hagar and the people of Israel in a way similar to Levenson (1985, 13, 21–25). However, she draws the conclusion that Hagar experiences "promise without fulfillment" (28). In her interpretation there is no consolation for Hagar other than that she manages to have Ishmael married to a non-Israelite woman (27). Ultimately, Hagar is someone with whom "all sorts of rejected women" can identify themselves (28).

This is not the place to pass judgments on the critical work of these scholars. The point we want to make is that when the contextual perspective of the reader in her or his life-situation is taken into account, the "detour" of God's promise cannot be looked upon from a supposed neutral point of view as in the interpretation of von Rad. The Jewish perspective of Levenson and the feminist perspective of Trible play an essential role in making the interpretation both academically and ethically responsible. The vulnerability of Hagar, an important theme of the text, is disregarded by von Rad. Thus, his supposed scholarly neutrality does not make his interpretation more rigorous, in a critical analytical sense, than the other two interpretations. As compared with those interpretations, he has missed an important feature of the text (Grenholm 1996, 186–98). Furthermore, he was blind to this feature, not because he did not bring with him a contextual perspective to the text, but because he has chosen a perspective that comes naturally in his Christian European androcentric context: he sides with Abraham and Sarah, not observing that this implies he also sides with the God who is not on the side of the oppressed.

Acknowledging that a text can be read from the perspective of different contextual life-situations facilitates the shift in the interpretive practice of Levenson. Although his interpretation is similar to von Rad's in that it shares the emphasis on the chosen people (although not defining it in the same way), he opens up, rather than closes, the possibility of debating the theological issues concerning the election of Israel as the chosen people. Furthermore, because his perspective allows him to see as significant certain features of the text regarding Hagar, he does justice to her role and her point of view, affirming her vulnerability, and in the process he opens up the possibility of reflecting on the implications of this text for the situation of the oppressed.

Trible goes one step further in her presentation of Hagar as a representative of rejected women (see also Williams 1990, 15–33). Her feminist perspective — another contextual perspective from a specific life-situation — underscores as most significant certain features of the text regarding Hagar and the nonfulfillment of the promise made to her. Ignoring Hagar in the process of interpretation, as von Rad did, does not automatically mean that one supports oppressive structures. Still, every time such structures are left without comment, they are tacitly affirmed. Von Rad's interpretation is not harmless.

This example illustrates five important points that help us to envision a tripolar practice.

- Each of these three interpretations, including von Rad's, was framed by the interpreter's contextual life-situation perspective. So is the case with all critical biblical studies, although many scholars are still not ready to acknowledge the role of social, political, economic, and cultural concerns and issues in their interpretive practices.

- In each case, the contextual perspective focused the interpreter's attention on certain features of the text viewed as most significant, and led her or him to consider other textual features as less significant, and eventually to ignore these.

- The limitations of each analytical interpretation are not to be viewed as a lack of critical rigor. It is when these limitations and the role of the interpreter's contextual perspective are not acknowledged that an interpretation lacks critical rigor.

- A tripolar interpretive practice is not foreign to Trible, Levenson, and even to von Rad. Each of them proceeded to interpret text, life, and religious perception of life in terms of each other. The less aware they were of it, the less explicit they made it, and the less they assume responsibility for it.

- It is through the comparison of interpretations by readers from different life-contexts and with different religious perceptions of life that the tripolar character of each interpretation became apparent.

From the preceding points, it also becomes clear that scriptural criticism as an interpretive practice that makes explicit its tripolar character does not necessarily involve the production of a new interpretation. Its main goal might be the assessment of existing interpretations — including the reader-believers' own, so as to help them to recognize that they have a choice among several interpretations. Then the question is, Which interpretations are, consciously or not, tripolar? Only those by biblical scholars such as von Rad, Levenson, and Trible? Of course not! Interpretations by ordinary believers, by preachers, and by theologians are tripolar also. Yet, in the same way that when we want to make a fire we self-consciously bring together two ingredients, fuel (wood, coal) and lighter (matches), and forget that oxygen is a necessary third ingredient, these interpreters' practice is often tripolar, even though they might not be self-consciously aware of it.[33]

Some theologians, especially feminist and liberation theologians, as well as some preachers, make explicit the tripolar character of their integrated scriptural critical practices. An examination of how these theologians and conscientious preachers, as well as pioneering educators who devise innovative programs in theological education, integrate basic modes of interpretation into their tripolar scriptural critical practices will put us in a position of formulating methodological steps for the practice of scriptural criticism that we propose to use in this and subsequent volumes of the Romans through History and Culture series.

A Model of Tripolar Scriptural Critical Practice and Its Promises

A brief review of the interpretation of the "father" language in Jesus' teaching (including in the Lord's Prayer, Matt. 6:9) by systematic theologian Elizabeth A. Johnson illustrates a tripolar practice at work. Reading her from the perspective of the preceding discussion, we can readily identify how she allows the three poles to interact with each other and to weave together basic modes of interpretations in a dynamic through which they inform each other rather than compete for primacy.

Johnson's interpretation includes a close reading of the biblical texts aimed at elucidating "the variety and plurality in Jesus' speech about

God" in the Gospel tradition (1992, 81; analytical mode of interpretation). On this basis, she draws this conclusion: "Jesus' Abba signifies a compassionate, liberating God who is grossly distorted when made into a symbol and supporter of patriarchal rule" (82). She underscores that the father image used by Jesus can be framed in different ways—that is, in terms of different religious perceptions, including a variety of viable "models of revelation" (77), as well as in terms of different life-context issues, especially sexism, patriarchalism, and androcentrism (77–78). Depending on the religious perception and the contextual issue used as a frame for the interpretation of "father" language, other images of God also found in Jesus' teaching might be included or excluded from the interpretation. Being inclusive, she analyzes the symbols of spirit, wisdom, and mother:

> In most of the texts where these symbols appear they are enmeshed in an androcentric framework, and so cannot be taken simply at face value. They need to be recovered within an egalitarian framework in order to release their emancipatory potential. (82)

Johnson sees a dynamic involving the *critical* analytical interpretation of the text, the *theological* conclusions drawn from a study of the religious symbols used, and *pragmatic* assessment of the life-context, which can be androcentric or not. Here we catch a glimpse of a process that involves more than moving from one point (critical analysis) across a gap to another point (religious perception of life; for her, a "hermeneutic of revelation" [1992, 76–77]). It is a tripolar dynamic process that includes not only these two poles, but also life-context as a third pole.

From the tripolar practice of Johnson as feminist theologian, we learn that in order to insure the dynamics of the interpretive process, one needs to constantly explore the diverse ways in which each pole can be constructed, and how choosing one construction for one pole affects the way one construes the other poles.

Thus, regarding the *religious perception of life*, Johnson explores different ways in which "revelation" can be, and has been, construed. Rather than revelation as conceptual truth in verbal form, she opts for revelation as liberating historical event, "or as inner experience, or as dialectical presence, or as new awareness, or as symbolic mediation" (1992, 77). As a theologian and Catholic believer, and in agreement with Vatican II—"all of Scripture is affirmed to be inerrant in what matters '*for the sake of our salvation*' " (78 [italics added])—Johnson deliberately gives priority to this religious perception pole and thus to theological and hermeneutical modes of interpretation.

Regarding *the scriptural text* as pole, this means that for her the textual features that point to "what matters 'for the sake of our salvation' " are particularly significant. She makes it explicit: "The healing, redeeming, liberating gestalt of the story of the God of Israel, the God of Jesus, in the midst of the disasters of history guides the reading of texts, becoming the principle by which some recede and others, long neglected, advance in importance" (1992, 77). Thus, because of her theological/ hermeneutical choice, "all historical, geographical, chronological, and scientific details" (78) as well as individual propositional statements — such as Jesus' isolated utterances about God as father — are features of the texts that are not in and of themselves particularly significant. Thus, Jesus' "father" language must be read together with all the other figures he used for God, and beyond this, with other scriptural texts that point to the liberating presence of God (82–103).

The role of the third pole, *life-context,* is no less prominent. Johnson's contextual concerns for the evil of sexism and other social oppressions further defines her religious perception of life: "for the sake of our salvation" also means for the sake of our liberation from sexism and social oppressions. These contextual concerns further focus the reading of the text on the textual features commonly used as a basis for sexist and patriarchal interpretations, namely, Jesus' "father" language, as well as on the textual features that challenge these interpretations, namely, the diverse and colorful language Jesus uses about God (1992, 80). Conversely, her religious perception of life (revelation as liberating event) and her reading of the text (as presenting a healing, redeeming, liberating gestalt) affects how she conceives the problems posed by sexism and patriarchalism in present-day life-situations. Thus, she chose, among many possibilities, certain kinds of "women's interpreted experience" as the most plausible assessments of the life-contexts of women (61–75).

Integrating Three Basic Modes of Interpretations in Scriptural Criticism. Both the theologian and the biblical critic, as coauthors of this overture, readily agree: Johnson's tripolar practice provides us with an excellent general model for scriptural criticism and its dynamic interweaving of basic modes of interpretations. Together with our colleagues in the Romans through History and Cultures project and the conscientious preachers who, collectively or individually, have integrated interpretive practices, Johnson presupposes that basic modes of interpretation long viewed in scholarship and in theological education as incompatible with each other are actually closely interrelated. As such, these practitioners of scriptural criticism contribute to redefining the relationship between modes of interpretations and disciplines, and consequently to redefining the goals envisioned for theological education.

Farley's detailed analysis of theological education clarifies what is at stake in this integration of basic modes of interpretation.[34] According to the old conventional wisdom, we academicians conceive of our disciplines as independent from each other. Because of our fragmented view of knowledge, each discipline has integrity in and of itself. Thus, much of our energy as academicians is devoted to protecting the rigor of our disciplincs by surrounding them with strict boundaries (Farley 1988, 29–55). As we reexamine this conception of our disciplines, we have to acknowledge, with Farley, that we conceive of them in terms of an "authority paradigm" according to which scholars are supposed to master the material and impart it to other people. Similarly, we conceive of theological education as "a cluster of sciences based on a priori authority" (128; see 103–32).

The new trends in theological education, as well as the practioners of scriptural criticism as a tripolar interpretive practice, call us to conceive of our disciplines outside of this authority paradigm. This involves recognizing that they belong together in a theological reflection always situated in actual life-contexts. Far from being the juxtaposition of discrete disciplines, this integrated theological reflection — or what we call scriptural criticism — would then be characterized by basic modes of interpretations devoted to "the *paideia,* or education, of believers [which is] a disciplining of the interpretation of the events and texts of traditions, of the interpretation of the vision or content under the posture of truth and reality, and of the interpretation of these things under the posture of praxis or action" (Farley 1988, 138).

In our vocabulary, this integrated interpretive practice — scriptural reading — is already practiced by believers and becomes self-conscious in scriptural criticism. "Disciplining" this scriptural reading, that is, bringing it to understanding, involves becoming aware that this interpretive practice weaves together the interpretation of three poles: the scriptural text (or more generally "the events and texts of traditions"), the religious perceptions of the believers' relation to life ("the vision or content under the posture of truth and reality"), and life-context ("these things under the posture of praxis or action"). Thus, as Farley underscores, these three basic modes of interpretation do not originate with the scholars. They are already used by believers. Consequently, we concur with Farley when he says that "the aim of theological study is to discipline, or rigorize, the basic modes of interpretation that already exist in the situation of faith" (1988, 71).

As we, the editors of this volume, reread Farley's analysis of the significance of the trends that he sees emerging in theological education, we are struck by the similarities with what we recognized in the interpretive practice of the conscientious preachers we took as models, and in the cross-disciplinary discussions among theologians, church historians, biblical critics, and specialists of reception of biblical texts taking place in the Romans through History and Cultures project.

In this project, consciously or not, our colleagues and we have begun implementing, though somewhat haphazardly, Farley's theoretical proposal as a collective interpretive practice. This involves recognizing that

our role as scholars and teachers is neither to master data (about biblical texts, religious perceptions of life, or believers in certain life-contexts)
that we would subsequently impart to others,[35] nor to define basic modes
of interpretation that we, as methodological masters, would train others
to use. Rather our twofold role is (1) to acknowledge that scriptural readings of biblical texts already exist and that they result from the believers'
use of basic modes of interpretation that are appropriate in and of themselves; and (2) to help believers to bring to understanding their scriptural
readings (both as a process and a product; see Patte 1995, 113–29), so as
to help believers "discipline, or rigorize, the basic modes of interpretation
that already exist in the situation of faith" (Farley 1988, 171).[36]

Tools for a Practice of Scriptural Criticism: Elucidating the Analytical, Hermeneutical, and Contextual Frames of Receptions of Romans

The Scope of Our Studies of Romans through History and Cultures

From what precedes, it becomes clear that our originally open-ended intention to investigate the relationship between receptions of Romans and
critical biblical studies of this text led us, the participants in the Romans
through History and Culture project, to a collective integrated critical
practice in line with and supportive of recent innovations in theological education. As we, the coauthors of this overture, reflected on this
collective practice, we progressively came to understand the process of
reading a scriptural text, Romans, as a tripolar dynamic practice. This
practice, scriptural reading, is spontaneously used by Christian believers as they read Romans as Scripture, but also by anyone who reads
a New Testament text with the awareness that it is held as Scripture by
Christians. Scriptural criticism is, therefore, the critical approach through
which the tripolar integrated practice of scriptural reading is brought to
understanding. Because this task involves elucidating how basic modes
of interpretation are interwoven, it calls for the resources of different
disciplines, as is the case in our project.

Even as collective undertaking, the elucidation of the dynamic process
represented by many receptions of Romans through history and cultures
can quickly become a daunting task. The number of receptions is overwhelming. The lack of data would, in many cases, make it impossible to
provide a description of the factors involved in the interpretive process
followed by the interpreter. It is clear that we must delimit the scope of
our task as scriptural critics.

The problem of numerous receptions is easily resolved. We cannot pre-
tend to be comprehensive. Our collective work focuses on a few selected

receptions of Romans. Our sampling aims at diversity, including receptions by well-known figures, such as Augustine, as well as by ordinary interpreters, such as Celia Enriquez, a church musician in the present-day Philippines. And we do not forget that critical studies of Romans are also receptions, even if their hermeneutical-theological and contextual dimensions remain in the background. Each volume in the Romans through History and Cultures series is focused on certain types of receptions that might be related, because they concern the same passages in Romans (as is the case in the present volume about receptions of Romans 4 and 9–11), or the reception of a single major figure (Augustine in volume 2), or, in subsequent volumes, a period (early church, Middle Ages, Reformation, contemporary) or a certain theme (patriarchy, gender). In order to help pastors, priests, seminarians, and their teachers to self-consciously choose the interpretation that in their judgment is most appropriate for a given life-context — what they should do as practitioners of scriptural criticism — it is enough to provide a critical description of a diversity of scriptural readings of Romans, each time making sure to include interpretations that we can anticipate are prevalent among contemporary readers of Romans.

The problem raised by the lack of data concerning the factors involved in the interpretive process followed by the diverse interpreters is more substantial. In order to avoid any confusion, we need to address it head-on by underscoring that, in the volumes of this series, we *do not* present practices of scriptural criticism.[37] We simply provide tools to facilitate this practice. Let us explain.

In the preceding pages, we have spent much time elucidating the process of scriptural reading as a tripolar interpretive dynamic practice that interrelates the following:

- *three basic modes of interpretation (methodologies):* the analytical, contextual-pragmatic, and hermeneutical-theological modes used for the interwoven interpretation of the three poles

- *three poles (what is interpreted):* the scriptural text, the believers' life-context, and the believers' religious perceptions of life, which are interdefining each other on the basis of the believer-interpreters' three modes of existence

- *three modes of existence (aspects of the believer-readers' existence):* autonomy, relationality, and heteronomy — that is, respectively, each believer-reader's sense of personal identity; her or his place in the web of social relations, including power/authority relations; and her or his religious experience, including encounter or lack of encounter with the holy and a sense of the presence or absence of the divine

Scriptural criticism is the interpretive practice that Christian believers (including pastors, priests, seminarians, and many of their teachers) who want to assume responsibility for their own interpretations should use. Why? Because this practice is an effective tool to help them become aware of the choices they make as they themselves interpret the text.[38] Interpreters practice scriptural criticism in order to assess their own interpretations. This practice does include assessing other people's interpretations. Yet, because interpreters do so primarily in order to determine whether or not such interpretations would be appropriate alternatives for them in their specific life-context and with their specific religious perceptions of life, they can do so from the outside. This assessment from the outside requires the identification of *characteristics of these other scriptural readings as final products,* but not necessarily of the characteristics of the process of interpretation that led to them.

Even when one has a limited knowledge of the specific views an interpreter had of the modes of existence, of the poles, and of the basic modes of interpretation during the process of interpretation, one can still analyze a scriptural interpretation as *final product* and describe its characteristics as scriptural reading. The interwoven use of the basic modes of interpretation in terms of specific views of the three poles and of the modes of existence frame the interpretation as final product, and one can describe how this interpretation as final product is framed in a threefold way. Three frames are inscribed in each scriptural interpretation as final product — such as the receptions of Romans. We name them in such a way that their relationship with the modes of interpretations will be clear:

- *three frames of a scriptural interpretation (features of the interpretation as final product)*: the hermeneutical, analytical, and contextual frames

An analogy might help us better understand the threefold framing involved in the process of scriptural reading that is inscribed in the scriptural interpretation as final product. The scriptural reading of a biblical text is somewhat like taking a picture. As we take a picture, consciously or not (automatic cameras do much of this by themselves), we frame it in three different ways: (1) we select a subject (a flower, a group of persons, a landscape) by locating it through the viewfinder, and in the process we exclude many other things in front of us; (2) we focus the lens on the subject, making sure that all its details (the petals, the faces, the trees) are clear, even though the foreground or the background might become blurry; (3) we adjust the speed of the shutter (or use a flash) in order to take into account the specific contextual situation — day or night, sunny or cloudy, indoors or outdoors, and so on. Similarly, any scriptural reading frames the text in a threefold way by choosing (1) a *hermeneutical* frame, through which we identify the subject matter of the reading (in the case of E. A. Johnson's interpretation, a specific view of revelation and of God); (2) an *analytical* frame (which brings into sharp relief the most significant textual features regarding, for Johnson, "the variety and plurality in Jesus' speech about God"); and (3) a *contextual* frame (which bridges the gap between text and life by taking into account the specific situation of the reading process, for Johnson, "women's interpreted experience").

On the basis of the picture as final product, we can readily describe the frames of the picture by asking questions such as, What is its subject, and is it well centered? Is it well focused or blurry? Is the lighting appropriate or not? But we might have a hard time saying exactly how this picture was framed and produced and why, especially if we do not know what other pictures could have been taken in this specific context, what kind of camera was used, what kind of flash was used if any, and so on. Similarly, we did not have any difficulty describing the frames inscribed in Johnson's interpretation, although much speculation would be required to elucidate how and why she chose these frames.

As editors of this volume, our role is to clarify as much as possible the hermeneutical, analytical, and contextual frames that characterize the interpretations of our colleagues, and that characterize the receptions discussed by our colleagues. We will do so in marginal comments throughout this volume. Since these marginal comments need to be short to be clear, we provide here a general description of the main characteristics of each type of frame.

There is no way of putting the different frames (and corresponding categories) in a definite order. In principle they are of equal weight. In practice one or two may dominate. This time we start with the contextual frames, as is appropriate when the perspective of believers is emphasized.

Contextual Frames and Their Bridge Categories

Believers gain from the text a new perspective on their lives through an ongoing two-way process. Believers read the biblical text with the expectation that this scriptural text in turn will "read them." The believer-readers' true needs, problems, concerns, and interests are brought to light when they allow the scriptural text to read their life-situations. A contextual frame is posited.

A contextual frame is most readily identified through the reference to a given context. Thus, in the marginalia, we readily designate them by referring to social and/or religious locations (post-WWII Germany, Lutheran, post-Holocaust, etc.). Yet, in order to recognize the characteristics of the contextual frame of a scriptural reading, we need to identify the bridge-categories that relate life and text. It is therefore these bridge-categories that we emphasize in the marginalia about contextual frames. It is helpful at this point to list four major types of bridge-categories, with the emphasis that this list is partial and that each type can take many concrete forms.

A scriptural reading brings to light the believer-readers' true needs, problems, concerns, and interests in a given life-context and eventually equips them to provide solutions for these problems and concerns and helps them address these needs and interests. Consequently, the easiest way of presenting these four types of bridge-categories through which life and text can be related is to list the four main problems for which the text is expected to provide solutions as it transforms the reader-believers' lives. In a specific context, the believers (or would-be believers) might have the following:

- A *lack of knowledge* or a *wrong knowledge* regarding aspects of their lives, what is true or false about life; or regarding issues that are important for life, what is good or bad to do. In this case, identifying the life-text contextual frame involves elucidating the specific lack or error of knowledge that the teaching of the text overcomes. The following marginalia fall into this category: "Dialectical struggle for the truth of the text and of the reality of our lives" (Parker's essay); "Readers sharing the cultural repertoire" (Brawley's essay).

- A *lack of will* (not wanting to do something) or a *wrong will* (wanting to do the wrong thing). In this case, identifying the life-text contextual frame involves elucidating the specific lack of will or wrong will that the teaching of the text overcomes or reorients. The following marginalia fall into this category: "The *Shoah* as providing a sense of responsibility" (Wasserberg's essay); "Empathic response to Augustinian and Reformation readings" (Campbell's essay).

- A *powerlessness* resulting from one's personal mental or physical limitations, or from a situation where individuals are overpowered and/or oppressed by external forces, be they natural, social, political, economic, or religious. In this case, identifying the life-text contextual frame involves elucidating the specific way in which the teaching of the text empowers the powerless. The following marginalia fall into this category: "Encounter of Christians and Jews after the *Shoah*" (Sievers's essay).

- A *lack of vision for life in community* or a *wrong ideology*. In this case, identifying the life-text contextual frame involves elucidating the specific world view — including its power and authority structures — that the text offers. This latter type of bridge-categories also relates the believer-readers' life-context and their religious perceptions of life. The following marginalia fall into this category:

"Arguments against the adoption of the Jewish identity by Gentile Christians in Paul's time and today" (Nanos's essay); "After the *Shoah* one needs to envision Paul as a faithful Jew and as proclaiming that Jesus is the Messiah for Gentiles" (Wasserberg's essay).

Clearly, these four types of bridge-categories are broad. Each of them potentially encompasses many different ways of relating life and text, since lives and texts are variables.

Hermeneutical Frames and Their Theological Categories

Believer-readers gain from the text new understandings of the religious perceptions they have of their relation to their life-context by entering into dialogue with the text about these perceptions. This is the hermeneutical process that Gadamer described as a "fusion of horizon," when this dialogue is euphoric, peaceful, and amiable; but this dialogue might also be a painful one, where no fusion is possible, as the practitioners of "hermeneutics of suspicion" underscore.

Hermeneutical frames are made of two kinds of theological categories: (1) those aspects of religious perceptions of life that are the subject matter of the dialogue; and (2) the views of Scripture, revelation, and religious authority that sustain the hermeneutical dialogue.

The theological categories that express a certain religious perception of life and are the subject matter of the hermeneutical dialogue are readily identifiable. As in the case of a live conversation with another person, entering into dialogue with a text involves finding an issue, a topic, a matter about which both of us are interested, though we might have different levels of knowledge about it. In a scriptural reading, this involves choosing an aspect of one's religious perception of life that is also dealt with in the text — a *theological category* (in the broadest sense of "theological," including ideological views of human beings, history, what makes life worth living, etc.). Entering into dialogue with the text involves learning about the text and its views on this theological category, as in a dialogue one learns about the person and her or his views. But beyond this small first step, true hermeneutical dialogue about one's religious perceptions of life is intersubjective and thus reciprocal, because it becomes a heteronomous dialogue that involves daring to share the most fundamental characteristics of one's existence.

Heteronomous dialogue with someone requires the establishment of a trusting relationship. Heteronomous dialogue with a text requires a view of the text as Scripture. Heteronomous dialogue with someone requires that I "learn this person"[39] with full respect for his or her mystery as an Other who always surprises me with new views, new insights, new perspectives, different from mine. So with a biblical text. When I read a text as Scripture, I respect its mystery, expecting that it will surprise me and challenge my views. Conversely, this intersubjective learning requires that I bring to the other person or to the text my own views, insights, perspectives into the conversation, with the confidence that they will be respected and affirmed in their differences. In the trusting relationship of a truly heteronomous dialogue, I gain new perceptions about an aspect of life, not because I have had to abandon my views for those of the other person or text, but because I now also view my perception of this aspect of life from the perspective of the other person or scriptural text. We now understand each other about the subject matter of our dialogue.

In order to identify the characteristics of the hermeneutical frame of a scriptural reading, one needs to identify the views of Scripture, revelation, and religious authority. These are the views that sustain the hermeneutical dialogue by establishing some kind of trusting relationship. More often than not they also mediate experience of the mystery of the Other, as apprehended in private religious experience or in relational life.

We have already given brief descriptions of several of these views of Scripture, revelation, and religious authority. These are sufficient for identifying most hermeneutical frames. Yet, lest subtler hermeneutical frames be missed, we need to add a few comments.

In a euphoric heteronomous dialogue with a person or a scriptural text, a fusion of horizon may take place: our two different perceptions of the aspect of life that is the subject matter of our dialogue become a single shared perception beyond words, which is now much richer than either of the original perceptions. But a heteronomous dialogue might also be dysphoric when one of the two partners brings into the dialogue a perception of life deeply marked by hurt, by suffering, by a sense of abandonment ("My God, my God, why have you forsaken me?"), by despair ("Wretched person that I am! Who will rescue me from this body of death?"), by suspicion, by heart-rending pain. No fusion of horizon is possible. No euphoria. What is shared is the mystery of what cannot truly be shared — suffocating pain, the silence of God, distrust, angry questioning — and a suspicion of any claim from the partner/text that this dreadful pain can be alleviated or even understood. In the silence of this dialogue in tears and beyond tears, when the theological category is the silence of God at Auschwitz (see Cohen 1981) or in one's dreadful private life, and there is a deep-seated suspicion vis-à-vis the biblical God about whom it is too easily said, "nothing will be able to separate us from the love of God in Christ Jesus our Lord," one's perception of this suffocating pain is, nevertheless, paradoxically transformed, because one can recognize it as a pain that is respected as ineffable, as a mystery that is beyond sharing. Then, the view of Scripture and of divine revelation is ambivalent, as is the case for many feminists:

Feminist hermeneutics, then, is profoundly paradoxical. It sees the Bible as both ally and adversary in the struggle for human rights, equality, and dignity. The biblical God, both helper and enemy, friend and tormentor, cannot simply be identified with God. (Schaberg 1990, 8)

Analytical Frames and Their Critical Categories

Finally, believer-readers frame their interpretation by focusing their reading upon certain textual features that they perceive as more significant than others. This framing is analytical, in the sense that it takes place through an analysis of the text in terms of certain critical categories. Since these critical categories are those used in critical methods, they are well known to pastors, priests, seminarians, and their teachers. The only points to be underscored are that each of these analytical methods frames scriptural readings in a different way, and that a given reading often focuses upon several categories (as a critical study often uses several methods). Thus, it might be helpful to classify these critical categories in terms of the special kind of analytical framing they provide.

A reading of a text can be focused upon its

- *Window dimension* — what is "behind" the text, be it the historical Jesus, early traditions, or the redactor's intention, is most significant (studied by different kinds of historical methods). Wasserberg and Nanos emphasize this critical category, which is also important for Campbell and Sievers.

- *Story dimension* — the development of the plot, the characters, their interrelations are most significant (studied by methods of narrative criticism). Brawley emphasizes this critical category.

- *Symbolic message* — metaphors, symbols, their constructions as coded features, and the symbolic organization as conveying a religious vision are most significant (studied by redaction criticism in a history of traditions perspective, by the history of religions approach, and by certain literary approaches). Most of Wasserberg's analytical frames and many of Campbell's belong to this category.

- *Transformative thrust*[40] — narrative and rhetorical transformations of characters and implied readers in thematic organization are most significant (studied by methods of structural and rhetorical criticism). Parker (following Barth) emphasizes this critical category.

- *Subversive thrust*[41] — social, economic, political, and religious structures of authority presupposed, advocated, or rejected by the text, as well as the traces of struggles for justice behind and

within the text, are most significant (studied by methods of social, economic, political, feminist, and postcolonial critical studies).
Grenholm, Patte, and Boyarin emphasize this critical category.

- *Voices from the margin*[42] — the voices that reflect a different social
  and cultural construction of reality are most significant (studied by
  methods of postcolonial and cultural criticism). Grenholm, Patte,
  and Boyarin emphasize this critical category also.

Marginalia Highlighting the Frames of the Interpretations of Romans 4 and 9–11

To facilitate the practice of scriptural criticism by Christian believers, including pastors, priests, seminarians, and many of their teachers, these
reader-believers need to be in a position to compare the features of their
own interpretations of Romans 4 and 9–11 with those of other interpretations. The point of this comparison is to help the readers of this volume
to recognize the choice they made, and thus the distinctiveness of their
interpretation. For this purpose, the greater diversity of options, the better. Consequently, instead of limiting our marginalia to the frames used
by the author of each essay, we highlight the frames of each of the numerous interpretations presented in this volume. As we formulate these
marginalia, we keep in mind that each interpretation as final product is
framed in its own way. Because of the comparative character of the essays, each of them refers to several interpretations of Romans, from the
(reconstructed) interpretations of the first readers to present-day receptions. Thus, in the margins, we signal the presence of several kinds of
analytical, hermeneutical, and contextual frames.

Analytical Frames (▲ in the margins and corresponding notes) involve
critical categories, which can be defined either in terms of textual features
and characteristics (the rhetoric of the text, its logic, etc.) or in terms of
the analytical model (e.g., canons of consistency, one or another kind
of "thrust" or "voice," etc.). Because the analytical frame reflects the
autonomous mode of existence, it concerns either features of the text
as autonomous object that can be analyzed or features of the particular
analytical ways of thinking of given interpreters (in the latter case, the
critical category is at times closely related to an ideological category of
a hermeneutical frame).

Hermeneutical Frames (■ in the margins and corresponding notes) involve *theological* or *ideological categories* defined in terms of the religious
perception of life either of the interpreters or of the text. Theological categories are easily distinguished from the critical categories. Ideological
categories of the interpreters are, at times, closely related to the critical
categories used by the interpreters. This is especially true when a critical approach is primarily characterized by a specific critical way of

thinking, which of course reflects a certain religious or ideological perception of one's relationship to other people and thus to their texts. In such cases, rather than cluttering the margin with both categories, we often chose to highlight a single one.

Contextual Frames (**C** in the margins and corresponding notes) involve *bridge-categories,* which are context specific and defined in terms of relational issues. The web of relationships in a given situation includes all the relations governed by structures of power and authority, and thus by structures of inclusion and exclusion. Since bridge-categories may concern relations among individuals or among groups, within and among secular or religious institutions, and even between believers and God, they are closely related to religious perceptions of life. For instance, the relationship between Jews and Christians, between Israel and God, and thus all the issues of the inclusion and exclusion of the Jews from salvation are contextual issues that are bridge-categories between life and texts, such as Romans 4 and 9–11. Yet, obviously, in each case such bridge-categories are supported by religious perceptions of life, and thus embody certain theological or ideological categories of corresponding hermeneutical frames.

Interplay of Frames (**I** in the margins and corresponding notes) involves situations where two or three frames — analytical, hermeneutical, or contextual frames — are at play simultaneously.

Reading Israel in Romans

The following essays are focused on Romans 4 and 9–11. Therefore, the issue of the relationship between Jews and Christians comes again and again to the fore in the interpretations of our colleagues as well as in the receptions of Romans they present. In order to better compare the respective hermeneutical and contextual frames of these interpretations, we propose to highlight the ways in which these readings construct "Israel."

The constructions of Israel in these interpretations concern their contextual frames, and more specifically all the issues about relationality — including the relationships between groups such as Jews and Christians; who has authority, is empowered, and takes the initiative to define these relationships, and thus to define Israel; the politics of identity in all its complexity (see Boyarin 1994); the role or lack of role of knowledge; the role or lack of role of motivation; and so on.

Yet, the constructions of Israel also concern the hermeneutical frames of these interpretations. Speaking of Israel is also speaking of chosenness, of election, of revelation, of religious experience, and ultimately of the place of Israel in the overall religious perception of life.

Although the constructions of Israel primarily concern the contextual and hermeneutical frames of the interpretations, they also concern the analytical frames, because each construction of Israel in a scriptural reading grounds itself on some textual features viewed as particularly significant while other textual features are bracketed out. Thus, we will also note which textual features are viewed as particularly significant in these readings of Israel in Romans.

Reading Israel in Romans will provide us with a means to compare more easily the different interpretations and receptions. As we use the three frames as a heuristic tool, we analyze our colleagues' interpretations in terms of categories that they may not have had when writing. We hope that we have not in any way distorted their interpretations. Rather, the use of these categories allows us to highlight, both in our reviews as well as in our marginal notations, the characteristics of the interpretive frames that our colleagues have chosen to emphasize.

Notes

1. During the last several years, this dialogue about receptions and critical studies of Romans took place among scholars gathered since 1997 first in a consultation and then in a seminar of national meetings of the Society of Biblical Literature.

2. Scriptural readings of Romans by Augustine, the bishop of Hippo, is the topic of the second volume of this series. Scriptural reading of Rom. 1:16–17 by Celia Enriquez, a church musician in the present-day Philippines, is presented and discussed in Revelation Velunta's "Ek Pisteōs eis Pistin and the Filipinos' Sense of Indebtedness" (to be published in a forthcoming volume of this series). See in the present volume the essay "Romans 9–11 and Jewish-Christian Dialogue: Prospects and Provisos" by Günter Wasserberg, who teaches New Testament at Christian Albrechts University, Kiel, Germany.

3. Nonreligious readings of biblical texts have in principle the same components, as we clarify below by noting that the threefold interpretive process is related to the threefold mode of human existence.

4. With Schneiders (1991, 11–26), we claim that no interpretation of a New Testament text can truly ignore that this text is Scripture for Christian believers, and thus that each interpretation presupposes a certain view of Scripture — although it might be aimed at showing the lack of validity of a given interpretation of the text according to this view, as many critical interpretations do.

5. The research program "Subordination in Theology: Fundamental Principle or Heavy Deadweight?" is directed by Cristina Grenholm (who works on a feminist theology relating the experience of childbirth to the story of the virginal birth and the doctrine of incarnation) and involves at present four other scholars: Annika Borg (on women's subordination as a hermeneutical category in contemporary exegeses of the household codes), Maria Jansdotter (on ecofeminism as an example of theological reflection that does not accept subordination and hierarchies), Maria Södling (on gender construction in the Church of Sweden between the World Wars), and Madeleine Åhlstedt (on the ambivalent relationship between women's movements outside of the church and their counterparts within the church). This program focuses on the interplay between gender theory, con-

temporary theology, and the Bible. These projects are framed by the fact that the God-man-woman hierarchy is a fundamental principle in Christian thinking. This is also the case of the principle of the equal value of human beings. There is a tension between the subordination and equality of women. The purpose of the project is to critically analyze tensions, divergences, and new constructions in contemporary patriarchal, feminist, and so-called gender-neutral theologies with methods from gender theory, hermeneutics, philosophy, and history.

6. Yes, we point to exemplary interpreters of the Bible who practiced scriptural criticism before we even dreamt of it. Yes, we point to innovations in theological education which presuppose scriptural criticism. Yes, it is appropriate to say that we found something, and did not invent it. But *we* are doing the pointing! *We* are identifying certain practices as more significant than others.

7. For Patte, this conviction reflects his structural interpretation of Rom. 1:18–31 in the context of Romans as a whole, which emphasizes idolatry, its deadly power over humans, and the gospel as the power through which they are eventually freed from this power. This conviction also refers to his interpretation of 1 Cor. 13:9–12. See Patte 1983, 256–95, 310–12.

8. In his essay (Jeffner 1987), which opened up for us helpful ways of conceptualizing scriptural criticism, the noted Swedish theologian first underscores that for him the concept of truth (including in theology) concerns the truth of assertions about "what is the case in the real world" (31). As we shall see, scriptural criticism seeks to bring to critical understanding and to assess existing scriptural interpretations, which can be viewed as assertions concerning the relationship between text and life. Jeffner then analyzes the different roles of a theologian and the different sets of criteria of truth he or she uses in each instance. Theologians as members of a society use in their daily life empirical and scientific criteria (32–33). As readers of the Bible (for Jeffner, biblical studies and theology should not be separated), theologians use the critical methods of biblical scholars and their criteria (33). As doctrinal theologians, they use criteria based upon human tradition, and ultimately upon religious experience (33–36). Finally, as preachers, theologians have to give up the *prima facie* truth of Biblical assertions (36). As is clear, "the sets of criteria belonging to different roles cannot readily be reconciled" (32). Yet, theologians often use several without making it explicit, and thus fail to integrate them (37–40). For Jeffner, a good theologian as preacher integrates the four different sets of criteria, through an emphasis on religious experience (41–44). In our conceptualization, the fourth set of criteria (giving up the *prima facie* truth of biblical assertions) is part of the interpretive practice through which conscientious preachers and other responsible believers ideally integrate the three other sets of criteria in their practice of scriptural criticism.

9. See also Jeffner (1982, 11–21), where he defined views of life as consisting of three constitutive parts: beliefs, values, and basic attitudes toward life. The beliefs concern a view of history, human beings, the universe, etc., and relate to the mind. The values concern the will. The last category gives an answer to the question of what it feels like to be alive. These three constitutive parts of a view of life are, of course, related to the different kind of truth-claims he underscores in 1987.

10. See Hampson (1996, 1–11) on autonomy and heteronomy, Grey (1989) on

relationality and autonomy, and Schüssler Fiorenza (1995, 50–57), who critiques the feminist relational Christology of Grey.

11. The concepts of heteronomy and of heteronomous religious experiences are thus different from Tillich's concept of heteronomy, which he understands as a negative category overcome by theonomy (1964, 163–66). David Tracy identifies theology as "the attempt to establish mutually critical correlations between an interpretation of the Christian tradition and an interpretation of the contemporary situation" (1985, 36). Thus, Tracy emphasizes the collective aspect of theology. In our view, heteronomous experience can be individual or communal. See also Collange's tripolar model (developed for his work in ethics), according to which *identité* (corresponding to autonomy, though for him, and we appreciate this point, it can be either individual or collective) and *altérité* (corresponding to relationality, though for him, and once again we agree, it includes relationship with others different from us, including with God) are held together by *le religieux* (religious experience, corresponding to heteronomy).

12. As much of biblical scholarship does, as Harvey (1966) points out when exploring the relationship between the historian and the believer.

13. See Schüssler Fiorenza 1988, 1999; Patte 1995, 1999. In her later book Schüssler Fiorenza (1999, 8) deplores the fact that Patte does not "critically analyz[e] the marginalizing discourses of malestream biblical studies and their silencing power" in *Ethics of Biblical Interpretation* (1995). Patte does so in *The Challenge of Discipleship* (1999, 190–210, and passim) as well as in Patte 1996, 353–96, for which *Ethics of Biblical Interpretation* was a prolegomenon.

14. There are many types of heteronomous experiences, which each time involve making oneself vulnerable to an Other. Thus the nature of the letting go of oneself, the emptying of oneself, is clearly different in the cases of relationship to a newborn child, a lover, a task, or God, or more generally to a dependent, an equal, or someone or something hierarchically superior. Yet, what is most significant is how this heteronomous relationship is constructed. Making oneself vulnerable in a heteronomous experience too often leads into being victimized, when the "Other" betrays the heteronomous relationship and becomes an abusive other, as feminists have rightfully emphasized (Coakley 1995, 106–11). One always has to challenge any reinscription of power relationships (Schüssler Fiorenza 1995, 50–57) not only in relationality, but also in heteronomous relationships, which, by definition, should be free from power and authority structures. Nevertheless, one should be wary of "another, and long-term, danger to Christian feminism in the *repression* of all forms of 'vulnerability,' and in a concomitant failure to confront issues of fragility, suffering or 'self-emptying' except in terms of victimology" (Coakley 1995, 106). The heteronomous relationship may also be empowering, and in fact is in quite a number of cases. Thus, with fear and trembling, both the feminist theologian and the biblical critic in our team recognize the importance of acknowledging the role of heteronomous experiences in the interpretive process. We do so because of our awareness that failing to account in the interpretive process for the role of heteronomous experiences and of the religious perceptions they engender has the disastrous consequence of universalizing and absolutizing them along with the interpretations, which, then, are triumphalist and oppressive.

15. Coakley deconstructs Hampson's view of heteronomy by reviewing numerous receptions of Philippians 2 and *kenōsis* through history, showing the many different ways in which they can be constructed. Thus, Coakley (1995, 82) readily agrees with Hampson (1996, 2) that a view of *kenōsis* that requires that Christians give up their autonomous self and identity in self-sacrifice and submission to some kind of patriarchal authority is a paradigm that, to put it mildly, is far from helpful for women. Yet, contrary to Hampson's expectations, Coakley shows that there are other possible views of *kenōsis* and heteronomy that do not require giving up autonomy in submission to a patriarchal authority.

16. The religious perception of the relation of believers as autonomous individuals to the actual conditions of their daily lives arises out of a particular heteronomous religious experience through which believers envision their relationship to the life-situations in which they are. Here, we paraphrase Althusser's neo-Marxist definition of ideology: "Ideology is a 'representation' of the imaginary relationship of individuals to their real condition of existence" (Althusser 1984, 36). We find Althusser's definition helpful because of his basic insight that ideology is tripolar and not bipolar. Traditional understanding of ideology (in Feuerbach and the early works of Marx) conceives of it as (1) the "imaginary/illusory representation" of (2) the "real conditions of human existence" (of life in the "real world"). Althusser recognizes in addition the essential role of a third pole, namely, the autonomous human beings who live by this ideology that puts them in "relationship" with the real world and who participate in the "imaginary" experience through which it is constructed. Thus, ideology is (1) a representation (for instance, in the interpretation of a biblical text) of (2) the imaginary relationship of individuals to (3) their real conditions of existence. As such ideology governs relational life (e.g., as political ideology), even as it shapes heteronomous religious perceptions of life (e.g., a view of sacred history or a modern secular view of history) and as it constructs autonomous views of one's identity. By contrast, a "dead ideology" is an ideology that is reduced, with disastrous consequences, to one of its three roles (see Havel 1999, 59). Consequently, for us, hermeneutical and analytical interpretive frames have "ideological" characteristics, as much as the contextual/pragmatic frame does.

17. Our emphasis on incarnation and present Christic manifestations does not mean that we fail to see God as holy and different from us. On the contrary, we affirm as an essential aspect of the believers' experience their encounter with the holy in the mystery of whom they dare to abandon themselves, giving up control over their own selves and over their lives in relation with others.

18. Our description of pastors and priests preparing their sermons by practicing scriptural criticism might seem idealistic. But even if they are a minority, such conscientious preachers do exist. We had the privilege to hear some of their sermons in Sweden, in the United States, in the Philippines, in France, in Congo-Brazzaville, and elsewhere. As academicians, we marveled each time. What exceptional interpretive skills in striving to interrelate the three interpretive moments! We also admired the oratory gifts that some of these preachers displayed. Yet what makes their preaching and ministry so substantive is their disciplined practice of scriptural criticism.

19. For both the feminist theologian and the biblical critic as post-Holocaust

reader, it is essential to recognize that the dreadful experiences of total vulnerability in the absence of God are genuine religious experiences. See Grenholm 1999a; Patte, "A Post-Holocaust Biblical Critic Responds" (chapter 9 in the present volume), who refers to Buber, Cohen, and Fackenheim.

20. This interweaving of the three modes of interpretation, and thus of the three sets of criteria and truth-claims, is often done subconsciously and hidden under the cover of "hermeneutics" (as Jeffner [1987, 37] points out).

21. Here we are not referring merely to traditional religious traditions. We affirm that there are many kinds of traditions, formally authorized as well as not formally authorized.

22. The text is then an "autonomous" locus of revelation.

23. A remarkable expression of this view of revelation is presented by Weems (1999, 42–49, and passim).

24. On aesthetics as a key component of true ethics, and thus, we extrapolate, of responsible interpretive practices, see Welch 1999, 119–36.

25. Generally speaking, this is the kind of scriptural reading one finds in Bernard de Clairvaux's commentary on Song of Songs. See, for instance, W. C. Smith 1993, 28–33.

26. And also its role as "talking book" in the spirituality of Asian women (see Kwok Pui-lan 1995, 44–56) and its role as conjuring a new reality in African-American traditions (see T. Smith 1994; Blount 1997, 262–84).

27. A bipolar reading, be it a pragmatic reading or an aesthetic reading, cannot have the integrative role that scriptural readings and, more generally, religious readings have, as Griffiths underscores (1999, 7–9, 22–59).

28. Thus, feminist biblical scholar Sharon Ringe writes, "A critical feminist reading of the Bible entails perspective, experience and commitment. The perspective is that of the multi-faceted social location occupied by women. Perspective is largely a given of the data of one's existence: gender, race, class, ethnicity, physical condition, relationships in which one is involved, and so on. Those data are transformed into experience as one becomes aware of how the data of social location intersect with events of personal, local and global history to result in suffering or well-being, inclusion or marginalization, participation as the subject of one's own life or merely as the object of others' decisions and actions. The commitment that makes a reading from such a perspective and experience specifically 'feminist' is commitment to the physical, psychological and social well-being of all women through the unmasking, revisioning and transformation of the institutions, social systems and ideologies that define women's lives in 'kyriarchal' social realities — that is, those in which a small group of elite males is dominant over all women and many men" (1997, 156). Similarly, theologian Edward Farley questioned the biblical critic's assumption that only one thing, the text, was interpreted: "And what is interpreted is not only one thing, the authoritative text, but everything that presents itself: the tradition, the local and even global situation, the paradigms that are disposing the interpretation, the acts and communications of other people" (1988, 128).

29. Heteronomous experiences might be punctual, fleeting but powerful encounters of the Other in surprising holy times separated by long periods of ordinary times marked by silence and absence of heteronomous encounters. In

such cases, the scriptural text as a pole might be limited to a few verses, a few words, or a symbolic story. But heteronomous experiences might be more diffuse, enduring, and peaceful encounters with the Other, a readily available Presence that one can meet in the quiet. In such cases, the scriptural text as a pole might become broader.

30. See, for instance, the history of this debate presented from a post-Bultmannian perspective in Harvey 1966.

31. Cf. Schüssler Fiorenza (1999, 9) on the original meaning of critical: "Since the words *critique* and *critical* are often understood in a negative, deconstructive, and cynical sense, I use these terms in their original sense of crisis. This expression is derived from the Greek word *krinein/krisis,* which means judging and judgment, evaluation and assessment. A critical approach is interested in weighing, evaluating, and judging texts and their contexts, in exploring crisis situations and seeking their adjudications. Its goals and functions are opposite to those of a positivist approach of 'pure' science."

32. While affirming this bipolar practice, we broaden the definition of these poles. In Stendahl's 1962 essay, the bipolar model "what the text meant" versus "what the text means" was exclusively formulated in terms of a historical paradigm. By defining the relationship between the two poles as "scriptural text" versus "the believers' religious perceptions of life," we keep open the possibility of conceiving it in terms of other paradigms, including a postmodern paradigm that underscores that any description of the text is focused on a specific textual dimension viewed as particularly significant in a sociocultural or religious context.

33. The fire analogy was suggested to us by Betsy Cagle.

34. This is not the place to discuss the many resources regarding theological education produced in the last twenty years or so. Our concern here is with the call to redefine the academic fields by "shifting boundaries," which our reflections include, and the fact that this call is heard and partially heeded, even as it is muffled by the resistance of the disciplines. We, the editors of this volume, believe that the theologians, church historians, biblical critics, and specialists of reception in the Romans through History and Cultures project heed this call to shift boundaries through our ongoing collaborative project. See Wheeler and Farley 1991 and bibliography. For a detailed "archeology" of the history of clergy education, see Farley 1983. Looking toward the places where transformation in theological education programs are ongoing, we refer to an experiment conducted by the Chicago Theological Seminary. In this project, developed under the leadership of the seminary president, feminist theologian Susan Thistlethwaite, the seminary community (students and faculty), and the "transformed and transforming communities of faith" are full-fledged partners in learning and teaching at the core of the curriculum. This innovative program promotes in North America the de-centering of theological education that one finds in other parts of the world through the deliberate contextualization of the programs, and consequently of the different disciplines. It is enough to mention here a few remarkable examples. For several decades, Union Theological Seminary of Philippine Christian University, Dasmariñas, Cavite (Philippines), has included within its core curriculum the study of the Protestant "revolutionary spirituality" that developed in

the Filipino colonialist context (Apilado 1999) and the formulation of this spirituality as inculturated Filipino theology (Aoanan 1998). Similarly, the Instituto Superior Evangélico de Estudios Teológicos, Buenos Aires, Argentina, integrated critical biblical studies and praxis in a life-context (Croatto 1987). Similarly, at the School of Theology at the University of Natal in Pietermaritzburg, South Africa, contextual theology (Draper 1998ff) and contextual biblical studies (West 1993, 1995) that deliberately find their starting points with the faiths and ideologies in southern African cultural settings have long been a part of the core curriculum.

35. This is the "banking concept of education" that Freire decries (1971, 57–74).

36. A similar point is made by Schüssler Fiorenza (1999, 38): "Since most biblical readers are not located in the university but in communities of faith, the religiously based paradigm of biblical studies must not be eclipsed."

37. Works inviting readers to different kinds of practice of what we call scriptural criticism include books by Grenholm (1990, 1996), E. A. Johnson (1992), Patte (1999), and Schneiders (1991).

38. Note that we presuppose that an interpreter by herself or himself cannot fully be aware of the interpretive process she or he used. This awareness comes through comparison with other interpretations.

39. As Luke Johnson (1998) says about Jesus.

40. See Kitzberger 2000.

41. See Wainwright 1994, 635–77.

42. See Sugirtharajah 1991.

References

Althusser, Louis. 1984. *Essays on Ideology.* London: Verso.

Aoanan, Melanio La Guardia. 1998. *Ecumenical and Prophetic: The Witness of the United Church of Christ in the Philippines.* Quezon City, Philippines: Claretian Publications.

Apilado, Mariano C. 1999. *Revolutionary Spirituality: A Study of the Protestant Role in the American Colonial Rule of the Philippines, 1898–1928.* Quezon City, Philippines: New Day.

Barr, James. 1980. *The Scope and Authority of the Bible.* Philadelphia: Westminster.

———. 1992. *The Garden of Eden and the Hope of Immortality: The Read-Tuckwell Lectures for 1990.* London: SCM; Minneapolis: Fortress.

Biderman, Shlomo. 1995. *Scripture and Knowledge: An Essay on Religious Epistemology.* Studies in the History of Religions 69. Leiden, New York, and London: Brill.

Blount, Brian K. 1997. "Righteousness from the Inside: The Transformative Spirituality of the Sermon on the Mount." Pp. 262–84 in *The Theological Interpretation of Scripture: Classic and Contemporary Readings,* ed. Stephen E. Fowl. Cambridge, Mass. and Oxford: Blackwell.

Boyarin, Daniel. 1994. *A Radical Jew: Paul and Politics of Identity.* Berkeley, Los Angeles, and London: University of California Press.

Brenner, Athalya, and Carole Fontaine, eds. 1997. *A Feminist Companion to Reading the Bible*. Sheffield: Sheffield Academic Press.

Buber, Martin. 1952. *Eclipse of God: Studies in the Relation between Religion and Philosophy*. New York: Harper.

Bultmann, Rudolf. 1960. "Is Exegesis Without Presuppositions Possible?" Pp. 289–96 in *Existence and Faith: Shorter Writings by Rudolf Bultmann*, ed. S. Ogden. Cleveland and New York: World Publishing Company.

Burgess, John P. 1998. *Why Scripture Matters: Reading the Bible in a Time of Church Conflict*. Louisville, Ky.: Westminster John Knox.

Carroll, Jackson W., Barbara G. Wheeler, Daniel O. Aleshire, and Penny Long Marler. 1997. *Being There: Culture and Formation in Two Theological Schools*. New York: Oxford University Press.

Chop, Rebecca. 1995. *Saving Work: Feminist Practices in Theological Education*. Louisville, Ky.: Westminster John Knox.

Coakley, Sarah. 1995. "Kenōsis and Subversion: On the Repression of 'Vulnerability' in Christian Feminist Writing." Pp. 82–111 in *Swallowing a Fishbone? Feminist Theologians Debate Christianity*, ed. Daphne Hampson. London: SPCK.

Cohen, Arthur A. 1981. *The Tremendum: A Theological Interpretation of the Holocaust*. New York: Crossroad.

Collange, Jean-François. 1998. "Qu'est-ce qu'une religion? Le religieux entre identité et altérité." *Études Théologiques et Religieuses* 73:557–70.

Croatto, J. Severino. 1987. *Biblical Hermeneutics: Toward a Theory of Reading as the Production of Meaning*. Maryknoll, N.Y.: Orbis.

Draper, Jonathan A. ed., 1998ff. *Bulletin for Contextual Theology in Southern Africa and Africa*. Pietermaritzburg, South Africa: University of Natal Press.

Fackenheim, Emil L. 1990. *The Jewish Bible after the Holocaust*. Bloomington and Indianapolis: Indiana University Press.

Farley, Edward. 1983. *Theologia: The Fragmentation and Unity of Theological Education*. Philadelphia: Fortress.

———. 1988. *The Fragility of Knowledge: Theological Education in the Church and the University*. Philadelphia: Fortress.

Fewell, Danna Nolan, and Gary A. Phillips, eds. 1997. *Bible and Ethics of Reading*. Semeia 77. Atlanta: Scholars Press.

Freire, Paulo. 1971. *Pedagogy of the Oppressed*. Trans. Myra Bergman Ramos. New York: Herder and Herder.

Gabler, Johann Philipp. 1980. "On the Proper Discrimination between Biblical and Dogmatic Theology and the Specific Objective of Each." *Scottish Journal of Theology* 33:133–58. (Original, "De justo discrimine theologiae biblicae et dogmaticae regundisque recte utriusque finibus," 1787.)

Grenholm, Cristina. 1990. *Romans Interpreted: A Comparative Analysis of the Commentaries of Barth, Nygren, Cranfield and Wilckens on Paul's Epistle to the Romans*. Studia Doctrinae Christianae Upsaliensa 30. Uppsala: Acta Universitatis Upsaliensis.

———. 1996. *The Old Testament, Christianity and Pluralism*. Tübingen: J. C. B. Mohr/Paul Siebeck.

————. 1999a. *Barmhärtig och sårbar: En bok om kristen tro på Jesus* [Merciful and Vulnerable: Contemporary Christian Faith in Jesus] Stockholm: Verbum.

————. 1999b. "The Doctrine of Justification: A Feminist Perspective." In *Justification in the World's Context,* ed. Wolfgang Greive and Viggo Mortenson. Geneva: Lutheran World Federation.

Grey, Mary. 1989. *Feminism, Redemption, and the Christian Tradition.* London: SCM.

Griffiths, Paul J. 1999. *Religious Reading: The Place of Reading in the Practice of Religion.* New York and Oxford: Oxford University Press.

Hampson, Daphne. 1996. "On Autonomy and Heteronomy." Pp. 1–16 in *Swallowing a Fishbone? Feminist Theologians Debate Christianity,* ed. Daphne Hampson. London: SPCK.

Harvey, Van. 1966. *The Historian and the Believer: A Confrontation of the Modern Historian's Principles of Judgment and the Christian's Will-to-Believe.* New York: Macmillan.

Havel, Václav. 1999. "The First Laugh," *New York Review of Books* 46, no. 20:59.

Isasi-Diaz, Ada Maria, and Yolanda Tarango. 1988. *Hispanic Women: Prophetic Voice in the Church.* San Francisco: Harper and Row.

Jeffner, Anders. 1982. "Att studera livsåskådningar" ["To Study Views of Life"]. Pp. 11–21 in *Aktuella livsåskådningar I: Existentialism och marxism* [*Contemporary Views of Life I: Existentialism and Marxism*], ed. Carl Reinhold Bråkenhielm et al. Lund: Doxa.

————. 1987. *Theology and Integration: Four Essays in Philosophical Theology.* Studia Doctrinae Christianae Upsaliensa 28. Uppsala: Acta Universitatis Upsaliensis.

Johnson, Elizabeth A. 1992. *SHE WHO IS: The Mystery of God in Feminist Theological Discourse.* New York: Crossroad.

Johnson, Luke Timothy. 1998. *Living Jesus: Learning the Heart of the Gospel.* San Francisco: HarperSanFrancisco.

Kasper, Walter. 1984. *God of Jesus Christ.* Trans. Matthew O'Connell. New York: Crossroad.

Kitzberger, Ingrid Rosa, ed. 2000. *Transformative Encounters: Jesus and Women Reviewed.* Biblical Interpretation Series 43. Leiden: Brill.

Kwok Pui-lan. 1995. *Discovering the Bible in the Non-Biblical World.* Maryknoll, N.Y.: Orbis.

Levenson, Jon. 1993. *The Death and Resurrection of the Beloved Son: The Transformation of Child Sacrifice in Judaism and Christianity.* New Haven and London: Yale University Press.

Lévinas, Emmanuel. 1985. *Ethics and Infinity.* Pittsburgh: Duquesne University Press.

Mananzan, Mary John. 1998. *Challenges to the Inner Room: Selected Essays and Speeches on Women.* Manila: Institute of Women's Studies.

Morgan, Robert, and John Barton. 1988. *Biblical Interpretation.* Oxford Bible Series 10. Oxford: Oxford University Press.

Patte, Daniel. 1983. *Paul's Faith and the Power of the Gospel: A Structural Introduction to the Pauline Letters.* Philadelphia: Fortress.

———. 1995. *Ethics of Biblical Interpretation: A Reevaluation.* Louisville, Ky.: Westminster John Knox.

———. 1996. *Discipleship According to the Sermon on the Mount: Four Legitimate Readings, Four Plausible Views of Discipleship, and Their Relative Values.* Harrisburg, Pa.: Trinity Press International.

———. 1997. "When Ethical Questions Transform Critical Biblical Studies." Pp. 271–84 in *Bible and Ethics of Readings,* ed. Danna Nolan Fewell and Gary A. Phillips. *Semeia* 77. Atlanta: Scholars Press.

———. 1999. *The Challenge of Discipleship: A Critical Study of the Sermon on the Mount as Scripture.* Harrisburg, Pa.: Trinity Press International.

Ringe, Sharon H. 1997. "An Approach to a Critical, Feminist, Theological Reading of the Bible." Pp. 156–63 in *A Feminist Companion to Reading the Bible,* ed. Athalya Brenner and Carole Fontaine. Sheffield: Sheffield Academic Press.

Schaberg, Jane. 1990. *The Illegitimacy of Jesus: A Feminist Theological Interpretation of the Infancy Narratives.* New York: Crossroad.

Schneiders, Sandra M. 1991. *The Revelatory Text: Interpreting the New Testament as Sacred Scripture.* San Francisco: HarperSanFrancisco.

Schüssler Fiorenza, Elisabeth. 1988. "The Ethics of Interpretation: De-Centering Biblical Scholarship." *Journal of Biblical Literature* 107:3–17.

———. 1995. *Jesus: Miriam's Child, Sophia's Prophet: Critical Issues in Feminist Christology.* New York: Continuum; London: SCM.

———. 1999. *Rhetoric and Ethic: The Politics of Biblical Studies.* Minneapolis: Fortress.

Segovia, Fernando F., and Mary Ann Tolbert, eds. 1998. *Teaching the Bible: The Discourses and Politics of Biblical Theology.* Maryknoll, N.Y.: Orbis.

Smith, Theophus. 1994. *Conjuring Culture: Biblical Formations of Black America.* New York and Oxford: Oxford University Press.

Smith, Wilfred Cantwell. 1993. *What Is Scripture? A Comparative Approach.* Minneapolis: Fortress.

Stendahl, Krister. 1962. "Biblical Theology, Contemporary." Pp. 418–32 in *The Interpreter's Dictionary of the Bible,* vol. 1., ed. George A. Buttrick. Nashville: Abingdon, 1962.

Stuhlmacher, Peter. 1994. *Paul's Letter to the Romans: A Commentary.* Trans. Scott J. Hafemann. Louisville, Ky.: Westminster John Knox.

Sugirtharajah, R. S., ed. 1991. *Voices from the Margin: Interpreting the Bible in the Third World.* Maryknoll, N.Y.: Orbis.

Thistlethwaite, Susan B., and George F. Cairns, eds. 1994. *Beyond Theological Tourism: Mentoring as a Grassroots Approach to Theological Education.* Maryknoll, N.Y.: Orbis.

Thistlethwaite, Susan B., and Mary Potter Engel, eds. 1990. *Lift Every Voice: Constructing Christian Theologies from the Underside.* New York: Harper and Row.

Tillich, Paul. 1964. *Systematic Theology.* Vol. 1. 4th ed. Digswell Place, England: James Nisbet.

Tracy, David. 1985. "Theological Method." Pp. 35–60 in *Christian Theology: An Introduction to Its Traditions and Tasks,* ed. Peter C. Hodgson and Robert H. King. 2nd ed. Philadelphia: Fortress.

Trible, Phyllis. 1985. *Texts of Terror: Literary-Feminist Readings of Biblical Narratives.* Overtures to Biblical Theology 2. Philadelphia: Fortress.

von Rad, Gerhard. 1987. *Genesis: A Commentary.* Rev. ed. Old Testament Library. London: SCM. (Original, *Das erste Buch Mose: Genesis.* Das Alte Testament Deutsch 2–4. Göttingen: Vandenhoeck and Ruprecht, 1964.)

Wainwright, Elaine. 1994. "The Gospel of Matthew." Pp. 635–77 in *A Feminist Commentary.* Vol. 2 of *Searching the Scriptures,* ed. Elisabeth Schüssler Fiorenza. New York: Crossroad.

Weems, Renita J. 1999. *Listening for God: A Minister's Journey through Silence and Doubt.* New York: Simon and Schuster.

Welch, Sharon D. 1999. *Sweet Dreams in America: Making Ethics and Spirituality Work.* New York and London: Routledge.

West, Gerald. 1993. *Contextual Bible Study.* Pietermaritzburg, South Africa: Cluster Publications.

———. 1995. *Biblical Hermeneutics of Liberation: Modes of Reading the Bible in the South African Context.* Rev. ed. Pietermaritzburg, South Africa: Cluster Publications; Maryknoll, N.Y.: Orbis.

Wheeler, Barbara G., and Edward Farley, eds. 1991. *Shifting Boundaries: Contextual Approaches to the Structure of Theological Education.* Louisville, Ky.: Westminster John Knox.

Williams, Delores S. 1990. *Sisters in the Wilderness: The Challenge of Womanist God-Talk.* Maryknoll, N.Y.: Orbis.

Wood, Charles M. 1985. *Vision and Discernment: An Orientation in Theological Study.* Atlanta: Scholars Press.

Wren, Brian. 1990. *What Language Shall I Borrow? God-Talk in Worship: A Male Response to Feminist Theology.* New York: Crossroad.

Part 1

RECEPTIONS AND CRITICAL INTERPRETATIONS OF ROMANS 4

-ONE-

Abraham, Father of Us All, in Barth's *Epistle to the Romans*

Thomas D. Parker

———— ◆ ————

Although it was the second edition (1922) of Barth's *Epistle to the Romans*[1] that initiated widespread discussions of the new "dialectical" theology, the guiding hermeneutical assumption of the entire theological movement was stated in the first edition (1918): "Our problems are **C** the problems of Paul; and if we be enlightened by the brightness of his answers, those answers must be ours" (Barth 1933, 1). Barth includes himself, his readers, and Paul and his readers in a wide circle that implicitly embraces all human persons. The letter addresses not only the **H** community of Christians at Rome, and by extension all other ancient Christian communities, Jewish and Gentile, but human beings simply as such. The body of the commentary makes clear that the subject matter is "our" concern; "we" are part of the conversation between the ancient wisdom and the wisdom of tomorrow. This places Barth's commentary firmly in a line of theological exegetes such as Luther and Calvin extending to our own time. This line includes Barth's contemporaries Rudolf **A** Bultmann and Friedrich Gogarten, both of whose existential exegeses later diverged markedly from Barth's own.

Who are "we"? Barth answers: we are human beings who confront **H** the *krisis* of finitude, existing in the contradiction of time and eternity **A** (Barth 1933, 10). The theme of Romans is how human beings can be **A** righteous before God their creator ("Origin"). Negatively, "we" are not

---

C Our problems are the problems of Paul.

H Romans as Scripture universally addresses all human beings in any time and place.

A Different forms of existential exegesis.

H The subject matter of the text is the *krisis* of human finitude.

A Discerning what Romans says about this subject matter.

God. Positively, "we" show up in the world and exist by virtue of what we are not, God. A correct reading of the text will be linked to concern for this shared subject matter (11). But this interpretation can be justified only by patiently working through the text to discern the truth of its discourse. Any commentary must deal with linguistic and historical matters, but in Barth's view, too few deal with the subject matter (*die Sache*) of the text.

C   Barth's focus on human beings simply as such shifts the discussion away from the intraecclesial conversations that concerned Luther and Calvin, however. Barth does not argue with earlier interpreters about such disputed questions as Phineas's justification by sacred violence (Ps. 106:30; Calvin 1960, 86–87) or the exegesis of Psalm 32 (Luther 1961, 123–45) in arguing against the scholastics. The question of whether Paul got the Genesis texts right is bracketed in a way neither Luther nor Calvin

A   could do. Barth relies on the exegetes of his time (e.g., Jülicher) for such discussions, not the history of ecclesial interpretation.

H   The question of what constitutes the subject matter of the text of Scripture was at issue in Reformation exegesis as it is in Barth's (or any other) work. The common tradition in the West held that there were four possible meanings to any text: the literal or historical, the ethical (tropological), the doctrinal (allegorical), and the mystical (anagogical). According to Thomas Aquinas, the latter three senses together are the

A   spiritual meaning. The literal or historical sense is primary, since the things signified by the words have themselves a deeper spiritual meaning (Aquinas 1945, 16–17). For both Luther and Calvin, the literal and spiritual meanings were inseparable. For a text like Romans, the literal meaning is the spiritual sense, for the things referred to are themselves spiritual realities. Barth agrees.

C   But how shall an interpreter discern the subject matter of Paul's Romans? The historical precedent of Luther especially and also of Calvin points the way: after establishing what stands in the text, the interpreter is to wrestle with it, to rethink it, until "the walls that separate the sixteenth century from the first become transparent," relativizing the distinction between yesterday and today (Barth 1933, 7) in struggle for the truth of the text and our lives as human beings who write them and read them. Thus, existential references to the "situation in which we are" (11) join with historical parallels and other contextual references (e.g., the exeget-

---

C Not ecclesial, but universal.

A Barth relies on the exegetes of his time.

H Literal meaning as spiritual meaning.

A Literal meaning as the most significant textual dimension.

C Dialectical struggle for the truth of the text and of the reality of our lives.

ical tradition) to establish a dialectical relation of text and reader. The voices in Romans and the voices in the reader's situation engage each other because both are concerned with the reality of human life in the world under God. This is Paul's subject matter and the reader's situation; an interpreter must be a skilled reader of both.[2]

The figure of Abraham is, for Barth, more than an exemplar of Paul's **H** teaching on faith as the meaning of the law, as it was for Calvin (1960, 7, 82 — an authoritative example for Christians). Barth's reading of the text is more in line with that of Luther (1961, 122): Abraham is the father of us all because he exists in that relation to God which is ours. In the *krisis* of all things human, he relies on God alone to secure his future. All witnesses to faith form one essential unity with Jesus (Barth 1933, 117) in whom the generic human situation vis-à-vis God is revealed and overcome. Without Abraham (and Dostoevsky!), Jesus is not the Christ.

> Jesus is established as the Christ, if his light is none other than the light of the Old Testament and of the whole history of religion and of all history, if the miracle of Christmas be the Advent of that light, for which the whole world of nature and of men, the whole creation visible and invisible, waits as for its fulfillment. (118)

The Christian community at Rome itself is included in this essential unity with Christ. Their "fidelity" in the face of the divine faithfulness manifests the resurrection of Jesus and his appointment as Son of God (32).

Romans 4 is thus not a stand-alone text describing an important his- **A** torical precursor, but the heart of the subject matter of which Paul writes. The argument of Romans leads from universal problematic of the righteousness of God through faith to the "we" of the epistle who themselves are realizations of the *krisis* and faith: "Therefore since we are justified by faith..." (Rom. 5:1). The rhetoric thus leads readers via Abraham from the meaning of Jesus Christ for the universal crisis of human faith and unbelief to understand how they are personally implicated in the way of faith revealed in Jesus the Christ. Romans 4 is the hinge joining the **C** general descriptions of the human condition and faith with the believer's personal situation.

H As witness of faith, Abraham exists in the universal *krisis* relation to God.

A Heart of the subject matter of Romans as a whole.

C Romans 4 joins general and personal.

Generic Traits of Humanity before God

A Barth reads the first three chapters of Romans as a generic description of the religious situation of human beings, simply as such, within which the appearance and destiny of Jesus Christ are to be understood.[3] This description is sketched in a rhetoric of conversation with persons and/or
H positions assumedly known to the readers and, by extension, to us.[4] It is depicted against background beliefs that Paul takes for granted, such as the human question of salvation (Rom. 1:16) in the face of pervasive destructiveness (1:18: unrighteousness) and the eternal power and deity of God, which limit and undergird human history (1:17: righteousness). The effect of these chapters is to focus on the tragic existential elements of the human situation rather than the merely moral ones — being in the right, so to say, rather than doing right things.

H   What is the truth about us as human beings confronted by the mystery of our origin and end and subjected to the ambiguities of history? We are as those "imprisoned" (Barth 1933, 37) who yet long for release only to find that there is no way out of our history except death. The hope of something more fuels the drive to transcend the conditions of finitude through a variety of cultural projects, chief among which are morality and religion. But no human project escapes the experienced reality of history: our best achievements are interlaced with sin and evil, confronted by disintegration and death. Barth takes these negations as determining the human condition. Human life is a "being unto death" (Heidegger, later), and no attempt to escape from evil can do more than increase
C its hold. The self-destruction of European culture and civilization in the First World War gave ample evidence of the *krisis* that lies at the heart of history.[5] "We" live the "universal questionableness of human life" (40 [Rom. 1:16–17]).

    Into this situation the gospel of Jesus Christ appears as the power of salvation to all who believe, the gospel of which Paul is not ashamed. Why should he be? There is no other. The gospel is a recollection of God, Creator and Redeemer, the primal Origin and End of all things. In
H a dialectical reversal, the gospel sets the inner questionableness of history itself in question. The conditions of finitude are themselves bounded by the mystery of the eternal. Beyond the line of death, the gospel proclaims resurrection (Rom. 1:16–17). In the midst of history's implacable judg-

---

A Romans 1–3 as description of the human religious situation in a rhetoric of conversation.

H The tragic in the human situation.

H Humans imprisoned in history.

C Self-destruction of European culture and civilization in WWI.

H The gospel sets the questionableness of history into question.

ments, the gospel proclaims mercy. In the face of human efforts to deny death through various "immortality projects," the gospel proclaims the futility and destructiveness of efforts to escape from evil and invites a wholly different way of being human.

Faith is that wholly different way. It is "the fidelity of men encounter-   H ing the faithfulness of God" (Barth 1933, 32). The faithfulness of God is manifest in two ways: God does not cease to create and govern the universe, nor does God cease offering a way through the negativities of history. The world endures and the conditions of history are maintained from beyond themselves. There is a term set to sin, death, and evil: they are bound by the conditions of history themselves, and not ultimate powers or meanings. But more. The very negations that throw down everything in history invite humans to look elsewhere for their source and sustenance. The "No" of God against destructiveness is the "Yes" of God to something beyond it, the faithfulness of God that overturns it and opens a future from God.

The primary word of faith is "nevertheless" (Barth 1933, 39). The divine faithfulness is encountered in the world that contradicts it. As all human beings live in that world, all have the possibility of faith.

> As surely as no one is removed from the universal questionableness of human life, so surely is no one excluded from the divine contradiction that is in Christ, by which this questionableness seeks to make itself known. (40)

Apart from faith that sees the negativities as divine judgment and the opening of another way, sin, death, and evil appear as wrath (Rom. 1:18), history as a kind of punishment for real or imagined wrongs. But in faith, human beings live from God's creativity and redemption, trusting what is beyond history for their life within history. "The possibility of hearing the Gospel is as universal as is the responsibility to hear it, and as is the promise vouchsafed to them who do hear it" (40).

Unfaith resists the judgment and so shuts itself up against the possibility of grace beyond history's negations. In place of the hidden grace of God it sets up the pseudograce of "No-God," the idols of the marketplace, theater, courtroom, and temple. Seeking release from negation, "we" fashion new forms of domination that only make matters worse. When these are swept away in history's judgment, the divine grace is again manifest, inviting faith. The "wrath" of God in history becomes the grace of God in history and the hope of all who are hemmed in by its negations. Paradoxically, the destruction of destruction is grasped by faith as good news, as the gospel of resurrection, the presence of the hidden God from beyond history creating life in the midst of death.

H Faith as a wholly different way.

H   This answer to the question of the truth about ourselves is the heart of what critics called Barth's "dialectical" theology. Barth intended it as more than a reading of the religious situation of the immediate post–World War I era, however. He put it forward as a reading of the perennial religious situation of human beings and therefore also of Paul, his op-
C   ponents, and his readers. It is buttressed with references to the cultural world in which the commentary is set but claims to wrestle with the question as it appeared in Paul's world.[6] The commentary details the way Paul's text addresses the questionableness of human religiousness as such, and its resolution through faith as attested in the gospel, rather than the ecclesial issues that so occupied Luther and Calvin.

Human Righteousness in the Face of the Righteousness of God

A   "The wrath of God is the judgment under which we stand insofar as we do not love the Judge" (Barth 1933, 42 [Rom. 1:18]), that is, apart
H   from and without Christ (43). With these words Barth begins his sketch of human religion as law in contrast to faith, and human righteousness as sin in contrast with grace. The first chapter of Romans details Paul's interpretation of the universality of sin as turning away from a knowledge of God the Creator (1:21) and the construction of alternative ultimates: images of things held divine without paradox, without the power to call their creators into question (1:22–23).

The result of turning away is more than refusal to live within the negativities of history; it is a positive defection from human vocation to accept the conditions of finitude and recognize the limit as gift (Rom. 1:22). The available, the desired, the arbitrary now become what is valued and relied on instead of fear and trembling in the face of God. The relation to God becomes ungodly, and human righteousness thinks to create a counterpart god that sacralizes God-forgetfulness. Godlike humans can allow themselves everything, however, and recognize no limit. In the end, humans in this condition are incapable of awe before what is other. They are "given up" to inordinate longing and social chaos (Barth 1933, 52–53 [1:24, 26]). This is the prison humans devise to escape the inescapable *krisis* and its resolution in faith.

H   The righteousness of God is manifest at the boundary of human life,

---

H Paul's text reads the perennial human situation.

C Religious situation in Paul's and Barth's cultural worlds.

A Romans 1–2 as description of human and divine righteousness (throughout this section).

H Human religion as law versus faith; human righteousness as sin versus grace.

H God's righteousness at the boundary of human life.

creating and sustaining all things within the limits of finitude (Rom. 3:1–4). God is not one thing (or many things) among others but the Origin and End of all things. God's righteousness is not identical with human righteousness, but stands in contrast to it. It is revealed in history as judgment on all human righteousness that refuses to acknowledge its dependence on God's goodness and gifts (Barth 1933, 80 [3:1–4]). It leads to repentance (2:3–5) not to religious self-justification.

The accidents of history, whether one is a Jew with a religious law or **C** a Gentile without one, do not affect the relation of human beings and God. How could they? Human beings are, irrespective of their cultures, **H** both recipients of the Creator's gifts and deniers of God's justice. The impartiality of God of which Paul speaks (Rom. 2:11) is an impartiality of both judgment and grace (2:6–10). Within the context of a wider Christian community that embraces Jews and Gentiles, Paul wrestles with the issue that concerns all without exception. With or without the law, human beings confront the *krisis* of all things human and the constant gift of God by which they are sustained. With or without the law human beings can turn from trust in idols to rely on that faithfulness of God.

Accepting the sentence of death on all things, persons of faith may turn to the source of life. In this turning, the origin and end of all things stands forth as God. It is revelation (Barth 1933, 63–70 [2:12–13]).

The Righteousness of God in the Face of Human Righteousness

What then of religion, of piety, of the law? Are not these the responses **A** of faithful persons, who express what they have heard and seen in the *krisis* as persons who have let God be God rather than seeking to justify themselves? If we follow their path, will we also not come to faith and be justified? Barth hears Paul wrestling with the question religious people must ask themselves: Of what value is being religious? Much and none! Precisely because the law (or piety, etc.) is a witness to the judg- **H** ment and grace of God, it is not itself the source of either. The witness is the historical "impression" (Barth 1933, 65) of revelation, not itself revelation. The witness can increase awareness of the *krisis* but cannot resolve it. The witness can create a clearing within which persons can be confronted with God. This is its value: to attest the reality of faith it cannot itself secure.

C Accidents of history, being Jew or Gentile, do not matter.

H Relation to God unaffected by history.

A Romans 3 as description of God's righteousness (throughout this section).

H Religion as witness of judgment and grace.

The law belongs to history, the realm of relative (only human) good and evil (Barth 1933, 77 [Rom. 3:1ff.]). The judgment of God is the "end of history," the righteousness of God as creator and sustainer of all. The relativization of all historical differences before God reveals their true meaning: dependence of God for their final meaning and justification. Yet the law remains a signpost or parable of God's righteousness (79 [3:1–4]) upon which faith relies. The question of whether God is righteous does not depend on human performance or nonperformance (3:5–8). That good may come in the face of evil is no commendation of evil, therefore, but a powerful witness to God's faithfulness.[7]

The perception of world as merely world and history as nothing more than history depends on perceiving it in contrast with an otherness neither world nor history: the nonhistorical origin and end of all things, the creative and sustaining power by which all things are (Rom. 3:21–22). This otherness runs through all culture and religion, and it generates the sense of *krisis*. It is the "impress" of revelation (1:19), apart from the law. Yet, the otherness is not merely a negation. It is the righteousness of God, the affirmation of God's "association with us" (Barth 1933, 93) as our God, in wrath and in forgiveness. Though we are imprisoned by our turning from God, God has not turned from us. Both judgment and forgiveness appear in human history from beyond, from God, who brings life from death (4:17) and righteousness from sin. The meaning of history is its redemption from beyond itself, from beyond law, and works, idolatries, and inhumanities.

The law and the prophets thus bear witness to the meaning of all religion (Barth 1922, 95). It becomes peculiarly visible in this history of judgment and promise. Within the history marked out by these witnesses, Jesus of Nazareth as the Christ appears. He is the definitive "impression" of God's faithfulness and righteousness, joining all other points in history that manifest it.

> Our discovery of the Christ in Jesus of Nazareth is authorised by the fact that every manifestation of the faithfulness of God points and bears witness to what we have actually encountered in Jesus. (Barth 1933, 96)

But he trusts in God as he sacrifices every historical claim and stands as a sinner among sinners. "He takes his place where God can be present only in questioning about Him" (97). Indirectly he bears witness to the faithfulness of the greater God.

H God's otherness is not merely a negation.

H Jesus as the definitive impression of God.

Jesus is the Christ for those who believe in him as they rely on God's **H** faithfulness beyond every human security. They are converted to a new disposition in relation to God and to all finite reality. This is faith, the **C** scandal of living in the *krisis* on the basis of the Unseen, irrespective of historical difference. This attitude is a new creation by the Word of God, a manifestation of God's grace, the promise of a "new man, . . . of a new world, . . . of the Kingdom of God" (Barth 1933, 103).

The revelation of the kingdom of God in Jesus as the Christ is a matter **H** of faith. He is the site at which the Word of God judges human pretensions and saves human creatureliness. Barth builds on Paul's use of redemption as the reconciliation set forth by God, a *Versöhnungsdecke* (1922, 79–80 [Rom. 3:24–25]).[8] "God gives life only through death" (Barth 1933, 105), that is, through a faithfulness that persists beyond the negations of history and directs faith to God's kingdom as the only true hope for humankind (106). Everywhere human beings have existed, forgiveness and the divine mercy have been poured out by divine patience, now in Jesus "we" have been given eyes to see God's faithfulness exhibited (3:27). The righteousness of God displayed in Jesus is mercy that leads to repentance. It is also that which, by leveling human distinctions in the face of God's forbearance everywhere, enables "us" to believe in ourselves and in all others as God's good creation (107; cf. Calvin 1960, 77).

Comparisons between Jews and Gentiles, those bound by the law and **H** those bound by conscience, are utterly beside the point in the face of the divine righteousness that justifies human beings on a wholly different basis. "In Jesus everything that occurs in the world is bent under the judgement of God and awaits His affirmation" (Barth 1933, 111 [Rom. 3:27–28]). Since the reality of deity depends on its universality (113), then, the most basic question of religion is raised here in the context of the issue of the relation of faith and the law as Paul presents it. And it is answered without equivocation: God is not found in any historical magnitude more than another. "He is, rather, the ground of all elements, by whom they are measured and in whom they are contained" (13). Law, conscience, and religious and nonreligious works all can be signposts to the righteousness of God only insofar as God is greater. Apart from a grace we do not possess, they manifest human sin and wrath, not a new creation.

H Faith in Christ beyond historical differences.

C Disregarding historical differences.

H Christ judges human pretensions and saves human creatureliness.

H Neither Jews nor Gentiles are right.

The Reality of God's Faithfulness
and Human Faith in Abraham

A
H
In Romans 4 Paul turns to the figure of Abraham, in whom the reality of God's faithfulness and human faith are actualized for all to see: the deepest significance of the law is established wherever human beings exist in the *krisis* of their history before God in faith. Alongside Jesus and authenticated by him is the paradigmatic figure of Abraham, father of all the faithful and, by extension, of all without exception for whom God is **H** merciful. Barth follows Luther (1961, 122–23) and Calvin (1960, 83–84) in taking Abraham's faith in the general sense as reliance on God alone for all things, and not just reliance on God for this and that, for land or descendants. It covers his calling from Haran as much as the specific promises. His reliance on God alone is his righteousness, not his virtue in believing (Calvin 1960, 84–85).

Historical achievement is set aside as a mark of distinction before God by the same grace that establishes them as persons.

> Jesus would not be the Christ if figures like Abraham . . . remained contrasted with Him, merely figures in past history, and did not constitute in Him one essential unity; if their positions were merely dissolved [*aufgehoben*] by the negation He proclaims and were not at the same time established. (Barth 1933, 117–18)

If Abraham had a claim to honor because of his righteous works, he would be worthy of great respect — but not before God, and therefore not in truth (Rom. 4:1–2). If, accordingly, historical achievement is decisive, then all is lost in the play of historical difference, and Abraham's greatness has nothing to do with Jeremiah or Jesus or us (117). As a sign of God's "unhistorical" righteousness, however, Abraham is one with Jesus and us. His righteousness is repentance and faith (119). The dissolution of all claims to virtue is the basis for human solidarity in the *krisis* of death and life, in sin, and in faith.

All great historical figures such as Abraham show their limits, and therefore indirectly the divine grace by which they live. The bookkeeping analogy ("reckoned to him for righteousness," Rom. 4:5) refers not to a possession of a better humanity but to the grace of One who "justifies the ungodly" (4:5). Genesis and Dostoevsky know this other way: human beings created, judged, and affirmed by God in spite of their defection in the crises of history (Barth 1933, 122–23). "If the line of death — his

---

A Romans 4 as paradigmatic actualization of God's faithfulness and human faith.

H The meaning of the law is the *krisis* of human history.

H Faith as reliance on God alone for all things.

human disestablishment through his establishment by God — be removed from Abraham's faith, its whole significance is removed" (121).

David attests this reality (of faith) as well (Rom. 4:6–8). The Bible shadows humanity with the light of eternity. In that light humans do not proclaim their greatness but their brokenness and their dependence on God alone above all in the face of their incapacity (Barth 1933, 123). As Luther (1961, 123) and Calvin (1960, 84–85) note in the context of discussion of religious good works, good works are acceptable to God and praised because God accepts the person, not vice versa. In faith, good works are calling upon God for grace not reward. They indicate the reliance of faith, not the perfection of love. Luther adds that perfect love of God is eschatological: God's love is given to those who believe, not to those who try to merit it (129).

As Paul reads the Genesis story, the narrative sequence attests this generic predicament and the resolution of faith.[9] Abraham's faith is his righteousness apart from circumcision, which attests it (Rom. 4:9–12). The divine forgiveness establishes the meaning of the sign, but remains **A** free from it and for it. Both Jews and Gentiles, at one in the face of death and in sin, at one in the promise of God's righteousness, are one in the faith of Abraham. As both uncircumcised and circumcised, Abraham lives by relying on the divine faithfulness. He is "father" of both or neither. Barth does not enter into the ecclesial question of the validity of a sacramental sign, so important for Luther and Calvin among earlier exegetes. For Barth, a true sign is precarious: it attests a founding grace beyond all signs.

The call of God precedes religion; the reality of revelation precedes its **H** impressions. Religion is unavoidable; it is the "reflection in the soul — in experience — of the miracle of faith which has occurred to the soul" from beyond it (Barth 1933, 128–29). Thus, true religion — e.g., circumcision (conscience?) — reminds humans they are not established by God by religion, and confirms their already real faith. If there is a difference between the religious and nonreligious, faith is void.[10] Nonreligion and antireligion (e.g., Nietzsche) are subject to the same critique as religion: insofar as they claim a higher and superior position (to be beyond the *krisis*), they are annulled by the judgment of God in the mode of wrath (136–37).

In Rom. 4:13–17a, the universality of the promise to Abraham and **H** his descendants that they should inherit the world is also undercut if

---

A The sign is of limited importance.

H Religion is annulled by God's judgment.

H Faith as recognizing that when God negates our possibilities, God gives us back our lives.

the parity of all people under God is infringed and God is understood as being partial to some human accomplishments but not others. This invalidates faith. While the Genesis account does not speak of the universal inheritance of all who share his faith in these words from Paul's religious world, through or outside the law, it does speak of his being a father of many nations. This means (for Barth, as for Luther [1961, 148–49] and Calvin [1960, 94–95]) that the word on which Abraham relied cuts through every human particularity: "Through the emergence of that status which men have in God, every human status is established by dissolution" (Barth 1933, 139). Seen in Christ, this father of the one nation is the father of us all on the same spiritual basis. "The historical framework is broken through when the secret of history is laid bare" (39).

Paul concludes that God, who gives life from the dead and calls nonexistent things into being (Rom. 4:17b), is the sole hope for Abraham against all historical possibility and impossibility (4:18–21). In a dialectical way, Barth notes, God is pure negation standing over against the negations of history (1933, 141). That God negates our possibilities means that God gives us back our lives on a new basis. Referring to Luther and Calvin, Barth notes that faith embraces the faithfulness of God in the face of ordinary human historical assessments. Abraham and Sarah face the same situation that all who rely on God alone to establish their lives face — and all others as well. The significance of their lives is a gift, not an achievement that will be washed away in the negations of history. Paradoxically, to recognize the end of history is to begin it anew as history (144).[11]

Summary of Barth's Reception of Romans 4: Abraham, Father of Us All

C Barth's theological exegesis of Romans stands self-consciously in the series of evangelical commentaries that looks back to Luther and Calvin, and beyond them to medieval and ancient models. Theological exegesis draws on its reading of the religious situation of its time in order to receive the text as an existential challenge as well as bearing cultural historical interest. Barth, and Bultmann with him, read that situation in the light of a cultural repertoire that included philosophical and literary modes of thought as well as traditional doctrinal ones. As Barth put it, when this letter is received as concerned with humanity before God, with its negative and positive meaning (the *krisis*), it is read as dealing with Paul's subject matter. Since that is a matter that concerns contemporary

---

C No disinterested reading.

readers, the letter is addressed to all readers with an existential challenge. One does not read Romans disinterestedly.

What of plural readings? Barth knows that there are others, which make different contributions, and that his own reading is merely historical, all-too-human, one of a series with no particular privilege. While this **H** reading cannot substitute for the readings that focus on Paul's historical and literary situation in a detached manner, or for readings dealing with other questions of existential moment, it claims to focus on the deepest concern that drives Paul as he struggles with the many local problems facing the Christian community at Rome he knows only at second hand. And it does so as a letter for the postwar generation in Germany.[12]   **C**

Accordingly, the "we" of the letter is read to include not only Paul **A** and Jewish and Gentile Christians, including those whose critical voices are heard, but Christians at all times, including Barth's readers. "We" is read confessionally and inclusively. Paul's distance from the Christian community in Rome provides a context for transcending the details of his personal situation to focus on the generic meanings of God's righteousness and of faith.

In sum, three themes are prominent in the argument of the letter lead- **H** ing up to and exemplified in Paul's treatment of Abraham before God. First, there is the theme of God's deity over against earthly historical humankind, the Origin and End of all creaturely reality. Barth rejects "inventory theism," as if God were one of a number of things on a list of things in the universe. Such a "God" is really not God at all, but the projection of human interests on the cosmos. The voice of Calvin echoes in the emphasis on God's deity: not just "greater" but "other."

The effect of this is to relativize historical difference. Within history, **C** which is all we can know, everything is equally subject to the judgment of time and circumstance. This solidarity under judgment connects humans with each other and with everything else at the same time that it removes all possibility of transcending the human condition. Everything is subject to death and dissolution. But it is also affirmed by the divine life-giving creativity. Humans die as those whose life was given them from beyond their own will and act, from the eternal God, whose creative goodwill remains the source of hope in the face of death and sin. This is the basis for insisting on the divine impartiality: God is judge and savior of all.

H The deepest concern of Paul.

C A letter for the postwar generation in Germany.

A Romans reflects Paul's distance from Christians in Rome.

H God as Other.

C Relativizing historical difference.

H   Second, there is the theme of the tragic character of human life that overcomes all moralism. In history, good and evil are mixed. Paul sees sin and relative righteousness among Jews and Gentiles alike. In the face of human sin, all our best goods are compromised, but none are without claim to be relatively good. Under the conditions of finitude, however, no good or evil can finally determine human life. Great achievements lead to crushing consequences, as the events of Barth's time showed. The voice of Luther sounds again in the recognition of the futility of good works *in loco justificationis.*

The effect of this is to lift up God's righteousness rather than human righteousness as the hope for salvation. God is righteous in judgment and in grace; in the former, one God limits the effects of good and evil, and in the latter, God establishes human beings as creatures, simply as such. For those who resist the judgment, history is experienced as wrath, the implacable no to any kind of utopia. For those who accept the judgment, history is experienced as the falling of the idols and as a clearing in which to rely on the divine faithfulness. Paul's move beyond moralism to faith in the promise of God is a witness to this wider context. Because he knows that only God can justify, he resists all attempts to enmesh God in the net of religiousness (or antireligiousness).

H   Third, there is the theme of faith (and hope) actualized in Abraham and decisively revealed in Jesus. Faith stands as a miracle over against human boasting: it has no foundation that would make it a matter of course or a crown of human achievement. It is simple acknowledgment that nevertheless God is God, and that salvation can only come from **C**   God, the creator and redeemer. This is the secret of Jesus' life that makes his life the site of reconciliation, the clearing where God's life-giving grace becomes a Word of gospel inviting our trust. It is the secret of Abraham's life (and David's) as well as our own.

A   The effect of this is to make Jesus the centerpoint of a narrative that includes us as well as the father of the faithful. The light thrown upon Abraham by the "gospel of God" illumines Abraham in such a way that readers can see not only the *krisis* he shares with them, but the One who stands behind the *krisis* and within it, offering life in the midst of death and justification for the ungodly. This is the divine righteousness. Because God is righteous, human beings may rely on God in hope. This is faith.

C   In the rhetoric of the letter, Abraham is the pivotal point at which the

---

H Faith beyond the tragic character of human life and its moralism.

H Faith actualized in Abraham and revealed in Jesus.

C Salvation as shared secret of human life.

A Jesus as the centerpoint of both Abraham's narrative and ours.

C The universal way to find our lives.

reality of faith in God, revealed in the gospel of God (Romans 1–3), is rendered in such a way that the connection between Jesus as the Christ and the Jewish and Gentile Christians, who rely on God's faithfulness revealed in him, is joined. In Romans 5, Paul can turn to the life of those who, through faith, now have peace with God. Far from being merely an example to secure an argument, Barth's Paul teaches that the reality of faith actualized in Abraham *is* directly the reality of faith experienced by Jewish and Gentile Christians on the basis of the gospel and, by extension, by all who accept the judgments of history and the grace of eternity. For there is finally no other way to found our lives.

Notes

1. All references to *The Epistle to the Romans* are to the English translation of the sixth edition (Barth 1929) by Edwin C. Hoskins (Barth 1933). This is a revision of the second edition (1922).

2. Barth's view was charged with importing meanings from his world into the text rather than extracting meanings from it. Aside from the fact that two-way traffic between world and text is unavoidable, his own view is limited to the assumption of an ontological difference between God and creatures that has a negative as well as a positive significance. Negatively, creatures are not divine but finite and temporal, existing within nature and history. Positively, creatures exist by virtue of a primal origin, a creativity entirely beyond their control. This ontological difference qualifies everything historical and makes any relation to God a critical one. In the preface to the second edition he connects this view with Kierkegaard's insistence on the infinite qualitative distinction between time and eternity (1933, 10). In the body of the commentary other elements of nineteenth-century intellectual culture are drawn on.

3. Compare Calvin's statement of the theme: "Man's only righteousness is the mercy of God in Christ, when it is offered by the Gospel and received by faith" (1960, 5).

4. Barth's text is sprinkled with the names of outsiders to the theological discussions of the nineteenth century: Franz Overbeck, Nietzsche, Dostoevsky, and Kierkegaard, as well as of insiders such as Calvin, Luther, Augustine, and, of course, Plato.

5. In a later reflection Barth acknowledged that his own decisive turn took place when the intellectual representatives of Christendom lined up in moral support of the war. Christianity itself is subject to dissolution and death.

6. The world of Barth's interpretation is the world of modernity that has cast off more explicitly religious meanings. Calvin and Luther saw the crisis of faith first of all within the ecclesial world of religious insecurities and religious works. The universal human predicament was implicated in its ecclesial form.

7. Barth sees the whole of history manifesting the judgment against history. Philosophers (e.g., from Plato through Nietzsche) and prophets (Jeremiah through Overbeck) display the root problem of finitude. Radical criticism's

"negation is all-embracing since it proceeds from an all-embracing affirmation" (1933, 87). The negativities of history prepare for the true God (Rom. 3:19–20).

8. Second edition. A term used in the first edition is *Versöhnungsgabe*. Our attempts to make a *Sühnesgabe* can be no more than representations of our need to be reconciled. When God stands forth in the middle of such an expiatory gift it becomes a means of reconciliation. See the first edition (reprint 1963), pp. 66–69. Neither Luther (1961, 116) nor Calvin (1960, 76–77) focuses on a narrow idea of expiation or satisfaction. For both, the central reality of Christ's self-offering is the offer of redemption (Calvin: blood stands for the whole) and forgiveness of sins.

9. Faith is, in this connection, "the impossibility from which all possibility emerges, the miracle from which proceeds all human experience, the paradox by which all direct and visible human being and having and doing is limited and rendered questionable ... and is established and affirmed ... as the divine 'nevertheless' and not as a divine 'therefore,' as forgiveness and not as an imprimatur upon what men are" (Barth 1933, 123).

10. "To be pilgrims means that men must perpetually return to the starting-point of that naked humanity which is absolute poverty and utter insecurity. God must not be sought as though he sat enthroned upon the summit of religious attainment" (Barth 1933, 132). Thus, faith is always miracle, surprise, the incalculable, rather than the security of banked virtues and achievements.

11. "This God, and the transformation of all things in relation to him — I saw a new heaven and a new earth — is the faith of Abraham, the radiance from light uncreated, the Genesis narrative, and the LOGOS of all history" (Barth 1933, 142). Before God, Abraham is the father of us all, irreligious and religious. As a postscript, Barth observes that apart from this presupposition, there is no meaning to history at all except the succession of epochs and events (145). But insofar as Abraham's situation is ours, history can reveal its value through such "communing": to display the *krisis* (146) in which all history stands, its "sickness unto death." "We" form one solidarity with Abraham and with Jesus as the Christ, in whom Abraham finds his ground in the "unhistorical" (faith) that forms the "substance" of all history (147).

12. As is well known, Barth turned to other things himself. In the years following the Second World War, he was critical of his stress on the negations of history rather than the actuality of God's grace operating in it (1960, 38–46). Characteristic positions of the Romans commentary remain presuppositions throughout his *Church Dogmatics*, however: the brokenness of theology, the criticism of religion as refined idolatry and of bourgeois Christianity in particular, the priority of God's grace and judgment (in that order), and faith as relying on the divine faithfulness.

References

Aquinas, Thomas. 1945. *Summa Theologica* 1.1.10. Pp. 16–17 in *Basic Writings of St. Thomas Aquinas,* vol. 1, ed. Anton C. Pegis. New York: Random House.

Barth, Karl. [1918] 1963. *Der Römerbrief*. Reprint, Zurich: EVZ.

————. [1922] 1929. *Der Römerbrief.* Munich: Christian Kaiser.

————. 1933. *The Epistle to the Romans.* Trans. Edwyn C. Hoskyns (from 6th ed.). London: Oxford University Press.

————. 1960. *The Humanity of God.* Trans. John Newton Thomas. Richmond: John Knox.

Calvin, John. 1960–61.*The Epistles of Paul the Apostle to the Romans and to the Thessalonians.* Calvin's Commentaries. Trans. Ross MacKenzie. Grand Rapids: Eerdmans.

Domanyi, Thomas. 1979. *Der Römerbriefkommentar des Thomas von Aquin: e. Beitr. zur Unters. seiner Auslegungsmethoden.* Basler und Berner Studien zur historischen und systematischen Theologie 39. Bern: Peter Lang.

Luther, Martin. 1961. *Luther: Lectures on Romans.* Library of Christian Classics 15. Trans. and ed. Wilhelm Pauck. Philadelphia: Westminster.

Rogers, Eugene F. 1995. *Thomas Aquinas and Karl Barth: Sacred Doctrine and the Natural Knowledge of God.* Notre Dame, Ind.: University of Notre Dame Press.

Steinmetz, David C. 1988. "Calvin and Abraham: The Interpretation of Romans 4 in the Sixteenth Century." *Church History* 57:443–55.

-TWO-

Multivocality in Romans 4

Robert L. Brawley

——— ◆ ———

A
C From the beginnings of its history of reception Romans speaks with multiple voices. Its language and rhetoric derive from an indeterminate intertextuality that already represents a host of voices (Kristeva 1980, 36–37, 64–66; Barthes 1977, 146–48). But on a discernible level, readers have access to multiple voices that give Romans rich textures. Layers of voices create patterns of reiteration that reinforce, redirect, elaborate, or contest one another (Suleiman 1980; Savaran 1988). Voices that reinforce one another contribute to determinate meaning. Voices that redirect or elaborate one another contribute to revisions of readers' anticipations in the progressive discovery of what is true in the world of the discourse. Voices that correct one another contribute to ambiguity and rivalry and create possibilities for distinct readings and for internal debate within Romans (Bakhtin 1984, 106; Kristeva 1980, 36–37, 66, 69).

This essay listens to varieties of voices via two methods. One is literary characterization inasmuch as some voices are overtly characterized (Brawley 1990, 107–58; Darr 1992). The second is intertextuality inasmuch as there are explicit and implicit repetitions of and variations on textual patterns from the cultural repertoire (Hays 1989; Brawley 1995). Characterization occurs through systems of epithets, relationships, actions, and evaluation that reiterate one another under proper names or designations of inanimate voices (such as Scripture). By intertextuality I mean an interplay of precursor and successor texts that offers readers new perceptions beyond the independent voices of the precursor and successor. This discussion offers highlights of both approaches. Because characterization is cumulative, I begin with progressive charac-

---

A Discerning voices of Romans through literary characterization and intertextuality.

C European-American theory.

terization in Rom. 1:1–3:31 from which the voices in Romans 4 trace their genealogy.

The Authorial Voice

The authorial voice concretizes itself in the proper name Paul and locates [A] itself in a triadic and mutually interactive relationship with God and the authorial audience. The authorial voice expresses a relationship to the authorial audience by giving thanks for and remembering them; the same thanksgiving and memory express a relationship to God through Jesus Christ; and the God to whom the authorial voice prays is a witness to the authorial audience of Paul's beneficence on their behalf.

A mutual benefit for the authorial voice and the authorial audience [A] is part of Paul's commission to proclaim good news. Paul's claim not to be ashamed of the gospel implies opponents who engage him in an honor/shame contest. In the honor/shame contest, God authenticates the authorial voice because the good news (Rom. 1:15–16) is nothing less than the power of God.

At Rom. 1:18 the authorial voice becomes an unobtrusive narrator of a drama of divine wrath (Wilckens 1964, 590; 1969, 52). This voice shifts in the diatribe of 2:1–29 as the authorial voice takes on the character of a debater engaging an imaginary interlocutor (Stowers 1981, 95–96 and passim). The situation is ambiguous at 3:1: "Then what is the advantage of the Jew?" Though likely part of the diatribe, the rhetorical question does not permit distinguishing between an address to an imaginary interlocutor (Stowers 1981, 119–54) or to the authorial audience or simply third-person discourse. According to Stanley Stowers, the diatribe style indicates that the first-person plural in 3:5 represents a teacher and an imaginary Jewish interlocutor (1994, 180–81). But God's judgment of the world in 3:6 and the power of sin over everyone in 3:9–19 incline toward construing "our" in 3:5 as universal. "The problem is extended to every human being and to God's trial with the whole world" (Käsemann 1980, 81–82). At 3:7 the discourse shifts to first-person singular. This too can be speech-in-character in a diatribe (Stowers 1994, 16–20), though actual opponents in 3:8 keep the section from being pure diatribe. Alternatively, it can be a concrete instance of a universal predicament. But this is complicated by the reference to opponents through which readers detect voices that accuse the authorial voice. The authorial voice reciprocates and condemns the opponents. Thus two voices contest each other.

[A] Triadic relation: Paul-God-authorial audience.

[A] Authorial voice, successively: in relation to authorial audience; in honor/shame contest; as narrator; diatribe debater; against opponents.

Romans 3:27 raises ambiguity. Are the rhetorical questions focalized through third-person narration or does the authorial voice address either the authorial audience or an imaginary interlocutor? The ambiguity is resolved slightly in favor of an address to the authorial audience by the use of the first-person plural in 3:28. For Stowers, "we hold that a person is justified by faith" is an agreement between a character in a diatribe and an interlocutor (1994, 180–81). But certainly there is agreement with the authorial audience. The same ambiguity and the same degree of resolution apply to the rhetorical questions in 3:29 and the recurrence of the first-person plural in 3:31.

The Authorial Audience

A The authorial audience is characterized as Gentiles located in Rome (Rom. 1:5–6). They too are in a triadic relationship with God and Paul. They are beloved by God and the object of Paul's divinely given commission (1:10–15).

At Rom. 1:18 the authorial audience appears to become spectators of a drama of God's wrath. The authorial audience views those who crush truth as actors on a stage before them. But a virtually unavoidable sting dupes the authorial audience. In 2:1 passing judgment on others renders the one who judges inexcusable. Judging on the first level is not unavoidable. Readers may be tolerant of people whose behavior is the same as theirs. But they can hardly tolerate hypocrites who judge others. **H** They inevitably judge hypocrites and thereby judge themselves. Even the authorial voice covers itself with the same blanket. Therefore, readers join the actors on the stage in the drama of God's wrath.[1]

Romans 2:17 does not unambiguously identify the authorial audience as Jewish. First, in the diatribe the one who hypothetically claims to be a Jew is an imaginary interlocutor. "One should not confuse depicting a Jew with encoding a Jewish audience" (Stowers 1994, 44; see 31, 143–75; 1981, 85–96). Further, everything in 2:17–23, 25 is either conditional or interrogative so that the addressee is indeterminate. Even the allusion to Isa. 52:5 in Rom. 2:24 does not establish the authorial audience as Jewish. It could apply to Gentiles who rely on the law but violate it. The sense could be that on account of such Gentiles, God's name is blasphemed among other Gentiles.[2]

In Rom. 3:21 a drama of God's justice that contrasts with the drama of God's wrath begins also as a third-person description with readers

---

A Authorial audience, successively: Gentiles in Rome; spectators then actors of the drama of God's wrath; possibly, Jewish audience; spectators and/or actors of the drama of God's justice.

H Judging hypocrites who judge others.

as potential spectators. But because readers become participants in the drama of God's wrath, they may also participate in the drama of God's justice. Thus Käsemann takes this drama as universal with cosmological dimensions of the power of God's grace (1980, 92–94). But if cosmological, God's justice is qualified for human beings: "for all who believe" (3:22). Readers are included among those who participate in faith. Further, they have a faith that enables Paul to anticipate reciprocal benefits of faith with them. Therefore, the "we" of 3:31 implicates the authorial audience as people of faith.

Jesus

Though Jesus does not appear in Romans 4 until v. 24, and though his **A** voice is silent in the chapter, he figures prominently in other characterizations. Further, he is present by implication, particularly in the links between 3:21–31 and ch. 4. He first appears in a relationship with Paul, his servant, and he is designated Christ. It is conventional to speak of Christ as Paul's second name for Jesus. But this is inadequate in 1:1–6 (see also 9:5; Dahl 1953, 86–87, 91–92). He is messianic as God's son and as a descendant from David. Readers likely construe ὁρισθέντος ("declared") in 1:4 as the validation of Jesus by God's power that raised him from the dead. Thus, descent from David according to the flesh stands in antithesis to the resurrection from the dead (Dahl 1953, 90). The epithet "lord" also characterizes Jesus and places him in relationship with people of faith.

Ambiguity appears in Rom. 1:9. God's "son" is theoretically either the **H** source of the gospel or its content. The genitive here is likely objective — a reiteration of God's son as the content of the gospel in 1:3. After 1:9 Jesus vanishes until 3:22, though he remains the content of the gospel mentioned in 1:15–16.

Jesus reappears at Rom. 3:22 with weighty ambiguity. God's justice is **H** modified by διὰ πίστεως Ἰησοῦ Χριστοῦ. The genitive can be either subjective (the faith Jesus has [Hays 1983, 157–84]) or objective (faith that others have in Jesus). But because readers encounter this in a sequence following references that characterize Jesus as one who mediates grace, readers can construe Jesus as one who mediates the disclosure of God's justice.[3] Alternatively, faith in Jesus can be the means of the disclosure of God's justice. In this case Jesus is the object of faith.

A Jesus before Romans 4 and by implication.

H God's son as source or content of gospel.

H Faith of Jesus or faith in Jesus.

Similar ambiguity surrounds the redemption that is in Christ Jesus in Rom. 3:24, where the syntax closely parallels 3:22:

διὰ πίστεως Ἰησοῦ Χριστοῦ (v. 22)
διὰ τῆς ἀπολυτρώσεως τῆς ἐν Χριστῷ Ἰησοῦ (v. 24)
("through the redemption in Christ Jesus")

H   Jesus may mediate redemption or redemption may be located in him. A relationship with God is reiterated in that God provides Jesus as a ἱλαστήριον ("mercy seat," v. 25). The ἱλαστήριον is more mysterious than ambiguous but likely characterizes Jesus' death as atonement. The atonement echoes Jesus' relationships both with God and with all who believe (vv. 22–24). Διὰ πίστεως, however, also modifies ἱλαστήριον with ambiguity. It may refer to the faith of all who believe or to Jesus' faithfulness (Hays 1983, 172–73; Stowers 1994, 201, 214, 240–41).

Jesus' characterization through relationships with God and with all who believe is reiterated in Rom. 3:26. Here again ἐκ πίστεως Ἰησοῦ raises ambiguity. Does God justify the one who has faith in Jesus or the one who has faith(fulness) like the faith(fulness) of Jesus?

God

C
A   God enters Romans from a cultural repertoire as Israel's God of the ages. A promise maker who spoke through Israel's prophets, God is the source of good news as both a promise of the past and a reality for the present (Rom. 1:1–3). God is characterized by acting with power to raise Jesus from the dead. It is difficult to discern whether "according to the spirit" (1:4) is an epithet for God or a qualification for Jesus. Because of the parallel with "according to flesh" in 1:3, it is possible to construe the Greek as referring to Jesus in his spiritual nature (Schweizer 1969, 417). But if "according to the spirit" modifies God's power, it identifies God.

C   God is characterized also by a relationship with Jesus. But relationships with Paul and the authorial audience mediated through Jesus also char-
H   acterize God. As the one who calls and bears witness to Paul (1:1, 9), God legitimates the epistle itself, and consequently God's voice speaks in the entirety of Romans.

God is further characterized by God's power for salvation (Rom. 1:16). This power indicates not only God's activity but also a relationship

---

H Jesus mediates redemption or redemption is located in him.
C Cultural repertoire of Israel's God of the ages.
A God's righteous voice and actions.
C Relationship of God with Paul and authorial audience.
H God's voice in the entirety of Romans.

with everyone who has faith. Through faith, God stands in a relationship to both Jews and Gentiles as the God of their salvation.

God is directly characterized by the advent of δικαιοσύνη ("justice," Rom. 1:17). But this raises again the problem of the objective/subjective genitive. Is justice a divine attribute or divinely attributed? According to the progressive development of what is true in the discourse, the answer is closely related to the advent of God's wrath in 1:18. Fitzmyer judges that the contrast with God's wrath makes justice a divine attribute (1993, 257; see Käsemann 1980, 35). But wrath is not merely a divine attribute in 1:18–3:20 because it invades human existence. Justice and wrath characterize God by implied actions toward humanity. Reiteration thematizes character, and three times Romans 1 repeats God's act of handing human beings over to themselves (1:24, 26, 28).[4] In an implied chronology, the advent of God's wrath has both priority and simultaneity with God's justice. The simultaneity is that God's power and divinity are perceptible but not perceived. Therefore, the advent of God's wrath breaks into history with chronological priority over the advent of God's justice.

Characterization of God as rich in kindness, forbearance, and patience **H** both stands in tension with and contributes to God as judge (Rom. 2:4). According to the implied chronology, God is first kind and patient in order to evoke repentance. But in the absence of repentance, the forbearance reinforces all the more God's just judgment. God is related to humanity with one of two faces, goodness or wrath; but also with one face, impartiality (2:11).

Readers learn in the progressive discovery of what is true in the dis- **H** course that a relationship with God's law is distinct from a relationship with God. Three honor/shame contests appear in Romans 2: in 2:17 a hypothetical interlocutor boasts in God in a contest for honor; in 2:23–24 God's honor itself is at stake; and in 2:27 people for whom circumcision is a matter of the heart acquire honor. In the first, the interlocutor in 2:17 depends on the law and boasts in God only to discover that God is not an agent of social vindication in the honor/shame contest implied by boasting (Malina and Neyrey 1991, 27–36; 1988:35–36). In the second, those who boast in God's law but transgress it effectively label God a social deviant. That is, they locate God outside social norms, and the audience for the social confirmation of this honor/shame contest is the Gentiles. In the third, God gives the verdict on the honor/shame contest. By an implied antithesis, those who boast in God but transgress the law may receive a social evaluation of praise from human beings. But those for whom circumcision is a matter of the heart receive no positive social

---

H The two faces of God.
H God's law is distinct from God.

evaluation from human beings. Rather, God's praise confirms them as authentic winners of the honor/shame contest (2:29).

In the progressive development of what is true in the discourse, God entrusts τὰ λόγια τοῦ θεοῦ ("the oracles of God") to the Jews (Rom. 3:2). When in spite of τὰ λόγια human beings are unfaithful, God's response is fidelity. The authorial voice negates even the possibility that human response annuls God fidelity and evaluates God as truthful in contrast to the falsehood of every human being. Axiomatically God is just (3:4–6).

In addition, Scripture's voice underlies the authorial voice, and the multiplicity of voices reiterates and thematizes God's justice. Romans 3:10–20 is an extended repetitive characterization of God in contrast to human beings. This also appeals to and clarifies the content of 1:18–3:8. A series of antitheses points to the characterization of God in contrast to culpable human beings: just/unjust, benevolent/malevolent, truthful/deceptive, nourishing/poisonous, blessing/cursing, sweetness/bitterness, saving life/shedding blood, preserving/ruining, blessing/misery, peace/conflict.

God's wrath and justice are simultaneous but also successive. Therefore, all of the characterization of God in Rom. 1:18–3:20 falls under the canopy of God's wrath. Even God's justice in 3:1–8 justifies God's wrath. But God's justice achieves preeminence with νυνὶ δέ ("but now") in 3:21. Thereafter readers revise the characterization of God under the canopy of God's justice.

God's grace qualifies God's character in relation to humanity. Now God does function as an agent in an honor/shame contest to vindicate believers. Moreover, the ἱλαστήριον in Christ that God puts forth qualifies grace because it demonstrates God's justice in passing over former transgressions. But further ambiguity also vexes readers. Does the ἱλαστήριον become effective through faith in Jesus' blood? Does the ἱλαστήριον in Jesus' blood become effective through faith? Does the ἱλαστήριον in Jesus' blood become effective through Jesus' faithfulness? Interpreters tend to make ἱλαστήριον a heavenly place of transaction between God and Jesus. But it is also possible to understand Jesus' blood as a reference to the crucifixion. God's passing over former sins, then, is concretized in forgiving the sin manifest in the crucifixion of Jesus (Stowers 1994, 37–38). Consequently, God is characterized as just and a justifier.

God's relationship to humanity that rests on faith is itself grounded in a further feature of God's character. God is one (Rom. 3:30). This

---

🔲 God is axiomatically just.

🔲 From God's wrath to God's justice.

🔲 Monotheism.

reinforces and develops God's impartiality (2:11; 3:22). Thus, radical monotheism is fundamental to God's character as both judge and justifier.

The Scriptures and the Prophets

Romans 1:2 appeals not to Scripture in its entirety but to prophetic me- **A** diation of God's promise. The voice of God is embedded in voices of **H** prophets that are in turn embedded in the voice of Scripture. Though **C** the scriptural voice is concealed in γέγραπται ("it is written") in 1:17, readers who know the cultural repertoire can identify Habakkuk's voice. But ambiguity accompanies the citation. Εκ πίστεως ("from faith") can denote either having faith or being faithful, and the phrase can modify either δίκαιος ("just") or ζήσεται ("will live").

Romans 2:12 introduces νόμος ("law"). Romans 2:14 specifies that the law is a Jewish possession in contrast to the Gentiles. There is no **H** necessity to consider law as Scripture except that 2:15 implicitly contrasts an external written law with an internal reality. At least the work of the law is γραπτόν ("written").

The characterization of the law is intricate. On the one hand, it may be equated with what is written (διὰ γράμματος, "through letter," Rom. 2:27).[5] On the other hand, it may be the laws contained in what is writ- ten — such as prohibitions against stealing, adultery, and idolatry (2:22). Thus, 2:26 speaks of τὰ δικαιώματα τοῦ νόμου as just decrees that per- tain to the law. This reiterates the language of 1:32, and readers may deduce that at least one way to know God's decree is through Scripture. But another part of the intricacy is that in the midst of a discussion *about* **H** Scripture, 2:24 cites a passage *from* Scripture — Isa. 52:5 LXX.

In Isa. 52:5 God's name is blasphemed because Gentiles have taken away God's people. But Rom. 2:24 argues that transgressors of the law cause God's name to be blasphemed among Gentiles. This may appear to be a manipulative prooftext, but readers who know the cultural reper- toire may take it as intertextual interplay. Such readers hear two voices reverberating back and forth: the authorial voice and the prophetic voice- over. When readers hear the two voices in interplay, they also hear the irony that Romans inverts the places Jews and Gentiles occupy in Isaiah, and that very plot plays out in the argument of Romans 4.

Readers may be perplexed about whether τὰ λόγια (Rom. 3:2) means

---

A Ambiguity and paradox embedded in voices of Scripture as cultural repertoire.

H Scripture as mediation of God's promise.

C Readings sharing the cultural repertoire will identify ambiguity and paradox.

H The law as Jewish Scripture.

H Scripture interprets Scripture.

Scripture or not.[6] But two associations make it likely. One is the association of τὰ λόγια τοῦ θεοῦ with circumcision in 3:1 as a part of τὸν διὰ γράμματος in 2:27. The other is the association of τὰ λόγια with God's fidelity, presumably God's fidelity to promises in Scripture. Further, 3:4 appeals to Scripture by citing Ps. 51:4 (Ps. 50:6 LXX), which is attributed to David. So the voice of David is embedded in a voice of Scripture that is embedded in the authorial voice. The citation is construed so as to show God's fidelity. This divine fidelity reinforces the thematization of the gospel as a scriptural promise that first appears in 1:1–2.

H   Another appeal to Scripture contrasts human infidelity with divine fidelity (Rom. 3:10–18). Not only is the appeal a composite of texts, but also, voices are embedded in voices.[7] When readers hear the authorial voice in this catena of texts, they hear multiple voices of Scripture. But the multiple voices of Scripture speak in the authorial voice.

In Rom. 3:19–20 the law possesses the trait of speaking. It renders all humanity accountable to God, and it mediates recognition of sin. This contrasts sharply with prophetic promises in Scripture in 1:1–3 and the thematization of God's fidelity to τὰ λόγια in 3:2. Again, in speaking about the law Paul makes a strong allusion to Scripture with a virtual citation of Ps. 142:2 LXX. For readers who know the cultural repertoire there is irony because the first half of the sentence from which the allusion comes is a plea against judgment. The psalm beseeches God (1) on the basis of the common guilt of everyone (2) not to judge. But apparently for Paul the logic of the psalm skips a step: (1) on the basis of common guilt (2) God judges everyone (3) so that the only way God does not judge is to have mercy. Therefore, Ps. 142:2 LXX can be the negative counterpart to the promise of divine mercy for all. Here again the argument of the discourse plays out the plot of the psalm.

Romans 3:31 claims that the faith it espouses upholds the law. Doubtless this refers backward to πίστις Ἰησοῦ Χριστοῦ. But in anticipation of the case of Abraham, it forms a bridge to Romans 4. God's justice for Abraham upholds the νόμος with the paradox that the νόμος will demonstrate that justification does not come from the νόμος (Hübner 1984, 53).[8]

Romans 4

A   Is the authorial audience included in the "we" in Rom. 4:1? According to Stowers, readers still hear the interlocutor of the diatribe who raises a false objection to which the example of Abraham responds. Though

---

H Multiple voices of Scripture.

A The "we" as dialogical or Paul and Jewish compatriots or authorial audience.

Stowers alleges Hellenistic parallels, the text lacks clues for readers to shift back and forth from the voice of a teacher to the voice of an interlocutor (Stowers 1982, 136; 1994, 232; Hays 1985, 79 n. 13). Stowers obviously demonstrates a reading of Romans 4 in which the voice of a teacher answers an interlocutor's question, and in this case "we" is "dialogical." But in the progressive development of the discourse, do readers gain insight for construing the first-person plural in Romans 4 differently?

Naming Abraham "our progenitor" may mean that Abraham is **H** (1) Paul's ancestor, (2) the ancestor of the Jewish people excluding the authorial audience, or (3) the ancestor of the Jewish people including the authorial audience. If Abraham is the physical progenitor of the Jews, the third alternative would characterize the authorial audience as Jewish. This is problematic because they are already characterized as Gentiles. But does κατὰ σάρκα ("according to flesh") designate Abraham as the progenitor of the Jewish people only? Romans 4:18 recalls a divine promise that Abraham will be ancestor of πολλῶν ἐθνῶν ("of many nations [Gentiles]"). Further, in Romans 4 κατὰ σάρκα in the first instance refers to Abraham before he was circumcised, and apparently in 9:8 Abraham's children according to the flesh are not the descendants of Isaac but of Hagar's and Keturah's sons. Does Paul view Abraham as an Adamic progenitor—the father of many nations? Certainly not altogether in the literal sense of genealogy. Rather, Abraham as progenitor is qualified by the heirs of his faith and by the faith of his heirs. Klein concurs with hyperbole: "Abraham is no one's father—he becomes father in and through faith" (1963, 436; see Wilckens 1964, 599–600; Kertelge 1967, 194).

In addition, the initial reference to Abraham contains grammatical **A** and syntactical ambiguity that allows for multiple readings of Rom. 4:1. (1) What did Abraham our ancestor discover with respect to the flesh? (Dunn 1988, 198). (2) What did Abraham our ancestor according to the flesh discover?⁹ (3) Have we found Abraham to be our ancestor according to the flesh? (insinuating that the answer is no) (Hays 1985). Therefore, "we" in 4:1 can include the author and authorial audience in a confessional "we," or can denote the dialogical voices of speech-in-character of a teacher and an interlocutor, or can indicate Jewish compatriots of the authorial voice, or can redefine Abraham's relationship with the authorial audience beyond Jewish identity. In face of this indeterminacy, it remains to see if the progressive discovery of what is true in the discourse will enable readers to gain clarity.

H Constructing Abraham as "our progenitor."
A Abraham, ancestor of whom?

A
C   In retelling Abraham's story, Romans 4 is an intertextual interplay with a cultural repertoire that embraces Scripture and tradition. Käsemann avers that Paul's argument from Scripture is ineffectual for modern readers because it disregards the historical meaning of Scripture (1980, 115). But he fails to consider the way intertextuality involves revisionary interplay between a precursor and successor text. Readers catch revisionary irony only as the successor transforms the precursor. Thus, Abraham's story is repeated from a cultural repertoire that includes Scripture and tradition, but with a twist.

C   Even readers unfamiliar with the cultural repertoire can overhear the hypogram of the tradition, that is, that which a text presupposes and engages in interplay (Riffaterre 1978, 12–13 and passim). For example, Abraham possesses ascribed honor as a venerable ancestor and acquired honor as a heroic protagonist. He stands in a relationship with God so that none other than God is the agent who acclaims his honor. Moreover, his relationship with God is distinguished by a divine promise that the authorial voice presumes is a shared datum of the cultural repertoire (Rom. 4:13).

More explicitly, the voice of Scripture speaks through the citation of Gen. 15:6, the backbone of Romans 4 (Hahn 1971, 100–101). In addition, Ps. 31:1–2 LXX gives an explication of the blessedness Abraham received according to Genesis (Hanson 1974, 53–58). Further, the discourse in Romans 4 implies the details of Psalm 31 LXX beyond the citation so that readers who know the cultural repertoire can hear further reaches of the psalm.

A   But Scripture also speaks with competing voices. The citation of Gen. 15:6 and Ps. 31:1–2 LXX and the whole story of Abraham reflect a positive voice of Scripture, so that in harmony with Rom. 3:21 readers can understand that the law attests God's justice.[10] On the other hand, law is not the means through which the promise came to Abraham (4:13). Klein hears primarily a polemical voice in Paul's retelling of Abraham's story because he hears a Jewish version that Romans contradicts (1963). Wilckens hears rather a more positive voice in Paul's emphasis on God's grace in relation to Abraham's justification (1964).[11] Further, the law speaks with the voice of wrath by identifying transgressions (4:15) (Hübner 1984, 79–80). This doubled voice of Scripture, positive and pejorative, reiterates and therefore thematizes 3:21, where though law attests God's justice, the disclosure of God's justice is apart from law.

A Romans 4 as intertextual interplay with Scripture and tradition.

C Readers are getting a new view on their cultural repertoire.

C Readers unfamiliar with cultural repertoire overhear tradition.

A Competing voices of Scripture.

In this sense 3:31 claims to uphold law against the supposition that the argument overthrows law.

Abraham's voice in Romans 4 corresponds to prophetic voices in 　**A**
Scripture, but it is also distinct in that Abraham is a protagonist in a narrative. In Romans 4 his voice is never overt, but under the third- 　**H**
person discourse readers nevertheless hear Abraham say, "I believe." His belief is reiterated in 4:17, 18, 20–21. Under the allusion to Scripture in 4:18, readers hear Abraham say, "I believe that I shall be the father of many nations [Gentiles]."

Abraham's voice speaks differently, however, in Rom. 4:17 and 20–21. In the case of 4:17, voices are mixed with voices. Under the third-person discourse, readers can hear Abraham say, "I believe in the God who makes the dead alive and calls into existence things that do not exist." Here Abraham's scriptural voice is mediated through the cultural repertoire. Obviously his belief recalls creation in Genesis 1. But Genesis 1 LXX takes a retrospective view toward God's creative speech so that the verbs are in the aorist. In Romans 4 God's act of calling into existence is in the present tense and is expressed with the verb καλέω ("I call") in harmony with the present tense of the same verb in Isa. 48:12–13 LXX (cf. Wisd. 11:15). Though Isa. 48:13 LXX has reference to creation, it even employs καλέω in the future tense. Καλέω is also reminiscent of Philo: τὰ γὰρ μὴ ὄντα ἐκάλεσεν εἰς τὸ εἶναι ("for he has called the things that exist into being," *Spec. Laws* 4.187 [cf. *Creation* 81; *Alleg. Interp.* 3.10; *Names* 46; *Jos. Asen.* 8:2, 9; *2 Bar.* 21:4; 48:8]) (Delling 1963, 31 n. 3). Further, parallel use of καλέω in Hellenistic religions may extend the cultural repertoire through which Abraham's voice is mediated (Schmidt 1965, 490).

Abraham's belief according to Rom. 4:17 also parallels *Shemoneh Es-* 　**H**
reh 2: "YHWH who makes the dead alive." Readers who know this textual pattern in the cultural repertoire can hear Abraham's voice in 4:17 in play with another voice (Käsemann 1980, 121). All of these voices are finally embedded in the authorial voice, and perhaps in 4:20–21 readers can hear a hypogram of Abraham's belief related only to an indeterminate cultural repertoire: "I am convinced that God is able to accomplish what is promised."

Abraham's voice is also mediated through Paul's notion that God has acted in Jesus' death and resurrection. In light of the developing voices in Romans 1–3, the absence of Jesus until 4:24 is conspicuous. But he is hardly out of sight, because parallels between 3:21–31 and ch. 4 induce

---

A Abraham's voice.

H Constructing Abraham's confession.

H Constructing Abraham's belief.

readers to view Abraham's story through messianist lenses. According to 3:25, God displayed Jesus publicly as a demonstration of God's justice in the remission of former transgressions. This line of thought has strong parallels in ch. 4, where God justifies the ungodly (4:5). The beatitude in 4:7–8 then makes Abraham a case in point of those whose sins are forgiven (Hanson 1974, 52–66; Wilckens 1961, 112; Dunn 1988, 229; in contrast, Fitzmyer 1993, 375). But 3:25 views God's dealings with former sins through God's act in Jesus, and so ch. 4 nuances Abraham's story

H from a christological perspective. As a consequence, Abraham's belief in the face of his own impotence (as good as dead) and Sarah's barrenness (postmenopausal in the superlative degree) can be equivalent to resurrection faith (Käsemann 1980, 123).[12] Belief in the God who gives life to the dead refers to life from Abraham's impotent body and Sarah's barren womb; however, it also has overtones of Jesus' resurrection.

Furthermore, because of the messianist perspective, the authorial voice also represses part of Abraham's scriptural voice. Jewish traditions that make Abraham heroic (*Jub.* 16:28; 17:15–18; 18:16; 19:8; 23:10; 24:11; 1 Macc. 2:50–52; Sir. 44:19–20; 2 *Bar.* 57:1–2; CD 3:2) show that he is capable of boasting, but the authorial voice silences his voice from such boasting. Further, the authorial voice silences Abraham's vacillation in Genesis so that he does not waver in his faith (Rom. 4:20).

A
H As with Abraham, the voice of Abraham's descendants also emerges in references to their belief. But a startling inversion occurs in identifying Abraham's descendants. Romans 1:16 establishes a pattern of "the Jew first and also the Greek" with respect to God's power for salvation. Romans 2:9 repeats the pattern ironically with respect to God's wrath. In spite of this ironic reversal, readers likely maintain expectations of the priority of Israel as Abraham's descendants. But 4:11–12 revises such expectations. Abraham is not first of all ancestor of Israelites but of Gentiles who believe. The purpose of his circumcision, then, is that he might also be the ancestor of Israelites who believe.[13] In this case, Israel is added to the Gentiles rather than the inverse.[14] Thus, readers can hear voices of both Gentiles and Jews: "I follow in the footsteps of Abraham."

In this fashion Abraham becomes "the father of us all" (Rom. 4:16). To return to the question of the identity of "we" in the chapter, Abraham's paternity is a part of the progressive development of what is true in the discourse that gives readers a retrospective clarification of "we" from 4:1 on. The "all" who have Abraham as father in 4:16 can hardly be confined to Stowers's dialogical "we" of a diatribe, because they are

---

H Faith in face of impotence and barrenness equivalent to belief in resurrection.

A The voice of Abraham's descendants.

H Inverting Gentiles and Jews.

further associated with many nations (or Gentiles) (4:17). Romans 4:23 reinforces this identity when the authorial voice claims that Gen. 15:6 "was written not for Abraham's account alone" but also for "our account." The first-person plural is further defined as "those who believe in the one who raised Jesus our Lord from the dead" (4:24–25). The inclusion of all who believe, and even those who will believe, in the first-person plural makes it implausible that "we" can be confined to a dialogical "we" in a diatribe.

Readers can also overhear God's voice even when God does not speak **A** overtly.[15] The commendatory voice of Scripture can be presumed to be **H** the voice of God, so that God speaks through the narration of Abraham's story. At another level, as the agent who pronounces the verdict of Abraham's honor, God speaks even when the text ascribes no direct word to God. At yet another level, God's voice, concealed in the divine passive ἐλογίσθη ("it was reckoned") in Rom. 4:3 (see 4:5, 9–10, 11), declares Abraham justified. Simultaneously, the authorial voice hears God's voice declaring that Abraham is not justified by works (Wilckens 1969, 65). God's voice underlies the divine passives in the citation from Ps. 31:2 LXX in 4:7–8 and in the repetition of ἐλογίσθη in 4:22. God's voice speaks, however, not only to Abraham but also to those identified as "we." Therefore, the divine voice in 4:23–24 declares those who believe justified. Here voices come in cascading layers. Readers hear the voice of Scripture, David's voice in the psalm, and God's voice. All these voices, however, also speak in the authorial voice.

In the hypogram of Rom. 4:13, God's voice makes a promise. The **H** promise raises questions concerning both (1) its recipients and (2) its contents. (1) The promise is addressed to Abraham and τῷ σπέρματι αὐτοῦ, ("to his seed"). In Gal. 3:16 Paul takes σπέρμα ("seed") as singular and interprets it christologically. By contrast, Rom. 4:11–12 makes Abraham the ancestor of all who have faith like his, and 4:16 makes certain that σπέρμα is collective (παντὶ τῷ σπέρματι, "to all his seed"; πατὴρ πάντων ἡμῶν, "father of us all") (Hübner 1984, 53; Beker 1980, 96). (2) The content of the promise is complex. On the one hand, God promises Abraham progeny, so that in the voice of Scripture God's voice declares, "I have made you the father of many nations [Gentiles]" (4:17). On the other, God astonishingly promises Abraham and his descendants nothing less than the world (4:13).

This promise comes not only through the righteousness of faith, as the text says, but also through the cultural repertoire. Clearly, the au-

---

A God's voice and the promise.

H God's voice in Scripture.

H Constructing God's promise for all the families of the earth.

thorial voice alludes to God's promises to make Abraham the ancestor of many nations and to make Abraham's descendants numerous (Gen. 15:5; 17:5; Rom. 4:17–18). But through the cultural repertoire, Rom. 4:13 also alludes to God's promise of (1) land and (2) blessing for all the families of the earth.

My claim that Rom. 4:13 alludes to the promise of blessing for all the families of the earth may require some defense. According to Hays's criteria for allusions (1989, 29–32), the volume of verbatim repetition of the promise is so low as to be inaudible. My claim fares better according to criteria of (1) availability and (2) recurrence. (1) The appearance of the promised blessing of all the families of the earth in Sir. 44:21 and Acts 3:25 as well as Gal. 3:8 confirms its availability in the cultural repertoire. (2) Galatians 3:8 demonstrates that it recurs elsewhere in Paul.

According to Gal. 3:8, Abraham received the gospel beforehand as God's promise to bless all the nations (Gentiles) in him. Thus, not only does Gal. 3:8 represent a recurrence, it also serves as a definition of the gospel that Abraham received as a promise. Romans 1:1–2 uses strong parallels to Gal. 3:8 when it speaks of God's gospel promised beforehand, so that if the definition of the gospel in Gal. 3:8 transfers to Rom. 1:1–2, it is possible to understand the hypogram of the gospel in Rom. 1:1–2 as God's promise to Abraham to bless all the nations (Gentiles) (Stowers 1994, 171; Käsemann 1980, 118). (I use Galatians to define Romans with caution. See Beker 1980, 94–95.)

A To return to the criterion of volume, Hays works on the level of ver- batim repetition. But repetition may also occur on the level of plot. This is precisely the case in Romans 4. The evidence that the inheritance in 4:13 includes the blessing of all nations is not so much in the verbatim repetition as in the argument. That is, Romans 4 argues for the blessing of all nations through Abraham.

C What is more, the explicit citations from Gen. 15:5 and 17:5 (Rom. 4:17–18) have parallels in Gen. 22:17–18. Genesis 22:17–18 reiterates the promise of numerous descendants and makes a promise of a future inheritance for Abraham's σπέρμα. Incidentally, the noun κληρονόμος ("heir") in Rom. 4:13 reiterates the verb κληρονομήσει ("he will inherit") in Gen. 22:17 LXX. Just at the point in Romans 4 where the parallels between Gen. 22:17–18 and 15:5 and 17:5 break off, Gen. 22:18 LXX continues: "And all the nations [Gentiles] of the earth shall be blessed in your σπέρμα." The suppression of verbal elements at the point where the precursor continues and the playing out of the plot of the precursor in the argument of the successor are inducements for readers who know

---

A Significance of the plot, as well as verbatim repetitions.

C Biblical citations and cultural repertoire.

the cultural repertoire to fill in a gap by recalling, "All the nations of the earth shall be blessed in your σπέρμα."

To reiterate, the allusion to the promise in Rom. 4:13 speaks through the voice of a cultural repertoire. God's promise of blessing in Gen. 12:3 is ambiguous. It can mean that Abraham will be a channel of universal blessing or that all the families of the earth will seek to be blessed the way God blesses Abraham. In favor of the first, Gen. 12:1–3 emphasizes blessing five times in contrast to the universal curse in Genesis 1–11, and the Yahwist emphasizes God's blessing elsewhere (Lohfink 1967, 83; von Rad 1961, 156). Furthermore, the Septuagint translates Gen. 12:3 unambiguously: "And in you all the nations [αἱ φυλαί, "tribes"; τὰ ἔθνη in Gen. 22:18] of the earth shall be blessed."

Moreover, the voice of the cultural repertoire also speaks with respect to the content of the promise as the inheritance of the world. According to some developments in tradition, the entrance of the Israelites into Canaan did not render the promise of land to Abraham obsolete (von Rad, 1965, 319–28; Foerster 1965, 779). Furthermore, Gen. 12:1–3 associates the promise of γῆ land with universal blessing. Evolving tradition pushed the promises into the future and expanded them universally. This development took God's promise of γῆ ("land," "earth") to Abraham as a promise of the whole world.[16] Thus, in the divine promises in Romans 4, readers hear not only an authorial voice, God's voice, and the voice of Scripture, but also the voice of the cultural repertoire.

Implications

This sample of multivocality in Romans has two quite diametrically ⊞ opposed implications for interpretation. (1) Voices that reinforce each other replicate systems that determine the limits of meanings. Thus, a reiteration of the authorial voice in prophetic voices, Abraham's voice, scriptural voices, God's voice, and the voice of a confessional "we" that includes the authorial audience forcefully determines that the just one is the justifier and that just one is God. (2) The multiplicity of voices has a capacity to thwart determinate meanings. Ambiguity and voices that correct one another mean that the text speaks with a nonreductive plurality of voices. In the development of Romans through ch. 4, there is indeterminacy about the meaning and function of law. The νόμος is upheld as νόμος when it shows that Abraham is not justified by νόμος but by God. (3) There is a third implication between the two diametrically opposite ones. That is, the multiplicity of voices has a capacity to revise meaning. In the progressive development of the discourse, voices that redirect earlier voices induce readers to revise their anticipations of what is true in

⊞ Centripetal and centrifugal effects of interplay of voices.

the discourse. A case in point is the subversion of readers' anticipations of the priority of Israel as Abraham's offspring and therefore heirs of *the* promise in an ironic reversal in which Israel and the Gentiles swap places.

Emphasizing certain voices over others is not the only factor in interpretation. Basically, I have focused on characterization, which Barthes called the code of semes. Barthes identified four additional codes, and even then did not consider the interpreter's location (1986). Nevertheless, emphasis on certain voices is one factor in diverse interpretations.

A Before drawing some connections between the multivocality and diversity in modern interpretations in Romans 4, I make some preliminary observations on interpretations of 3:1–8. When Stowers reads 3:1–8 with emphasis on the authorial voice, he hears a particular argument between a teacher and an imaginary interlocutor. By contrast, Käsemann attends primarily to the authorial voice and to the divine voice mediated through the authorial voice and offers a theocentric reading. Thus in 3:1–8 he hears a universal acclamation of God's faithfulness to all creation. Cosgrove attends to a combination of the voice of the authorial audience, the authorial voice, and the divine voice, and shows how the voice of the authorial audience refracts both the authorial voice and the divine voice. He imagines a Jewish reader in Rome who in hearing God's voice in 3:1–8 would emphasize God's fidelity to promises to Israel and a Gentile reader who would emphasize the universality of God's judgment, including God's judgment against Israel (1997, 13–16). In attending to voices of Scripture in 3:1–20, Hays emphasizes a universal vindication of God in both God's fidelity and judgment apart from particularities of the authorial audience and continues the theodicy to the end of ch. 3 (1988, 47–54).

In keeping with my earlier observations that the scriptural voice, the authorial voice, and the divine voice are embedded in each other, when Hays attends the scriptural voice in Romans 4, he hears authorial propositions about both God and Scripture. Paul's voice appeals to Scripture, but Scripture speaks in Paul's voice. Thus Scripture affirms that Abraham's story is a narrative of God's promises to justify both Jews and Gentiles on the basis of trust (1988, 54–55). Fitzmyer also reads for an authorial voice through which Scripture speaks. Thus he emphasizes a Pauline thesis: Abraham's story is primarily an illustration of justification by faith (1993, 369–70). Käsemann likewise reads for Paul's thesis of justification, as it is vindicated through Scripture, and thus privileges the authorial voice, though he acknowledges an opponent's voice in the diatribe style of Romans 4. Paul's thesis is therefore a message to "us." But Käsemann also hears a divine voice through the authorial voice so that he speaks of God's message or word of promise and God's cosmological claim over all creation (1980, 105–29). Though Cosgrove emphasizes

---

A Selecting certain voices as particularly significant.

reading through different perspectives from the authorial audience, he ultimately hears an authorial voice in Romans 4. That is, Paul argues "that Abraham's heirs are not restricted to his fleshly descendants but include those nondescendants who share Abraham's faith" (1997, 67). Kuss labels Romans 4 a proof from Scripture but hears both Scripture and the divine voice it mediates as messages of the authorial voice. In these three intertwined voices Kuss hears in Paul's argument a forceful divine voice in continuity with established revelation in Scripture. Though he identifies the actual audience as Gentile, Kuss hears a Pauline argument against Judaism (*sic*), for which he construes a dialogical voice as if the authorial audience is not merely Jewish but Judaism. Finally, in spite of a strong emphasis on God's grace, Kuss presents an anthropocentric reading in which Abraham is a model of correct behavior (1957, 1:178–95).

Ostensibly, Klein reads for an authorial theme. He acknowledges Paul's references to the law and the prophets as scriptural proofs but denies that they provide any prehistory for Paul's theme of justification, and the indicated break produces a desacramentalization and profaning of Judaism. Both the radical nature of the revelation of God's righteousness in the Christ event and Paul's violation of Scripture for his purposes swallow the voice of Scripture and break continuity with Scripture (and history) (1963, 424–47; 1964, 676–83). By contrast, Wilckens takes seriously Paul's claim that he does not overthrow the law (Rom. 3:31) as a validation of the voice of Scripture so that he hears a prominent continuing witness to God's righteousness, to God's promises, and to the God of promises. In short, Wilckens has a far more theocentric understanding of Romans 4 than does Klein (1961, 120–21; 1964).

Though Stowers agrees that Romans is theocentric, and though he defines νόμος as divine teaching, he rarely attends to a divine or scriptural voice. Rather his focus on dialogical voices of a teacher and an imaginary Jewish teacher and on the authorial audience (functioning in an ancient Mediterranean rhetorical world) produces a strongly anthropological reading in which Romans is the story of the loss and restoration of self-mastery. For him, in Romans 4, Abraham is a model not of belief but of how God fulfills promises. This sounds theocentric initially, but God's promise is fulfilled by Abraham's fidelity, acting as the circumstances required in the light of God's promises (an old man having intercourse). Further, Stowers relates Jews and Gentiles to Abraham in quite different ways, Gentiles through Christ and Jews through their heritage (Stowers 1994, 108, 241, and passim).

Diversity in interpretations of Romans 4 derives from a number of factors. But one of them is the variety of voices in the text. From the beginnings of its history of reception Romans speaks with multiple voices.

Notes

1. Stowers, adducing ancient diatribes, argues that Rom. 2:1–5 addresses an imaginary interlocutor and does not characterize the authorial audience (1981: 85–96). But none of Stowers's examples dupes the reader as does 2:1–5.

2. The plural δι' ὑμᾶς ("on account of you") appears rather than the second-person singular as in the remainder of Rom. 2:17–23. For Stowers, this is directed at imaginary Jewish teachers who are unfaithful to God's promise to Gentiles and seek rather to teach the law to Gentiles (1994, 150–51).

3. Klein (1963; 1964) and Wilckens (1964) debate whether God's act in Jesus breaks continuity with (Klein) or stands in continuity with (Wilckens) salvation history. See Beker 1980, 97–104.

4. For Stowers, Rom. 1:18–2:16 has to do with Gentiles collectively and is not universal (1994, 113). Against Stowers, Gentile idolaters are focal instances of what has gone wrong for all humanity.

5. In reference to Scripture, γρέμμα is always pejorative in Paul (Schrenk 1964, 746, 763–69; Käsemann 1980, 76–77).

6. On the basis of philology and context, Doeve argues convincingly that τὰ λόγια refers to revelation in Scripture with emphasis on God's promises (1953, 111–23). See Manson 1962, 87–104; Williams 1980. Williams takes τὰ λόγια especially as God's promise to Abraham to bless all the families of the earth. For Stowers, τὰ λόγια may be God's promises in general, but the deficiency for Paul's interlocutor is the Abrahamic promise (1994, 167).

7. Psalm 9 LXX is cited and its thematic development is reflected in Romans 1–3. See Stowers 1994, 120–22.

8. On interpretations of law in Rom. 3:31 see Luz 1968, 171.

9. Variant readings support different construals. One omits εὑρηκέναι ("to find") so that the verse is about Abraham according to the flesh. The Nestle-Aland 26th edition places εὑρηκέναι before Ἀβραάμ, but the majority group of manuscripts places εὑρηκέναι after προπάτορα ("forefather") and before κατὰ σάρκα, which supports construing the phrase with the infinitive. Fitzmyer judges this inconsistent with Paul (1993, 371). But as I show, it is consistent with Romans 4, and I suggest also with Romans 9. See Kuss 1957, 1:180.

10. As "testimony" to God's fidelity Scripture functions positively (Wilckens 1961, 120–21; 1964, 589–91). For Dunn, ἀνομία ("lawlessness") in Psalm 31 LXX characterizes Gentiles (1988, 206).

11. Klein distinguishes God's justice from the revelation of God's righteousness in Christ. The latter is apocalyptic and the former salvation historical (1964, 676–83).

12. For Käsemann, Abraham's faith anticipates the fulfillment of the promise and is identical with Christian faith (1969, 140, 148, 173). See Stuhlmacher 1965, 227; Hahn 1971, 105; Kertelge 1967, 193–95. For Boers the connection between Abraham's faith and Christian faith lies in Abraham's belief in the same God, though making the dead alive makes Abraham's faith a type of Christian faith (1971, 84, 96–98). See Guerra 1988, 264–69. Against direct connections between Abraham's faith and Christian faith, see Cranford 1995, 87–88. For Gaston, life for the dead means the creation of a church that includes Gentiles (1980, 57).

13. Klein judges that "the history of Israel is radically desacralized and paganized" (1963, 436). See Wilckens 1964, 596–600. But Wilckens mistakenly speaks of the physical mediation of Abraham's offspring through Judaism (1964, 600). See Klein 1964, 683. Fitzmyer misses the inversion (1993, 381). Paul makes Abraham the ancestor first of believing Gentiles.

14. Abraham is thus more than a figure who unites Jewish and Gentile Christians (contra Campbell 1981, 39). Rather, he gives a new perspective on the place of Gentiles and Israel in relation to each other.

15. Gen. 15:4 LXX mentions the "voice" of God in contrast to the "word" of God in the MT.

16. So Sir. 44:19–21; *Jub.* 17:3; 19:21; 22:14; 32:18–19; Rom. 4:13; 1 Cor. 6:2; Heb. 2:5; cf. Matt. 5:5; James 2:5; Philo, *Moses* 1.155; *Mek. Exod.* 14:31. According to *Sipre* on Deut. 34:1–4, on Mount Nebo God showed Moses the whole earth. Bailey shows how Abrahamic promises were universalized and spiritualized in the two pre-Christian centuries (1994, 59–69).

References

Bailey, Kenneth. 1994. "St. Paul's Understanding of the Territorial Promise of God to Abraham: Romans 4:13 in Its Historical and Theological Context." *Near East School of Theology Theological Review* 15:59–69.

Bakhtin, Mikhail. 1984. *Problems of Dostoevsky's Poetics*. Theory and History of Literature 8. Manchester: Manchester University Press.

Barthes, Roland. 1977. *Image, Music, Text*. New York: Hill and Wang.

———. 1986. *S/Z*. New York: Hill and Wang.

Beker, J. Christiaan. 1980. *Paul the Apostle: The Triumph of God in Life and Thought*. Philadelphia: Fortress.

Boers, Hendrikus. 1971. *Theology Out of the Ghetto: A New Testament Exegetical Study Concerning Religious Exclusiveness*. Leiden: Brill.

Brawley, Robert. 1990. *Centering on God: Method and Message in Luke-Acts*. Literary Currents in Biblical Interpretation. Louisville: Westminster John Knox.

———. 1995. *Text to Text Pours Forth Speech: Voices of Scripture in Luke-Acts*. Indiana Studies in Biblical Literature. Bloomington: Indiana University Press.

Campbell, William. 1981. "The Freedom and Faithfulness of God in Relation to Israel." *Journal for the Study of the New Testament* 13:39.

Cosgrove, Charles. 1997. *Elusive Israel: The Puzzle of Election in Romans*. Louisville: Westminster John Knox.

Cranford, Michael. 1995. "Abraham in Romans 4: The Father of All Who Believe." *New Testament Studies* 41:71–88.

Dahl, Nils. 1953. "Die Messianität Jesu bei Paulus." Pp. 83–95 in *Studia Paulina: In honorem Johannis de Zwann*, ed. J. Sevenster and W. van Unnik. Haarlem: Bohn.

Darr, John. 1992. *On Character Building: The Reader and the Rhetoric of Characterization in Luke-Acts*. Literary Currents in Biblical Interpretation. Louisville: Westminster John Knox.

Delling, Gerhard. 1963. "Partizipale Gottesprädikationen in den Briefen des Neuen Testaments." *Studia Theologica* 17:1–59.

Doeve, Jan. 1953. "Some Notes with Reference to τὰ λόγια τοῦ θεοῦ in Romans III 2." Pp. 111–23 in *Studia Paulina: In honorem Johannis de Zwann,* ed. J. Sevenster and W. van Unnik. Haarlem: Bohn, 1953.

Dunn, James. 1988. *Romans 1–8.* Word Biblical Commentary 38a. Dallas: Word.

Fitzmyer, Joseph. 1993. *Romans: A New Translation with Introduction and Commentary.* Anchor Bible 33. New York: Doubleday.

Foerster, Werner. 1965. "κληρονόμος." *Theological Dictionary of the New Testament* 3:776–85.

Gaston, Lloyd. 1980. "Abraham and the Righteousness of God." *Horizons in Biblical Theology* 2:39–68.

Guerra, Anthony. 1988. "Romans 4 as Apologetic Theology." *Harvard Theological Review* 81:264–69.

Hahn, Ferdinand. 1971. "Genesis 15:6 im Neuen Testament." Pp. 90–107 in *Probleme biblischer Theologie: Gerhard von Rad zum 70. Geburtstag,* ed. H. Wolff. Munich: Christian Kaiser.

Hanson, Anthony. 1974. *Studies in Paul's Technique and Theology.* London: SPCK.

Hays, Richard. 1983. *The Faith of Jesus Christ.* Society of Biblical Literature Dissertation Series 56. Chico, Calif.: Scholars Press.

———. 1985. "Have We Found Abraham to Be Our Forefather According to the Flesh? A Reconsideration of Rom 4:1." *Novum Testamentum* 27:251–70.

———. 1989. *Echoes of Scripture in the Letters of Paul.* New Haven: Yale University Press.

Hübner, Hans. 1984. *Law in Paul's Thought.* Edinburgh: T. & T. Clark.

Käsemann, Ernst. 1969. *Paulinischen Perspectiven.* Tübingen: Mohr (Siebeck).

———. 1980. *Commentary on Romans.* Grand Rapids: Eerdmans.

Kertelge, Karl. 1967. *'Rechfertigung' bei Paulus: Studien zur Struktur und zum Bedeutungsgehalt des paulinischen Rechfertigungsbegriffs.* Münster: Aschendorff.

Klein, Günter. 1963. "Römer 4 und die Idee der Heilsgeschichte." *Evangelische Theologie* 23:424–47.

———. 1964."Exegetische Probleme in Röm 3,21–4,25." *Evangelische Theologie* 24:676–83.

Kristeva, Julia. 1980. *Desire in Language: A Semiotic Approach to Literature and Art.* New York: Columbia University Press.

Kuss, Otto. 1957. *Der Römerbrief: Übersetzt und erklärt.* 2 vols. Regensburg: Pustet.

Lohfink, Norbert. 1967. *Die Landverheissung als Eid: Eine Studie zu Gn 15.* Stuttgarter Bibelstudien 28. Stuttgart: Katholisches Bibelwerk.

Luz, Ulrich. 1968. *Das Geschichtsverständnis Paulus.* Munich: Christian Kaiser.

Malina, Bruce, and Jerome Neyrey. 1988. *Calling Jesus Names: The Social Value of Labels in Matthew.* Foundation and Facets: New Testament. Sonoma, Calif.: Polebridge, 1988.

————. 1991 "Honor and Shame in Luke-Acts: Pivotal Values of the Mediter-
    ranean World." Pp. 25–65 in *The Social World of Luke-Acts: Models for
    Interpretation,* ed. J. Neyrey. Peabody, Mass: Hendrickson.
Manson, T. W. 1962. "LOGIA." Pp. 87–104 in *Studies in the Gospels and
    Epistles.* Manchester: Manchester University Press.
Rad, Gerhard von. 1961. *Genesis.* Old Testament Library. Philadelphia: West-
    minster.
————. 1965. *The Theology of Israel's Prophetic Traditions.* Vol. 2 of *Old
    Testament Theology.* New York: Harper and Row.
Riffaterre, Michel. 1978. *Semiotics of Poetry.* Bloomington: Indiana University
    Press.
Savaran, George. 1988. *Telling and Retelling: Quotation in Biblical Narrative.*
    Indiana Studies in Biblical Literature. Bloomington: Indiana University Press.
Schmidt, Karl. 1965. "καλέω," *Theological Dictionary of the New Testament*
    3:487–91.
Schrenk, Gottlob. 1964. "γράμμα." *Theological Dictionary of the New Testament*
    1:741–73.
Schweizer, Eduard. 1969. "πνεῦμα." *Theological Dictionary of the New Testa-
    ment* 6:389–455.
Stowers, Stanley. 1981. *The Diatribe and Paul's Letter to the Romans.* Society
    of Biblical Literature Dissertation Series 57. Chico, Calif.: Scholars Press.
————. 1994. *A Rereading of Romans: Justice, Jews, and Gentiles.* New Haven:
    Yale University Press.
Stuhlmacher, P. 1965. *Gerechtigkeit Gottes bei Paulus.* Göttingen: Vandenhoeck
    and Ruprecht.
Suleiman, Susan. 1980. "Redundancy and the 'Readable' Text." *Poetics Today*
    13:119–42.
Wilckens, Ulrich. 1961. "Die Rechfertigung Abrahams nach Römer 4." Pp.
    111–27 in *Studien zur Theologie der altestamentlichen Überlieferungen,* ed.
    R. Rendtorff and K. Koch. Neukirchen: Neukirchener Verlag.
————. 1964. "Zu Römer 3,21–4,25: Antwort an G. Klein." *Evangelische
    Theologie* 24:586–610.
————. 1969. "Was heißt bei Paulus: 'Aus Werken des Gesetzes wird kein
    Mensch gerecht.'" Pp. 51–77 in *Vorarbeiten.* Vol. 1 of Evangelisch-
    katholischer Kommentar zum Neuen Testament, ed. E. Schweizer et al.
    Neukirchen: Neukirchener Verlag.
Williams, Sam. 1980. "The Righteousness of God in Romans." *Journal of Biblical
    Literature* 99:241–90.

THREE

Multivocality and Multiplex Perspectives in the Interpretation of Romans

Robert L. Brawley and Thomas D. Parker

———— ◆ ————

If the well-known optical puzzle is white on black, a viewer beholds a goblet. If it is black on white, the same viewer discerns two silhouettes facing each other. This indicates that one element in vision is a mental construal associated with what we also name perspective. The construals stand in relief against each other but also have limits such that an observer sees either the goblet or the silhouettes — not both simultaneously. By analogy, interpreting Romans involves complex textual puzzles with mental construals that can be mutually illuminating and/or mutually limiting. A part of both the mutually illuminating and mutually limiting possibilities is the multivocality that readers' perspectives, themselves multiplex, engage.

A   Chapter 2, "Multivocality in Romans 4," attempts to name some voices implicated in the text: the authorial voice, the voice of the authorial audience, the voice of Jesus, the voice of God, the voice(s) of Scripture and the prophets, and the voice(s) of the cultural repertoire. Though these voices are themselves products of an interpreter's reading, they raise the issue of determinacy and indeterminacy, mutually illuminating and mutually limiting possibilities, as it were, before reading. By

H   contrast, chapter 1, "Abraham, Father of Us All in Barth's *Epistle to the Romans*," shows how a particular reader and some predecessors construe Romans 4, its multivocality included.

A Naming competing voices implicated in the text.
H How a reader construes the voices.

Interpretations inevitably include voices other than those of the text. **C**
We readily attribute a portion of the construals of Luther, Calvin,
and Barth (or Käsemann, Hays, and Stowers) to their social locations.
Further, the Western theological tradition distinguished multiple levels **H**
beyond the literal in the function of biblical language. According to
Thomas Aquinas, representing a highly developed consensus of scholas-
tic interpretive theory, the literal is primary. Spiritual meanings (moral,
doctrinal, mystical) are built upon it because what is represented literally has spiritual meaning in itself. In this case, the meanings, though
complex, are not competing voices but compose a unified voice.

For Reformation exegesis on Romans, as represented by Luther and **H**
Calvin, the intended literal subject matter is the spiritual meaning. So
Paul is writing literally about spiritual realities when he writes about
Abraham in Romans 4. For those exegetes, these realities are not behind,
in front of, at the side of, or vaporized out of the text. Nor is this a
matter of readers arbitrarily generating meanings from their own stock
of prior conceptions, as if Scripture were an empty cup waiting to be
filled with some inimitable contents. Properly read, the text (with its
inner dynamic of voices in conversation) informs and corrects readers'
preunderstandings, bringing them into agreement with what Calvin and
Luther believe is the gospel. In this way Scripture builds a salvific world,
makes ethical demands, and envisions lives illumined by God's glory.

The commentaries of Luther and Calvin on Romans arise in differ- **C**
ent contexts and deal with different issues than that of Barth. Luther's
Lectures on Romans arises in the universe of an ecclesial discourse. He
therefore cites great exegetes from the past, argues with the scholastics,
and discusses the scholarly work of his peers. He dialogues especially with
Old Testament scholars — peers from his own academic focus. Not sur- **A**
prisingly, therefore, he is particularly attentive to the voice of Scripture
in Romans 4.

Calvin also struggles with the scholastics and his contemporaries. Yet, **C**
in distinction from Luther, he reads Paul more historically in relation to **A**
his concern with the issue of Jews and Gentiles in the church at Rome as
the site for his reflections on the righteousness of faith. Luther graphically
equates "legalistic Jews" with the scholastics who oppress conscience.

C Role of social locations.

H Several levels contributing to a unified voice.

H How the text's literal subject matter informs and corrects readers' preunderstandings.

C Luther: ecclesial scholastics, Old Testament scholars.

A Focus on voice of Scripture in Romans 4.

C Calvin: the church in struggles with scholastics and contemporaries.

A Historical relation between Jews and Gentiles.

But for Calvin, Jews and Gentiles are not mere tropes for righteousness by works over against faith. They are specific populations who in their own ways bear witness to the reality of God's judgment and grace. In this connection, Calvin comments specifically on the concreteness of

H Paul's situation. In keeping with the Western interpretive tradition, however, he extends the significance of Abraham and of Paul's presentation of Abraham beyond the literal historical level to their significance for the church. In contrast with Barth (see below), Calvin stops short of envisioning a universal significance of Paul and Abraham for unbelievers as well as believers. Rather, Paul is applying what is written about Abraham to the *universal church,* and Abraham mirrors a pattern of righteousness also to the *universal church.*

H Barth's *Epistle to the Romans* stands in this line of interpreters from Aquinas through Luther and Calvin. For Barth, Paul is writing about the "veritable gospel," the truth about the human situation vis-à-vis the Origin and End of all things, that is, God the Creator, Judge, and Renewer. In the line of the Western tradition, the veritable gospel is no epiphenomenon of the literal things arising from their representation in writing. Rather, the literal and spiritual meaning is unified, though the

A various levels of meaning are complex. But the unified understanding of meaning notwithstanding, these complex levels of meaning arising in Western theological interpretations go beyond what we might attribute to Romans in its historical and literary situation. In fact, Barth contends with a purely historical reading of Abraham as producing an Abraham that does not concern "us." Therefore, we frame the question as the

C relation among voices outside the text and those inside, although it is invariably outside readers who discern voices in the text.

C In contrast with Luther and Calvin, Barth is intentionally nonecclesial. He brings a "post-Christendom" cultural repertoire into play with his radical critique of Feuerbach, Kierkegaard, Overbeck, and Nietzsche

H with rhetorical reference to Dostoevsky and other outsiders. These are his interlocutors, as scholastics and theologians were the interlocutors of Luther and Calvin. In contrast with the sharp polemics of Calvin and Luther against opponents, however, Barth accepts his interlocutors as illuminating the perennial *krisis* of being human in the world, alienated from and longing for their Origin and End. On the other hand, he ar-

---

H Abraham as pattern of righteousness for universal church.

H The veritable gospel as meaning.

A Literal meaning not limited to the historical and literary.

C To be heard, the voices of the text need readers.

C A post-Christendom cultural repertoire.

H Post-Christendom interlocutors illuminating the perennial *krisis* of humans in the world.

gues with religion and its apologists, with bourgeois Christianity and its spokespersons in the liberal tradition, and with academic exegesis that focuses on historical meaning alone.

This means that we have evidence of specific intellectual traditions **C** out of which Luther, Calvin, and Barth produce their readings of Romans, even though we barely scratch the surface of their social locations. Granted that social location is one of the factors in distinctive readings, we can also discern how the prominence that interpreters grant to certain voices inscribed in the text influences their interpretations.

Barth makes a direct identification between his authorial audience and **A** Paul's authorial audience. In so doing, he defines the authorial audience **H** not in terms of its characterization in the text but in terms of his postulate of a universal address to humanity. The authorial audience is representative of human beings as such. This is not merely the presupposition that Romans is canonical. The subject matter is universal — geographically and temporally. The subject matter renders "a distinction between yesterday and to-day...impossible" (1933, 7). This enables Barth to make modern believers correspond to "those who are going to believe" in Rom. 4:24. Thus, he redefines the authorial audience that is implied **C** in the text by extending it to universal proportions, certainly including a confessional "we," but also embracing the likes of Socrates.

By stark contrast, Stowers takes his interpretive cues from the Hellenis- **C** tic literary environment in which Romans was written, thus masking his own voice and the perspectives of his readers. On this basis, he limits the **A** "we" of Rom. 4:1 to the voices of a debater and interlocutor in a diatribe. Barth and Stowers are heirs of different interpretive traditions, Barth of the Western theological tradition and Stowers of the post-Holocaust historical critical tradition of biblical interpretation. Moreover, these interpretive heritages are parts of their social location that influence which voices they hear in the text. Nevertheless, their attention to different voices in the text contributes to distinctive readings that are mutually illuminating and mutually limiting.

Barth's attention to a universal voice enables him both to recognize **C** and to overlook the inversion of the place of Gentiles and Jews in Rom.

C Producing readings out of intellectual traditions and social locations.

A Barth: focus on subject matter.

H Authorial audience representative of universal audience.

C Universal human situation.

C Hellenistic literary environment.

A Hellenistic categories: diatribe.

C No distinction between Jews and Gentiles.

A 4:11–12. On the one hand, he catches the irony that here Jews are added on to Gentiles rather than the customary presumption that Gentiles are added on to Jews. This is a revision in readers' anticipations that Fitzmyer
H misses altogether. But Barth then universalizes out of his Western interpretive tradition to claim that the Jews (Barth also means Christians and all religious people) must first become Gentiles; that is, the religious must become irreligious in light of a pure faith, which (again out of his Western interpretive tradition) is faith without circumcision, that is, apart from religion. Thus, Barth's reading disregards the issue of the relationship between Jewish and Gentile Christians in Paul's world. He does not hear this voice of the cultural repertoire. By contrast, Klein, by attending to the voice of the antithesis to Paul's story — that is, Klein's reconstruction of a Jewish story of Abraham against which Paul struggles — radicalizes Paul's inversion of Jew and Gentile to the point of breaking Paul's gospel off from Judaism. Kuss likewise attends to the voice of an antithesis to Paul's story and thus hears a Pauline argument against Judaism. Hearing no such hypothetical antithetical Jewish story, Wilckens reads Paul's inversion of Gentiles and Jews rather in terms of continuity between Israel and Christianity. Again, attention to distinct voices contributes to distinct readings that are mutually illuminating and mutually limiting.

A   From Barth's perspective, he is reading for an authorial voice. What are the issues that Paul faces? Fitzmyer and Käsemann likewise read for an authorial voice that they take to be a Pauline thesis — justification by faith. But Barth could hardly reduce the subject matter to a Pauline thesis. He universalizes the issues that Paul faces. The questions that engage Paul are the questions that engage all humanity, and the answers he gives are answers for all humanity. This is because for Barth, Paul struggles with the ultimate concern that perturbs all human beings. In this sense, the authorial voice in Romans is in the end also the voice of the authorial audience, just as the voice of the authorial audience is also the voice
H of all humanity. Käsemann hears rather a divine voice that is mediated through the authorial voice, and instead of making a universal claim for human concerns, Käsemann makes a universal claim for God. The divine voice embedded in the authorial voice makes a cosmological claim over all creation. For his part, Barth, along with Luther and Calvin, assumes this claim in God's "No" and "Yes" of judgment and justification.
A   Whereas as a voice in Romans 4, Jesus, though present by implication

---

A Inversion of Jews and Gentiles.

H Faith versus religion.

A Human voices about universal ultimate concern versus divine voice about theological thesis.

H Universal claim for humans versus universal claim about God.

A Due to ambiguities in Greek, Jesus' voice heard differently.

(especially through relationships that characterize other voices and by parallels between Romans 3 and 4), is essentially silent, Barth gives him a universal voice. In Brawley's reading, Paul's gospel is about Jesus (1:3, 9, 16). But the faith "of" or "in" Jesus (subjective or objective genitive in Greek) may be construed as either Jesus' fidelity that mediates God's justice or Jesus as the object of faith in which a believer's act of faith mediates God's justice. Stowers can then give Jesus prominence as one who acts in fidelity to God, whereas Barth gives him prominence also as the indirect object of faith. Here, distinct readings are partially due to the inherent ambiguity in the Greek text, and the distinct readings confirm a level of indeterminacy in interpretation.

As he does with Jesus, so Barth also gives Abraham a universal voice. **C** What is visible in Abraham is just this: how human beings, aware of the *krisis* of historical being in the world, deal with their precarious but promising existence, either in faith (Abraham) or in unbelief (religious and cultural projections that mask humanity's true condition). Because Abraham's situation is directly our own, simply as human beings, Abraham's story is our human story. Thus, without annulling the historical distinction between Abraham and other human beings (Abraham cannot be our contemporary), Barth liberates Abraham, as he does Paul, from human particularity on the basis of the universal importance of his history, so that Abraham is the "father of us all." Jesus, **H** however, is the center of the story of which Abraham and his "descendants" are a part. The gospel is not merely a Christian story but the story of all humanity centered in Jesus, because Jesus' life and fate is the site where the *krisis* of historical being in the world becomes most acute.

Barth pays scant attention to the voice of God that overlays the voice **A** of scripture and (in witnessing to Paul's legitimacy [Rom. 1:9]) also overlays the authorial voice. His discourse is rather far more about God than listening to God. Aside from Scripture, he hears the voice of God in the "No" and "Yes" of judgment and justification experienced in our history and biography. He apparently does hear a divine voice overlaying **H** the voice of Scripture in the promise to Abraham in 4:13, the promise that Abraham and his descendants would inherit the world. But this divine voice is universalized into God's "Yes" for all humanity inasmuch as the promise is to Abraham, who is the "father of us all." Käsemann likewise universalizes the promise not only on the basis of 4:13 but also

---

C Universal: Abraham liberated from human particularity.

H Jesus as center of universal history.

A Listening or not listening to God's voice.

H God's voice heard in Scripture.

by hearing the voice of the cultural repertoire in which the promise to Abraham was already pushed into the future and universalized. By similar attention to the cultural repertoire and to an authorial voice enhanced by Paul's use of Abraham in Galatians, Käsemann, Stowers, and Brawley hear God's promise to bless all the families of the earth also in the promise to Abraham. Here, distinct readings are mutually illuminating and mutually limiting.

A
H   Furthermore, Barth keeps God's voice at arm's length when he looks at the value of religiosity. Religiosity witnesses to God's judgment and grace, but as a witness is not itself revelation. Even Christ is likewise a witness to God's fidelity, albeit a definitive witness, the center of the biblical story. Käsemann attends to a divine voice mediated through the authorial voice and offers a theocentric reading, but nevertheless agrees with Barth that Rom. 3:1–8 is a universal acclamation of God's faithfulness. Hays accentuates the dimension of the scriptural voice in his reading of 3:1–20, but

H   also emphasizes a universal vindication of God. We thus have here a case where attention to different voices produces congruent readings, a case in point for voices that reinforce one another. Furthermore, it serves to illustrate Brawley's contention that the scriptural voice, the divine voice, and the authorial voice are embedded in each other. Cosgrove hypothesizes not a monolithic authorial audience but a complex one in which he hears on the one hand God's fidelity and on the other hand God's judgment, and so splits the two apart. Barth, Käsemann, and Hays, however, combine God's fidelity and God's judgment. By contrast, in reading the same text, Stowers focuses on the authorial voice and emphasizes the argument of a debater and an imaginary opponent.

A
H   To return to Barth, visual rather than verbal imagery characterizes his christological witness. In Jesus we have been given *eyes to see* God's faithfulness. God's righteousness is *exhibited* or *displayed* in Jesus. Nevertheless, Barth detects a divine voice in God's justice, which he hears as a "No" to human efforts to establish themselves and a "Yes" to God's own fidelity. Barth hears this divine "No" particularly in Romans 1 as an account of the universality of divine judgment against human independence from God, and God's "Yes" in the justification of the ungodly. Käsemann likewise sees the drama of God's wrath and grace as universal, whereas Stowers takes Romans 1 as having to do only with Gentile idolatry.

A Attention to different voices embedded in each other.

H Witnesses are not revelation.

H Congruent readings are theologically construed.

A Visual rather than verbal imagery.

H Visual christological imagery, except for divine "No" and "Yes."

In a strongly implicit way, Barth hears Abraham's voice as a declaration of utter dependence upon God. This is at the same time a scriptural voice as Gen. 15:6 is appropriated in Rom. 4:3. Likewise, Barth hears David's voice simultaneously as a scriptural voice from Ps. 32:1 (31:1 LXX), though not nearly so distinctively as does Luther — the Old Testament professor. Further, he discerns a scriptural voice in Paul's reading of Abraham's story. Barth takes the law primarily as religiosity. But 3:19–20 ascribes a voice to the law: it speaks as Scripture. Barth, however, suppresses the voice of Scripture because Scripture both hides and reveals **H** God's voice. He hears here only the voice of religion and piety, which for him is the meaning of the law. Of course, even as religion and piety the law has a voice, but only as a secondary witness to God.

The failure to discern multivocality also leaves its impress on the his- **A** tory of interpretation. For example, Barth gives the citation of Isa. 52:5 in Rom. 2:24 a universal voice, whereas Käsemann gives the citation from Isaiah only a historical voice. Both thereby restrict the possibility of hearing intertextual voices, and they miss the irony that in citing Isa. 52:5, Rom. 2:24 inverts the place of Jews and Gentiles — an inversion that Paul makes more explicit in Rom. 4:11–12. Klein hears behind Abraham's story an alleged version that Paul contradicts. This transforms Paul's Abraham into a polemic, and also obviates the interplay between Romans and Genesis.

This attempt to interpret a minute slice of the history of the interpretation of Romans is susceptible to its own criteria. As authors, we readily **C** acknowledge that we interpret out of our social locations, including our own heritage from interpretive traditions. Our readings are also subject **H** to different construals. But a part of the mutually illuminating and mutually limiting possibilities is the multivocality that we, our multiplex perspectives notwithstanding, engage. This is to confirm our contention **A** that all readers have access to multiple voices that give Romans rich textures. Diversity in interpretations of Romans 4 derives from a number of factors. But one of them is the inherent multivocality in the text. From the beginnings of its history of reception Romans speaks with multiple voices.

H Scripture both hides and reveals God's voice.

A Failure to discern multivocality in history of interpretation.

C Interpretations related to social locations.

H Readings subject to different construals.

A Romans speaks with multiple voices.

References

Barth, Karl. 1933. *The Epistle to the Romans*. London: Oxford University Press.

Calvin, John. 1961. *The Epistles of Paul the Apostle to the Romans and to the Thessalonians*. Grand Rapids: Eerdmans.

Cosgrove, Charles. 1997. *Elusive Israel: The Puzzle of Election in Romans*. Louisville: Westminster John Knox.

Hays, Richard. 1983. *The Faith of Jesus Christ*. Society of Biblical Literature Dissertation Series 56. Chico, Calif.: Scholars Press.

———. 1983. "Have We Found Abraham to Be Our Forefather According to the Flesh? A Reconsideration of Rom 4:1." *Novum Testamentum* 27:251–70.

Fitzmyer, Joseph. 1993. *Romans: A New Translation with Introduction and Commentary*. Anchor Bible 33. New York: Doubleday.

Luther, Martin. 1961. *Lectures on Romans*. Library of Christian Classics 15. Philadelphia: Westminster.

Käsemann, Ernst. 1980. *Commentary on Romans*. Grand Rapids: Eerdmans.

Klein, Günter. 1963. "Römer 4 und die Idee der Heilsgeschichte." *Evangelische Theologie* 23:424–47.

Kuss, Otto. 1957. *Der Römerbrief: Übersetzt und erklärt*. 2 vols. Regensburg: Pustet.

Stowers, Stanley. 1981. *The Diatribe and Paul's Letter to the Romans*. Society of Biblical Literature Dissertation Series 57. Chico, Calif.: Scholars Press.

———. 1994. *A Rereading of Romans: Justice, Jews, and Gentiles*. New Haven: Yale University Press.

Wilckens, Ulrich. 1964. "Was heißt bei Paulus: 'Aus Werken des Gesetzes wird kein Mensch gerecht.'" Pp. 51–77 in *Vorarbeiten*. Vol. 1 of Evangelisch-katholischer Kommentar zum Neuen Testament, ed. E. Schweizer et al. Neukirchen: Neukirchener Verlag.

A Theologian and Feminist Responds

Cristina Grenholm

——— ◆ ———

My response is given from the perspective of *scriptural criticism*. I read Thomas D. Parker's and Robert L. Brawley's essays as examples of final products of scriptural interpretation. Thus, I continue the reflection that has already started in the marginalia. I also inquire how the analytical, contextual, and hermeneutical frames are interrelated.

It is legitimate to ask whether my endeavor can be justified, even considering that Parker and Brawley belong to the collective of scholars within the Society of *Biblical* Literature eagerly trying to come to grips with the different dimensions of biblical interpretation. Still, they did not intend to answer all the questions that were later articulated. However, I think Francis Watson is right in expressing the same doubt and immediately rejecting it. In a review of James Dunn's commentary on Romans, Watson writes,

> I have perhaps done him an injustice in raising controversial hermeneutical issues about which he has little directly to say. . . . I have tried to show, however, that the hermeneutical issue of the relation between author, text and interpreter cannot ultimately be divorced from the practice of exegesis, since the direction of exegesis is always determined not just by the desire to reproduce the original as faithfully as possible but by prior hermeneutical decisions. (1991, 252)

In my view (as shown in the overture), I do not think there is any way in which we can avoid somehow touching upon all three kinds of frames, either explicitly or implicitly. On the other hand, I do not think it is possible to constantly be self-conscious about the whole process. Rather, critical awareness of the process becomes possible in the collective discussion among scholars, believers, and nonbelievers. In Brawley's terminology, I add another voice. This implies that my own views are brought into play as I reflect on the material provided by my colleagues.

What are "my own views"? What makes them different from subjective and arbitrary perspectives? Being trained as a scholar implies being aware of many possibilities in the world of theology. When our personal choices are made, they are based on our knowledge of these options. Skillful analyses also help. But they do not fully account for convictions and beliefs. Life-contexts also provide a basis for convictions. Our whole "set" of religious perceptions does not stem from scholarly reflection, but from things we took to be self-evident, possibly part of a tradition. Nevertheless, scholarly responsibility involves integrating knowledge and conviction. Thus, we do not need to agree on personal convictions in order to remain scholars. Disagreement on personal convictions does not prevent scholars from being scholars. But we should agree on the principles according to which such convictions should be assessed.

As I add my voice to those of Parker and Brawley, I bring in not only my scholarly knowledge, but also some of my convictions. My view of God, my understanding of the authority of Scripture, of universalism, and of patriarchy will come into play. I am a systematic theologian[1] and a feminist. I will also reflect on my Swedish context, since it is called for as I try to enter the dialogue on Romans 4 between two Americans. However, I am as much susceptible to self-deception, lapses of thought, and simple unawareness of what is really going on in my writing as anybody else. I add a voice. I do not claim it is the best.

Important Themes When Interpreting Romans 4

The title of this book is *Reading Israel in Romans.* Thus, Romans 4 comes naturally to mind. By means of a major figure in Jewish self-understanding, Christians have also found a basis for their self-understanding in Abraham as father of us all.

We can imagine Paul reviewing his upbringing. As a Jew, he could regard Abraham as his father. Has his faith in Christ changed this relationship? However, this question comes less naturally for Christians living at the turn of the millennium. Abraham is not a figure we relate to, unless we are taught to do so. Furthermore, the idea of a common father, a father of us all, creates at least two problems. Postmodernism has taught us to be suspicious of universalism, in a broad sense of the term.[2] We have also become aware of the oppressive character of patriarchy. Adopting a father does not come without a question mark.[3]

Reading Israel in Romans is impossible without addressing the three issues of the relationship between Jews and Christians, the claim for universalism implied in a common father, and the patriarchal bias of that claim.

Each of these issues can be framed in three different ways. Analytically, the issue of Jews and Christians can be taken as a historical problem, also wrestling with the concept of Gentiles. Contextually, it is hard to justify neglecting the experience of Jewish people. Hermeneutically, we have to pay attention to the different religious perceptions by which we conceptualize what is at stake here.

In a similar way, the issue of universalism can be approached with different kinds of analytical framings, often supported by a hermeneutical counterpart. If Abraham is understood as expressing human nature, he should not be analyzed as if he were a historical figure. The contextual frame determines, for example, whether he is viewed against a purely Christian background or not.

Finally, using patriarchy as an analytical frame makes the interpreter focus on the distribution of power revealed in the text. Its context can either be viewed primarily historically or be related to the effects the text has on contemporary society. The hermeneutical frame may include a critical view of patriarchy, objecting to its claim for unequal means of distributing goods and power.

The Contextual and Hermeneutical Frames

When I first met with the group of scholars gathered to examine receptions and critical studies of Romans, I had a problem following the discussions after the presentations. It was clear that something important was at stake. It was less clear what this was.

There are several explanations for this. Not everything is said. There is no need to restate both the points about which many participants agree and points about which they disagree. In the former case, much is shared, because there is a shared context. In the latter case, the situation is more complicated. People may not find it necessary or even desirable to bring conflicts to the surface. Thus, there can be a tacit agreement on the conflicts. But it may also be too difficult to identify disagreements in a constructive way. This calls for more reflection.

This can be the role of the newcomer who shares neither the context nor the hermeneutical frame in play. By taking as my starting point my own context, I have been able to conceptualize its hermeneutical frame in a new way, which in turn has revealed some of the characteristics of the American discussion.

When listening to my colleagues, I see clearly that the historical problems discussed relate to controversial issues of our time. However, it is not clear to me how the two interconnect. To put it bluntly, What does Paul have to do with the injustices committed against the Jewish people? Is Paul but a catalyst for the discussion or could he really help us out here in some way? My questioning sounds insensitive, yet since it is obvious to many participants in this discussion that there is a connection and less obvious how it should be characterized, I think it worthwhile to follow this track.

The hermeneutical frame helps us enter into dialogue with the text. Parker and Brawley do not make explicit their religious perceptions of the relationship between Jews and Christians. Still, it is clear that Parker, following Barth, includes Jews and Christians in a universal humanity. Brawley argues that the point of Romans 4 is that the Jews are included among the Gentiles who believe, and not the other way around. Admittedly, this is not the same as saying that Gentiles equal Christians, but it is very close, since the characteristic of the Gentiles is their faith.

The largely implicit contextual counterpart to this hermeneutical frame is the Holocaust. However, it is mixed with the "normal" scholarly interest in the historical questions raised by the text of Romans. I am familiar with the latter, but not with the former. I have to ask myself, How shall I characterize the context in which I have been reading Romans?

I have been working with interpreting Romans from a systematic theological perspective since the middle of the 80s. I have to face it: the issue of Israel and the Jewish people has not been on the agenda in Sweden. Instead, we continue to ask the question of how to relate law and gospel. Sweden is dominated by the Church of Sweden, which is Lutheran. Still, the reason for putting energy into discussing this is hidden under the surface — as in the American situation. It was not until recently that I discovered where the drive for dealing with different understandings of *nomos* came from. The hermeneutical frame relating to my context was hard to locate.

Jan Bonda's book *The One Purpose of God: An Answer to the Doctrine of Eternal Punishment* made me realize where the vigor in our discussions came from. Bonda writes from a Calvinistic perspective. The pressing issue concerns the doctrine of predestination in Bonda's context. Ultimately, he has to ask why God has chosen most people for eternal punishment. Is there a limit to God's will to save?

Reading Bonda's book gave me a hermeneutical frame that, although stemming from a different context than my own, helped me clarify both my context and the hermeneutical frame of the discussion on law and gospel.

If there is a limit to God's will to save, the law forms the dividing line. Since God's law must be universal, human divisions do not count. Although the Church of Sweden does not hold to the doctrine of eternal punishment, it seems to share its structure.[4] All are condemned by the law and all are offered salvation by grace through faith.[5]

With the assistance of Bonda we can put it this way: traditionally Christian theology in my context has operated with the dichotomy of election and exclusion by means of the law and gospel distinction. Some are held to be excluded, and Israel is the paradigmatic example. At the same time, election and exclusion have been primarily understood as universal. This is similar to the way Barth deals with the issue.

We have now come to a point where I think it is possible to sort out differences and similarities between the American and the Swedish contextual and hermeneutical frames.

In the Swedish situation, the contextual frame has yielded to universalism, making religious perceptions the primary counterpart for critical analysis. The tripolar character of biblical interpretation collapses into a bipolar balance that does not connect to the realities of life.

In the American situation, the context seems to be clearer, although mostly kept implicit. The scholarly milieu contains Jews and Christians. Universalism cannot easily be held to. (This is also the case of Parker's interpretation of Barth. It is impossible to neglect the fact that there are no disinterested readings.) The Holocaust is present both in the voices of the Jewish believers and in those of Christians struggling with how to cope with a harmful heritage. However, it is my impression that the hermeneutical frame connected to this context is not elaborated enough to make the discussion fruitful.

Thus, I see a need for combining the contextual awareness of the American discussion with the theological discussions familiar to me. However, this will change the contents of theology.

No doubt, there are theological reflections on the Holocaust and religious dialogue. However, such developments are rarely related to Romans. Krister Stendahl's *Paul among Jews and Gentiles* needs and deserves a follow-up.

The Connection between Analysis and Hermeneutical Frames, according to Barth

This is where Karl Barth's commentary on Romans is of continual interest when we are investigating how to read Israel in Romans. It provides a hermeneutical frame clearly related to the analytical. Let us study its theology. Barth begins his analysis by positing a specific view of human life as universal context. Then, his interpretation involves a hermeneutical frame with at least two constituent parts, one philosophical and one theological: existentialism (human beings live in the *krisis* of finitude) and the idea of God as the Other.

When Barth interprets Romans 4, these constituent parts come clearly to the fore. The *krisis* of the human situation is repeatedly underlined (1933, 118, 123, 146). It is also expressed in poignant ways, as, for example, "We stand at the barrier between death and life, between deep-seated human corruption, which is the denial of God, and the righteousness of God, which is the denial of men" (147). Human beings are defined primarily by their ungodliness (123). Consequently, God is "pure negation" (141).

According to Barth, all of this comes clearly to the fore in the figure of Abraham. Barth readily admits that it would be a problem for contemporary Christians to identify with Abraham were it not for the fact that there exists an "objective link between all then and now, and here and there" (1933, 117). Abraham as father of us all has a "non-historical radiance" (140). This is what counts and what in the end makes the Jewishness of Abraham irrelevant:

> Abraham is, of course, the father of a single nation, Israel; but we have seen that, because in Christ he is the father of this one nation, he is also, at the same time and in consequence, the father of many nations. The historical framework is broken through when the secret of history is laid bare. (139)

Human beings are existentially godless, whether they are Jews or Christians. There is no mutuality between us and God. On the contrary, we are separated by a gulf that cannot be bridged except by God in a world that we do not have access to. Israel is constructed as a part of a negative description of humanity.

A Change of Context

Parker holds that what Barth does is similar to what Luther and Calvin did, merging theology and exegesis, not separating the literal and spiritual meanings. The highlighted difference between Barth, on the one hand, and Luther and Calvin, on the other, is that Barth is not referring to an ecclesial context, but to human beings as such. He groups Jews with the religious and ecclesiastical "men" (1933, 40). Although Parker points out that Luther and Calvin approach universal problems in ecclesial terms, a difference remains.

What are the implications of such a shift from an ecclesial context to universal categories? It seems to be an opening toward humanity in general, as Parker notes. Consequently, God can be known outside an inner circle, whether it is an inner circle of chosen ones, of believers, or some other kind of persons.

Barth allows borders to be crossed, but from a negative point of view. Rather than being joined in a knowledge of God, human beings are all in the same situation, because they misunderstand God. They are united in their ungodliness.

Understood from a Barthian point of view, Abraham unites humanity in its weakness. However, there are other possibilities. Universalism can be positively interpreted in Romans 4, especially when read with Rom. 5:1–11 rather than Romans 1–3. Such an interpretation seems to be more fruitful, because it allows us to adopt a theological position that emphasizes a positive connection between all human beings, including their hope for a good, ultimate power of the universe.

Assessing Universalism

Should we regard the shift provided by Barth from the ecclesial to the universal as a shift of context? I do not think so. Barth's description of humanity is deprived of contextual characteristics. It is precisely when contextual differences are disregarded, as in the case of Abraham, that the religious meaning of the text becomes clear. Barth poses a rhetorical question: "Is not the blessing pronounced upon him in the non-particularity of his humanness and createdness?" (127). This is the opposite of contextualization. The kind of universalism put forward by Barth and others prevents us from paying attention to real people in the real world. Naming the context "universal humanity" becomes a way of hiding or even neglecting the real world. Stating that accidents of history do not matter, since they do not affect the relationship between humans and God, is neglecting important dimensions of life. Although nuances can be added to this image of Barth, and we can adjust his theology, the problem with universalism as an escape from down-to-earth realities remains.

Similarly, the Holocaust cannot be understood in exclusively universal terms. It is a dreadful historical example of what happens when theology meets with the real world.[6] Although I do not think that theology is exclusively to blame for the oppression of the Jewish people — or of women — there is a connection between the specific and the universal that cannot be overlooked.[7] Universalism always runs a risk of becoming insensitive to the contexts that it claims to describe.

Multivocality and Harmony

Brawley presents a different approach that allows for a deconstruction of universalism. He uses multivocality as an analytical frame. The analysis is thought provoking and helpful in many respects. According to Brawley, voices relate to each other in three different ways. The first option is that they are in harmony and thus reinforce each other. The second and third options show different degrees of dissonance. Either there is a kind of two-step relationship between the voices so that the reader can discern a development, or there is a more severe tension that is not resolved.

In characterizing the different relationships between the voices it becomes obvious that the characterization itself implies the presence of a listener who hears the voices, that is, a reader. The reader approaches the text with the question of what it means and with some anticipations of what to expect.

The *reinforcing* voices help the reader determine the meaning of the text. The *elaborating* voices seem to have a persuasive character, according to Brawley. They revise the anticipations of the reader. The *corrective* voices leave the reader in some kind of ambiguity that can be resolved in different ways. Brawley holds that they can lead to different interpretations.

Brawley seems to understand reading reinforcing voices as non-problematic. He also seems to presuppose that elaborating voices can be dealt with without any hesitation or resistance on the part of the reader. However, what happens if these voices threaten the reader? Brawley does not address the issue of how to deal with the possible violence of texts (cf. Butler 1997, 1–13, 43–69). The reader may not want her or his anticipations revised in the way that the text suggests. The corrective voices seem to provide a basis for a more sympathetic reading of the text than the others, according to my preferences. The reader has a say. She or he can wrestle with the ambiguity of the text.

When Brawley's identification of the different voices is used the way he does toward the end of his essay, we find a possibility for going one step further with the questions I raised concerning the reinforcing and elaborating voices. Provided the knowledge of the many voices of Romans, we can analyze the analyses of its interpreters by identifying the voices that are lifted up by them. However, we then have to ask, Why were these voices brought to the fore and not others? In so doing, we raise contextual and hermeneutical issues. What happens if we ask these questions regarding Brawley's text?

An Alternative Hermeneutical Frame

One example of a corrective voice that results in what Brawley calls "a startling inversion" concerns the identification of Abraham's descendants. Contrary to what the readers expect, Israel is second and the Gentiles are first. By a series of elaborating voices the readers are led to this conclusion. This is good news for the Gentile audience.

What difference does it make if readers other than the authorial audience are taken into consideration? This is something Brawley does not discuss, remaining as he does on the analytical level. Even in the original context, the letter was likely to have an effect on those described in it. There were Jews in Rome, even if they did not form part of the Christian congregation, as Brawley argues. To be sure, they knew who were enemies and friends. This construction of Israel seems to me to be more natural if Jews are not directly included in the contextual frame, either historically or in our time. Brawley does not mention the implicit offense in incorporating within one's self-understanding a group that has its own distinctive self-understanding.

However, Brawley adds something else. The importance of his thesis is emphasized by his claim that God speaks through the narration of Abraham's story. This is a hermeneutical frame, providing a view of Romans as authoritative Scripture. God's voice is added as *the* corrective voice.

At this point, reading Parker and Brawley together clarifies the issue. They actually present (individually and in their joint essay) the contours of a hermeneutical frame proposed as an alternative to that of Barth. This frame concerns the existential connection between the text and our world (according to Barth, human beings live in the *krisis* of finitude), the image of God (God as the Other), and the view of the authority of Scripture.

Parker agrees with Barth and the reading of Paul he presents. Yet, in holding that Paul reads the universal religious situation of humanity, Parker does not underline the *krisis* character of that situation. He also notes that Barth changes his mind over time, being less pessimistic about the flux of history. To me it seems likely that Parker shares this latter position to some extent. The existential connection is kept, but it is depicted in a less dialectical way.

The issue of how to understand the character of the voice of God in Scripture is first presented by Brawley in the discussion of the inclusion of the Jews among the Gentiles. He identifies the voice of God on a textual level. The divine voice is distinct from the other voices in the epistle. The voice of God has different connotations from, for example, the authorial voice or the voice of the prophets. The voice of God designates revelation, God making Godself known. Thus, when Brawley writes that God legitimates the epistle and that God's voice is heard in its entirety, this has broader implications than pointing to yet another voice. If God speaks through Romans, it is truly revelatory.

Using a simple distinction, I can say that Brawley tends toward a construction of scriptural authority that affirms Romans as Word of God rather than as words about God. The voice of God is somehow mediated through Romans. This becomes even clearer in the critique of Barth delivered by Parker and Brawley in their joint essay. They criticize Barth for speaking indirectly about God rather than listening to God's voice. While Parker and Brawley encourage the reader to listen and adjust to the voice of God, they contend that Barth keeps it at a distance. Barth's construction of scriptural authority allows for the reader to enter as a dialogue partner with the text in a different way (cf. Grenholm 1996, 137–56). As I understand it, Barth does not overlook the voice of God. Rather, he has a different understanding of the relation between Romans and the Word of God.

Who is this God speaking in Romans? Brawley is explicit concerning this part of his hermeneutical frame. The focus is on God's justice. Furthermore, it is underlined that God is one. I am led by my thoughts to hear the deep voice of a good, but stern, judge. We can trust his judgment, but we fear it all the same. The combination of this view of scriptural authority and this image of God makes the divine voice predominant. The multiple voices seem to become a choir accompanying the soloist.

Brawley operates primarily with reinforcing and elaborating voices in his analysis. Although his theory of multivocality would allow him to make explicit a contextual frame, Brawley, following the common usage in critical biblical studies, focuses on the analytical frame of interpretation. There is a tension between the theory and its application. A closer look at how the analysis is pursued explains why.

The multiple voices of Romans force the reader to organize them in some way. One way of organizing them that Brawley uses is the concept of cultural repertoire. In some cases, the reference is beyond dispute, but it seems reasonable to assume that the cultural repertoire is so rich that it contains a wide range of possibilities that cannot all be detected.

What can be said concerning how Brawley handles this choir of voices? The example just mentioned concerning the Jews being included among the Gentiles shows that a possible ambiguity of the text (Brawley characterizes these voices as corrective) is resolved by stressing the text as Word of God. It is clear that the voices of the Jews are not heard, and neither is the voice of Paul, originally a Jew. Putting the contextual frame into play would provide another result. The voices would become embodied.

Let me take another example of how the cultural repertoire is constructed, this time from the essay by Parker. It is clear that Barth likewise operates with multiple voices. When commenting on this, Parker names the following "outsiders": Overbeck, Nietzsche, Dostoevsky, Kierkegaard; and at the same time the following "insiders": Calvin, Luther, Augustine, and Plato. Why are the outsiders not included in the cultural repertoire by Parker? What makes a voice an outsider?

I agree that there is a difference between the writer Dostoevsky and the Reformer Luther. Still, when they are used as contextual frames providing religious perceptions, do they not both serve the same function of enhancing certain aspects of the multivocality of the text?

The analytical frame of the multivocality of the text opens the possibility of fruitful contributions with different kinds of contextual and hermeneutical frames. For systematic theology, it is certainly inspiring. The voices of tradition can be heard in resonance with the voice of Paul. In my view, the challenge of the dissonant voices has to be met. Instead of yielding to harmony, it is interesting to see where embracing the ambiguities of the text takes us. Brawley repeatedly points to alternatives presented by Romans. Let me explore one of these tensions, bringing in the two-nature christological doctrine of the Nicene Creed as a hermeneutical frame. What happens if we try to remain within the creative space[8] of the potentialities of an unresolved tension?

Brawley characterizes the voice of Jesus as highly ambiguous: there is an antithesis between his descent from David and his resurrection from the dead (human versus divine). There is an ambiguity concerning the faith of Jesus and faith in Jesus in Rom. 3:22. Furthermore, there is an ambiguity concerning whether Jesus mediates redemption or redemption is located in him (3:24). From a theological point of view, this is telling. Could it be that the fundamental mystery of Christ concerning his relation to God is mirrored in linguistic or textual ambiguities? Could there be a resistance of the text against explicating the inexplicable? Brawley at least points toward the potential power in not just striving for harmony when searching the Scriptures for Jesus Christ. Interpretations focusing on ambiguities on the analytical level have interesting connections to one of the main ambiguities in Christian theology at the hermeneutical level, best known in the Chalcedonian formula of the two-nature christological doctrine.

If this connection is to be further explored, my suggestion is not that this preliminary result of the analysis of the ambiguous character of the voice of Jesus supports the doctrine. Rather, this analysis underlines the character of the creeds as a summary of biblical stories. Thus, it opposes the view that the creeds are to be regarded as checklists for correct belief.[9]

Adopting Abraham as Our Father

Let us continue along this path, expanding on what is already in Brawley's analysis by altering the hermeneutical frame. It should be clear that this requires an alternative view of scriptural authority, understanding Romans as words about God rather than as a medium of the divine voice. Still, the analytical frame remains the same.

One example of elaborating voices, which Brawley gives, is the tension between the voices of the author and Isaiah in Rom. 2:24. The readers hear an irony, according to Brawley. The same is the case in 3:19–20, where Ps. 142:2 LXX brings another irony about.

When approaching what Paul says on Abraham, Brawley comes across another tension. In the Hebrew Bible Abraham is in fact capable of boasting, while Paul frees him from that weakness. What conclusions should be drawn by present readers who have also the cultural repertoire of the Hebrew Bible? Either we can accept the character of Abraham as retouched by Paul (Brawley's view) or we can imagine Abraham as an imperfect father.

Let us consider the ambiguous image of Abraham as boasting and having faith in the sense of not relying on oneself, which Brawley identified but did not explore. This is an image of a human being that combines weakness and strength, rather than being purely pessimistic or optimistic. Related to such an anthropology as a hermeneutical frame, Abraham, father of us all, includes all boasters who nevertheless can find peace in moments of trust despite their own weakness.

Regarding this image of Abraham as imperfect, is he not a father we could consider adopting? Abraham is not free from human weaknesses. He boasts. He can be said not to treat well either his wife or his concubine. He is prepared to sacrifice Isaac and agrees to send a mother and her child into the desert. And still he is capable of faith, of leaving all his efforts and mistakes aside, trusting in God's good purposes of life. His example can be liberating if it is not used to legitimate oppression. But is it possible to do otherwise?

Family images seem impregnated with patriarchy. That could be a reason for ceasing even to discuss them. Still, this seems to be a dangerous strategy. Harmful structures remain harmful unless we confront them.

Father of Us All?

How is the fatherhood of Abraham constructed? Let us twist the question around and ask, How can we be incorporated into his family? There are at least three possibilities. We can belong to the family by means of a specific characteristic: we are circumcised Jews or Christian children of faith. Or, we can belong by means of a universal characteristic: for example, we are all human beings and because of that we are boasting sinners or people of faith. We fit indisputably into a universal pattern. Or, we can belong because we fit in a sense that combines the first two alternatives, allowing for both the specific and the universal. An example of this will be given below.

Both Parker and Brawley choose the second possibility, universalism. However, they construe it in different ways. Parker, following Luther, Calvin, and Barth, understands Paul as describing the human situation beyond particularities. Brawley reads the message of Romans to be that the Jews are incorporated among the Gentiles. Abraham is first the father of the Gentiles and then also of the Jews.

From the perspective of the postmodern critique of universalism, the beauty of this idea is easily overlooked. In Abraham as father of us all we can see a mythological expression of the principle of the equality of all human beings, never mind the differences. Since the combination of Jews and Gentiles includes all of humanity, Abraham as father of us all provides a basis for seeing a sibling in the other. Like Schüssler Fiorenza, we do not want to rid ourselves of this basis for political action. This is an obvious risk if we emphasize contextuality at the expense of general emancipatory goals. Oppressive divisions may be reinforced (1995, 9–10).

However, there are several problems related to claiming Abraham as our mutual father. Equality is qualified. We are equal *in faith*. This raises the problem of the limits within the community at two different levels. At a level of religious dialogue we see that the Jews belong to the same community not only by disregarding their characteristic, a covenantal piety expressed in loyalty to the Torah (as also Wasserberg's essay points out), but also by adopting faith as a characteristic of Christians. Israel is reconstructed according to a Christian pattern.

At a level of religious perceptions, reflecting on conditions of life, the problem of the distinction between creation and salvation comes up. On the one hand, faith is something that, according to Romans 4, characterizes Abraham as a symbol of the basic unity of Jews and Gentiles. On the other hand, faith is related to Jesus Christ.

This touches on the complex relationship between the two Testaments of the Christian Bible. Let us contrast two views. A common view is that Jesus Christ is the fulfillment of revelation. This makes christological interpretations of the Christian Old Testament possible. An alternative view is that the relationship between Jesus and his tradition is far more complex and ambiguous. With Barr, we can affirm that the original problem "was not how to understand the Old Testament but how to understand Christ" (1982, 139).

Especially in the Reformed traditions, but also in general, the first view has been prevalent. The concept of faith can then be understood as a prerequisite for salvation. If combined with the first way to become incorporated in Abraham's family — belonging because one shares a specific characteristic — faith as defined by Christians is required from all. As we have seen, this is the view of neither Parker nor Brawley. Rather, they have an inclusive understanding of faith, especially clear in Parker and his presentation of Barth. Yet the fact that it is combined with the idea of fulfillment in Christ keeps the privilege of definition within Christian circles.

Let us explore a third possibility: the combination of a positive evaluation of differences and a nonhierarchical view of the relationship between Jesus Christ and his tradition.[10] Then we can affirm a close connection between faith as trust in God and faith as belief in Christ. Could not the fascinating idea of the kinship of all human beings in their trust in God be developed?

The positive potentiality and the factual conflict implicit in the image of Abraham as father of us all have been well expressed and presented by Jewish scholar Jon Levenson in his book *The Death and Resurrection of the Beloved Son: The Transformation of Child Sacrifice in Judaism and Christianity*. He presents a hermeneutical frame based on a critical analysis and clearly related to his own context as a rabbi. His interpretation can be read as an opening to an exploration of the third possibility we are looking for.

Levenson lifts up a pattern that connects the Hebrew Bible with the New Testament in an ambiguous way. There is a competition between the firstborn and the beloved sons. This is the case with Abraham, and Ishmael and Isaac. According to this pattern, the beloved son takes the place of the firstborn by means of a symbolic death that both humiliates and exalts him. Isaac takes the place of Ishmael when he is symbolically sacrificed by Abraham. There is an obvious parallel to Jesus, who dies but rises and replaces Isaac as the chosen son, explicitly named the beloved son of God. (See especially ch. 15, "The Displacement of Isaac and the Birth of the Church.")

Thus, there is a competition between the sons wherein the one originally having the privileges and the duties is replaced by the beloved. Levenson does not suggest any solutions to this tension, but he points out clearly why the fact that somebody is acknowledged as a brother (or sister) does not automatically result in mutual love. The tension is kept for us to deal with.

Construing a Father
While Taking Diversity into Account

Levenson challenges us to give a response from Christian theology. Is there any possibility of overcoming the competitive relation between the children of Abraham? Parker and Brawley point out the necessity of construals in biblical interpretation. Let us try one way of handling the dilemma pointed out by Levenson. How can we relate to the competing sons?

Theoretically, regarding the hermeneutical frame, I believe that what unites them — the universal aspect — should be envisioned as a part of a religious perception of humanity. However, universality needs to be kept in creative tension with an awareness that life is always contextualized. Thus, universalism can never be the whole truth.

When discussing universalism and context above, I opted for a positive rather than negative description of humanity. Our common origin in Abraham on a mythological level at least relativizes the distinction between Jews and Gentiles. They are all people of faith. This need not imply only a theoretical acknowledgment of equality, neither need it be restricted to be a negative common characteristic, as in the case of Barth's theology.

In my view, a responsible interpretation requires us to take note that a primarily negative definition of what unites all the children of God does not give us anything to hold on to. It does not connect with our actual lives in history. It does not call for universal celebration. However, if the universal understanding of human beings as children of God is connected to our different experiences of something beyond all of us wherefrom we expect to receive all good things, or at least the hope of such an ultimate power, then we have a reason to celebrate together. If for our hermeneutical frame we adopt faith as an act of trust in a God who can be met in this world, we need not end by affirming the competitive relationship between those who came first and those who did not come until later on.[11]

This may still be a Lutheran way of understanding faith. My proposal can be understood as even more narrow than the position that all Jews are actually Christians. Now they are all Lutherans! No doubt, Lutheran theology is a source of inspiration for me, but at this point I do not propose that it should be understood in a specific confessional sense. Rather, trust in something good outside ourselves is a possible phenomenological definition of religious belief with a wide range of applications, including a multitude of religions as well as other views of life.

In Tillich's terminology, faith is relying on one's ultimate concern (1964, 234ff.). Beyond Tillich, when those concerns are not evaluated from a religious point of view, people of faith includes all human beings; all have an ultimate concern. Perhaps the paradigmatic figure of Abraham is big enough to include nontheistic, secular, human longing. In effect, this is what Barth did, as Parker and Brawley point out. However, Barth addresses post-Christendom from his pessimistic perspective. The idea seems worth expanding from a more positive point of view in order to avoid excluding nonreligious people from our vision of what the image of Abraham as father of us all may contain.

This path can be combined with different views of the relationship between promise and fulfillment. Let us again briefly glance at two alternatives. From a Christian point of view one can pose the question of what difference there is between sharing a promise in faith (the promise was indeed given in the old covenant) and believing in the fulfillment of that promise. Do they not both express trust in God? Belief in Jesus is belief in his resurrection as a sign of what will happen to all who believe. It is still the time of the promise. From this theological point of view it is not important to establish clear boundaries between different kinds of reliance on a promise. Waiting for the Messiah to come or to come back may not be so different.

Following Leenhardt and Patte, we could try another path.[12] By viewing Abraham as a type fulfilled in Christ Jesus and in the experience of the believers, fulfillment circumscribes time in a proleptic way. Understood in this way, faith is being fulfilled in everyone's experience, although only believers recognize it.

It is beyond the scope of this essay to develop these alternative ways of finding a positive connection between universal phenomena as trust or glimpses of fulfillment, on the one hand, and specific traditions, on the other. However, what has been sketched should be enough to show that these alternatives are available. The basis for this in Christian theology is the doctrine of incarnation, telling us that God shares life in this world. This can at least be understood as meaning that God can be perceived in any culture and in any part of creation.

What is at stake here is not only how Israel is read, but how the father, to whom universal fatherhood is attributed, is construed.

A Feminist Warning and a Suggestion

What has prevented us from using the image of Abraham as father of us all to promote and celebrate unity despite difference? Maybe the problem is patriarchy. Equality is forever impossible to base in hierarchy. No father can grant the equality of his children. Rather, they are most likely to compete.

Danish exegete Kristen Nielsen considers the father-son image as a biblical root metaphor in her book *Satan: The Prodigal Son? A Family Problem in the Bible.* She expresses the hierarchical character of the relationship between the father and his sons:

> Authority and solicitude belong to the father role. The father has begotten the sons, who are dependent upon him and who owe him respect and love. In return, he provides for their needs and protects them from external threats and dangers. (1998, 42)

This is the image of the patriarchal father. However, fatherhood can have other implications. Although Nielsen focuses on Satan as the son of God, her theme has close connections with ours, and her conclusion is valid for us:

> The biblical texts form part of an intertextuality open to different interpretations, and it therefore never leaves us in peace. But if we are to emphasize just one characteristic it must be the father's love for *both* his sons. This love is not without its problems; it is in fact bound up with pain and suffering, since it forms part of the image of active family life. (1998, 184)

Yet we need not get stuck with the patriarchal pattern. For this, it is enough to contextualize the father-son metaphor primarily in the complexity of family life as we know it. Ideally, family life is primarily mutuality. The close relationships both in origin and often in daily life make us vulnerable to one another. Contextualized in this way, the metaphor opens possibilities for further exploration of the positive connotations of the phrase "Abraham, father of us all."

A patriarchal father has authority that cannot be put in question. A reading of Romans 4 that relates to a hierarchical view of Scripture is likely to be combined with an Abraham inscribed in patriarchy. A horizontal view of Scripture, on the other hand, gives the reader permission to approach Abraham on equal terms and without fear.

I suggested earlier that viewing Abraham as a boaster who nevertheless trusts God helps us to see Abraham as our equal. Yet, it was pointed out long ago that boasting (*hybris*) is a sin of the privileged that is not equally distributed among men and women (Saiving 1960). Perhaps it is even more fruitful for a nonpatriarchal understanding to focus on another feature of the text's description of Abraham: an impotent man having descendants.

The theme is brought up in a straightforward way by Brawley. Following Käsemann, Brawley relates Abraham's awareness of his impotence and Sarah's barrenness to the resurrection. I would choose another point of connection: descendants and, therefore, birth. Although not explicitly mentioned, the birth of Isaac pervades our reading of the text. This child, who is beyond the words of the text, can be seen as a paradigm for human mystery.

The absent yet present child evokes Abraham's awe and wonder before the fulfillment of the promise. Like Abraham and Sarah, we, in beholding a newborn, are filled with awe and joy originating in deep respect for life itself and in humble ignorance of what will become of this child. We do not know, and yet, with trust and hope, we prepare ourselves to receive the baby, to encourage and nourish it.

Beholding the child, we can perceive ourselves as sprung from the same root. As children of the human family, we also experience the vulnerability of life. But more than anything, we can rejoice at the miracle of being alive — the vulnerable embodiment of a promise we can trust to be fulfilled.

Notes

1. Although my discipline is called "studies in faiths and ideologies."

2. See, for example, Thiselton 1995 and Tilley 1995.

3. In discussing whether the image of the father can be used about God in a patriarchal context, Johnson concludes that "such symbols in fact do not function to emancipate women, however much they may be adjusted toward kindness and other desirable characteristics" (1992, 40). See also pp. 33–41. Cf. McFague 1987, ch. 4.

4. Cf. Keller on the apocalyptic pattern as prevalent in Christian culture. She argues against the common opinion that apocalypse is a marginal phenomenon. On the contrary, its sharp distinction between the faithful and the condemned can be discerned even in feminism, which programatically opposes to dualistic thinking (1996, 257, 260–64).

5. *Confessio Augustana*, art. 4.

6. Cf. Hick 1993, 80–83.

7. Cf. Schüssler Fiorenza, who points to the connection between the anti-Jewishness of historical Jesus research and feminism that also needs to be confronted (1995, 82–96).

8. Cf. Schüssler Fiorenza, who envisions the empty tomb as an "open space" that invites contemporary readers to "meaning-making" (1995, 124–25). See also pp. 3–4 on her hermeneutical point of departure.

9. Cf. Young (1992, 1–15) concerning the character of the creeds as stories. Originally, creeds were not systems of doctrine, but summaries of the Christian story. "They tell who God is and what he has done. They invite the convert to make that story and that affirmation his or her own" (12).

10. Hick presents such a pluralistic understanding of Christianity (1993, 140–49). However, it need not be adopted in that form.

11. Lutheranism is often accused of being as pessimistic as the Reformed tradition. However, there are different strands within it. The one I side with emphasizes Luther's celebration of creation. See, for example, Løgstrup 1997. Although I still believe there is much to learn from the distinctive feature of the Lutheran tradition — the emphasis on sin and forgiveness — I do not believe it is sufficient for interpreting life in all its dimensions. Cf. Grenholm 1999.

12. See Leenhardt 1961, 113–20; Patte 1983, ch. 7.

References

The "Augsburg Confession." 1959. Pp. 23–96 in *The Book of Concord: The Confessions of the Evangelical Lutheran Church*. Trans. and ed. Theodore G. Tappert, with Jaroslav Pelikan, Robert H. Fischer, and Arthur C. Piepkorn. Philadelphia: Fortress.

Barr, James. 1982. *Old and New in Interpretation: A Study of the Two Testaments*. 2nd. ed. London: SCM.

Barth, Karl. 1933. *The Epistle to the Romans*. Trans. Edwyn C. Hoskyns (from 6th ed.). Oxford: Oxford University Press.

Bonda, Jan. [1993] 1998. *The One Purpose of God: An Answer to the Doctrine of Eternal Punishment*. Trans. Reinder Bruinsma. Grand Rapids and Cambridge: Eerdmans.

Butler, Judith. 1997. *Excitable Speech: A Politics of the Performative*. New York: Routledge.

Grenholm, Cristina. 1999. *Barmhärtig och sårbar: En bok om kristen tro på Jesus [Merciful and Vulnerable: Contemporary Christian Faith in Jesus]*. Stockholm: Verbum. (English translation forthcoming.)

Hick, John. 1993. *The Metaphor of God Incarnate*. London: SCM.

Johnson, Elizabeth A. 1992. *SHE WHO IS: The Mystery of God in Feminist Theological Discourse*. New York: Crossroad.

Keller, Catherine. 1996. *Apocalypse Now and Then: a Feminist Guide to the End of the World*. Boston: Beacon.

Leenhardt, Franz J. 1961. *The Epistle to the Romans*. London: Lutterworth.

Levenson, Jon D. 1993. *The Death and Resurrection of the Beloved Son: The Transformation of Child Sacrifice in Judaism and Christianity*. New Haven and London: Yale University Press.

Løgstrup, K. E. [1956] 1997. *The Ethical Demand*. Notre Dame, Ind.: University of Notre Dame Press.

McFague, Sallie. 1987. *Models of God: Theology for an Ecological, Nuclear Age*. London: SCM.

Nielsen, Kirsten. [1991] 1998. *Satan: The Prodigal Son? A Family Problem in the Bible*. Biblical Seminar 50. Sheffield: Sheffield Academic Press.

Patte, Daniel. 1983. *Paul and the Power of the Gospel: A Structural Introduction to Paul's Letters*. Philadelphia: Fortress

Saiving, Valerie. 1960. "The Human Situation: A Feminine View." *Journal of Religion* 40:110–12.

Schüssler Fiorenza, Elisabeth. 1995. *Jesus: Miriam's Child, Sophia's Prophet: Critical Issues in Feminist Theology*. New York: Continuum; London: SCM.

Stendahl, Krister. 1976. *Paul among Jews and Gentiles, and Other Essays*. Philadelphia: Fortress.

Thiselton, Anthony C. 1995. *Interpreting God and the Postmodern Self: On Meaning, Manipulation, and Promise*. Grand Rapids: Eerdmans.

Tilley, Terrence W. 1995, *Postmodern Theologies: The Challenge of Religious Diversity*. With John Edwards et al. Maryknoll, N.Y.: Orbis.

Tillich, Paul. 1964. *Systematic Theology*. Vol. 1. 4th ed. Digswell Place, England: James Nisbet.

Watson, Francis. Review of *Romans 1–8* and *Romans 9–16*, by James D. G. Dunn *Journal of Theological Studies* 42: 252–54.

Young, Frances. 1992. *The Making of the Creeds*. London: SCM; Philadelphia: Trinity Press International.

Part 2

RECEPTIONS AND CRITICAL INTERPRETATIONS OF ROMANS 9–11

–FIVE–

"God's Gifts and Call Are Irrevocable"

The Reception of Romans 11:29 through the Centuries and Christian-Jewish Relations

Joseph Sievers

———— ◆ ————

Introduction

Romans 11:29 in Its Modern and Pauline Contexts

To study a single verse of Paul's Epistle to the Romans is problematic, **A**
to say the least.[1] Taking a statement out of its context, one risks not
understanding it or, worse, misunderstanding its intended meaning. In
Romans 9–11, Paul is struggling with questions for which he had no
immediate or established answer. Accordingly, attempts to interpret these
chapters have not been easy, and the areas of scholarly consensus are
limited (Räisänen 1988).

If, then, I take only one verse and try to show how it has been interpreted and used from the patristic era to the present, it is in part to
keep this essay within reasonable limits. Yet the passage was not chosen arbitrarily. In recent statements and discussions on Christian-Jewish **C**
relations, Rom. 11:28b-29 appears to be the most frequently cited biblical text (Hoch and Dupuy 1980, Scripture index). On the other hand,
exegetes warn against using chs. 9–11 uncritically for the definition of
Christian views of Judaism (Kümmel 1997, 32–33; Sanders 1983, 197; **H**
Wasserberg in this volume).

A One verse as an object of analysis.

C Recent discussions on Christian-Jewish relations.

H Christian views of Judaism.

It is universally recognized that Romans 9–11 forms a special section
of the letter, rarely judged a later insertion (Dodd 1932, 150). Refoulé,
while defending the absolute coherence of chs. 9–11 (1987, 239–42),
concludes that they are unconnected with the remainder of Romans
(1995, 193) or even incompatible with Pauline authorship (1991, 79).
On the basis of the lack of scriptural quotations in 11:28–32, Ponsot considers these verses a possible "addition actualisante" (1988, 169 n. 60).
A Against these, a large majority of scholars considers chs. 9–11 an integral part of the letter, linked thematically and stylistically to the rest of
it (Räisänen 1988, 180; Aletti 1991, 150–55, 199–203).

Recently, a renewed emphasis has been placed on the rhetorical model
underlying Romans in general (Aletti 1991, 31–36) and Romans 9–11
in particular (Siegert 1985), a concern found already in Melanchthon
(Schäfer 1963). It is generally recognized that 11:25–32 forms the last
subunit of these chapters before the final doxology (11:33–36). Bultmann did not have much use for these verses and declared the mystery of
salvation history in 11:25ff. to be a product of speculative fancy (1984,
484). Käsemann, commenting on these same verses, pointedly disagrees,
emphasizing the painstakingly careful dialectic by which Paul reaches the
A end of ch. 11 (1980, 311). Similarly, other exegetes consider 11:25–32
the culmination of chs. 9–11 (Luz 1968, 268; Stuhlmacher 1971, 557).

Within this text segment our verse represents part of the elaboration
of the argument, or, in the words of one recent commentator, "[Rom.]
A 11:29, if not 11:28 and 11:29, constitutes the apostolic summary appli-
cable to all three chapters" (Schatzmann 1987, 18). Kühl had already
noted that 11:29 is one of the clearest expressions of Paul's idea of God
(1913, 394). According to K. Barth, chs. 9–10 are to be understood
in light of 11:29 (1942, 332). Holtzmann called 11:29 the formula on
which Paul's entire doctrine of justification is built (1926, 663). Others
see such a summing up in 11:32, which, however, closely corresponds to
11:29 (Barrett 1957, 224; Stuhlmacher 1971, 558, 567). The centrality of
11:29 appears beyond doubt if, in Räisänen's words, "it is now generally
agreed that [Paul's] real concern [in chs. 9–11] is the question of the trustworthiness of God as regards his promises to Israel" (1988, 178). Kuss
considers one of Paul's principal questions in chs. 9–11 whether God has
"repented of" and withdrawn his gifts and calling (1978, 663), and sees
in 11:29 the basic insight of a Jewish-Pauline view of God (1978, 809).
Gaston declares that "Romans as a whole can be understood to center on

---

A Romans 9–11 connected with the rest of Romans, despite the views of some scholars.
A Rom. 11:25–32 as the culmination of Romans 9–11, despite the views of some scholars.
A Rom. 11:29 central in Romans 9–11.

the theme of the faithfulness...of God" (1987, 60; cf. Räisänen 1989, 91–92; Donfried 1989, 771–72).

Despite its importance, Rom. 11:29 has received comparatively little attention. Many commentaries, patristic as well as modern, skip it entirely or merely paraphrase it. None of the Latin church fathers *stricto sensu* (i.e., not counting Ambrosiaster and Pelagius) comments on this part of Romans. Augustine refers to 11:29, mostly in connection with his teaching on grace and predestination (Platz 1938, 197 n. 2). Thomas Aquinas's commentary on Romans remains to this day among the fullest treatments of our verse (1953, 924–29). Refoulé's work on 11:25–32 (1984) is the most thorough, though unconvincing, discussion. The scholarly neglect of our verse despite its theological importance was pointed out by Spicq (1960, 210). This neglect has changed, largely however, **C** only in writings concerned with Christian-Jewish relations.

Purpose and Structure of the Present Essay

An urgent desideratum is the integration of (1) a critical exegesis of **I** Romans 9–11, (2) insights received through the tragic history of this century and through changing relations between Jews and Christians, and (3) theological reflection on the meaning of God's faithfulness. Although this essay can in no way accomplish such a task, it may at least lay out the data in a somewhat systematic fashion and point out some of the pitfalls and accomplishments of past and present exegesis and theology.

This essay attempts to present not only the current state of scholarship, but to pay close attention to past exegetical and theological evaluations. In fact, theology and exegesis have influenced each other, positively as well as negatively, although at times they seem to be going their separate ways, to the detriment of both. Here it is impossible to enter the debate about theological hermeneutics in general, but Rom. 11:29 seems to be a good test case to investigate what hermeneutical principles have been at work in the past or are currently being applied more or less consciously in using the Scriptures in theological discourse. As to ideas that recur in the literature, I have tried to indicate their earliest appearance in print, but obviously, it is often impossible to be sure of their origin.

The first purpose of this essay is to give an overview of the different interpretations of Rom. 11:29. It will, secondly, attempt to indicate where and how this verse has been used in redefining Christian attitudes vis-à-vis the Jewish people, paying attention to hermeneutical, exegetical, theological, and historical questions.

The essay is structured to proceed from the more technical philological questions (first section) and other exegetical questions (second

---

C Neglect of Rom. 11:29 in commentaries, except in Christian-Jewish discussions.

I Interplay of analytical, contextual, and hermeneutical frames.

section) to the theological concerns (third section) found in Rom. 11:29. In the fourth section it will attempt to document how this verse has been used for Christian-Jewish relations and to note theological advances or at least soundings into as yet uncharted waters that may be found in such documents and studies.

Exegesis of Romans 11:29 in Past and Present

Romans 11:29 consists of nine Greek words: ἀμεταμέλητα γὰρ τὰ χαρίσματα καὶ ἡ κλῆσις τοῦ θεοῦ ("For God's gifts and calling are irrevocable"). Textcritically it presents no problems and no significant variants (Spicq 1960, 210 n. 1). Nestle-Aland's 27th edition lists no variants.[2] Translation has never presented major problems, even though the meaning of ἀμεταμέλητα has been interpreted in different ways. The Latin *sine poenitentia enim sunt dona et vocatio Dei* ("For without repentance are God's gifts and calling") is a basically correct though weak translation. It appears unchanged, except for slight differences in spelling, from the Old Latin (Sabatier 1751, 638) until the most recent edition of the Neo-
A Vulgata.[3] Unfortunately, by rendering the Greek adjective as a noun, the Latin has obscured the fact that the gifts, and hence the giver, not the beneficiary, are "without repentance." It may have been this ambiguity that led Ambrosiaster (1966, CSEL 81.1.384–87) to conclude from this
H verse that God's grace is given (in baptism) without requiring prior repentance. In the *Quaestiones Veteris et Novi Testamenti,* now generally considered the work of Ambrosiaster, 11:29 is used in a similar sense: "Finally he remits all sins at once to believers who have converted to him, without prior penitential lamentation. Therefore the Apostle Paul says: God's gifts and calling are without repentance" (Pseudo-Augustinus 1908, CSEL 50.207). One should note, however, that in a fragmentary commentary on Lamentations attributed to Origen there is a reference to baptism in connection with 11:26–29. Baptism is seen as the cause of the removal of "lawlessness," which is essential for salvation (Origen 1983, 3:278.12). Similarly, John Chrysostom, writing at approximately the same time as Ambrosiaster, apparently sees in the irrevocable character of God's gifts and calling a foreshadowing of future baptism.[4] Thus Ambrosiaster might have tried to give a textual basis to an interpretation that was already then current, even in the Greek East.

Ambrosiaster's influence appears in Pelagius. After stating that God does not repent of the promises to Abraham's seed, he adds as an alternative meaning: "Or: those people will be saved without the affliction of

---

A Ancient philology; "without repentance" in Rom. 11:29 referring to beneficiaries or to gifts and giver.

H No need of repentance for believers, but God's gifts are conditional.

penance, if they believe" (1926, 92). Here we note not only the misinterpretation of ἀμεταμέλητα but also the allusion to Rom. 11:26a, "and thus all Israel will be saved," and the addition of the condition "If they believe," probably derived from 11:23, "if they do not persist in unbelief" (or perhaps from 10:9).

Ambrosiaster's commentaries were generally attributed to Ambrose of Milan until the sixteenth century.[5] Therefore, for many centuries these commentaries carried all the prestige of that church father. Lanfranc of Bec (1003–1089), archbishop of Canterbury, explains that, to those to whom God gives the gift of faith, he gives it without their prior repentance; but, showing some awareness of the problems of this interpretation, he adds, "Or: those whom he has chosen for eternal life, he has chosen without changing his plan" (*PL* 150.144). Anselm of Laon (d. 1117) included in his gloss on Rom. 11:29 an interpretation that follows Ambrosiaster: *Remissio peccatorum in baptismo* ("Remission of sins in baptism"). His gloss became part of the frequently reprinted *Biblia Latina cum glossa ordinaria* (1480–1481, 298), a standard reference work for several centuries. Even Zwingli still copied Ambrosiaster's explanation, although he also noted Erasmus's unambiguous and correct translation (Corpus reformatorum 99.34; cf. 99.1).

These two elements — the conditional character of the gifts, and the lack of need of repentance — remain staple fare in Latin exegesis until the time of Erasmus, and even beyond. Cornelius a Lapide (1567–1637), a Jesuit, points out this error not only in Ambros[iaster] and Aquinas, but criticizes this interpretation also in an unnamed reformer. He even cites Calvin to the effect that Paul here refers to the election not of individuals but of the whole Jewish people (1617, 161). Erasmus did clarify the meaning of the text by rendering it *Nam dona quidem et vocatio Dei eiusmodi sunt, ut eorum illum penitere non possit* ("For God's gifts and calling are such that he cannot repent of them") (1509, 340). In his *Annotationes,* first published in March 1516, Erasmus explained ἀμεταμέλητα as something that cannot be regretted by the one who gave or promised it, in other words, unregrettable (*impoenitibilia*) (1535, 407; 1994, 311). Luther received an early copy of this work while he was still preparing his 1515–1516 lectures on Romans. He used Erasmus beginning in Romans 9 (Flicker 1908, xlvi) and followed him also in 11:29, noting in his scholia that *amitamelita* means *impenitibilia* and refers not to human repentance but to God's not changing his mind (*WA* 56:440).

Melanchthon's comments on Rom. 11:29 are somewhat disappointing. In his 1529 commentary he simply offers a rough paraphrase (1848, 481). In later editions (1540 and, quoted below, 1556) he seems to misrepresent 11:29 entirely, because he interprets 11:28–32 to mean, "He exhorts all to repentance, after which he equally offers consolation to all who are doing penance" (1848, 997; cf. 700). Since Paul does not

(1968, 296 n. 129). Luz may be basically correct, but the meaning of "calling" (κλῆσις) should not be restricted too narrowly, as we shall see presently.

The "Calling"

A It has been claimed that "the doctrine of vocation as it appears in the NT finds its most articulate expression in Pauline theology" (Scheef 1962, 792). Certainly we have to see the reference to "God's calling" in Rom. 11:29 also in this framework. Weiss noted correctly that it would be arbitrary to limit "the calling" specifically to Israel's missionary vocation (1899, 500). Many commentators, including Zahn (1910, 527) and K. Barth (1942, 332), point out that "calling" and "election" are used here almost synonymously. Wilckens asserts on the basis of 9:24ff. that the "calling" refers to the Christian proclamation (1980, 258).[7] In 9:24–26, however, the verb "to call" (καλέω) is used three times, twice meaning "to name." Wilckens also seems to overlook God's calling Jacob in 9:12 (cf. 9:7). Fitzmyer argues that "that 'call' refers to the initial summons of Abraham (Gen 12:1–2), which became in time the election of Israel as God's 'chosen' people (Deut 7:6–7). But now that call must also include God's summons of Israel by the gospel" (1993, 626).

Most authors, however, do not pronounce themselves on the precise meaning of "the call of God." Käsemann proposes, "It is the power of God's address and claim which takes place with every charisma. The term is interchangeable with charisma as in 1 Cor 7:15ff., for in his gifts the saving will of God comes on the scene as task or mission. God does not give gifts without calling and *vice versa*" (1980, 316). Other authors see the call as the most important or most exalted one of the gifts of grace (Cornely 1896, 622; Jülicher 1908, 300; Bardenhewer 1926, 173; Joachim Jeremias 1977, 202; Michel 1978, 358), or as "the sum and purpose of them all" (Black 1973, 148). Cranfield, however, points out that aspects of the divine calling such as "task," or "commission," do not naturally fall under the description of "gift." He suggests that "by ἡ κλῆσις here we may understand God's calling of Israel to be His special people to stand in a special relation to Himself and to fulfill a special function in history" (1981, 581). Dunn takes a mediating position, holding that the views of Käsemann, Michel, and Cranfield are not mutually exclusive: "Paul would no doubt have been happy to own all three" (1988, 686).[8]

A "Calling" meaning the election of Israel; or of Christians; or of Israel to the gospel; or attached to every gift; or to a task or mission.

The Form of Romans 11:29

God's faithfulness is a central affirmation of the Hebrew Bible and the **A**
New Testament as well as of extracanonical Jewish and Christian writings (Hofius 1973; Jörg Jeremias 1975, 119). It is expressed in brief, poignant form in Rom. 11:29. The verse as a whole is judged to be in form and content a fixed religious axiom (Kühl 1913, 394; Michel 1978, 357).

Implicitly this fact was acknowledged since early times, when the verse was used outside its Pauline context of the gifts given to Israel. We have already seen the (mis)use made by Ambrosiaster, but even earlier a liturgical fragment seems to point to the broader application of the sentence. It reads in part, "of your irrevocable gi[ft]s through your only son."[9] Cornely is one of few commentators who warn of simply taking Rom. 11:29 as a universal affirmation (1896, 622). He points to the definite articles as indicators that specific gifts and a specific calling are meant. Thus both the general validity and the special occasion of the statement have to be kept in mind.

The Beneficiaries of God's Gifts and Calling

Who are the intended beneficiaries of God's gifts and calling? This is in **I**
the first instance an exegetical problem, but the solutions are (and have to be) influenced by theological concerns. On the surface, there is a simple answer: the Israel of Rom. 11:25–26 is the natural referent, since "all **A**
Israel" is, with the exception of the deliverer (11:26b), the last personal subject before 11:29. Israel in turn comprises or is identical with the "Israelites" of 9:4. As we have already seen, the "gifts" of 11:29 are generally identified with those listed in 9:4–5. Paul there speaks of the beneficiaries as "my kin according to the flesh, who are Israelites" (9:3–4). From the way Paul agonizes about them, they seem identifiable as those Jews who do not believe in Jesus Christ.[10]

Thus, according to Refoulé, the only difficulty in Rom. 11:29 is the question of who is called (1984, 210). This question has infrequently been addressed directly. Rather, it has been treated mostly in conjunction with the interpretation of "all Israel" in 11:26a, because almost all authors agree that the reality called "all Israel" is also the object of God's love (11:28b), and therefore the beneficiary of God's gifts and calling. Augustine, following Origen, considered it a stupid idea to think that the

---

A Rom. 11:29 as a fixed religious axiom about God's faithfulness; or as a specific statement.

I Interplay of analytical and hermeneutical frames.

A Beneficiaries being Israel not believing in Christ (Rom. 11:25–26; 9:4).

same persons can be enemies of God and beloved by God (*Praed.* 16.33). Modern authors are generally less scandalized by such a polarity of expressions. Refoulé represents a broad consensus when he includes those designated as "enemies" among the "beloved" (1984, 198–99, 206). The consensus, however, does not go much further.

A According to Dreyfus, the calling in Rom. 11:29 is that of the patriarchs (1977, 145 n. 26). For him, "calling" and "election" are used almost synonymously in Paul. Thus he also asserts that election can only be individual, even though subsequently its beneficiaries may constitute a community (140). Stated deliberately in extreme terms, his thesis is that for Paul Israel has never been rejected, because Israel as a sociological entity has never been elected (144). Following Dreyfus, Refoulé emphasizes that God's calling according to Paul is always directed toward individuals (1984, 213; 1991, 75). However, he does not restrict the calling to the patriarchs but, using the terminology of chs. 9–11, develops the following equation: Israelites = God's children = beloved = elected = called. All the links of this equation for Refoulé, however, represent only "the remnant," including the remnant that is momentarily hardened (1984, 215).

For Dreyfus, the elect have the function of representing the entire people, and the people in its totality has been and still is the object of God's special love (1977, 144). For Refoulé, instead, the Jewish people as such is never considered at all in Romans 9–11. According to him, Paul here knows only two kinds of Israel, one elected and the other religious yet hardened (1984, 166–67). Refoulé suspects of eisegesis those who see a positive function of "the remnant" on behalf of the entire people (1984, 149). The prooftext he mentions concerning Sodom and Gomorrah (Rom. 9:29 = Isa. 1:9), however, seems to confirm such a function: if there is a sufficient remnant, as few as ten people, there is hope of salvation also for the others (cf. Gen. 18:26–32).

A The question, then, of who is meant by "all Israel" is not as simple as it might appear. Its meaning has been subject to debate since early Judaism and the early church. Recent discussion has been summarized by Refoulé (1984, 36–45; 1991, 76–79; earlier discussion in Caubet Iturbe 1962; cf. Sievers 1997a, 397–400). A schematic overview of the different positions, in addition to his own proposal, is given by Nanos (1996, 256–59).

The overwhelming majority of exegetes takes "all Israel" as a reference to "historical Israel," that is, the Jewish people (Cornelius a Lapide 1617, 160; Cornely 1896, 616; Sanday and Headlam 1902, 335; Lyonnet in

---

A Beneficiaries being the patriarchs and other individuals (not community); the remnant.

A Beneficiaries being all Israel: historical Israel and the Jewish people; or the remnant as a limited group of elect.

De Lorenzi 1977, 50; Mussner 1979, 57; Walter 1984, 182; Fitzmyer 1993, 623). Dunn notes "a strong consensus that πᾶς Ἰσραὴλ must mean Israel as a whole, as a people whose corporate identity and wholeness would not be lost even if in the event there were some (or indeed many) individual exceptions" (1988, 681).

Wright takes a different position: "In this context (Rom 11:26) 'all Israel' cannot possibly mean 'all Jews.' It is impermissible to argue that 'Israel' cannot change its referent within the space of two verses, so that 'Israel' in v. 25 must mean the same as 'Israel' in v. 26: Paul actually began the whole section (9:6) with just such a programmatic distinction of two 'Israels'" (1991, 250; cf. Refoulé 1984, 144–83). While he is right that probably Paul did not mean to exclude possible individual exceptions, it would be difficult to demonstrate that Paul used "all Israel" in a more restrictive sense than unqualified "Israel" in the preceding verse and indeed in the same sentence. To restrict the meaning of "all Israel" to only a limited group of the elect thus seems to be uncalled for and not in Paul's intention. It would make 11:25–32 an anticlimactic diatribe that does not fulfill any of the expectations raised by Paul's solemn language.

Theological Questions

It remains amazing how great a variety of approaches has been taken over the centuries, even though the key issue seems to remain that of the beneficiaries of God's gifts and calling. One central question that haunts **H** Jewish as well as Christian theology is whether or not God can "repent" or "change his mind." A talmudic dictum recounts that a voice from heaven is heard asking to be freed from the bond of an oath, but without a human response God cannot release himself from his obligation (*b. B. Bat.* 74a). In a similar vein, Buber emphasized during a dialogue session in the dramatic circumstances of January 1933 that for himself and for the Jewish people the covenant had not been canceled. He made this assertion while recounting his experience of visiting the city of Worms, admiring first the perfect artistic greatness of the Romanesque cathedral before moving on to the nearby Jewish cemetery (with the exception of catacombs, the oldest one extant in Europe). The cemetery evokes for Buber death and decay and chaos. Yet he sees it also as a sign of a covenant that has not been canceled, enduring despite everything (Buber and Schmidt 1933, 273; cf. Backhaus 1996, 33–34).

Jörg Jeremias has devoted a study to the idea of divine repentance in the Hebrew Bible. He asks whether such a concept is irreconcilable with Rom. 11:29 and concludes that both the stories of the flood and of Saul

---

H Can God repent? No. Covenant with Israel endures.

that speak of God "repenting" serve to underline that such actions will never be repeated by God (1975, 36; cf. 119).

The irrevocable character of God's gifts and calling asserted by Paul was seen as problematic by most church fathers who addressed this question. In her selective study of patristic material, Judant affirms against Journet (1961, 110) that exegetical and theological evaluations of a given text have to coincide (Judant 1969, 262). Based on this very problematic axiom, she elevates the interpretation of certain fathers to the status of exegetical and theological truths. She asserts that the Jews for whom "the gifts and calling of God are without regret" are those who belong to the church and that this is the interpretation of the entire patristic tradition of the first five centuries (262–63). Schelkle expresses the same problem quite differently. He surmises that early interpreters were almost unable to deal with Rom. 11:29 as it stands (1956, 403).

Luther, in a late polemical pamphlet very different in substance and style from many of his earlier writings including his lectures on Romans (WA 56:440; cf. 438), asserts that he sees no hope for the Jews and, above all, no scriptural basis for any hope for them (WA 53:579–80; cf. Kuss 1978, 813–14). Examples in similar directions could be multiplied, but I will refrain from doing so. It is clear, however, that in past centuries most exegetes and theologians, Catholic as well as Protestant, have found it difficult to consider God's love for the Jewish people a continuing reality.

Can the Beneficiaries Change?

With regard to Rom. 11:29, this has led to different views concerning the beneficiaries of God's gifts. The development of the tradition is complex and sometimes the view is expressed that the benefits have simply been taken away from the Jewish people and passed on to the church (Judant 1969, 261–62). This claim is certainly not self-evident today, but also in the past it has not been as widespread as is sometimes argued (Judant: 270) or assumed.

This view does not reflect the teaching of Origen or of other patristic authors. Origen offers the earliest complete commentary on Romans, unfortunately preserved only in a less-than-perfect translation by Rufinus.[11] Here he discusses at length Rom. 11:25–29. First of all, he affirms that the blindness that has come over part of Israel is due to the envy of the "angels of the nations" (1998, 700; PG 14.1196A), and is therefore not primarily due to culpability on the part of the Jews. He further admits that God alone and his only-begotten son, and perhaps some of his friends, know who is meant by "all Israel" that is to be saved (1998,

---

■ Interplay of analytical and hermeneutical frames.

⊞ Can God repent? Yes. Election endures only for those who belong to the church.

⊞ Beneficiaries not seen as changed from Israel to the church, except in the views of a few.

702; *PG* 14.1197B). Commenting on 11:28–29, Origen does suggest that God's gifts are not dependent on the worthiness of the recipient. In the end, he distinguishes between those Jews who were opposed to Jesus ("enemies") and those who followed him ("beloved"). For the latter only, "God's gifts and calling are irrevocable" (1998, 705; *PG* 14.1199A-B). Yet, in his (apparently later) commentary on the Song of Songs he refers both expressions of 11:28 ("enemies" and "beloved") to one and the same people Israel (*GCS* Origen, 8.113.24–28; cf. Cocchini 1986, 85 n. 100; Tyconius 1989, 18, 20). In any event, Origen advocates at most a restriction but not a change of the beneficiaries.

Similarly, Cyril of Alexandria affirms that after the calling of the Gentiles, Israel too will be saved (*PG* 74.849D). No restriction or change is evident in a fragment attributed to Gennadius of Constantinople (d. 471), who states, "Even though now too they collide with you over the Gospel and you have been instead brought into it, yet because of the Fathers they too have been granted (God's) love. For it is right that somehow all God's gifts remain trustworthy and reliable" (Staab 1984, 401). Similarly, Oecumenius states rather unequivocally, "Even though they themselves because of their disbelief are not beloved, yet thanks to the fathers they are still being loved, and from this they also await salvation. The calling, he says, regards that issued concerning the (Jewish) people" (Staab: 430; cf. xxxvii). John Damascene, after quoting Rom. 11:28–29, comments briefly on these verses: "Since you have been called, those have become more contentious. But even so, God has not canceled their call, but waits for all those of the gentiles who are going to believe to come in, and then those too will come" (*PG* 95.536). Again there is no trace of supersessionism, even though in this view the effects of the gifts and the calling have been put on hold until the Gentiles have come in.

The first to speak of a transfer of *charismata* from the Jewish people to the Christian community appears to be Justin Martyr, but even though part of his statement is couched in the most general terms, he is referring more specifically to the gift of prophecy and makes no allusion to Rom. 9:4–5 or 11:29: "For with us are, even up to now, prophetic gifts. From this you too must understand that those (gifts) which formerly belonged to your people have been transferred to us" (*Dial.* 82.1). Thus, Justin claims for (Gentile) Christians the status of true Israelites and descendants of Abraham.[12] However, he never alludes to or cites 11:25–32 or the issues concerning Israel raised there.

An anonymous ninth-century commentary concludes its exposition of Rom. 11:28–29, "We have said that on account of Christ's death for our salvation the Jews are enemies of God, yet I do not (want to) fail to mention that some considered that their being enemies is to be referred to the apostle himself, as if the apostle were saying that the Jews were his enemies because he preached Christ to the Gentiles" (CChr.

CM 151.109–10). Here the Jews do not seem to come into view even as possible beneficiaries of God's gifts and calling; the only question is whose enemies they are, God's or Paul's.

Very different on this point is Abelard's commentary on Romans, written between 1135 and 1137 (Buytaert 1969, xxiv, 37). Although in his commentary on Romans Abelard followed some of the then current conventions, a study of even one verse shows how he grappled with the text and refrained from simply compiling previously known works. He is one of the few authors who does not even take into consideration Ambrosiaster's interpretation of Rom. 11:29. Instead, he addresses precisely the question of whether divine displeasure over any malice of the descendants can cause the revocation of God's promises to the fathers, and answers with an emphatic no: God never regrets to have given something or to have called someone to the faith, because his will is truly entirely unchangeable (CChr. CM 11.270.471–74). Having said this, he explains that where there is talk about God repenting, it is not repentance as normally used in the human sense.

Abelard tries to combine these insights with Paul's statement that "all Israel will be saved." He observes, on the one hand, that God's gifts precede and prepare for God's call: "In God's chosen ones, his gifts precede their call. God in the meantime prepares their will so that when he calls them to himself they give their assent and when he commands (them) they obey (him)" (CChr. CM 11.270.481–83). On the other hand, he recognizes that not all Jews but only a remnant will be among these elect.[13] On the composition of this remnant he offers several hypotheses in connection with Rom. 11:26. Not all individuals but many from all the different tribes of Israel will in the end be converted through the preaching of Enoch and Elijah.[14]

Calvin expresses a view that extends the name Israel to, as he puts it, the whole people of God, including Jews who will in the end accept the faith (*Iudaei ex defectione se ad fidei obedientiam recipient*) (Calvin 1540, 256). Lyonnet criticizes Calvin, especially in his interpretation of Rom. 11:25, for not leaving any room for a future conversion of Israel (Huby 1957, 629–30; Lyonnet 1962, 135–36). Yet, Calvin's statement does not reflect a supersessionist but rather an "integrationist" model (Klappert 1980, 17–18).

Are Benefits Lost or Put on Hold?

Frequently raised is the question of whether benefits originally bestowed by God may be lost, forever or temporarily. Biblical precedents for an affirmative answer are found especially in the stories of the flood and of Saul but also in other situations where God is said to have revoked a prior decision. Theodoret of Cyrrhus (d. 466) mentions the examples of Saul, who lost his calling, and of Solomon, who lost the peace assured to him by God. They lost these gifts because of their ungratefulness. A similar threat applies to Gentile Christians, who may be deprived of the grace they received. Thus, Theodoret assumes a conditional character of God's gifts, but suggests that Rom. 11:29 is meant as an exhortation for the Jews (*PG* 82.181).

Ephraem Syrus (d. 373) emphasizes that conversion and penance are ◫ needed in order to benefit from the gifts and calling issued to the patriarchs (1893, 38). Similarly, Pelagius emphasizes the conditional character of God's love: "if they believe, they are beloved." He interprets Rom. 11:29 as follows: "If they believe, (their) sins will not be able to be imputed to them because God does not repent of what he promised to Abraham" (1926, 92). Pelagius's argument follows a similar line as that in Origen's commentary on Romans. A specific dependence of Pelagius on Origen is argued by Smith on the basis of a systematic comparison (1919, 168–69). In a similar vein, John Chrysostom asserts that the virtue of the ancestors is of no use, if their descendants do not believe (*PG* 60.592). The same line of reasoning is followed by Chrysostom's one-time assistant and frequent opponent Severianus (Staab 1984, 223; Schelkle 1956, 403–4) and by many later patristic and medieval commentators.

Augustin Calmet (1672–1757), a Benedictine and one of the most influential Catholic exegetes of the eighteenth century, discusses at some length the fact and the conditions of the irrevocable character of God's gifts and calling. In contrast with the conditional gifts to Saul and Solomon, he considers the promises to Abraham and his descendants as unconditional and therefore irrevocable. He states, "Without fail He will put his word into practice, if not for all of Israel at least for its better part. He will convert them and call them back to himself; He will give them faith and the grace of his calling" (1730, 219). Thus, even though God's gifts are irrevocable, they become effective only after the conversion. Such a view is very widespread among medieval and more recent exegetes (Migne 1840, 277). Sickenberger compares the status of Israel to that of the prodigal son, not to his older brother. God's love for him will be fully realized when he converts (271). Huby succinctly states a common view: "Israel as a people remains called to enter the reign of God; one day it will enter" (1957, 404).

Augustine and Predestination

Frequently, predestination has been considered the principal focus of Ro- ◫ mans in general and of 8:28–11:36 in particular. Such an interpretation owes its origin ultimately to Augustine. As is well known, his *Confessions* and other works are deeply influenced by his understanding of

---

◫ Benefits and irrevocableness as conditional upon conversion.

◫ Predestination of individuals or of Israel as a people through the centuries.

Romans. He gave up on his projected commentary on Romans, begun about 394, in order to devote himself to "easier" tasks (*Retract.* 1.24 = CSEL 36.114). He returned to the exegesis of 7:7–25 and 9:9–29 in his response to questions by Simplicianus, written in 397. This work was decisive for the development of his doctrine of grace, as he himself admitted in one of his last writings.[15] Augustine starts referring to 11:29 in a letter to Paulinus, written between 414 and 416, early in the Pelagian controversy. There he defends his idea of predestination: In his opinion God's gifts and calling are irrevocable for "those who are among the predestined" (*qui pertinent ad numerum praedestinatorum*) (*Epistula* 149.2.21 = CSEL 44.367). Later, in several anti-Pelagian writings, he has recourse to 11:29 in order to prove a double calling, of those who are elect and of those who are not. He does not speak of "double predestination," but affirms that God's grace, gratuitously given, precedes any human response. He explains 11:29 by saying that gifts and calling are "without change, permanently set" (*sine mutatione stabiliter fixa sunt*) (*Praed.* 16.33 = PL 44.985).[16] Positive predestination means an assurance of God's faithfulness until the end, even though no one can be sure before death whether he or she is to be numbered among the predestined. If someone does not persevere, this means that he or she has not received such a call from God. In any event, in opposition to Pelagian teachings, he categorically denies the importance of personal merit (*Persev.* 16.41 = PL 45.1018).

In the end, Augustine confesses that divine choice remains a mystery, but that it is not up to human beings to impugn God's choice or justice: "From all this it is shown with sufficient clarity that the grace of God, which both begins a person's faith and enables it to persevere unto the end, is not given according to our merits, but is given according to his own most secret and at the same time most righteous, wise and beneficent will; since those whom He predestined He also called, with that calling of which it is said, 'The gifts and calling of God are without repentance' " (*Persev.* 13.33 = PL 45.1012).

Concerning predestination, Augustine asserts that he is preaching simply "what every Christian confesses" and what has been taught by Cyprian before him (*Persev.* 13.36 = PL 45.1015). But certainly Cyprian had no developed concept of predestination, nor was it universally held by other Christians. Thus, the idea of predestination is invariably and justifiably linked to the name of Augustine. His work has been so influential that until this century Romans 9–11 could be called simply a treatise on predestination (Jülicher 1908, 279; Maier 1929, 5; Caird 1956–1957).

A commentary earlier attributed to the Venerable Bede (673–735), but actually written by Florus of Lyons (790–860) (Spicq 1944, 45) bears the revealing title *Expositio in Epistolas Beati Pauli ex operibus Sancti Augustini collecta.* Regarding Rom. 11:28–29, reference simply is made to Augustine's *De praedestinatione sanctorum.* This type of explicit citation of sources seems to have been inaugurated by the Venerable Bede (Spicq 1944, 29). Also the commentary by Haymo of Auxerre in his discussion of 11:29 sees vocation, and thus election, as a fruit of predestination (*PL* 117.466; cf. *PL* 134.246).

Several centuries later, Luther too uses predestinarian language in his gloss explaining our verse: "he does not regret, nor does he change, because he has predestined to give and to call" (*non penitet eum nec mutat, quod predestinavit dare et vocare*) (Flicker 1908, 107). After these and other predestinarian interpretations of Romans 9–11 in general and 11:29 in particular, it comes as a surprise that Calvin, the proponent par excellence of double predestination, does not use predestination language at all in his commentary on this verse. Also, he does not emphasize the individual's fate but God's faithfulness to the election of his people: "He is not, we must remember, dealing now with the private election of any individual, but the common adoption of a whole nation, which to outward appearances might have seemed to have fallen for a time, but which has not been cut off by the roots" (1540, 259; trans. MacKenzie [Calvin 1980, 257]). Calvin reaffirms that God is faithful to his original call, and adds that, according to Paul, there is no contrast between gospel and election, for God calls those whom he has chosen.

Beyond Calvinist circles, predestination remained (as mentioned above) one of the principal keys to reading Romans 9–11 in general and 11:29 in particular. Calmet begins his commentary on Romans with a *Dissertation sur la prédestination, et la réprobation des hommes* (1730, xi–xlvii), in which he asserts, "It is a dogma of Christian religion that from all eternity people are irrevocably either predestined for glory or reproved and destined to eternal unhappiness. Furthermore, it is a point on which all Catholic theologians are in agreement that the predestination to grace and the calling to faith are absolutely free gifts of God" (1730, xi). He concludes his detailed exposition on 11:29 with a comment on double predestination. Those who are predestined to glory may temporarily fall into sin, but cannot suffer eternal condemnation. Those others who have received *only* the grace of vocation or faith may live for a long time in God's love, but they will not have the gift of perseverance and will not go to heaven (Calmet 1730, 220). Perhaps frequent contact with Jansenist circles in Paris led him to such a position.[17]

Aquinas's commentary on Rom. 11:29 may be counted to this day among the most extensive treatments. In accordance with his usual technique, he carefully contextualizes the verse, trying to determine the structure of Paul's argument. This organic versus atomistic construction of Aquinas's commentaries is one of their most original elements in contrast with their predecessors (Spicq 1944, 215). Aquinas starts from this objection: though once beloved, the Jews have no possibility of future salvation because of their enmity to the gospel (1953, 924). He considers

11:29 the most appropriate response to it, citing in support 1 Sam. 15:29 and Ps. 109:4 LXX (110:4 MT) in order to emphasize God's unfailing fidelity. Aquinas cites further possible objections (925), based on accounts where God is said to be sorry for what he has done or promised (Gen. 6:6; Jer. 18:9–10). He answers this objection by stating that these are anthropopathic expressions that only try to describe the consequences of God's action, not God's inner emotions, just as God's wrath is not an inner sentiment but an outward expression so understood by humans. Aquinas deals with one further objection, the possible loss of the gifts and calling, citing Matt. 25:28 and 22:14. Against this he asserts that the gift here stands for a promise, given in accordance with God's foreknowledge or predestination. Similarly, the call here is equivalent with divine election. Thus, even though Aquinas is indebted to Augustine, he emphasizes much more than does Augustine the permanence of every God-given gift and calling. Aquinas does allow for the possibility that human beings reject God's grace, but there is nothing that could cause God to change his decision (1953, 926).

After this surprisingly thorough exposition, Aquinas turns his attention to the alternative interpretation based on Ambrosiaster's commentary and gives it about equal space. Since Aquinas did not know Greek, he apparently took Ambrosiaster's interpretation as a valid alternative literal reading of the text. He introduced this section by stating, "What is said here may also be understood differently.[18] We may say that God's gifts which are given in baptism and the calling, by which the baptized is being called to grace, exist without repentance on the part of the baptized" (1953, 927). He immediately adds that this is so that no one should despair of the future salvation of the Jews, even though they do not seem to repent of their sin. Aquinas is perhaps the only medieval commentator who links also this (mis)interpretation to the eventual salvation of the Jews.

Salvation History

C A concern with postbiblical Israel's place in salvation history is found in few commentators on Rom. 11:29. Isaac La Peyrère (1596–1676) **H** seems to be a lonely and controversial voice in the Baroque period. He belonged to a well-to-do Calvinist family from Bordeaux, possibly of Marrano origin (Popkin 1987, 22–25). In his *Du rappel des Juifs,* published anonymously in 1643, he comments on Romans 11, including v. 29, suggesting that the Jews will be called again by God, after being temporarily rejected. Their renewed call will lead to acceptance of Christ

---

C Postbiblical Israel.

H Postbiblical Israel's place in salvation history.

as well as to a return to the Holy Land, under the guidance of a king of France.

Godet proceeds much more cautiously. After having stated that in Romans 11 Paul's intention is not to address the question of a *temporal* reestablishment of the Jewish nation in Palestine, he asks himself, "Will a national restoration of a political nature go along with this general conversion of the people?[19] Will it precede it or follow it?" He avers that such are not legitimate questions for exegesis to try to answer, but it is noteworthy that he dared raise them in a serious exegetical commentary, years before the rise of political Zionism (1890, 411–12).

Theodicy

Sometimes, a principal element in the interpretation of Romans 9–11 in ▣ general and 11:29 in particular is a defense of God's way of acting. Theodore of Mopsuestia categorically asserts that God did not reject the Jews because he repented of the election of the fathers, but they themselves, in the perversity of their minds, became the cause of their separation from God (Staab 1984, 159). Schelkle calls this a rather rationalistic solution of the problem, intended to defend God's immutability (1956, 403).

An element of theodicy is to be found also in Hatto of Vercelli, when at Rom. 11:29 he comments on Saul's rejection (following in some way Theodore of Mopsuestia). He explains that it is not a matter of God's mutability, but that God's decision changes depending on human merits (*PL* 134.246B; cf. *RBMA* §3126, §1959).

Hervaeus Burgidolensis (1080–1150) explains that the irrevocable character of God's gifts applies to his unconditional promises (*promissa Dei gratuito facta*). Similarly, God's calling of those whom he chose before the world's creation remains forever valid, and they will bear lasting fruit (*PL* 181.759A-B).

Cajetan too defends divine immutability by distinguishing between "gifts and calling of God...that proceed from his election" — that is, gifts which God indeed never regrets (*quorum deum nunquam poenitet*) — and those gifts that do not proceed from election. The latter are merely of a temporary or material nature and may be withdrawn by God. He would count God's regret for having created humankind (Gen. 6:6) in this second category (1540, 78b). Even though Cajetan here develops a line of thought that may be traced back to Augustine, he states the double meaning of gifts and calling more radically than his predecessors.

Cornelius a Lapide cites Cajetan (along with Aquinas) for the idea of the two types of calling. He specifies that the proposition of Rom. 11:29 is true of an efficacious and absolute calling, which reaches its desired effect, as in the case of people who are predestined. As an example

---

▣ Theodicy.

of conditional and ineffective gifts, he cites the fertility of the land of Canaan: "Thus God called the Hebrews and promised them the fertility of the land of Canaan, under the condition: if you implement my law." Because the Jews (here *Judaei* and no longer *Hebraei*) did not fulfill this condition, God did not carry out his promise. But for his part, he had fulfilled his promise, because he was ready to give, and in fact would have given, this fertility, if they had abided by his condition, that is, his law (1617, 161). Thus, Cornelius a Lapide vindicates God's reliability and his justice. A similar line of reasoning is followed by Calmet a century later. He too, after having emphasized God's fidelity, discusses the conditional and unconditional nature of God's gifts. Promises to Saul, to Solomon, and regarding the fertility of the land were conditional and therefore subject to change, whereas those concerning the coming of the Messiah and God's kingship over all "true" Israelites are absolute and never revoked ("sont des promesses absolues, que le Seigneur n'a jamais révoqué" [1730, 220]).

Kühl entitles his comments on Romans 9–11 "Die paulinische Theodizee," a title taken from an earlier monograph by Beyschlag (1913, 310). Kühl concludes this section with a chapter on "Basic Principles of Pauline Theodicy" (403–11). Against this interpretation, Michel argues that Paul's statements in chs. 9–11 may not be understood as timeless truths or as a philosophical theodicy; instead, Paul responds, in accordance with the gospel, to the problem of Israel in salvation history (1978, 364). Kuss warns of an anachronistic interpretation of Paul: it would be imprecise to say that in chs. 9–11 Paul wanted to explain his "doctrine of predestination," his "theodicy," or his "theology of history." On the other hand, chs. 9–11 undoubtedly do offer important contributions concerning these questions, which, however, owe their formulation to later situations (1978, 665).

God's Fidelity

H   As already noted, God's fidelity and trustworthiness are often seen as a principal theme of Romans. An emphasis on this aspect of God's nature can be found in some earlier commentaries, at times couched in predestinarian language. Among the medieval authors who pay closest attention to the question of God's abiding fidelity are Abelard and Aquinas. In a similar vein, Erasmus states, "God does not, in our human way, promise a gift or receive into adoption only to repent later and change his mind. He is absolutely immutable, for just as he never errs, neither does he ever need to repent." Erasmus adds, however, the proviso, "He will remember his promise as soon as they cease to reject it" (1984, 68).

H   God's fidelity and human freedom coexist.

Not much later, God's fidelity may be called the principal theme in Brenz's exposition of Romans 11:29. His deliberate attention to our verse is perhaps in direct contrast to Melanchthon's neglect of it. Even though Brenz emphasizes several times the necessity of faith, the main thrust of his argument is God's faithfulness to his promises, that is, his gifts and calling (1538, 364.25–30). Brenz expressed this emphasis on God's faithfulness in a parable of a castle into which a king admits us. Even if we of our own will should leave it and surrender to the enemy, the king would not destroy the castle but would continue to admit all those who want to take refuge in it. God has his castle always open because "he does not repent of his gifts and calling" (366.4–13). While Brenz applies 11:29 at first to Jews, he also finds it appropriate for Christians who may lose their baptismal innocence. The temptation is to despair of salvation, even though one does penance. Brenz here uses *poenitentia* deliberately both of humans, who need it, and of God, who never repents (365.33–35). Here seems to be the earliest explicit reference in interpretations of 11:29 to the fact that God's covenants (*pacta*) are irrevocable.

God's fidelity is stressed also by Cornelius a Lapide: "Even though the Jews are still incredulous, God does not revoke what he unconditionally gave or promised." A Lapide counts among these gifts the promises made to the patriarchs and their descendants. He believes that gifts and calling will become effective at the end of the world (1617, 161).

God's fidelity to the Jewish people to the end of the world is emphasized by several little-known nineteenth-century authors (e.g., Reithmayr 1845, 621; Maunoury 1878, 278). Kühl follows a similar line of thought: Israel in its entirety is destined by God for salvation, and all Israel (*Gesamtisrael*) will reach this goal as surely as God's gracious promises are irrevocable (1913, 404).

God's fidelity, however, does not constrain or contradict human freedom. God's plan in history will definitely be accomplished, even though individuals are free to refuse his call (Godet 1890, 411). Lyonnet sees God's fidelity expressed in a special way in Rom. 11:29, because here the object is not promises that might be conditional but gifts that are unconditional (1962, 139).

Universal Applicability of Romans 11:29

As already noted, Rom. 11:29 is sometimes seen as a universally valid **H** theological axiom. Dunn acknowledges that 11:29 may be applied beyond its specific meaning: "Since the statement is made as a general principle, the gentile (and subsequent) readers would be justified in ap- **C** plying it more broadly to their own calling and foundational gifts of

---

H Rom. 11:29 as a universal theological axiom.

C Rom. 11:29 applied to Gentiles or to the Jewish people.

grace; the continuity of election always includes but is not limited to Israel, since it is a continuity of grace" (1988, 686). A general application
of 11:29 was offered also in an address by Pope Paul VI (1974, 881).
Although the general applicability of 11:29 remains, in recent times the
verse has been used primarily with reference to the Jewish people and its
continuing covenant relationship with God.

Romans 11:29 in the Context of Christian-Jewish Relations

As I have amply documented, Rom. 11:29 has been interpreted by exegetes and theologians to refer to God's faithfulness and to the reliability
of his gifts and promises. Yet, the question of how this might apply to
contemporary Jews and Judaism has almost never been asked. Generally,
it was thought that the gifts and calling had either passed entirely to the
Christian church, or that these benefits had been put on hold for the Jews
until in the end they, or at least a more-or-less large and representative
number of them, would be converted to Christ.

As already noted, however, some lonely voices even in past centuries
referred to Rom. 11:29 in the context of relations with contemporary
Jews. Léon Bloy (1846–1917) took up the issue most forcefully, at first
in his 1892 essay *Le Salut par les Juifs*. His essay was judged, hyperbol-
ically, to be a paraphrase of Romans 11, and Bloy himself considered it
the most energetic Christian testimony in favor of the Jewish people since
Romans 11 (1905, 7). Bloy was used to expressing himself in extremes,
which gained him some followers and many enemies. Raïssa and Jacques
Maritain were profoundly influenced by Bloy, through whom they both
converted to Catholicism in 1906. Jacques, certainly because of the Jewish origin of his wife, Raïssa, but perhaps also through the earlier contact
with Bloy, took up the fight against anti-Semitism in various publications
as early as 1926 in a response to Jean Cocteau (1965, 13). He cites Romans 11, especially 11:28, as a prohibition against anti-Semitism. Also
in a published address of February 1938 he showed that anti-Semitism
is incompatible with Christian teachings, quoting Romans 11, includ-
C   ing 11:29, in support (81). Similarly, he opened a 1937 essay, originally
entitled "L'impossible antisémitisme" and later reedited as "Le mystère
d'Israël," by suggesting that in order to understand anti-Semitism, one
has to evoke the entire question of the Jewish Diaspora. And in this he
sees "un mystère d'ordre sacré" (24), which has been treated in its principal elements in Romans 9–11, of which he proceeds to quote ample
portions, including 11:29.

C Rom. 11:29 against Nazi anti-Semitism; for contemporary Israel's unique mission?

A strong influence of Bloy and of the Maritains may be detected in the work of the Swiss theologian and cardinal Charles Journet (1891–1975). As early as 1935, and especially in his book *Destinées d'Israël*, he wrestled with an interpretation of Romans 9–11 in light of his theological outlook as well as in response to Nazi anti-Semitism.[20] Journet quotes 11:29 in a broader discussion of ch. 11 (1945, 326), yet he insists that the old covenant finally has to die for the new to flourish (1945, 343). In subsequent publications he seems to have modified this view (1956, 83). In fact, he struggled to explain theologically the present reality of the Jewish people, and he affirmed that Israel's religious mission remains unique and distinguished it irrevocably from all the other peoples (1969, 454; cf. Kamykowski 1994, 206).

The Contribution of Karl Barth (1886–1968)

While the work of the previously mentioned authors remains important, **C** Karl Barth was undoubtedly the most influential theologian to connect Romans 9–11 organically not only to Israel's past and eschatological future but also to its present. In his commentary on Romans (1922), we find him almost at the antipodes of such a step. For Barth at that time, Paul was addressing the church. Barth sees in Romans 9–11 the affliction, guilt, and hope of the church, and expresses this in his chapter headings. Thus, he interprets 11:29 ecclesiologically: the divine mission **H** of the churches remains irrevocable, in spite of all the churches' failings (1922, 405). It must be noted that Barth does not here simply attribute to the church the gifts once given to Israel, but he interprets chs. 9–11 as a critique of the church (*kirchenkritisch*) and not of Israel (*israelkritisch*). Thus, at a deeper level, there is at least implicitly a solidarity between the church and Israel, just as Barth interprets 9:1–5 as a declaration of solidarity with that same church that causes unspeakable pain to any sincere proclaimer of the gospel (1922, 16–19). A similar identification, which here has supersessionist overtones, is still found in his *Church Dogmatics* where he simply speaks of the people of God, called Israel in the Old Testament and Church in the New Testament (1942, 89). In the same volume, however, he develops his doctrine of Israel in a detailed theological commentary on chs. 9–11. This chapter (§34) covers over one hundred tightly printed pages and has been the subject of several monographs (Marquardt 1967; Klappert 1980; Sonderegger 1992). It cannot be our purpose here to deal with it in its entirety, though it is especially hazardous to take one small part of Barth's dogmatics out of its context.

C Rom. 11:29 and Romans 9–11 as a critique of the contemporary church; as indicating solidarity between the church and Israel; or as supersessionist.

H Ecclesiology.

C   It is possible to discover at least part of Barth's process of rethinking
since the second edition of his commentary on Romans. He was invited
to preach on Rom. 15:5–13 at the University of Bonn on 10 December
H   1933. It is here, at the end of the first fateful year of Nazi rule, that Barth
for the first time points out the theological significance of present-day
Jews and Judaism and their special relationship to Jesus: "*This* people's
blood was in his veins the blood of the Son of God" (1933, 14). It is the
ontological distinction between Jews and Gentiles that enables Barth,
in 1933, to discover a strictly christologically founded solidarity with
the Jews as such (Takeda 1981, 118). This form of argumentation finds
its fullest expression in volume 2.2 of his *Church Dogmatics* of 1942.
Barth was breaking new ground in offering a strictly theological view
also of postbiblical Judaism (Marquardt 1967, 15). Baumbach concurs
and emphasizes the influence Barth's discovery has had on documents
concerning Christian-Jewish relations (Baumbach 1993, 552–53).

Barth's views of Judaism were not without problems or without a
heavy debt to earlier teachings in which Judaism served only as a foil
for Christianity. Though he considers Israel and the church as one community in two expressions, Israel is for him a sign of God's judgment,
whereas the church is a sign of God's mercy (1942, 215). Barth's complex attitude toward Judaism has been scrutinized and at times severely
criticized by his own students and their students (Marquardt 1967; Klappert 1980; Takeda 1981) as well as by others. A fresh general evaluation
is not our task here. Instead, we concentrate on Barth's ample treatment of Rom. 11:29 in his chapter on the election of the people of God.
Barth suggests that 11:29 is a key to understanding chs. 9–10 in that
11:29 underscores the unshakable foundation of God's love for and election of Israel. He emphasizes that this axiom is neither a philosophical
statement about divine *immutabilitas* nor an expression of a stubborn
affirmation of Jewish prerogatives. Instead, he sees it as an affirmation
of Christian hope in the unshakable character of God's mercy demonstrated in Jesus' resurrection (1942, 332–33). If God is faithful, then
this faithfulness has to extend to Israel's past, present, and future. Barth
emphasizes that 11:28b ("beloved for the sake of the fathers") finds its
strongest confirmation and motivation in 11:29, and that this affirmation
refers to each and every member of the Jewish people at all times (1942,
333). For him, 11:30–32 offers a development (*Entfaltung*) of 11:29,
and here again the present reality of God's mercy that extends to Jews
and Gentile Christians is unmistakably emphasized. An attentive read-

---

C Rom. 11:29 indicating that God's faithfulness extends to Israel's present (1933–1942)
and future.

H Israel and the church as one community in Christ (Israel as sign of God's judgment and
the church as sign of God's mercy); hope in the unshakable character of God's mercy.

ing of these verses makes it impossible to remove "the Jewish question" from the present into an eschatological future (1942, 335). This theological argumentation for the present relevance of the Jewish people may be considered one of the unique achievements of Karl Barth. It has had a profound influence also on Catholic theology (Rosato 1986, 661–67).

The rethinking of Christian-Jewish relations that occurred at Vatican II **C** may owe much to Barth's innovative interpretation of Romans 9–11. In fact, John M. Oesterreicher, who authored the first draft of the document that later became Vatican II's declaration *Nostra Aetate*, adopted a Barthian expression, "arch of the one covenant" ("Bogen des einen Bundes" [Barth 1942, 220]), for the title of his discussion of covenant and people of God and developed the idea further in the direction suggested by Barth. Several other passages of the *Church Dogmatics* are cited by Oesterreicher (1974, 27, 29, 39). He published this article after the Vatican Council, but it is quite likely that he and other members of the committee that drafted the document on the church's relations with non-Christian religions were familiar with Barth's *Church Dogmatics* during their conciliar work.

Allusions and Citations in Church Documents

Romans 11:29 was never cited in official Catholic pronouncements be- **C** fore Vatican II (DS, Scripture index). In two statements of the Confessing Church in Germany, dated 12 December 1938 and 17 October 1943, Romans 9–11 is alluded to, but only in the context of references to baptized Jews (Heydenreich 1962, 235, 247). The earliest direct citation of 11:29 seems to have occurred in a 1948 declaration by the World Council of Churches: "For many the continued existence of a Jewish people which does not acknowledge Christ is a divine mystery which finds its only sufficient explanation in the purpose of God's unchanging faithfulness and mercy (Rom 11:25–29)" (Croner 1977, 70). This **H** statement is made in a context that calls for an intensified but sensitive Christian mission among Jews and declares anti-Semitism a "sin against God and man." It has remained the only primarily theological statement on Christian-Jewish relations made by the World Council of Churches, although there have been later condemnations of anti-Semitism that also touch on theological issues. Rendtorff comments that so far there has been no ecumenical statement comparable to *Nostra Aetate* (Rendtorff and Henrix 1988, 323).

On a national level, on 21 May 1949 the Dutch Reformed Church issued a position paper concerning its confessional foundations and per-

---

C Christian-Jewish relations in Vatican II.

C Rom. 11:29 in church documents since 1938.

H Anti-Semitism as sin and Christian mission among Jews.

spectives. The document opens its reflections on Israel's present and future with a reference to Rom. 11:29. On the one hand, it is affirmed that the people Israel is not rejected or abandoned by God; on the other hand, the Jewish people is seen, in a traditional formulation used also by Karl Barth, as a sign and a mirror of God's judgment (Rendtorff and Henrix 1988, 445).

H   The 1950 synod of the Evangelische Kirche in Deutschland in Berlin-Weißensee issued a brief statement on "the Jewish question" that shows a similar openness to the continued validity of God's election. Taking Rom. 11:32 as its motto, it affirms that God's promise concerning the chosen people Israel remains in force even after the crucifixion of Jesus Christ (Rendtorff and Henrix 1988, 549). Even though 11:29 is not cited, it clearly is at the root of such an affirmation (Baumbach 1993, 536). This declaration has been considered pathfinding in that it overcomes the centuries-old traditional church teaching of substitution, or supersessionism (536). It should be noted, however, that the Dutch document of the previous year had pointed in the same direction and that the 1948 declaration of the World Council of Churches had at least opened a window toward such an understanding. While there have been many declarations by Protestant as well as Catholic church authorities on issues connected with Christian-Jewish relations, theological reflection on the subject did not resurface until Vatican II (Rendtorff and Henrix 1988, 231–42, 527–54).

        At the Second Vatican Council, the first reference to Rom. 11:29 is found in the dogmatic constitution *Lumen Gentium (LG)* in the context of the church's relations with non-Christians. Romans 9:4–5 and 11:28b-29 are quoted in support of the thesis that the Jewish people, due
H   to its original election and the irrevocableness of God's gifts and call, is in a special way linked to the church: "Finally, those who have not yet received the gospel are in various ways related to the People of God. There is, first, that people to which the covenants and promises were given" (*LG* 16). Here, the term "people of God" is applied to the church (but not limited to its institutional expressions) and not to the Jewish people. Similar language is used in *Nostra Aetate (NA)*, Vatican II's declaration on the relation of the church to non-Christian religions. There, however, these ideas are developed further. Despite the fact that a majority of Jews did not accept the gospel and many opposed its spreading (Rom. 11:28a is cited), they "remain beloved by God, whose gifts and call are without regret" (*NA* 4). This affirmation is followed by the expression of the firm hope for the day known only to God "in which all people will call

---

H God's promise to Israel remains in force.

H Jews are specially linked to the church and remain beloved by God.

on the Lord with one voice and will 'serve him shoulder to shoulder' (Zeph. 3:9)."

Among various criticisms regarding the inadequacy of *Nostra Aetate,* it may be noted that reference to present-day Jewry is almost completely lacking, except in a recommendation to foster mutual knowledge and understanding and in a generic warning against anti-Semitism. While such criticisms are understandable, they do not sufficiently take into account the context of this conciliar statement. One may further note that the citation of Rom. 11:28b-29 forms a link between past, present, and eschatological future, expressed in theological and not christological terms through the quote from Zephaniah.

As is evident now, over thirty years later, the importance of *Nostra* **C** *Aetate* consists not only in what it affirms but, above all, in the consequences it has had. While it has not been fully assimilated into the life of the church everywhere, it has had a considerable impact expressed in many later documents, and not only those emanating from Catholic sources. Indeed, *Nostra Aetate* has been instrumental in bringing about a radical paradigm shift in Christian-Jewish relations.

After the Second Vatican Council, the Holy See's Secretariat (now, Pontifical Council) for Promoting Christian Unity, with its Office for Catholic-Jewish Relations, as well as many bishops, synods, and episcopal conferences in the United States, Europe, and Latin America issued statements regarding Catholic-Jewish relations. They offer various suggestions on how to apply the teachings of *Nostra Aetate* in the various local situations. Many of these documents allude to or cite Rom. 11:29.[21]

An important and controversial document was issued on 16 April **H** 1973 by the French Bishops' Committee for Relations with Judaism (Croner 1977, 60–65). It was meant to offer pastoral orientations concerning Christian attitudes toward Judaism, taking its cue from the basic insights of *Nostra Aetate.* It rightly considered the Vatican II Council declaration a beginning rather than a point of arrival. As scriptural basis for its section on the permanent vocation of the Jewish people, it referred to God's "eternal covenant" with Abraham (Gen. 17:7) and to Rom. 11:29. In one sense, this is a small step from *Nostra Aetate*'s citation of 11:28–29. Yet here, the connection between the irrevocable character of God's call and present-day Jews, implicit in *NA* 4, is made explicit. In a comment by the chief rabbinate of France it is noted that here for the first time in an official Catholic document the permanent vocation of the Jewish people is affirmed (*DC* 1631 [6 May 1973]: 422). This conclusion is not entirely correct, since already the U.S. National Conference of Catholic Bishops had spoken of, perhaps somewhat awkwardly, "an

---

C Changed relations between Christians and Jews.

H Permanent vocation of the Jewish people.

acknowledgment by Catholic scholars of the living and complex reality of Judaism after Christ and the permanent election of Israel, alluded to by St. Paul (Rom [11]:29), and incorporation of the results into Catholic teaching" (Croner 1977, 20). Reactions to the French document were animated. Some will be discussed below.

H   A further impulse for the interpretation of Rom. 11:29 came from Pope John Paul II in an address on 17 November 1980 to Jewish leaders in Mainz, Germany. In a frequently quoted statement, he remarked, "The first dimension of this dialogue, that is, the meeting between the people of God of the Old Covenant, never revoked by God (cf. Rom 11:29), and that of the New Covenant, is at the same time a dialogue within our Church, that is to say, between the first and the second part of her Bible" (John Paul II 1987, 35; German original: Rendtorff and Henrix 1988, 75). The pope's affirmation that the old covenant has never been revoked is only partly based on Rom. 11:29, because there, Paul does not directly address the question of covenant. Most exegetes, however, connect the gifts of 11:29 with the privileges listed in 9:4–5, among which Paul includes "the covenants" (several ancient mss use the singular). The pope's use of the phrase "the people of the Old Covenant, never revoked by God" has caused and continues to generate ample discussion (Lohfink 1989, 91–92; Vanhoye 1994; Main 1996).

In and of itself, the pope's phrase may be considered merely a logical continuation of the line of interpretation initiated by Karl Barth, given brief expression in *NA* 4, and developed in documents of the American, French, and German episcopates.[22] Yet, it presents also a radical novelty, because it clearly overcomes the still widespread doctrine of supersessionism, which considers the role of Israel entirely superseded by that of the church.

H   The remark by Pope John Paul II has frequently been cited, for example, in a document issued on 24 June 1985 by the Holy See's Commission for Religious Relations with the Jews (International Catholic-Jewish Liaison Committee 1988, 307). The use of Rom. 11:29 as a key text for a better understanding of Christian-Jewish relations is thus reaffirmed. This teaching finds expression also in the recent *Catechism of the Catholic Church*, which states that the privileges mentioned in 9:4–5 belong (present tense) to the Jewish people, because of the affirmation in 11:29 (§839). Similarly, the Pontifical Biblical Commission's document "The Interpretation of the Bible in the Church" (1993, 117) quotes 11:29 in its discussion of the limits of the actualization of biblical texts: "The tragic events of the past must...impel all to keep unceasingly in mind

H The old covenant never revoked; the role of Israel not superseded by the church.

H Authoritative statement from the pope.

that, according to the NT, the Jews remain 'beloved' of God, 'since the gifts and calling of God are irrevocable' (Rom 11:28–29)."

Questions on the Applicability of Romans 11:29

The use of Romans 11 in general and 11:29 in particular for the sake of a new biblically and theologically grounded view of the relationship between Christians and Jews did not remain uncontested. Several voices were raised especially in response to Vatican II's declaration *Nostra Aetate* and its various drafts (Judant 1969; Carli 1965, 1966; Vaccari 1964). Bishop Carli, the most vociferous opponent of *Nostra Aetate* among the Second Vatican Council Fathers, commented on a draft of the document that God's gifts are "without regret," but that for those who refuse them ⊞ or do not utilize them, they become cause for condemnation (1965, 201). He did not adduce any exegetical or theological justification for this view.

In response to the French bishops' 1973 statement, forty Jesuits working in Lebanon, while taking exception especially to the bishops' treatment of the situation in the Middle East, also contested the use of Rom. 11:29. They suggested that it must be read in light of the discussion of the covenants in the Epistle to the Hebrews (8:7, 13; 13:20), where the first covenant is described as "antiquated and near its end" (*DC* 1635 [1 July 1973]: 619). Similarly, the Catholic bishops of Egypt, ⒶA in a letter to the French bishops, offer a detailed criticism of the use of Rom. 11:29. They affirm that the irrevocableness of the gifts does not ⊞ imply their permanence but refers to the place they occupy in the plan of salvation; God's irrevocable gifts to the Jewish people were in view of the blessing of all nations in the descendants of Abraham (*DC* 1638 [9–23 September 1973]: 786–87). Cardinal Jean Daniélou took a similar position, stating, "It is a mistake to speak still today of a special election of the Jewish people.... To speak of a New Covenant means that the Old is obsolete" (*DC* 1635 [1 July 1973]: 621). Similarly A. Feuillet, alluding to Heb 8:13 stated that in Christian perspective the old covenant is obsolete and replaced by the new covenant.[23] Alongside these critical voices, others supported the bishops' use of Rom. 11:29. Congar saw in ⊞ the affirmation of the continuing theological significance of Judaism one of the principal contributions of the document. With reference to Rom. 11:29, he remarked that the election of Israel has introduced into history a structure whose permanence Paul recognizes. It applies also to the time of the church, as long as the fullness of time is not reached.[24]

⊞ Condemnation of the Jews.

Ⓐ Irrevocableness of the gifts meaning not their permanence but their place in the plan of salvation.

⊞ Theological significance of Judaism continuing or not.

⊞ Continuing theological significance of Judaism or not.

H   As previously stated, Pope John Paul II's reference to the "people of God of the Old Covenant, never revoked by God" has caused copious reactions. In an article on the universality of salvation in Christ and the validity of the old covenant, Vanhoye admits that the covenant with Abraham has never been revoked, but states, "The Sinai covenant has thus been revoked by God, but in the moment of rupture God has promised to replace it with a new and different covenant."[25] He further argues that, in accordance with Gal. 3:15–18, 29, *after Christ* the only way to enter into God's covenant with Abraham is by adhering to Christ. He summarizes Paul's thought to the effect that "the only way to have a covenant relation with God consists in accepting the justification God gives through faith in Christ, and not through the Sinaitic Law" (1994, 823). Nevertheless, he leaves open a slight possibility that non-Christian Jews can still be in a covenant relationship with God (826 n. 14).

Vanhoye makes several explicit references to the pope's remark, but tends to interpret it in a sense that would restrict the never-revoked covenant to Christians. He asks if "the people of God of the Old Covenant, never revoked by God" and "the present-day people of the Covenant concluded with Moses," cited in the same speech, are to be considered identical entities (1994, 816 n. 2). Further on, he answers this question for himself by declaring that the pope's statement, if read in the perspective of Gal. 3:15–18, 29, concerns a dialogue within the church, between its Judeo-Christian and Gentile Christian components. Vanhoye affirms that the pope's phrase suggests such an interpretation, but admits that another idea seems to be implied as well (821 n. 8).

Vanhoye's article has caused such reaction that the editors decided to print two responses (Main 1996; Martin 1996), plus a rectification by the author. Main points out that Vanhoye does not provide any credible proof for the revocation of the Sinai covenant (1996, 34, 38–40, 50). To the contrary, she asserts that the new covenant makes sense only insofar **C** as the Sinai covenant remains valid (56). Without entering into the question of Vanhoye's biblical exegesis (which does not touch Rom. 11:29), his interpretation of the pope's statement as referring primarily or exclusively to intraecclesial relations seems flawed. First of all, the pope's express concern in this address is interreligious dialogue (Rendtorff and Henrix 1988, 75–76; John Paul II 1987, 35). When he says that the first dimension of this dialogue is at the same time a dialogue within our church, then it is clear that the primary reference is *not* to the intraecclesial dimension, although this is important and deserves attention. When the pope further refers to "the present-day people of the Covenant concluded with Moses," it does not seem possible to infer that he refers to the

---

H Universality of salvation in Christ or not.
C Intraecclesial or interreligious relations.

people of a Sinai covenant that has been canceled. Vanhoye also does not seem to pay sufficient attention to the context. The pope was speaking to Jewish leaders. Is it conceivable that he came to tell them that God's irrevocable covenant is no longer theirs? Apparently, no one understood him to mean that, and the further use of this phrase seems to preclude such an understanding. Similarly, already the Good Friday prayer for the Jews according to the *Missale Romanum* of 1970 refers to the Jews' fidelity to his covenant (*in sui foederis fidelitate proficere*) (Rendtorff and Henrix 1988, 57). This formulation presupposes a continuing covenant relationship.

Developments Evidenced in Church Documents

In Catholic documents concerning relations with Jews, beginning with **H** *Lumen Gentium* and *Nostra Aetate,* Rom. 11:29 is one of the most frequently cited passages. It is taken as the main basis for the affirmation of God's fidelity that extends not only to individuals but in mysterious ways also to the Jewish people as such. Protestant documents since World War II occasionally do refer to Rom. 11:29 (Goldschmidt and Kraus 1962; Croner 1977, 70; Rendtorff and Henrix 1988, 445), but more often speak of God's faithfulness in connection with 11:1–2, 32 or other biblical texts, or without specific scriptural reference (Croner 1977, 78; Rendtorff and Henrix 1988, 471, 494, 561, 594–95, and passim).

Documents by different member churches of the World Council of Churches or their various organs evidence, of course, a great variety of theological and practical approaches. Yet, with some notable exceptions, one may observe, as in Catholic documents, a progressive overcoming of supersessionism and a growing acceptance of a continuing theological significance of Judaism and the Jewish people.

Conclusions

The history of the interpretation of Rom. 11:29 is long and intricate. The verse, perhaps the most concise statement of God's fidelity, has long been neglected or caused difficulties. For based on a Christian reading of other biblical texts, it seemed inconceivable that Jews who did not accept Jesus as the Christ could still be in a positive relationship with God. Thus, it was frequently argued that God's gifts and calling had either passed entirely to the Christian church or had been put on hold until the Jews' conversion.

Paul certainly struggled tremendously with the question of Israel's **A**

H Progressive overcoming of supersessionism; continuing theological significance of the Jewish people.

A Acknowledging a diversity of possible interpretations.

destiny. His answers are almost as complex as the question, and it has recently been argued that Romans 11 in effect says, "To read me rightly, you must deliberate with *me* about what *you* want the identity and destiny of carnal Israel to be" (Cosgrove 1996, 287). It must be acknowledged that Romans 11 has been read in a great variety of ways. Ruether claims that "contemporary ecumenists who use Romans 11 to argue that Paul does not believe that God has rejected the people of the Mosaic covenant speak out of good intentions, but inaccurate exegesis" (1974, 106). Daniel Harrington, on the other hand, after a careful analysis of Rom. 11:29 and its context, concludes, "What is clear . . . is Paul's endorsement of the continuing nature of God's election of Israel, even of those Israelites who have refused to accept the gospel" (1992, 64). Perhaps, then, we do not have to be as pessimistic as Cosgrove about the possibility of evincing Paul's intended meaning.

C   One element that has had hermeneutic importance is the "new" encounter between Christians and Jews, as human beings, as religious persons, and as people who live after the *Shoah*. Whereas Christian theology has often dealt with the continued existence of the Jewish people by ignoring it or by triumphalism, other ways have been sought, especially in the past fifty years. When Martin Buber claimed, "I have not been notified that my covenant has been revoked" ("der Bund ist mir nicht aufgekündigt worden") (Buber and Schmidt 1933, 273), his dialogue partner, Karl Ludwig Schmidt, and Protestant and Catholic theology with him, did not have any response. In some way, a response came almost fifty years later in the words of Pope John Paul II about the "Old Covenant never revoked by God."

C   Only after the onslaught of anti-Semitism in this century were eyes of Christian theologians, writers, exegetes, and church leaders opened to
A   the possibility that Rom. 11:29, in the context of Romans 9–11 rather than, for example, Hebrews 8, might provide a hermeneutical key to better understand the Jewish people's relations with God and with the church. The Catholic church since Vatican II, and many other churches over the past fifty years, have taken decisive steps in a direction of a better understanding of and relations with Jews and Judaism.

If Catholic and Protestant theologians have come to a more positive appreciation of Judaism, then this should not be interpreted as a caving in to political or other pressures.[26] It does not necessarily militate against the Christian belief in the universality of salvation in Jesus Christ, as Vanhoye and others seem to fear. Instead, it is perhaps one of the most

---

C Encounter of Christians and Jews after the *Shoah*.

C After the onslaught of anti-Semitism in the twentieth century.

A Reading Rom. 11:29 in terms of Romans 9–11 rather than Hebrews 8.

remarkable ways in which the Catholic church and other churches come to grips with, in the words of Vatican II, "the responsibility of reading the signs of the time and of interpreting them in the light of the gospel" (*Gaudium et Spes* 4; cf. *Unitatis Redintegratio* 4).

In this light, intensive study of Romans 11 in general and of 11:29 in ☐ particular can open one's eyes to the mystery (11:25) of God's fidelity. This has, of course, direct consequences for the question of Christian-Jewish relations and for a Christian theology of Judaism. But God's faithfulness to the Jewish people is also paradigmatic: for Gentile Christians, too, it can serve as a sign of the permanence of God's love. Indeed, this paradigm may be helpful for a Christian theology of vocation.

We have observed that Ambrosiaster's misinterpretation of Rom. 11:29, based on a simple error or on a somewhat forced theology of baptism, exerted its influence for over one thousand years, even beyond the Reformation. Erasmus and others corrected this error on the basis of exegetical considerations. Similarly, Augustine's teaching on grace and predestination, which made extensive use of Rom. 11:29, has had an enduring influence on Catholic and Protestant theology; yet, modern exegesis has shown that Paul's main concern here is not predestination. On the other hand, Karl Barth's theological approach, which grew out of his practical experience, has helped to frame the question of the meaning of Rom 11:29 in a new way, also for exegetes. Finally, important impulses for further exegetical and theological reflection have come through Vatican II and Pope John Paul II. Thus, in some small way, we may see here the complex and delicate, yet often fruitful, interaction between exegesis, theology, church teachings, and praxis.

Notes

1. For a fuller version of this essay with quotations in the original languages, see Sievers 1997a. All translations are my own, unless indicated otherwise. I am grateful to Jared Wicks, Jean-Noël Aletti, and Daniel Patte for their helpful comments. Responsibility for any remaining errors rests, of course, solely with me.

2. P46 (Chester Beatty Papyrus II, ca. 200 c.e.) reads κτίσις ("creation") instead of κλῆσις ("call"), apparently in error.

3. For Jerome's similar translation, see his commentary on Isa. 6:9–10 (CChr. SL 73.93.91–92).

4. *PG* 60.592 (652). Along with others, Chrysostom found forgiveness of sin through baptism predicted in Rom. 11:26–27 (Schelkle 1956, 402).

5. The coinage of the name "Ambrosiaster" is generally but erroneously attributed to Erasmus (*PL* 17.39–40; *DBSup, TRE, LTK3* s.v. "Ambrosiaster"; Souter 1927, 39; Vogels in CSEL 81.1.IX). For correction, see Hoven 1969, 173.

☐ The mystery of God's faithfulness to the Jewish people and to others.

6. Bruno adds, based on Ambrosiaster: "God's gifts, i.e., the remission of sins" (*PL* 153.98C). The *Glossa ordinaria* (*Biblia Latina* 1480–81:298) interprets *dona* simply as *promissiones*.

7. Similarly, Johannes Bengel (1687–1752) had already distinguished between gifts, for Jews, and calling, for Gentiles (1742, 600).

8. For divergent medieval interpretations of "the calling" in our verse, see *PL* 153.98C.

9. ἀμεταμελητῶν σου χαρι[σμά]των διὰ τοῦ μονογενοῦς σου παιδός (Wilcken 1934, 34). Also, *Odes Sol.* 4:11, "For there is no regret with you; that you should regret anything which you have promised," may echo Rom. 11:29.

10. Many scholars use the term "unbelieving Jews" or its equivalents without further qualification. Paul never used this terminology, although he spoke of those broken off from the olive tree because of their "unbelief" (Rom. 11:20, 23). As the term *perfidi Judaei* ("faithless Jews") has been eliminated from the Catholic Good Friday liturgy, its synonyms should be eliminated from scholarly discourse. Kuss pointedly refers to Jews as "of the old faith" (*altgläubig*) rather than "unbelieving" (*ungläubig*) (1978, passim).

11. Rufinus "gives a prolix but more or less faithful paraphrase, which frequently takes mild liberties with the text and pays no special heed to exactitude, but normally preserves the general sense" (Chadwick 1959, 15); cf. Hammond Bammel 1985, 43–104.

12. Justin Martyr, *Dial.* 11.5: Ἰσραηλιτικὸν γὰρ ἀληθινὸν πνευματικόν... ἡμεῖς ἐσμεν. Cf. *Dial.* 123.7; 135.3; *1 Clem.* 29:1–3; 30.1. Further early witnesses for the identification of Christendom with the (new) people of God are cited by Tison 1961, 98–106; cf. Fitzmyer 1993, 620.

13. So Peppermüller 1972, 155. Schreckenberg appears too optimistic when he asserts that Abelard considers truly "all Israel" as eschatologically saved (1988, 142). For Abelard's views on Judaism, see his *Dialogus inter Philosophum, Judaeum et Christianum*.

14. CChr. CM 11.265.307–13; 266.343–48. Enoch and Elijah are associated in their eschatological role in the second-century *Apocalypse of Peter* (ch. 2) and in Tertullian (*An.* 50.5 = CChr. SL 2.856.33–35). Abelard seems to be the first, followed by numerous others (*PL* 181.757C; 191.1489B; *Glossa Ordinaria* [in *Biblia Latina cum glosse ordinaria*]; Cornelius a Lapide 1617, 161; cf. Refoulé 1984, 59–60; Berger 1988, 432–41), to apply this idea to Rom. 11:26.

15. *Praed.* 4.8; cf. *Retract.* 2.27.3 = CSEL 36.132; Mutzenbacher 1970, xxiv.

16. Guillaume of St. Thierry, regarding Rom. 11:29 (CChr. CM 86.158.802–14), relies heavily on Augustine. Similarly, Peter Lombardus quotes this passage (*PL* 191.1490), but also adds a long disquisition based on the baptismal interpretation of Ambrosiaster (cf. *PL* 68.492D).

17. While writing his commentaries, Calmet lived in Paris at the abbey of Blancs-Manteaux, a meeting place of Jansenists (Marsauche 1989, 236).

18. Such phraseology is regularly used to introduce possible alternative readings and not a different (i.e., spiritual) sense of Scripture (Spicq 1944, 207).

19. Godet strongly insists against a great number of theologians that Rom. 11:26 refers to the idea of "the national conversion of Israel at the end of times" (1890, 406).

20. Journet 1945. The book appeared in March 1945, but its preface is dated in part to 30 September 1943, and in part to 22 July 1944. For a critical review, see Jean-Louis Leuba (*Judaica* 2 [1946]: 159). For a bibliography of Journet's writings concerning Christian-Jewish relations, see Kamykowski 1993, 336–37.

21. Texts in Croner 1977, 3, 9, 20, 21, 26, 33, 61; Rendtorff and Henrix 1988, 134, 139, 141, 144, 249, 269, 271; descriptive references in Sievers 1997a, 433 n. 206; 1997b, 348 n. 58.

22. The phrase used by the pope ("the people of the Old Covenant, never revoked by God") is itself not entirely new, as the title *Der ungekündigte Bund* of the proceedings of an earlier *Evangelischer Kirchentag* shows (Goldschmidt and Kraus 1962). Cf. *pacta Dei sunt irrevocabilia* (Brenz 1538, 365.35).

23. *L'Osservatore Romano*, 15 June 1973, cited in *DC* 1635 (1 July 1973): 621.

24. *La Croix*, 16 June 1973, cited in *DC* 1635 (1 July 1973): 622–23.

25. "L'alliance du Sinaï, a donc étéré voquée par Dieu, mais au moment même de la rupture, Dieu a promis de la remplacer par une nouvelle alliance, différente" (Vanhoye 1994, 831). I am grateful to Fr. Vanhoye for clarifying comments on this section.

26. "semantischer Einschüchterungsversuch" (Klein 1982, 411); "theologischer Besitzverzicht" (Grässer 1985, 286).

References

Aageson, James W. 1986. "Scripture and Structure in the Development of the Argument in Romans 9–11." *Catholic Biblical Quarterly* 48:265–89.

Abelard, Peter [Abaelardus, Petrus]. 1969. "Commentaria in Epistulam Pauli ad Romanos." Pp. 1–340 in *Petri Abaelardi Opera Theologica*, ed. Eligius M. Buytaert. CChr. CM 11. Turnhout: Brepols.

Alctti, Jean-Noël. 1991. *Comment Dieu est-il juste? Clefs pour interpréter l'épître aux Romains*. Paris: Éditions du Seuil.

Ambrosiaster. 1966. *Ambrosiastri qui dicitur commentarius in epistulas Paulinas. Pars I. In Epistulam ad Romanos*, ed. Henricus Iosephus Vogels. CSEL 81.1. Vienna: Hoelder-Pichler-Tempsky.

Aquinas, Thomas. 1953. *Super epistolas S. Pauli lectura*, ed. Raphael Cai. Vol. 1. 8th ed. Turin and Rome: Marietti.

Asmussen, Hans. 1952. *Der Römerbrief*. Stuttgart: Evang. Verlagswerk.

Backhaus, Knut. 1996. "Gottes nicht bereuter Bund: Alter und neuer Bund in der Sicht des Frühchristentums." Pp. 33–55 in *Ekklesiologie des Neuen Testaments*, ed. Rainer Kampling and Thomas Söding. Freiburg: Herder.

BAGD. 1979. W. Bauer, W. F. Arndt, F. W. Gingrich, and F. W. Danker. *A Greek-English Lexicon of the New Testament*. 2d ed. Chicago: University of Chicago Press.

Bardenhewer, Otto. 1926. *Der Römerbrief des heiligen Paulus*. Freiburg: Herder.

Barrett, Charles K. 1957. *A Commentary on the Epistle to the Romans*. Black's New Testament Commentaries. London: Black.

————. 1977. "Romans 9:30–10:21: Fall and Responsibility of Israel." Pp. 99–121 in *Die Israelfrage nach Röm 9–11,* ed. Lorenzo de Lorenzi. Monographische Reihe von "Benedictina." Bibl.-ökum. Abt. 3. Rome: Abtei von St Paul vor den Mauern.

Barth, Karl. 1922. *Der Römerbrief.* 2nd ed. Munich: Kaiser.

————. 1933. *Die Kirche Jesu Christi.* Theologische Existenz heute 5. Munich: Kaiser.

————. 1942. *Die kirchliche Dogmatik.* Vol. 2.2. Zurich: Evangelischer Verlag Zollikon.

————. 1950. "Die Judenfrage und ihre christliche Beantwortung." *Judaica* 6: 67–72.

Barth, Markus. 1977. "Das Volk Gottes: Juden und Christen in der Botschaft des Paulus." Pp. 45–134 in M. Barth et al., *Paulus — Apostat oder Apostel.* Regensburg: Pustet.

Baumbach, Günther. 1993. "Bedeutung und Deutung der Hileigen (*sic*) Schrift in deutschen kirchlichen Verlautbarungen zum christlich-jüdischen Gespräch seit 1950." Pp. 535–53 in *Die Bibel in jüdischer und christlicher Tradition,* ed. H. Merklein, K. Müller, and G. Stemberger. Bonner biblische Beiträge 88. Frankfurt: A. Hain.

Baumert, Norbert. 1986. "Charisma und Amt bei Paulus." Pp. 203–28 in *L'Apôtre Paul: Personnalité, style et conception du ministère,* ed. A. Vanhoye. Bibliotheca ephemeridum theologicarum lovaniensium 73. Leuven: Leuven University Press.

Bea, Agostino Cardinal. 1965. "Il popolo ebraico nel piano divino della salvezza." *Civiltà Cattolica* 2769:209–29.

————. 1966. *La Chiesa e il popolo ebraico.* Brescia: Morcelliana.

Bell, Richard H. 1994. *Provoked to Jealousy: The Origin and Purpose of the Jealousy Motif in Romans 9–11.* Wissenschaftliche Untersuchungen zum Neuen Testament 2.63. Tübingen: Mohr.

Bengel, Joh. Albert. 1742. "Annotationes in Epistolam Pauli ad Romanos." Pp. 530–620 in *Gnomon Novi Testamenti.* Tübingen: Schrammii.

Berger, Klaus. 1988. "Henoch." *Reallexicon für Antike und Christentum* 14: 473–545.

Beyschlag, W. 1868. *Die paulinische Theodicee Römer IX-XI: Ein Beitrag zur biblischen Theologie.* Halle and Saale: Strien.

Beza, Theodore. [1566] 1988. *Cours sur les épîtres aux Romains et aux Hebreux 1564–66 d'après les notes de Marcus Widler.* Travaux d'Humanisme et Renaissance 226. Geneva: Droz.

Biblia Latina cum glossa ordinaria. [1480–81] 1992. *Facsimile Reprint of the Editio Princeps Adolph Rusch of Strassburg 1480/81.* Vol. 4. Turnhout: Brepols.

Biblia Sacra cum glossa ordinaria. 1617. *Postilla Nicolai Lirani.* Vol. 6. Antwerp: Joannes Keerbergius.

Black, Matthew. 1973. *Romans.* New Century Bible. Grand Rapids: Eerdmans.

Bloy, Léon. 1905. *Le Salut par les Juifs.* 2nd ed. Paris: Demay.

Brenz, Johannes. [1538] 1986. *Explicatio Epistolae Pauli ad Romanos.* Vol. 1. Ed. Stefan Strohm. Tübingen: Mohr.

Brunner, Emil. 1948. *Der Römerbrief.* Stuttgart: Oncken.

Buber, Martin, and Karl Ludwig Schmidt. 1933. "Kirche, Staat, Volk, Judentum: Zwiegespräch im Jüdischen Lehrhaus in Stuttgart am 14. Januar 1933." *Theologische Blätter* 12, no. 9 (September): 257–74.

Bultmann, Rudolf. 1984. *Theologie des Neuen Testaments.* 9th ed. Tübingen: Mohr.

Buytaert, Eligius M., ed. 1969. *Petri Abaelardi Opera Theologica.* CChr.CM 11. Turnhout: Brepols.

Byrne, Brendan. 1996. *Romans.* Sacra Pagina 6. Collegeville, Minn.: Liturgical Press.

Caird, G. B. 1956–57. Predestination — Romans ix–xi. *Expository Times* 68: 324–27.

Cajetan, Thomas de Vio. 1540. *Epistolae Pauli et aliorum Apostolorum ad Graecam veritatem castigatae.* Rev. ed. Paris: Guillard.

Calmet, Augustin. 1730. *Commentaire littéral sur tous les livres de l'Ancien et du Nouveau Testament. Les Épîtres de Saint Paul.* Vol. 1. Paris: Emery, Saugrain, Pierre Martin.

Calvin, John. 1540. *Commentarius in Epistolam Pauli ad Romanos.* Ed. T. H. L. Parker. Studies in the History of Christian Thought 22. Leiden: Brill, 1981.

———. [1556] 1892. *Commentarius in Epistolam Pauli ad Romanos.* Cols. 1–292 in vol. 49 of *Calvini Opera.* Corpus reformatorum 77. Braunschweig: Schwetschke et filius.

———. 1980. *The Epistles of Paul to the Romans and to the Thessalonians.* Trans. Ross MacKenzie. Calvin's Commentaries. Grand Rapids: Eerdmans.

Carli, Luigi Maria. 1965. "La questione giudaica davanti al Concilio Vaticano II." *Palestra del Clero* 44:85–203.

———. 1966. "Chiesa e Sinagoga." *Palestra del Clero* 45:333–55, 397–419.

Catechism of the Catholic Church. 1994. Vatican: Libreria Editrice Vaticana.

Caubet Iturbe, Francisco Javier. 1962. "Et sic omnis Israel salvus fieret, Rom 11,26: Su interpretación por los escritores cristianos de los siglos III–XII." *Estudios Bíblicos* 21:127–50.

———. 1963. " '... Et sic omnis Israel salvus fieret' Rom 11,26." Pp. 329–40 in *Studiorum Paulinorum Congressus Internationalis Catholicus 1961.* Vol. 1. Analecta biblica 17–18. Rome: Pontifical Biblical Institute Press.

CChr. CM. 1969–. Corpus christianorum: Continuatio mediaevalis. Turnhout: Brepols.

CChr. SL. 1953–. Corpus christianorum: Series latina. Turnhout: Brepols.

Chadwick, Henry. 1959. "Rufinus and the Tura Papyrus of Origen's Commentary on Romans." *Journal of Theological Studies,* n.s., 10:10–42.

Cocchini, Francesca. 1986. *Origene: Commento alla lettera ai Romani.* Vol. 2. Genova: Marietti.

Cornelius a Lapide. 1617. *Commentaria in omnes D. Pauli Epistolas.* 2nd ed. Antwerp: Nutius.

Cornely, Rudolph. 1896. *Commentarius in S. Pauli Apostoli Epistolas I. Epistola ad Romanos.* Cursus Scripturae Sacrae NT 2.1. Paris: Lethielleux.

Corpus reformatorum. 1834–. Halle: Schwetschke et al.

Cosgrove, Charles H. 1995. "The Church *with and for* Israel: History of a Theological *Novum* before and after Barth." *Perspectives in Religious Studies* 22:259–78.

————. 1996. "Rhetorical Suspense in Romans 9–11: A Study in Polyvalence and Hermeneutical Election." *Journal of Biblical Literature* 115:271–87.

Cramer, J. A. 1844. *Catenae Graecorum Patrum in Novum Testamentum. Tomus IV in Epistolam S. Pauli ad Romanos.* Oxford: Oxford University Press.

Cranfield, C. E. B. 1981. *A Critical and Exegetical Commentary on the Epistle to the Romans.* Vol. 2. 2nd ed. International Critical Commentary. Edinburgh: T. & T. Clark.

Croner, Helga. 1977. *Stepping Stones to Further Jewish-Christian Relations: An Unabridged Collection of Christian Documents.* London and New York: Stimulus Books.

CSEL. 1866–. Corpus Scriptorum Ecclesiasticorum Latinorum. N.p.

DBSup. 1928–. *Dictionnaire de la Bible, Supplemént.* Ed. L. Pirot et al. Paris: Letouzey.

DC. 1919–40, 1944–. *Documentation Catholique.* Paris.

De Lorenzi, Lorenzo, ed. 1977. *Die Israelfrage nach Röm 9–11.* Monographische Reihe von "Benedictina." Bibl.-ökum. Abt. 3. Rome: Abtei von St Paul vor den Mauern.

De Lubac, Henri. 1964. *Exégèse médiévale: Les quatre sens de l'écriture.* Seconde Partie II. N.p. Aubier/Montaigne.

de Martel, Gérard, ed. 1995. *Expositiones Pauli Epistolarum. Ad Romanos, Galathas et Ephesios e codice Sancti Michaelis in periculo Maris.* Avranches, Bibl. mun. 79. CChr.CM 151. Turnhout: Brepols.

Dodd, C. H. 1932. *The Epistle of Paul to the Romans.* Moffat New Testament Commentary. London: Hodder and Stoughton.

Domanyi, Thomas. 1979. *Der Römerbriefkommentar des Thomas von Aquin: Ein Beitrag zur Untersuchung seiner Auslegungsmethoden.* Basler und Berner Studien zur historischen und systematischen Theologie 39. Bern: P. Lang.

Donfried, Karl P. 1989. Review of *Paul and the Torah,* by Lloyd Gaston, *Catholic Biblical Quarterly* 51:769–72.

Dreyfus, François. 1977. "Le passé et le présent d'Israël (Rom. 9, 1–5; 11, 1–24)." Pp. 131–92 (plus discussion on pp. 152–92) in *Die Israelfrage nach Röm 9–11,* ed. Lorenzo De Lorenzi. Monographische Reihe von "Benedictina." Bibl.-ökum. Abt. 3. Rome: Abtei von St Paul vor den Mauern.

DS. 1973. H. Denzinger and A. Schönmetzer, eds. *Enchiridion Symbolorum.* 35th ed. Freiburg i.B.: Herder.

Dunn, James D. G. 1988. *Romans 9–16.* Word Biblical Commentary 38B. Dallas: Word.

Encyclopedia of the Early Church. 1992. 2 vols. Cambridge: James Clarke.

Ephraem Syrus. 1893. *Commentarii in epistolas D. Pauli nunc primum ex Armenio in Latinum sermonem a Patribus Mekitharistis translati.* Venice: S. Lazarus.

Erasmus of Rotterdam, Desiderius. 1509. *Un inédit d'Érasme: La première version du Nouveau Testament copiée par Pierre Meghen 1506–1509. Contribution à l'établissement d'une édition critique du NT.* Angers: Gibaud, 1982.

———. 1535. *Erasmus' Annotations on the New Testament: Acts — Romans — I and II Corinthians. Facsimile of the Final Latin Text with Earlier Variants.* Ed. Anne Reeve and M. A. Screech. Leiden: Brill, 1990.

———. 1984. *New Testament Scholarship. Paraphrases on Romans and Galatians.* Vol. 42 of *Collected Works of Erasmus.* Ed. Robert D. Sider. Trans. and ann. John B. Payne et al. Toronto: University of Toronto Press.

———. 1990. *Parafrasi della Lettera ai Romani.* L'Aquila, Italy: Japadre.

———. 1994. *New Testament Scholarship. Annotations on Romans.* Vol. 56 of *Collected Works of Erasmus.* Ed. Robert D. Sider. Trans. and ann. John B. Payne et al. Toronto: University of Toronto Press.

Federici, Tommaso. 1966. *Il Concilio e i non cristiani: declaratio, testo e commento. Con un saggio introduttivo di Henri de Lubac.* Rome: AVE.

Flicker, Johannes. 1908. *Luthers Vorlesung über den Römerbrief 1515/1516.* Vol. 1 of *Anfänge reformatorischer Bibelauslegung.* Leipzig: Dieterich.

Fitzmyer, Joseph A. 1990. "The Letter to the Romans." Pp. 830–68 in *New Jerome Biblical Commentary,* ed. R. E. Brown et al.

———. 1993. *Romans: A New Translation with Introduction and Commentary.* Anchor Bible 33. New York: Doubleday.

———. 1995. *The Biblical Commission's Document "The Interpretation of the Bible in the Church": Text and Commentary.* Subsidia Biblica 18. Rome: Pontifical Biblical Institute Press.

Gaston, Lloyd. 1987. *Paul and the Torah.* Vancouver: University of British Columbia.

Gaugler, Ernst. 1952. *Der Römerbrief.* Prophezei Schweizerisches Bibelwerk für die Gemeinde. Zurich: Zwingli.

GCS. 1897. *Die griechischen christlichen Schriftsteller der ersten Jahrhunderte.* New ed., 1956–. Berlin: Akademie.

Getty, Mary Ann. 1988. "Paul and the Salvation of Israel: A Perspective on Romans 9–11." *Catholic Biblical Quarterly* 50:456–69.

Godet, F. 1890. *Commentaire sur l'Épitre aux Romains.* Vol. 2. 2nd ed. Neuchatel: Delachaux et Niestlé.

Goldschmidt, Dietrich, and Hans-Joachim Kraus, eds. 1962. *Der ungekündigte Bund: Neue Begegnung von Juden und christlicher Gemeinde.* Arbeitsgemeinschaft Juden und Christen beim Deutschen Evangelischen Kirchentag. Stuttgart: Kreuz-Verlag.

Gorday, Peter. 1983. *Principles of Patristic Exegesis: Romans 9–11 in Origen, John Chrysostom, and Augustine.* Studies in the Bible and Early Christianity 4. New York: Mellen.

Gore, C. 1900. *St. Paul's Epistle to the Romans: A Practical Exposition.* Vol. 2. London: Murray.

Grässer, Erich. 1981. "Zwei Heilswege? Zum theologischen Verhältnis von Israel und Kirche." Pp. 411–29 in *Kontinuität und Einheit,* ed. P.-G Müller and W. Stenger. Freiburg, Basel, and Vienna: Herder.

———. 1985. *Der alte Bund im Neuen: Exegetische Studien zur Israelfrage im Neuen Testament.* Wissenschaftliche Untersuchungen zum Neuen Testament 35. Tübingen: Mohr.

Grenholm, Cristina. 1990. *Romans Interpreted: A Comparative Analysis of the Commentaries of Barth, Nygren, Cranfield, and Wilckens on Paul's Epistle to the Romans.* Stockholm: Uppsala.

Hammond Bammel, Caroline P. 1985. *Der Römerbrieftext des Rufin und seine Origenes-Übersetzung.* VL aus der Geschichte der lateinischen Bibel 10. Freiburg: Herder.

Harrington, Daniel J. 1988. "Israel's Salvation According to Paul." *The Bible Today* 26:304–8.

———. 1992. *Paul on the Mystery of Israel.* Collegeville, Minn.: Liturgical Press.

Henrix, Hans Hermann. 1984. "Der nie gekündigte Bund: Eine katholische Beschreibung des Verhältnisses von Israel und Kirche." *IDCIV-Vorträge Nr. 7.* Vienna: n.p.

Hesse, Franz. 1981. "Die Israelfrage in neueren Entwürfen Biblischer Theologie." *Kerygma und Dogma* 27:180–97.

Hesselink, John. 1988. "Calvin's Understanding of the Relation of the Church and Israel Based Largely on his Interpretation of Romans 9–11." *Ex Auditu* 4:59–69.

Heydenreich, Renate Maria. 1962. "Erklärungen aus der Evangelischen Kirche Deutschlands und der Ökumene zur Judenfrage 1932–1961." Pp. 183–283 in *Der ungekündigte Bund: Neue Begegnung von Juden und christlicher Gemeinde,* ed. Dietrich Goldschmidt and Hans-Joachim Kraus. Arbeitsgemeinschaft Juden und Christen beim Deutschen Evangelischen Kirchentag. Stuttgart: Kreuz-Verlag.

Hoch, M.-Th., and B. Dupuy. 1980. *Les Églises devant le Judaïsme: Documents officiels 1948–1978.* Paris: Cerf.

Hofius, Otfried. 1973. "Die Unabänderlichkeit des göttlichen Heilsratschlusses: Erwägungen zur Herkunft eines neutestamentlichen Theologumenon." *Zeitschrift für die neutestamentliche Wissenschaft* 64:135–45.

———. 1986. "Das Evangelium und Israel: Erwägungen zu Römer 9–11." *Zeitschrift für Theologie und Kirche* 83:321.

Holtzmann, Oskar. 1926. "Der Römerbrief." Pp. 618–78 in *Das Neue Testament nach dem Stuttgarter griechischen Text übersetzt und erklärt.* Vol. 2 Giessen: Töpelmann.

Hoven, René. 1969. "Notes sur Érasme et les auteurs anciens." *L'Antiquité Classique* 38:169–74.

Huby, Joseph. 1957. *Saint Paul: Épître aux Romains.* Rev. ed. Ed. Stanislas Lyonnet. Paris: Beauchesne.

Hübner, Hans. 1984. *Gottes Ich und Israel: Zum Schriftgebrauch des Paulus in Römer 9–11.* Forschungen zur Religion und Literatur des Alten und Neuen Testaments 136. Göttingen: Vandenhoeck and Ruprecht.

International Catholic-Jewish Liaison Committee. 1988. *Fifteen Years of Catholic-Jewish Dialogue 1970–1985.* Vatican: Libreria Editrice Vaticana.

Jeremias, Joachim. 1977. "Einige vorwiegend sprachliche Beobachtungen zu Röm 11, 25–36." Pp. 193–205 in *Die Israelfrage nach Röm 9–11,* ed. Lorenzo De Lorenzi. Monographische Reihe von "Benedictina." Bibl.-ökum. Abt. 3. Rome: Abtei von St Paul vor den Mauern.

Jeremias, Jörg. 1975. *Die Reue Gottes: Aspekte alttestamentlicher Gottesvorstellung.* Biblische Studied 65. Neukirchen: Neukirchener Verlag.

John Paul II, Pope. 1979–. *Insegnamenti di Giovanni Paolo II.* Vatican: Libreria Editrice Vaticana.

———. 1987. *Pope John Paul II on Jews and Judaism 1979–1986.* Ed. Eugene J. Fisher and Leon Klenicki. Washington, D.C.: United States Catholic Conference.

Journet, Charles. 1945. *Destinées d'Israël: A propos du Salut par les Juifs.* Paris: Egloff.

———. 1956. "The Mysterious Destinies of Israel." Pp. 35–90 in *The Bridge: A Yearbook of Judaeo-Christian Studies,* ed. John M. Oesterreicher. Vol. 2. New York: Pantheon.

———. 1961. "La dialectique paulinienne des Juifs et des Gentils." *Nova et Vetera* 36:107–29.

———. 1969. *L'Église du Verbe incarné. III. Essai de théologie de l'histoire du salut.* Paris: Desclée de Brouwer.

Judant, Denise. 1969. *Judaïsme et Christianisme: Dossier patristique.* Paris: Cèdre.

Jülicher, Adolf. 1908. "Der Brief an die Römer." Pp. 217–327 in *Die Schriften des Neuen Testaments,* ed. Johannes Weiss. Vol. 2. 2nd ed. Göttingen: Vandenhoeck and Ruprecht.

Justin Martyr. 1909. *Dialogue avec Tryphon. Texte grec, traduction française, introduction, notes.* Ed. Georges Archambault. 2 vols. Paris: Picard.

Käsemann, Ernst. 1980. *Commentary on Romans.* Trans. Geoffrey Bromiley. Grand Rapids: Eerdmans.

Kamykowski, Lukasz. 1993. *Izrael I Kosciól Wedlug Charlesa Journeta (Israel et l'eglise d'après Charles Journet).* Krakow: Wydawnictwo Naukowe Papieskiej Akademii Teologicznej.

———. 1994. "Qu'est-ce qu'Israël? Examen de l'approche de Charles Journet." *Analecta Cracoviensia* 26:193–212.

Klappert, Bertold. 1980. *Israel und die Kirche: Erwägungen zur Israellehre Karl Barths.* Munich: Kaiser.

———. 1981. "Traktat für Israel (Römer 9–11): Die paulinische Verhältnisbestimmung von Israel und Kirche als Kriterium neutestamentlicher Sachaussagen über die Juden." Pp. 58–137 in *Jüdische Existenz und die Erneuerung der christlichen Theologie: Versuch der Bilanz des christlich-jüdischen Dialogs für die Systematische Theologie,* ed. Martin Stöhr. Abhandlungen zum christlich-jüdischen Dialog 11. Munich: Kaiser.

Klein, Günter. 1982. " 'Christlicher Antijudaismus': Bemerkungen zu einem semantischen Einschüchterungsversuch." *Zeitschrift für Theologie und Kirche* 79:411–50.

Klumbies, Paul-Gerhard. 1992. *Die Rede von Gott bei Paulus in ihrem zeitgeschichtlichen Kontext.* Forschungen zur Religion und Literatur des Alten und Neuen Testaments 155. Göttingen: Vandenhoeck and Ruprecht.

Kraus, Wolfgang. 1996. *Das Volk Gottes: Zur Grundlegung der Ekklesiologie bei Paulus.* Wissenschaftliche Untersuchungen zum Neuen Testament 85. Tübingen: Mohr.

Kühl, E. 1913. *Der Brief des Paulus an die Römer.* Leipzig: Quelle and Meyer.

Kümmel, Werner Georg. 1977. "Die Probleme von Römer 9–11." Pp. 13–33 in *Die Israelfrage nach Röm 9–11*, ed. Lorenzo De Lorenzi. Monographische Reihe von "Benedictina." Bibl.-ökum. Abt. 3. Rome: Abtei von St Paul vor den Mauern.

Kuss, Otto. 1978. *Der Römerbrief. Dritte Lieferung. Röm 8,19 bis 11,36.* Regensburg: Pustet.

Lagrange, M.-J. 1950. *Saint Paul Épître aux Romains.* 6th ed. Paris: Gabalda.

Landgraf, Artur. 1932. "Familienbildung bei Paulinenkommentaren des 12. Jahrhunderts." *Biblica* 13:61–72, 169–93.

La Peyrère, Isaac. 1643. *Du rappel des Juifs.* Paris: n.p.

Lohfink, Norbert. 1989. *Der niemals gekündigte Bund: Exegetische Gedanken zum christlich-jüdischen Dialog.* Freiburg: Herder.

LTK3. 1993. *Lexikon für Theologie und Kirche.* 3rd ed. Ed. W Kasper et al. Freiburg i.B.: Herder.

Lübking, H.-M. 1986. *Paulus und Israel im Römerbrief: eine Untersuchung zu Römer 9–11.* Europäische Hochschulschriften. Reihe 23, Theologie. Bd. 260. Frankfurt and New York: Lang.

Luz, Ulrich. 1968. *Das Geschichtsverständnis des Paulus.* Beiträge zur evangelischen Theologie 49. Munich: Kaiser.

Lyonnet, Stanislaus. 1962. *Quaestiones in epistulam ad Romanos. Series altera. De praedestinatione Israel et theologia historiae. Rom 9–11.* Rome: Pontifical Biblical Institute Press.

Maccoby, Hyam. 1991. *Paul and Hellenism.* London: SCM.

Maier, F. W. 1929. *Israel in der Heilsgeschichte nach Römer 9–11.* Münster: Aschendorff.

Main, Emmanuelle. 1996. "Ancienne et Nouvelle Alliances dans le dessein de Dieu: à propos d'un article récent." *La nouvelle revue théologique* 118:34–58.

Maritain, Jacques. 1965. *Le mystère d'Israël et autres essais.* Paris: Desclée De Brouwer.

Maritain, Raïssa. 1948. "Léon Bloy et Israël." Pp. 305–16 in *Bilan Juif. Confluences: Revue des Lettres et des Arts 7.*

Marquardt, Friedrich Wilhelm. 1967. *Die Entdeckung des Judentums für die christliche Theologie: Israel im Denken Karl Barths.* Munich: Kaiser.

———. 1971. *Die Juden im Römerbrief.* Theologische Studien 107. Zurich: Evangelischer Verlag.

Marsauche, Patrick. 1989. "Présentation de Dom Augustin Calmet (1672–1757)." Pp. 233–53 in *Le Grand Siècle et la Bible,* ed. Charles Kannengiesser. Vol. 6 of *Bible de tous le temps,* sous la direction de Jean Robert Armogathe. Paris: Beauchesne.

Martin, Vincent. 1996. "L'ancien et le nouveau." *La nouvelle revue théologique* 118:59–65.

Maunoury, A.-F. 1878. *Commentaire sur l'Epître de Saint Paul aux Romains.* Paris: Bloud et Barral.

Melanchthon, Philipp. 1848. *Opera quae supersunt omnia.* Ed. Carolus G. Bretschneider. Corpus reformatorum 15. Halle: Schwetschke.

Michel, Otto. 1978. *Der Brief an die Römer.* Kritisch-exegetischer Kommentar über das Neue Testament 4. 14th ed. Göttingen: Vandenhoeck and Ruprecht.

Migne, J.-P. 1840. *In Epistolas D. Pauli ad Romanos...commentarias.* Vol. 24 of *Scripturae Sacrae cursus completes.* Paris: Migne.

Möhler, Johann Adam. [1835–1837] 1990. *Vorlesung zum Römerbrief.* Munich: Wewel.

Munck, Johannes. 1967. *Christ and Israel: An Interpretation of Romans 9–11.* 2nd ed. Philadelphia: Fortress.

Murray, John. 1965. *The Epistle to the Romans.* Vol. 2. 2nd ed. New International Commentary on the New Testament. Grand Rapids: Eerdmans.

Mussner, Franz. 1979. *Traktat über die Juden.* Munich: Kösel.

Mutzenbacher, Almut. 1970. *Sancti Aurelii Augustini de diversis quaestionibus ad Simplicianum.* CChr. SL 44. Turnhout: Brepols.

Nanos, Mark D. 1996. *The Mystery of Romans: The Jewish Context of Paul's Letter.* Minneapolis: Fortress.

Niebuhr, Karl-Wilhelm. 1992. *Heidenapostel aus Israel: Die jüdische Identität des Paulus nach ihrer Darstellung in seinen Briefen.* Wissenschaftliche Untersuchungen zum Neuen Testament 62. Tübingen: Mohr.

Nygren, Anders. 1949. *Commentary on Romans.* Philadelphia: Fortress.

Oesterreicher, John M. 1974. "Unter dem Bogen des einen Bundes — Das Volk Gottes: Seine Zweigestalt und Einheit." Pp. 27–69 in *Judentum und Kirche: Volk Gottes,* ed. Clemens Thoma. Theologische Berichte 3. Zurich, Einsiedeln, and Köln: Benziger.

———. 1986. *The New Encounter between Christians and Jews.* New York: Philosophical Library.

Origen. 1983. *Jeremiahomilien: Klagliederkommentar; Erklarung der Samuel- und Königsbücher.* Vol. 3 of *Origenes Werke.* Ed. E. Klostermann. 2nd ed., ed. P. Nautin. Die Griechischen christlichen Schriftsteller der ersten Jahrhunderte. Berlin: Akademie.

———. 1998. *Der Römerbriefkommentar des Origenes: Kritische Ausgabe der Übersetzung Rufins. Buch 7–10.* Ed. Caroline P. Hammond Bammel, H. J. Frede, and H. Stanjek. VL aus der Geschichte der lateinischen Bibel 34. Freiburg: Herder.

Osten-Sacken, Peter von der. 1982. *Grundzüge einer Theologie im christlich-jüdischen Gespräch.* Abhandlungen zum christlich-jüdischen Dialog 12. Munich: Kaiser.

———. 1987. *Evangelium und Torah: Aufsätze zu Paulus.* Munich: Kaiser.

Pallis, Alex. 1920. *To the Romans. A Commentary.* Liverpool: Liverpool Booksellers.

Parker, T. H. L. 1986. *Commentaries on the Epistle to the Romans 1532–1542.* Edinburgh: T. & T. Clark.

Parry, R. St. John. 1912. *The Epistle of Paul the Apostle to the Romans.* Cambridge: Cambridge University Press.

Paul VI, Pope. 1974. *Insegnamenti di Paolo VI.* Vol. 12. Vatican: Libreria Editrice Vaticana.

Pelagius. 1926. *Pelagius's Expositions of Thirteen Epistles of St. Paul: Text and Apparatus Criticus.* Ed. Alexander Souter. Text and Studies 9.2. Cambridge: Cambridge University Press.

Penna, Romano. 1986. "L'evolution de l'attitude de Paul envers les Juifs." Pp. 390–421 in *L'Apôtre Paul: Personnalité, style et conception du ministère,* ed. A. Vanhoye. Bibliotheca ephemeridum theologicarum lovaniensium 73. Leuven: Leuven University Press.

Peppermüller, Rolf. 1972. *Abaelards Auslegung des Römerbriefes.* Münster: Aschendorff.

PG. 1857–66. Patrologiae Cursus Completus. Series Graeca. Paris: Garnier/ Migne.

PL. 1841–55. Patrologiae Cursus Completus. Series Latina. Paris: Garnier/Migne.

Plag, C. 1969. *Israels Wege zum Heil: Eine Untersuchung zu Römer 9–11.* Stuttgart: Calwer.

Platz, Philipp. 1938. *Der Römerbrief in der Gnadenlehre Augustins.* Würzburg: Rita-Verlag.

Ponsot, Hervé. 1988. *Une introduction à la lettre aux Romains.* Paris: Cerf.

Pontifical Biblical Commission. 1993. *The Interpretation of the Bible in the Church.* Vatican: Libreria Editrice Vaticana.

Popkin, Richard H. 1987. *Isaac La Peyrère (1596–1676): His Life, Work, and Influence.* Leiden: Brill.

Pseudo-Augustinus. 1908. *Pseudo-Augustini Quaestiones Veteris et Novi Testamenti CXXVII.* Ed. Alexander Souter. Corpus Scriptorum Ecclesiasticorum Latinorum 50. Vienna: Tempsky.

Quasten, Johannes. 1950–1960. *Patrology.* 3 vols. Utrecht: Spectrum.

Räisänen, Heikki. 1987. "Römer 9–11: Analyse eines geistigen Ringens." *Aufstieg und Niedergang der römischen Welt* 2.25.4:2891–939.

———. 1988. "Paul, God, and Israel: Romans 9–11 in Recent Research." Pp. 178–206 in *The Social World of Formative Christianity and Judaism,* ed. Jacob Neusner et al. Philadelphia: Fortress.

———. 1989. Review of *Paul and the Torah,* by Lloyd Gaston. *Theologische Literaturzeitung* 114:191–92.

RBMA. 1940–1980. *Repertorium Biblicum Medii Aevi.* Ed. Fredericus Stegmüller. 11 vols. Madrid: Consejo Superior de Investigaciones Científicas, Instituto Francisco Suárez.

Refoulé, François. 1984. *"...et ainsi tout Israël sera sauvé": Romains 11,25–32.* Lectio divina 117. Paris: Cerf.

———. 1987. "Unité de l'Épître aux Romains et histoire du salut." *Revue des sciences philosophiques et théologiques* 71:219–42.

———. 1991. "Cohérence ou incohérence de Paul en Romains 9–11." *Revue biblique* 98:51–79.

———. 1995. "Du bon et du mauvais usage des parallèles et des notes en Romains IX-XI." *Revue des sciences religieuses* 69:172–93.

Reithmayr, F. X. [1845] 1976. *Commentar zum Briefe an die Römer.* Regensburg. Reprint, Frankfurt: Minerva.

Rendtorff, Rolf. 1989. *Hat denn Gott sein Volk verstossen? Die evangelische Kirche und das Judentum seit 1945. Ein Kommentar.* Abhandlungen zum christlich-jüdischen Dialog 18. Munich: Kaiser.

Rendtorff, Rolf, and Hans Hermann Henrix. 1988. *Die Kirchen und das Judentum: Dokumente von 1945 bis 1985.* Paderborn: Bonifatius; Munich: Kaiser.

Rosato, Philip J. 1986. "The Influence of Karl Barth on Catholic Theology." *Gregorianum* 67:659–78.

Ruether, Rosemary R. 1974. *Faith and Fratricide: The Theological Roots of Anti-Semitism.* New York: Seabury.

Sabatier, Petrus. 1751. *Bibliorum Sacrorum Latinae versiones antiquae seu Vetus Italica.* Vol. 3. Part 2. Paris: Didot.

Sanday, William, and Arthur Headlam. 1902. *A Critical and Exegetical Commentary on the Epistle to the Romans.* 5th ed. International Critical Commentary. Edinburgh: T. & T. Clark.

Sänger, Dieter. 1994. *Die Verkündigung des Gekreuzigten und Israel: Studien zum Verhältnis von Kirche und Israel bei Paulus und im frühen Christentum.* Wissenschaftliche Untersuchungen zum Neuen Testament 75. Tübingen: Mohr.

Sass, Gerhard. 1995. *Leben aus den Verheissungen: Traditionsgeschichtliche und bibel-theologische Untersuchungen zur Rede von Gottes Verheissungen im Frühjudentum und beim Apostel Paulus.* Forschungen zur Religion und Literatur des Alten und Neuen Testaments 164. Göttingen: Vandenhoeck and Ruprecht.

Schäfer, Rolf. 1963. "Melanchthons Hermeneutik im Römerbrief-Kommentar von 1532." *Zeitschrift für Theologie und Kirche* 60:216–35.

Schatzmann, Siegfried. 1987. *A Pauline Theology of Charismata.* Peabody, Mass.: Hendrickson.

Scheef, R. L., Jr. 1962. "Vocation." Pp. 791–92 in vol. 4 of *Interpreter's Dictionary of the Bible.*

Schelkle, K. H. 1956. *Paulus Lehrer der Väter: Die altkirchliche Auslegung von Römer 1–11.* Düsseldorf: Patmos.

Schlatter, Adolf. 1935. *Gottes Gerechtigkeit: Ein Kommentar zum Römerbrief.* Stuttgart: Calwer.

———. 1995. *Romans: The Righteousness of God.* Trans. Siegfried S. Schatzmann. Peabody, Mass.: Hendrickson.

Schlier, Heinrich. 1977. *Der Römerbrief: Kommentar.* Herders theologischer Kommentar zum Neuen Testament 6. Freiburg: Herder.

Schmidt, Karl Ludwig. 1943. *Die Judenfrage im Lichte der Kapitel 9–11 des Römerbriefes.* Theologische Studien 13. Zurich: Evangelischer Verlag.

Schmithals, Walter. 1988. *Der Römerbrief: Ein Kommentar.* Gütersloh: Mohn.

Schmitt, Rainer. 1984. *Gottesgerechtigkeit-Heilsgeschichte — Israel in der Theologie des Paulus.* Europäische Hochschulschriften. Reihe 23, Theologie. Bd. 240. Frankfurt and New York: Lang.

Schoeps, Hans-Joachim. 1959. *Paulus: Die Theologie des Apostels im Lichte der jüdischen Religionsgeschichte.* Tübingen: Mohr.

Schreckenberg, Heinz. 1988. *Die christlichen Adversus-Judaeos-Texte (11.–13. Jh.): Mit einer Ikonographie des Judenthemas bis zum 4. Laterankonzil.* Europäische Hochschulschriften. Reihe 23, Theologie. Bd. 335. Frankfurt and New York: Lang.

Sickenberger, Joseph. 1932. *Die Briefe des Heiligen Paulus an die Korinther und Römer.* Vol. 6 of *Die Heilige Schrift des Neuen Testamentes übersetzt und erklärt.* Ed. Fritz Tillmann. 4th ed. Bonn: Hanstein.

Siegert, Folker. 1985. *Argumentation bei Paulus gezeigt an Röm 9–11.* Wissenschaftliche Untersuchungen zum Neuen Testament 34. Tübingen: Mohr.

Sievers, Joseph. 1997a. "A History of the Interpretation of Romans 11:29." *Annali di storia dell'esegesi* 14:381–442.

———. 1997b. " 'God's Gifts and Call Are Irrevocable': The Interpretation of Rom 11:29 and Its Uses." *SBL Seminar Papers* 36:337–57.

Smalley, Beryl. 1952. *The Study of the Bible in the Middle Ages.* 2nd ed. Oxford: Blackwell.

Smith, Alfred J. 1919. "The Commentary of Pelagius on Romans Compared with That of Origen-Rufinus." *Journal of Theological Studies* 20:127–77.

Sonderegger, Katharine A. 1992. *That Jesus Christ Was Born a Jew: Karl Barth's "Doctrine of Israel."* University Park, Pa.: Pennsylvania State University Press.

Souter, Alexander. 1922. *Pelagius's Expositions of Thirteen Epistles of St. Paul: Introduction.* Texts and Studies 9.1. Cambridge: Cambridge University Press.

———. 1926. *Pelagius's Expositions of Thirteen Epistles of St. Paul: Text and Apparatus Criticus.* Ed. Alexander Souter. Texts and Studies 9.2. Cambridge: Cambridge University Press.

———. 1927. *The Earliest Latin Commentaries on the Epistles of St. Paul.* Oxford: Clarendon.

Spicq, C. 1944. *Esquisse d'une histoire de l'exégèse latine au Moyen Age.* Bibliothèque Thomiste 26. Paris: Vrin.

———. 1960. "ΑΜΕΤΑΜΕΛΗΤΟΣ dans *Rom.* XI,29." *Revue biblique* 67:210–19.

———. 1978. "ἀμεταμέλητος." Pp. 72–74 in vol. 1 of *Notes de lexicographie Néo-Testamentaire.* Fribourg: Éditions Universitaires.

Staab, Karl. 1984. *Pauluskommentare aus der griechischen Kirche: Aus Katenenhandschriften gesammelt und herausgegeben.* 2nd ed. Münster: Aschendorff.

Stendahl, Krister. 1976. *Paul among Jews and Gentiles.* Philadelphia: Fortress.

Stowers, Stanley K. 1994. *A Rereading of Romans: Justice, Jews, and Gentiles.* New Haven: Yale University Press.

Stuhlmacher, Peter. 1971. "Zur Interpretation von Römer 11:25–32." Pp. 555–70 in *Probleme biblischer Theologie,* ed. Hans Walter Wolff. Munich: Kaiser.

———. 1989. *Der Brief an die Römer.* Das Neue Testament Deutsch 6. Göttingen: Vandenhoeck and Ruprecht.

Swidler, Leonard, et al. 1990. *Bursting the Bonds? A Jewish-Christian Dialogue on Jesus and Paul.* Faith Meets Faith Series. Maryknoll, N.Y.: Orbis.

Swiss Commission for Jewish-Roman Catholic Dialogue. 1992. "Anti-Semitism: A Sin Against God and Humanity." *SIDIC* (Journal of the Service Internationale de documentation judeo-chrétienne) 25.3:16–22.

Takeda, Takehisa. 1981. "Israel und die Völker: Die Israel-Lehre des Völkerapostels Paulus in seiner Bedeutung für uns gojim/ethne-Christen. Ein Weg zur Rezeption Israels als ein Weg zur biblischen Theologie." Th.D., Freie Universität Berlin.

Theobald, Michael. 1992. *Römerbrief Kapitel 1–11.* Stuttgarter kleiner Kommentar, Neues Testament 6.1. Stuttgart: KBW.

Tison, J.-M. 1961. "Salus Israel apud Patres primi et secundi saeculi." *Verbum domini* 39:97–108.

TRE. 1976–. *Theologische Realenzyklopädie.* Berlin: de Gruyter.

Tyconius. 1989. *The Book of Rules.* Trans. William S. Babcock. SBL Texts and Translations 31. Atlanta: Scholars Press.

Vaccari, A. 1964. "Irrevocabilità dei favori divini: Nota a commento di Rom XI,29." Pp. 437–42 in vol. 1 of *Mélanges Eugene Tisserant.* Vatican City: Bibliotheca Apostolica Vaticana.

Vanhoye, Albert. 1994. "Salut universel par le Christ et validité de l'Ancienne Alliance." *La nouvelle revue théologique* 116:815–35. (See also the author's "Rectification," *La nouvelle revue théologique* 118 [1996]: 66). An abridged Italian version of the article appeared in *La Civiltà Cattolica* 3467 (3 December 1994): 433–45.

WA. 1883. Luther, Martin. *Werke.* Kritische Gesamtausgabe [Weimarer Ausgabe]. Weimar: Böhlau.

Walter, Nikolaus. 1984. "Zur Interpretation von Römer 9–11." *Zeitschrift für Theologie und Kirche* 81:172–95.

Weber, E. 1911. *Das Problem der Heilsgeschichte nach Römer 9–11.* Leipzig: Deichert.

Weiss, Bernhard. 1899. *Der Brief an die Römer.* Kritisch-exegetischer Kommentar über das Neue Testament 4. 9th ed. Göttingen: Vandenhoeck and Ruprecht.

Wicks, Jared. 1991. "Biblical Criticism Criticized." *Gregorianum* 72:117–28.

Wilcken, Ulrich. 1934. "Ein liturgisches Fragment." No. 3, pp. 31–36 in *Mitteilungen aus der Würzburger Papyrussammlung.* Abhandlungen der Preußischen Akademie der Wissenschaften. Phil.-hist. Klasse 1933.6. Berlin: Verlag der Akademie der Wissenschaften.

Wilckens, Ulrich. 1980. *Der Brief an die Römer.* Evangelisch-katholischer Kommentar zum Neuen Testament 6.2. Zurich: Benziger.

Wolf, Jo. Christophorus. 1741. *Curae philologicae et criticae. Tomus III. In IV. priores Pauli epistolas quibus integrati contextus Graeci consulitur.* Basel: Johannes Christ.

Wright, N. T. 1991. *The Climax of the Covenant: Christ and the Law in Pauline Theology.* Edinburgh: T. & T. Clark.

Zahn, Theodor. 1910. *Der Brief des Paulus an die Römer.* Kommentar zum Neuen Testament 6. Leipzig: Deichert.

Zeller, Dieter. 1985. *Der Brief an die Römer.* Regensburger Neues Testament. Regensburg: Pustet.

Ziesler, John A. 1989. *Paul's Letter to the Romans.* Trinity Press International New Testament Commentaries. Philadelphia: Trinity Press International.

Romans 9–11 and Jewish-Christian Dialogue

Prospects and Provisos

Günter Wasserberg

———— ◆ ————

Preliminary Remarks on My Hermeneutic

C I was born and raised in postwar Germany.[1] These are givens in my life, not choices. When I traveled through Europe during my high school years I became increasingly aware of how people in other countries viewed Germany. Intrinsically linked to the name "German" are other names: Auschwitz, Treblinka, Bergen-Belsen, Birkenau — the *Shoah*. Once, at Speaker's Corner in London, I was confronted by a young Polish Jew when he discovered that I was a German. He yelled that I had killed his mother. I did not know what to say. Although I knew that I had not killed his mother, I nonetheless felt guilt. My attitude has changed over

H the years: I no longer feel guilty, but I do feel ashamed. And I feel the need to consciously and deliberately take on the responsibility to confront and deal with the German past — which is my past even if it precedes my birth. If we younger Germans are unwilling to hear the chorus of painful voices of the millions of Jews (and others) who were slaughtered, then no one in Germany will ever hear their voices. Most of my parents' generation have been unable to deal with its past. In this, but for quite different reasons, they strangely resemble those Jewish parents who until recently were unable to talk about the horrors of the *Shoah*.

C I am not only a postwar German, I am also a Christian brought up

---

C The *Shoah*.

H The shame and responsibility of being German.

C Lutheran tradition and German high culture.

in the Lutheran tradition. The horror of the *Shoah* is related not only to my national identity but also to my religious tradition. I am compelled to ask, How could the *Shoah* happen in the midst of a culture that rightly has been proud not only of Bach and Beethoven, Kant and Hegel, Goethe and Schiller, but also of Luther and the Reformation? It is not enough to point to some so-called Christian heroes such as Niemoeller or Bonhoeffer. In the case of Bonhoeffer we find a man who made great efforts to help Jews and to oppose Hitler, and was put to death as a result; yet, one should not forget what he said theologically about Judaism (see, e.g., Klein 1975, 118–19). We must not take comfort in creating heroes in order to ease a collective Christian conscience while not asking why the majority of Christians in Germany were silent when the deportation of their Jewish neighbors took place.[2] In what ways and to what extent Christian theology and practice are to be held accountable for the *Shoah* has been much discussed. But that Christians, with some notable exceptions, did not help prevent it is clear.

As a Lutheran, I also have to grapple with what Luther said about the Jews. I do not see a basic difference between the early and the late Luther in his writings on the Jews. What changes over time in Luther is his disappointment about the unwillingness of the Jews to become Christians after he had attempted to cleanse the gospel of what he saw as Rome's distortions of it. I find Luther's position on the Jews consistent from his early to his late writings in that if Christ is the ultimate offer of God's grace, then the Jews have lost the right to remain in their old, "legalistic" faith. If there is only one truth, then either "we" or "they" are wrong. Since we Christians cannot be wrong (says Luther), they, the Jews, must be wrong.

Disturbed by what I read in Luther, I turned to the New Testament. The New Testament (in combination with the Old Testament) is the central source of the Christian faith. Passages such as John 8:37–47 and Matthew 23, for example, are not the only ones that do not shed a favorable light on the Jews or the Pharisees. I have come to interpret the New Testament as in many ways a document about the evolving estrangement and separation of synagogue Jews and Christian Jews and Gentiles. This process was painful — on either side, although the New Testament tells the story only from the Christian perspective. One can read the New Testament as a grief document about this growing split within God's people.

In my dissertation (Wasserberg 1998) I took a closer look at Luke-Acts. Methodologically, I tried to allow "Luke" to tell his story instead of

---

H Luther: God's grace is in Christ, so Jews' legalistic faith is wrong.

A The New Testament as grief document about the estrangement of synagogue Jews, Christian Jews, and Gentiles.

imposing our contemporary needs to define appropriate parameters for Jewish-Christian dialogue. What is Luke-Acts' own self-understanding of Christian identity, and how does it view Judaism?[3] Is Luke's implied (or actual) audience already separated from the synagogue? My answer is

A that it is (and perhaps never had any real connection with the synagogue). Is Luke-Acts anti-Jewish? The answer depends on how one defines "anti-Jewish." At the least, it has polemical elements that come close to being identifiable as anti-Jewish.

H What is crucial in evaluating Luke-Acts is that the author (in my view) does not offer to us as modern readers a paradigm that would be helpful in Jewish-Christian dialogue if one approaches it (as I do) with the premise that Judaism is a religious entity that, theologically speaking, was and remains God's chosen people, even as Christians claim that they themselves are. The two religious traditions represent different responses to God's gracious love. Jews do not have to become Christians nor Christians Jews. The monotheistic religions Judaism and Christianity (and Islam) are self-sufficient religious systems. They are not lacking anything. They are not deficit entities. Each of them can stand on its own. Jews do not need Jesus, and Christians are not in need of Torah. I happen to be born into a Christian, Protestant, Lutheran environment; thus, I have to come to terms with my cultural-religious background as Jews and Moslems have to deal with theirs.

H Since the *Shoah,* for me (and many others) it is indisputable that we need to strive for an understanding of Christianity that is not anti-Jewish — an understanding that takes into account multiple ways to God. Exclusivity as practiced throughout the centuries is no longer acceptable. We must reject the narrow question about who is right and who is wrong. Multiple confessions of divine revelations, even competition between the different religious traditions, are warranted, though not at the price of claims of superiority. Feelings neither of superiority nor of inferiority should underlie the paradigm of mutual relations between Jews and Christians. Christians do not have to apologize for being Christians, nor Jews for being Jews.

C When I approach the New Testament with a hermeneutic such as this and an eye to Jewish-Christian dialogue or relations between Jews and Christians generally, the question arises whether the New Testament provides us with the kind of paradigm I have suggested. Then, in looking

---

A Luke's audience separated from the synagogue.

H Judaism as self-sufficient religious system of God's chosen people, even as Christians claim they themselves are.

H Non-anti-Jewish Christianity; thus, neither superiority nor inferiority between Jews and Christians.

C Jewish-Christian dialogue.

at the New Testament, surely (it might be said), if any of the New Testament documents comes close to what I regard as needed for a proper Jewish-Christian dialogue, Paul and his little treatise in Romans 9–11 on the relation of the Christian community to Israel fits the bill. To that question this paper is directed, and to those chapters I now turn, noting that what I outline below is very much a "work in progress" and inviting comments and criticisms as I seek better understanding of what for over twenty years has been my prime theological concern, Jewish-Christian relations and dialogue.

Romans 9–11 in the Context of Pauline Theology

Contrary to some interpreters of Paul, I regard it as important to view Romans 9–11 not only in the context of the entire letter but also in the framework of his theology as a whole. Granted, one has to be careful to read the undoubtedly Pauline letters as distinct entities. Nonetheless, I believe (and will seek to show) that Paul has a basic theological "core," 🅰 which in the process of his missionary efforts becomes clearer to him, and which he articulates more fully, as he encounters the various situations and problems that arise in the churches he founded or (in the case of Romans) that he surmises or conjectures. In that sense one can talk about different stages and developments of his theology.

Whatever the stages and developments, there is nonetheless a key to 🅰 Paul's theology (Becker 1993, 69–76): his "Damascus" experience which he describes in Gal. 1:15–16 in prophetic terms (cf. Jeremiah) as God's call — God revealed Jesus to him as God's son in order that Paul would proclaim him to the Gentiles. Luke's three reports of Paul's call (Acts 9, 22, 26) differ in many respects from Paul's own account in Galatians 1 and should therefore be examined separately; nonetheless, all three have Paul's sending to the Gentiles (9:15; 22:15, 21; 26:17) in common with Paul's own report. To be the apostle to the Gentiles is the specific profile of Paul's missionary efforts.

This view of Paul is probably one of the least disputed aspects of his theology. Of course, it does not exclude the possibility that Paul may have begun to carry out his call by preaching his gospel of Christ first to Jews. To think that Paul's call to be the apostle to the Gentiles immediately led him to leave his synagogue community is hard to believe. Rather, he will have started his mission, if not inside, then around the local synagogue community in Antioch in Syria. Had Paul preached only to Gentiles other than those whom Luke in Acts calls *sebomenoi (ton theon)* (Acts 13:50;

🅰 Romans 9–11 as expression of a stage of Paul's missionary theology.

🅰 Gal. 1:15–16: Damascus road experience as key to Paul's theology.

16:14; 17:4, 17; 18:7), that is, Gentiles who were more or less closely associated with the synagogue as sympathizers, then it would seem strange that Paul himself mentions Jewish persecutions and punishments (2 Cor. 11:24–26). Paul the missionary for Jesus Christ ran into trouble with synagogue authorities. But since that same Paul explicitly sees himself as the apostle to the Gentiles, it would seem that those Gentiles must have resembled — or included — those whom Acts designates as *sebomenoi*. The Gentiles to whom Paul addresses his gospel are most likely, by and large, sympathizers of the synagogue.

A   What is at the heart of Paul's gospel? It has as its source Paul's vision of Jesus as God's Son (Gal. 1:16). Even though Paul does not use many words in Galatians 1 when he talks about this turning point of his life, it nonetheless becomes clear that this vision is the reason why he can include himself among the apostles (1 Cor. 15:8) and claim his apostolic independence from Peter, James, and the Jerusalem church (Gal. 2:1–10). It is striking that Paul hardly ever uses Jesus traditions, even though he might well have heard more of them than he cites, not only from the Jerusalem church but most likely also from Christian Jews in Antioch. Paul displays little interest in the historical Jesus. His gospel focuses on the crucifixion and resurrection, and its source, he insists, is his own "Easter" experience of the risen Lord.

H   That experience meant for him *either* that for Gentiles Christ is the way Gentiles (but not Jews) enter into the covenant of God's chosen people, *or* that Jesus is the Messiah both for Gentiles and Jews. If the latter — universal salvation through Jesus the Messiah — that includes (indeed presupposes) Jews as addressees. But if the former is what Paul thought — Gentiles have Jesus as Messiah, Jews have the Torah — then

A   would he, a Jew, not continue to live as an observant Jew? In fact, he does not (Gal. 2:11–14): there is discontinuity between his life as a zealous Jew (Gal. 1:14) and his life after his encounter with the risen Lord, an experience that changes his understanding of Torah. His new identity as an apostle to the Gentiles presupposes Jesus' messiahship to Israel.[4]

H   The difference between the Jerusalem church and the Antioch church lies in the understanding each had of the meaning of Torah and thus in their understanding of Jesus as Messiah. The so-called apostolic agree-

A   ment that Paul refers to in Gal. 2:1–10 describes a kind of job sharing:

A Gal. 1:16 as Paul's own "Easter" experience.

H Jesus is the Messiah for Gentiles and Jews both.

A Discontinuity in Paul's life.

H Meaning of Torah and understanding of Jesus as the Messiah.

A Galatians 2: Christianity, most "successful" Judaism, denying centrality of Torah.

the Jerusalem church represented by Peter and James is to proclaim Jesus as Messiah among the circumcised, while the Antioch church represented by Paul and Barnabas will do so among the Gentiles. Since this proclamation of Jesus as Messiah to the Gentiles likely included or had as its consequence table fellowship of Jews and Gentiles (Gal. 2:11–14), this marks a decisive break with Jewish self-identity and lifestyle. Ironically, this break represented in Galatians by Antioch, a Jewish congregation that welcomes Gentiles in Christ as equals, becomes more successful than the Jerusalem church, a Jewish messianic party within the boundaries of Judaism. In this sense, one can say that Christianity (i.e., Judaism as a Gentile movement) is the most "successful" Judaism of all time (even as Paul, the "apostle to the Gentiles," is, ironically, the most famous Pharisee of all time). But one also has to be aware that this Christian version of Judaism cannot be harmonized with the Judaism from which it sprang, because it denies what is foundational to the Judaism of that day (and to this day): the centrality of Torah. In other words, a new understanding of Torah (which relativizes its centrality) is almost required and presupposed before Paul can go to the Gentiles and preach his "law-free" gospel.

Although Paul's understanding of Jesus as the Messiah marks a break **H** with "traditional" Judaism, he nonetheless sees his proclamation of that message as consistent with his Jewish identity: the God who is the father of Jesus the Messiah is the God of Israel who promised that Israel would be a blessing to the nations. Paul remains wholeheartedly Jewish and proud to be an Israelite (Rom. 11:1; 2 Cor. 11:22; Phil. 3:5). But that he focuses his gospel and his mission on Gentiles indicates a change in his **A** understanding of Judaism (Phil. 3:7–11) and in his self-understanding and his daily practice as a Jew. As is evident from 2 Cor. 11:24–26, for many Jews Paul had crossed the Torah line that set Jews off from Gentiles and threatened Jewish identity both through his message and his behavior in relation to Gentiles. For Paul, however, the Christ event marks a new definition of God's election. The Jews God's chosen people, and they will remain so (Rom. 11:1), but now the Gentiles also have unlimited access to the God of Israel.

This is how I see the theological framework for reading Romans 9–11. That theology is Jewish inasmuch as Paul claims that Jesus is a Jew **A** and the Jewish Messiah. But Jesus is the Messiah also for Gentiles, that is, for all peoples, whether Jews or Gentiles (Rom. 1:16). Paul's theology breaks with Torah Judaism inasmuch as he claims that the Torah has lost

---

H Christ event is God's election redefined; it is for Jews and also for Gentiles.

A Paul's Gentile focus indicating changes in his understanding of Judaism.

A The Jesus movement and the early Jerusalem church were Jewish.

H its binding authority. To perceive Paul as, on the one hand, remaining a faithful Jew while, on the other hand, proclaiming Jesus as Messiah for the Gentiles without the law seems to posit a certain schizophrenia in Paul. Dividing up Paul in this way does not represent what we find in

C Galatians, as I noted previously. But it does seem to fit our own need, after the *Shoah*, for a "harmonious" paradigm of Jewish-Christian relations and dialogue. While I understand this need — I am striving for some way to meet it for myself! — I am less optimistic than many others that it works, let alone whether it is Pauline.

Romans 9–11: Israel and Jesus Christ — God Interrogated

C If the gospel (of Christ) is God's power for salvation for the Jew first and also for the Greek (Rom. 1:16), then any Jewish refusal of this gospel poses a fundamental problem for the core of the Christ proclamation. As I have previously mentioned, with regard to Jesus, Paul focuses almost exclusively on the cross and resurrection. This is the basic point of the gospel. It is important to keep in mind that, unlike Abraham, Jesus did not die as an old man nor, Socrates-like, with his disciples gathered around him, imparting pearls of wisdom such as, "Now the Gentiles are equal partners in the people of God." Rather, he died young — a horrible death on a Roman cross. Nor do Gentiles appear to be the addressees of the earthly Jesus; nor did the first Easter experiences involve them. The Jesus movement and the early Jerusalem church were Jewish. The positive implications the Christ event might *also* have for Gentiles apparently were not at first realized within the Jerusalem synagogue-church — that evidently first came in Antioch. For Paul, Jews continue to be the primary addressees (Rom. 1:16, 2:10).

This then poses a fundamental problem for Christian proclamation: why do most Jews reject the gospel? Even if, as Gaston (1995) sees it, it were correct that Israel's misstep lies in the claim to expand the

A observance of Torah to the Gentiles (according to Acts), it still leaves unanswered the question of why Jews who proclaimed Christ to fellow Jews were expelled from Jerusalem (Acts 8:1b; 11:19). The interpretation of the Christ event must have been highly controversial within Judaism. Paul's struggle in Romans 9–11 is not about Christ; it is about God.[5]

H Paul cannot be a faithful Jew and proclaim Jesus as Messiah for Gentiles.

C After the *Shoah*, one needs Paul as a faithful Jew who proclaims Jesus as Messiah for Gentiles.

C Problem for early Christianity: why do most Jews reject the gospel?

A Acts: the interpretation of the Christ event was controversial within Judaism.

If Christ means salvation both for Jews and Gentiles, then any Jewish refusal of that claim calls God into question. This issue needs to be addressed. **H**

In his beginning remarks (Rom. 9:1–5) Paul expresses his deep sorrow and anguish over the fact that Israel has not yet come to faith in Christ, who is God (9:5).[6] This opening doxology sets the stage (while the doxology in 11:33–36 closes it) and demonstrates that for Paul, theology and Christology are so closely related that they become almost interchangeable. **A**

The focus here is not on the Gentiles but on Israel. The split over Christ within Israel raises the serious question as to whether God's word has failed (Rom. 9:6). God is being interrogated. Throughout the history of Israel God has shown that he elects whom he wills. His sovereignty **A** is beyond question. Paul extends this line of thought from Israel's patriarchs onward (9:9–13) to Egypt's Pharaoh (9:15–17) and then to all of humanity: the creature has no right to question the Creator (9:20–21). From this perspective there is no difference between Jews and other peoples. Thus, to be born a Jew is not a privilege in itself (cf. 10:12), because not all Israelites are Israel (9:6), that is, belong to the children of the promise (9:8). These children of the promise consist of Jews who believe in Christ — the "remnant" (9:27) — and of Gentiles, the newly elected people of God (9:24–26). The metaphoric language about the vessels of wrath and the vessels of glory in verses 9:22–23 on the one hand demonstrates God's free will and on the other hand hints already at ch. 11 with the solution of the problem of Jewish refusal of Christ. What seems to be destined for the detriment of Israel eventually is meant for the salvation of Jews and Gentiles both.

The Jews, who have tried to obtain "uprightness" through the law, have stumbled, whereas those Gentiles who believe in Christ have attained it through faith (9:30–32). Granted, the law is holy (7:12) — more so in Romans than in Galatians. The law reveals God's will to Israel, but in the course of time it became obvious that humanity failed to live according to the law. The blame rests on all humanity, first on Israel as God's chosen people (Rom. 2:17–3:20), but also on non-Jews, who have always had a basic understanding of what is right or wrong in the eyes of God (2:1–16). Therefore, Christ in his self-sacrifice on the cross is the *telos*, the culmination as well as the conclusion of the law (10:4). The law is not to be understood as "works-righteousness," a form of

---

H God called into question by the Jewish refusal of Christ.

A Opening and closing doxologies (Rom. 9:5; 11:33–36) indicate that theology and Christology are interchangeable.

A How God governs the history of Israel for the salvation of Jews and Gentiles both (Rom. 9:6–28).

self-justification (that is a Lutheran distortion). Rather, in the light of the Christ event the law has lost its function as the avenue to salvation. What Jews and Gentiles alike with their faith in Christ have already obtained (10:11–14), other Jews will also eventually come to realize. There is no question for Paul that Jews need Jesus as their savior as much as Gentiles do (10:13).

Still, the question remains why such a large portion of Israel thus far has not accepted the gospel. Paul says it is not because Christ has not been preached to Israel[7] — it even has been proclaimed unto the ends of the earth (Rom. 10:18). The proclamation of the gospel to the Gentiles also had the function of stirring the Jews in order that they too might come to faith in Christ (10:19–20; cf. 11:11). There is no excuse: in rejecting Christ, Israel has been a disobedient people (10:21).

But Jewish disobedience with regard to faith in Christ does not lead to rejection by God (Rom. 11:1). No "church" ever replaces Israel as God's chosen people![8] On this, Paul is emphatic: "Has God rejected his people? By no means! I myself am an Israelite, a descendant of Abraham, a member of the tribe of Benjamin. God has not rejected his people whom he foreknew" (11:1–2). God's election of Israel will never be abrogated. Paul's approach to Israel is dialectic: with regard to Christ there is no privilege on Israel's side. Jews and Gentiles alike become children of the promise (9:8; cf. Gal. 4:28). With regard to possible Gentile boasting over Israel Paul emphatically takes pride in his Jewish ancestry. But he also makes it clear that those in Israel who have not accepted Christ are hardened. That God is the agent of this hardening also is obvious and is backed up by Paul's reference to scriptural passages that he alludes to or quotes from (Rom. 11:8–10).

Thus, one last question remains: *Why* has God hardened the hearts of Israel? Answer: Israel's rejection of Christ is part of God's plan of salvation. Israel has stumbled but will not fall (Rom. 11:11) — which, again, indirectly shows that Israel is also supposed to come to believe in Christ. What is their *paraptōma* ("transgression," 11:11–12) but their refusal to believe in Christ? But since God is the agent behind this refusal, their transgression has to be seen in a salvific framework: through Israel's stumbling the Gentiles have gained access to God's salvation (11:11–12). This is part one of God's plan.

The second part, its flip side, is God's use of Gentiles coming to faith in Christ to incite the Jews, to make them jealous (Rom. 11:11, 13–14), so that they do not remain in a state of stumbling but (as it were) rise

---

A In rejecting the preaching of the gospel, Israel is disobedient (Rom. 10:14–21).

A Israel is not rejected but hardened; its not accepting Christ is a part of God's plan of salvation of all in covenant with Christ as foundation (Rom. 11:1–16).

from the dead and claim their rightful place in God's plan as the holy "first fruits" and the holy "root" (11:15–16). The ultimate goal of the second part of God's plan of salvation, then, is to bring both — Jews and Gentiles — into God's covenant with Christ as its foundation.

The final doxology (Rom. 11:33–36) is formulated "in pure God-language" (Stendahl 1995, 38), which need not surprise us because, as I stated previously, it is not the Christ event that is being questioned but God. Thus, Stendahl's question, "Why is Paul so overtly non-christological at exactly this point and so unlike the rest of the epistles?" (39), has to be answered as outlined above. To claim, as Stendahl does, that "Paul shatters universalism" (39) and upholds "the wonderful ◨ particularism of Israel" (44) misses Paul's point. As much as I agree with Stendahl's analysis of Paul with regard to the present-day situation of interdenominational and interreligious dialogue, I do not see how Sten- ◙ dahl's reading of Paul accords with Paul's thought. For Paul, Christ is the ultimate avenue to salvation for all, whether Jew or Gentile. It was the Jews' delay in coming to recognize Christ that had become an agonizing problem for his mission and for him personally. Insofar as one can, with Stendahl, describe Romans as a letter about "missiology, not soteriology" (41), it nonetheless has Christ as the foundation for the mission to Jews and Gentiles both. Stendahl's paraphrase of Paul's attitude towards Israel, "Get off the backs of the Jews, and leave them in the hands of God" (40), is right. I also wholeheartedly agree with the first part of Stendahl's following sentence: "God has the power to realize their (i.e., the Jews') salvation"; but to say that this salvation "is definitely not cast in christological terms" (40), while grammatically possible, is theologically dubious. In Romans 9–11 Paul has no need to expand further on his Christology (as soteriology) — that he has dealt with sufficiently in the first eight chapters of Romans. If faith in Christ is God's power to salvation for Jews *first* but also for Greeks (1:16), then Israel's attitude is indeed crucial, and Israel's rejection of that salvation calls God into question. What Paul in 11:25 calls *mysterion* is not something mysteri- ◧ ous in the sense of a riddle, but something that fills him with great awe and moves him to ponder in wonder God's ways. The only adequate response to this divine *mysterion* is to burst out in joyful exaltation in praise of God (11.33–36).

◨ Against Stendahl's nonchristological affirmation of Israel's particularism.

◙ Analysis of Paul shaped by contemporary interdenominational and interreligious dialogue.

◧ Christ as ultimate avenue of salvation for all, including Jews, is mystery (Rom. 11:25) consistent with the rest of Romans (cf. 1:16).

Conclusion

C If my reading of Paul has merit, then his paradigm cannot provide the model for Jewish-Christian relations. Paul hoped that Israel would not **A** remain aloof from salvation through Christ forever. To interpret Paul as advocating a two-scheme salvation — Torah for Jews, Christ for Gentiles — is, I believe, neither Pauline nor based on any other New Testament author. To be sure, such an interpretation seems to meet the requirements of what is needed after the *Shoah*. But it also seems to project onto Paul a modern kind of tolerance that would be alien to him. I do not think Paul was schizophrenic in dividing his understanding of God's salvation into two parts. After all, Paul was a Jew and continued to perceive himself as a Jew, one who believed in Christ. Whether he was aware that his understanding of Judaism in light of the Christ event in effect abrogated Judaism by denying to the law the position it occupied in much of Judaism in his day is a different question. He certainly did not think of himself as an apostate, but in the eyes of synagogue Jews such a verdict would make sense and would constitute grounds for inflicting punishment on him as a result.

A That some Jews found Paul's view of salvation difficult to accept is evident from Acts, where the author constructs a Paul who is Jewish in a way that Paul would not have been able to affirm. If one were to put the Lukan Paul into a room with the Paul of his letters, they would soon be arguing with one another. There is no way to harmonize these two Pauls.[9] But the fact that Luke constructs this Jewish-Pharisaic-Christian Paul is an indication that the "historical Paul" had gone way too far for other Jewish followers of Jesus to accept. This is one more indication to me that Paul was rightly perceived as a threat to Jewish identity. And he still is. He believed that Jews would have to come to accept Jesus as their Messiah and savior.

H This view of Jews "worked" as long as it was held within Christian walls, as it was for centuries, taking Jews as paradigms for human behavior in general (Augustine, Luther). In this I agree with the criticisms Stendahl has raised. It is a distortion of Paul's thought, taking it out of context. Nonetheless, in using Paul as a framework for their theology and reading him christologically — and exclusivistically — Augustine and Luther were, I believe, being true to what I have tried to outline as basic to his theology: Christ is a savior not only for the Gentiles, but also for the Jews. And that separates me from Paul. I do not regard Judaism as a deficient religion, although I am afraid that is exactly what is implicit and sometimes explicit in the New Testament. Therefore I fear that we have

---

C Christ as ultimate salvation for all is not useful in Jewish-Christian relations.

A Two-scheme salvation — Torah for Jews, Christ for Gentiles — is not Pauline.

A Lukan Paul differs from historical Paul.

H Judaism as paradigm of deficient religions.

to admit that Paul, and the New Testament generally, do not provide us with a paradigm that is useful or helpful for Jewish-Christian relations.

As long as I move in Christian circles, I might perhaps feel at ease with **C** a view of faith in Christ as savior of all and might wonder why Jews cannot see the advantages of Christianity. But as soon as I step outside and become aware of the synagogue, I come to the painful realization that not only is the New Testament perception of Jews negative and polemical but so too, by extension (or by our reading of it), is its view of Judaism today. I find that unacceptable. Jews are as much saved as are Christians, even as they are in as much need of God's love and forgiveness as are Christians. If we could perceive Judaism and Christianity as two different religious paradigms that are expressive of our human needs and strivings, I would be more at ease. But I fear that many Christians will not leave Jews in peace, because the Christian claim that Christ is the universal savior is directed also toward Jews. The Jewish "no" is a deep **C** wound to the Christian soul. That wound contributed to what happened in Germany under National Socialism. And as long as we do not perceive the problematic and potentially explosive dynamics underlying Christian texts and discourse about Judaism, similar *Shoahs* may result. That is my fear. Maybe I am wrong. I hope I am wrong.

While I have great respect for scholars such as Stendahl, Gaston, and **H** Nanos — I have learned much from them — I suspect that despite all their efforts to criticize anti-Jewish interpretations of Romans, they take too easy a way out of a fundamental problem inherent in Christianity. How can we resolve this problem, or at least leave it open in a way that respects both Judaism and Christianity? Despite all, what we can learn from Paul is to be reminded that Israel's election remains valid. How, then, to define Christianity in a way that does not deny Judaism the Torah as God's way of salvation for Jews? Or, in the phrasing of Rosemary Radford Ruether (1974), how to affirm Christian Christology without at the same time affirming its "anti-Judaic left hand?"[10]

Notes

1. I wish to thank Dr. Harold Remus, professor emeritus, Wilfrid Laurier University, for his help in editing this paper and in improving my English.

2. Christians living in other countries have their own questions to ask about the behavior of their governments when the exterminations were going on.

C Paul's views can be kept only as long as Jews are absent in closed "Christian circles."

C The Jewish "no" to Christ as universal savior is a deep wound to the Christian soul that engenders the *Shoah*.

H Christianity has an anti-Jewish "left hand."

3. I am aware of the artificiality of these terminologies: there is no one Judaism and no one Christianity. To describe these socioreligious entities adequately is difficult.

4. If Jesus is not the Messiah for Israel, but only for Gentiles, then (looking beyond Paul) that overlooks Jesus' own proclamation of the coming reign of God, which has Israel as the main addressee (Becker 1998). And if Christ died and rose only so that Gentiles might have access to God's covenant with Israel, then why do the first witnesses to the resurrection — all Jews — proclaim the risen Jesus as their own hope? Peter and the other apostles did not leave their Jewish context and seek to carry on a Gentile mission. Why did they proclaim Jesus as Israel's Messiah if the gospel was not aimed at Israel?

5. This, by the way, explains the rare explicit mentioning of Christ in Romans 9–11, which I believe leads Stendahl (1995, 38) in a wrong direction.

6. According to one punctuation (Fitzmyer 1993, 548–49).

7. Note in Rom. 10:17: the word of Christ not the law!

8. On the much discussed term "Israel of God" (Gal. 6:16), see Betz 1979, 322–23.

9. *Pace* Nanos, who takes the Lukan Paul for the Paul of the letters.

10. "The character of anti-Judaic thinking in the Christian tradition cannot be correctly evaluated until it is seen as the negative side of its christological hermeneutic" (Ruether 1974, 64).

References

Becker, Jürgen. 1993. *Paul: Apostle to the Gentiles.* Trans. O. C. Dean Jr. Louisville: Westminster/John Knox.

———. 1998. *Jesus of Nazareth.* Trans. James E. Crouch. New York: Walter de Gruyter.

Betz, Hans Dieter. 1979. *Galatians: A Commentary on Paul's Letter to the Churches in Galatia.* Hermeneia. Philadelphia: Fortress.

Fitzmyer, Joseph. 1993. *Romans: A New Translation and Commentary.* Anchor Bible 33. New York: Doubleday.

Gaston, Lloyd. 1987. *Paul and the Torah.* Vancouver: University of British Columbia Press.

———. 1995. "Israel's Misstep in the Eyes of Paul." Pp. 309–26 in *The Romans Debate,* ed. Karl P. Donfried. Peabody, Mass.: Hendrickson.

Klein, Charlotte. 1975. *Anti-Judaism in Christian Theology.* Philadelphia: Fortress.

Nanos, Mark D. 1996. *The Mystery of Romans: The Jewish Context of Paul's Letters.* Minneapolis: Fortress.

Ruether, Rosemary Radford. 1974. *Faith and Fratricide: The Theological Roots of Anti-Semitism.* New York: Seabury.

Stendahl, Krister. 1995. *Final Account: Paul's Letter to the Romans.* Minneapolis: Fortress.

Wasserberg, Günter. 1998. *Aus Israels Mitte — Heil für die Welt: Eine narrativ-exegetische Studie zur Theologie des Lukas.* Berlin and New York: Walter de Gruyter.

SEVEN

Divergent Images of Paul
and His Mission

William S. Campbell

Examples from the Reception of Romans
in the Twentieth Century

A certain duplicity in Paul's Epistle to the Romans has been observed by a number of interpreters from C. H. Dodd to more recent scholars such as Heikki Räisänen of Helsinki, Francis Watson of London, and Charles Cosgrove in the United States. Although there are several points where lack of clarity or consistency emerges, the most frequently discussed chapters tend to be Romans 9 and 11, which are seen by quite a few scholars as somewhat at odds with each other.

Dodd sets out the issue with exquisite clarity: "The fact is that the **A** whole argument of 3:1–8 is obscure and feeble. When Paul, who is normally a clear as well as a forcible thinker, becomes feeble and obscure, it usually means that he is defending a poor case. His case is inevitably a poor one, since he is trying to show that, although there is no par- **H** tiality about God, yet the Jew's superiority is, somehow, much in every way. It is no wonder that he becomes embarrassed, and in the end dismisses the subject awkwardly" (1932, 46). Dodd continues in similar vein on Rom. 3:9: "Well, now, are we Jews in a better position? Not at all. . . . Though temporarily and relatively the Jews have a certain advantage, yet in an absolute view of the matter, that advantage vanishes. This is very near to [Paul's] conclusions in chapters 9–11 and it is at least a possible interpretation of the Greek here" (47–48).

Dodd's diagnosis of the reasons for Paul's weak arguments was that Paul had argued from the promise to Abraham on two divergent and

A Inconsistencies in Paul's argument.

H God's impartiality versus favoritism toward Israel.

perhaps inconsistent lines (1932, 183), and his logic was vitiated by his emotional interest in his own people. Logically, the Jew can have no advantage whatsoever, but "the trouble is that the 'Jewish objector' is in Paul's own mind. His Pharisaism — or shall we say his patriotism? — was too deeply ingrained for him to put right out of his mind the idea that somehow the divine covenant with mankind has a 'most favoured nation clause' " (43).

A brief glance at Watson's criticisms will illustrate similar problems with Paul's argument: "It is ironic that Paul's arguments for the consistency of God in 9–11 are themselves inconsistent for Romans 11 is based on the definition of the chosen people rejected in Romans 9" (1986, 168). Heikki Räisänen's criticisms are similar. E. P. Sanders, on the other hand, **A** maintains that part of the problem with Paul is his method of argument — the apostle does not, as we would normally expect, argue from problem to solution but on the contrary, from solution back to problem (1977, 442ff., 499). Nevertheless, Sanders too admits in relation to chapters 9–11 that what is noteworthy is not so much the ideas they contain but the feelings of anguish, concern, and triumphant expectation that Paul expresses in relation to his own people (1983, 193). Paul's solution in ch. 11 is a "somewhat desperate expedient" to meet the problem of "competing convictions which can be better asserted than explained": reconciling native convictions with those received by revelation. Paul's anguish is that he seeks desperately for "a formula which would keep God's promises to Israel intact, while insisting on faith in Jesus Christ" **A** (1983, 197–99). That we are confronted by a variety of readings of Paul's letter is occasioned largely by the difficulty of his topic as much as by his style and method of argument — the use of diatribe style in large sections of the letter and the frequent recourse to the Hebrew Scriptures, especially in chapters 9–11, increase the potential for diverse readings and charges of at least apparent inconsistency. We are particularly in- **A** terested in the canons of consistency, the standards of measurement, the criteria by which we are to esteem one reading as more acceptable than another. In this regard it is illuminating to note the charges or explanations that are stated as reasons for Paul's failure to convince or to maintain consistency.

A   The apostle has confused relative advantage with absolute advantage, perhaps because of patriotic and emotional attachment to his own people (Dodd 1932, 43); anguish and concern to solve an insoluble problem

---

A Paul's arguments are inconsistent because they are emotional and go from solution to problem.

A Paul's arguments appear inconsistent.

A Interpreters' canons of consistency.

A Paul's and his interpreters' standards of consistency.

(Sanders 1983, 199; Räisänen 1988, 195–96); a new revelation received as Paul wrestled with the subject matter in writing Romans (Noack 1965, 165–66); if one does not wish to conclude that Paul was capable of thinking coherently only for very short periods of time and if one rejects an artificial harmonizing process, the only possible solution lies in examining afresh the social context and function of Romans in order to make coherent sense of it (Watson 1986, 170). I note in passing the need to be careful lest we seek anachronistically to judge Paul by our standards of logic and consistency, and the need also to maintain an awareness that Paul was operating in a culture very different from ours, where somewhat different standards of consistency — perhaps even of rationality — and methods of argument applied. Paul was, after all, seeking to convince a first-century audience, and we must not judge as if he had targeted us.

But allowing for all the explanations and reasons that help us to understand the apostle and his letters, it must still be noted that the most powerful voice that can be raised against the apostle is his own. This can have three main forms. The first form of Paul's voice comes from his other letters written prior to Romans. From them, particularly from Galatians, we know the content of Paul's gospel already, and we legitimately expect what we find in Romans to harmonize with this, the Early Paul, or at least the Earlier Paul. The second form of Paul's voice emerges not so much from what he said as from what he did — his missionary activity as apostle to the Gentiles; we expect him to fight for them and to uphold their rights. The third form of Paul's voice is, however, the most powerful of all, and it is this that raises such difficulties in Romans. In the earlier part of the letter, even up to the end of ch. 9, or perhaps for some, the end of ch. 10, many see what they recognize as the familiar (Earlier) Paul. But in ch. 11 another voice of Paul suddenly and surprisingly appears — what we might call the Later Paul. This Paul seems to some to be completely at odds with the Earlier Paul, and contrasts sharply with the previously well-known pattern of his life and his publicly proclaimed gospel in his letters to other churches. Is the different voice the result of the apostle facing a changed situation, or the outcome of a development in his thought?

Which is the genuine voice of Paul? Will the real apostle please stand forth! Various strategies may be adopted here. One is to put all the weight on Romans 1–8, 1–9, or even 1–10, and to interpret ch. 11 from the perspective of the rest of the letter, thereby reducing the significance of its specific contribution. This has been a dominant pattern among some Lutheran interpreters,[1] but there are many parallels in Dodd. Dodd was of

---

🅰 Paul's inconsistency in his "three voices."

🅰 Achieving consistency by forcing Romans 11 into chs. 1–10.

the opinion that Rom. 12:1ff. seems to be the real sequel to 8:39, rather than chs. 9–11, which are a somewhat self-contained unit, a treatise or sermon possibly in existence prior to the writing of Romans (1932, 148). The surprise resulting from the inclusion of chs. 9–11 at this point arises from the fact that Paul has earlier in the letter apparently spoken of the abrogation of the privilege of Israel in a dispensation in which no distinctions are drawn (151). This means in practice ignoring or dismissing at least part of ch. 11, and presuming we already know and understand the *authentic* Paul without the wisdom or otherwise of ch. 11. The outcome of this may well produce a view of Israel entirely at odds with Paul's con-
C clusion at the end of ch. 11. Israel is not saved but has lost any special status whatsoever; according to Klein, Paul's theology "radikal entheiligt und paganisiert... die Geschichte Israels" ("radically profanes and paganizes the history of Israel") (1963, 441). Klein's perspective typifies the approach of those who tend to force the contents of Romans 11 to fit the mold of the Paul they already know and understand from elsewhere — the apostle to the Gentiles or, more specifically, the Paul of Paulinism.

Klein's essay, of course, was written some thirty-five years ago, and we must allow for the changes and development in interpretation since then. Nevertheless, there are close parallels even in a very recent study. Cosgrove cannot help stressing what a surprise is the content of Rom. 11:25ff. in an otherwise coherent argument in Romans. Because of this, he remarks, "If what Paul affirms about Israel in Romans 11 comes as a surprise, that in itself shows how strong the countervailing reading of Romans 9 is" (1997, 29). Likewise, he questions, "If Paul's teaching about divine impartiality seems to contradict the notion of a special election of the Jewish people, is it reasonable to affirm that special election when one can also reasonably construe his arguments in a way that does not require this conclusion?" (37).

What emerges from the preceding overview of opinions is that Romans 11 has become a focal point in the discussion. This marks a refinement of the earlier view that sought to interpret chs. 9–11 from the perspective of chs. 1–8, and thus somewhat neutralize its contribution; but now it is recognized that chs. 9–10 fit reasonably well with the content of
A chs. 1–8. This in effect isolates ch. 11 and highlights apparent discrepancies between its contents and that of ch. 9 (cf. Watson 1986, 168–72; Räisänen 1988, 182, 192ff.; Cosgrove 1997, 30–37). Thus, Romans 11 and especially its conclusion come as a somewhat surprise intrusion in a letter that can be consistently interpreted in a direction other than what that chapter suggests. This probably indicates that the work done in recent years on the connections between chs. 1–8 and chs. 9–11 has been

---

C Israel is not saved, has lost its special status (Lutheran context of thirty-five years ago).

A Highlighting inconsistency between Romans 11 and chs. 1–10.

partially successful in demonstrating real links across these chapters. But the problem of perceived contradictions between the content of ch. 11 and that of ch. 9 or of the whole of the earlier part of the letter remains, for some scholars at least, a serious obstacle.

One possible explanation of this interpretive conundrum in the history of the exegesis of Romans is not just that there are divergent readings of the letter itself, but rather that there were already in existence, whether implicitly or explicitly, divergent understandings of the significance of **A** Paul's gospel and mission. It may in fact be the existence of these that forms part of the explanation for the parallel, if not conflicting, readings of his letter to the Romans.

Paul, Champion of the Gentiles: The Partisan Paul

If the Roman Christians were aware even indirectly of the contents of **C** Galatians and possibly of some of his other earlier letters, and knew a certain amount of information, reliable and otherwise, about the apostle to the Gentiles who had promised to visit them for some time now, then they already would have formed a specific view of Paul and his theological opinions, especially in respect to the Gentiles. They would certainly have been familiar with a rough outline of his gospel. We need to differentiate between what Paul knew of the Romans and what they thought they knew about him. Thus, although he had not yet been to Rome, Paul was not a complete stranger to the Roman Christians.

It would appear, however, that their perception of the apostle may, in fact, have been slightly misguided, especially as to how they understood the significance of his Gentile mission. Paul may have been understood by the Roman Gentile Christians as being pro-Gentile and, conversely, as being indifferent to Jews. Paul's inclusion in the letter of phrases such as "to the Jew first" may indicate a correction of their viewpoint in this area. This hypothesis would gain support also from the content of Rom. 11:13ff., where it is clear that Paul wishes to correct the Gentile Christians' self-understanding in relation to Israel.

If we can project an image of Paul as he can be understood from his personal experience in his call and so forth from his writings prior to Romans (or reports of same), and from the impression created by his mission to the Gentiles (such as the creation of mainly Gentile communities exercising a certain degree of freedom in relation to the Jewish law), then we can envisage how Paul might have been viewed by the Gentile

---

A Divergent understandings of Paul's mission.
C The Roman Christians' self-understanding and the pro-Gentile Paul.

Christians at Rome. He was probably seen as the champion of the cause of Gentiles throughout the church and at the council of Jerusalem and so forth — a pro-Gentile Paul committed to winning the Gentile world and indifferent to the concerns of Judaism.

[H]   In many ways this pro-Gentile Paul closely resembles the Paul of liberal scholarship as reflected in the work of someone like Dodd. The emphases on "no distinction" and on the universal scope of the gospel are only two aspects of this portrait. But it includes the assumption that Jews who accepted the gospel, even those not situated within the Pauline mission area, would cease to associate with the synagogue community and probably also cease to abide by the law. An associated mindset may have been the tendency to view almost all Paul's opponents as Judaizers. At every point of contact Paul seems to be in conflict with Jewish Christians and the Jerusalem Christian leaders. This reading derived much of its strength from the Lutheran tendency to stress the antithesis between the gospel and the law. It was therefore simply assumed that Paul and his Gentile mission were engaged in an ongoing war with Jewish Christians and Judaism — two competing cultures and missions. Existentialist theology, such as that of Rudolf Bultmann, did little to challenge the prevailing current of opinion, mainly because of a lack of interest in historical continuity between the old and the new. So the continuity between Paul's Gentile communities and the Jewish roots of their faith was seldom stressed, while radical discontinuity was everywhere assumed.

It is difficult to be precise in broad areas of interpretation such as these, but it would appear that here we have in outline the generally accepted image of Paul and his mission that continued to dominate until about 1970, and that is viewed by many as the norm even up to the present time.

[H]   An alternative opinion was already in process with the work of Johannes Munck in the 1950s.[2] Munck's interest in a fresh appraisal of Paul's thought, especially as represented in Romans 9–11 was, more than a decade later, advanced by Krister Stendahl's timely stress upon Paul's thought and mission as encompassing real Jews and Gentiles (1976a). The solid mold of Pauline scholarship had been broken and this opened up the way for a fresh appreciation of the apostle, particularly from the perspective of Romans, around which an increasing volume of scholarship would rapidly concentrate.

[H]   The outcome of this scholarly development has gradually led to a rediscovery of the Jewishness of Paul and therefore to a more bal-

---

[H] Lutheran discontinuity between old and new.
[H] Continuity between old and new.
[H] Jewishness of Paul.

anced reading of his theology and practice. The new perspective on Paul necessarily took account of a fresh understanding of Romans 9–11, particularly as these chapters could no longer be viewed as being simply an appendix of secondary importance in the interpretation of the letter. Assisted as it was by the growing interest in the relevance of the Holocaust **C** for the interpretation of the New Testament, by a blossoming interest **A** in a sociological approach to the study of the Christian origins,[3] and by recent critiques of the Lutheran understanding of faith and works, the scene was set for a revised understanding of Paul's thought and work. This radical reassessment of Paul is well demonstrated in the coining by James Dunn (1983) of the now well-known term "the new perspective on Paul."

In my opinion, the conflict surrounding the question of contradictions **A** in Paul's thought arises mainly from a debate as to what constitutes the "real Paul." Is he the heroic Paul who is depicted as the champion of the Gentiles, or is he the "revised Paul" of Romans, especially of Romans 11? To put it another way: is the real Paul to be identified with the previous pro-Gentile image of the apostle, or with the recent more Jewish Paul identified in Romans, particularly in chs. 9–11? Is the apostle really pro-Gentile, partial to Gentiles and their cause, or is his gospel — "to the Jew first and also to the Gentile" — inclusive and impartial?

The answer we give to these questions is crucial if we are not to be left with two strongly conflicting images of the apostle and his mission. Is it really likely that Paul would recognize the rights of Jewish Christians in certain situations to continue to abide by the law? Would he not have advocated that they forsake the synagogue? Did he recognize continuing distinctions between Jews and Gentiles even in Christ, so that ethnic differences remain a consideration in some contexts? Did he stress a certain priority for the Jew in the purpose of God, and did he really hold that God had not cast off Israel but would still save "all Israel" in some miraculous way in the future? It could, of course, be argued that this revised reading of Paul emerges from post-Holocaust guilt,[4] and that we are now trying to update our image of him to suit a revised understanding of what constitutes liberal Christianity. We are perhaps, after all, still "discovering" the image of Paul we expect to find. Whatever our response to this issue, it is necessary to look again at some of the texts where our conflicting images of Paul are generated, and to seek afresh to assess which image they most support.

C Relevance of the Holocaust for New Testament interpretation.

A Sociological approach to the study of Christian origins.

A Question of contradictions arises from debate about the "real Paul."

Continuity between Romans 3–4 and Romans 9–11

A There are obvious links between Rom. 3:1ff. and 9–11 that we do not need to discuss in detail here: the advantage of the Jew, the value of circumcision, and the faithfulness of God despite the faithlessness of Israel are clearly common themes noted in ch. 3 to be dealt with in detail later. There are, however, other points in ch. 4 that again point beyond themselves to an anticipated later sequel. Adolf von Schlatter correctly perceives the relevance of Abraham in ch. 4 for the rest of the letter: "If this section of the letter were missing, much of the clarity of the second part of the letter would be removed. Why are there two types of sons of Abraham, and why is Israel the olive tree into which the believer is grafted?"(1995, 107).

One of the more interesting of these "forward looking" passages is Rom. 4:16, where the aim of Paul's discussion of Abraham's faith is clearly indicated. In a tightly constructed argument, Paul asserts that faith and grace were necessary ingredients in guaranteeing that the promise would be realized for all the seed of Abraham, *not only* for those who adhere to the law, *but also* for those of the faith of Abraham. I wish to note the inclusive emphasis and form of argument here — "father of us all" — designed to specifically include both those who may be of Jewish origin as well as those of Gentile origin.[5] Paul does not argue exclusively — *either* Jews or Gentiles. He argues inclusively — not only A but also B — and the surprise use of *hoi tou nomou* in a neutral rather than a pejorative sense underlines that he specifically wishes to stress "the national reference,"[6] the inclusion of Jews *as Jews*. I want to insist that the emphasis here is not simply on the inclusion of Gentiles, but on the inclusion of Jews and Gentiles *both*.[7]

This form of argument is fairly typical of Paul's mode of arguing in the entire letter. Another interesting use of the same argument occurs at Rom. 9:24, again at the high point of a discussion. In 9:23 Paul speaks of "vessels of mercy" as the goal of the divine purpose, and in 9:24 he further elaborates on the composition of these vessels as being "not from the Jews only but also from the Gentiles." What is obvious here is that Paul uses a Jewish form of argument: "not only from the Jews" — as if there is no need to discuss this and as if what follows is the surprise element — "but also from the Gentiles" (Dahl 1969, 27–28). Now, it could be argued that in both places, 4:16 and 9:24, Paul's concern is to contend for the inclusion of Gentiles, as Gentiles, in the people of God. This is not, in my opinion, his primary intention.

It is clear that Paul is deliberately arguing for an inclusive salvation that includes Jews *as Jews* as well as Gentiles *as Gentiles*. Pointers such as

---

A Consistency of Paul's argument is found in inclusive passages.

these (more could be enumerated) indicate that there is a real continuity in subject matter as well as intent between Romans 3–4 and 9–11. There seems to be real continuity in substance between these sections. This will become clearer as we turn to consider the relationship between ch. 9 and ch. 11 as well as their place within the letter as a whole.

Romans 9 and the "Surprise" Ending to Romans II

Räisänen is certainly correct in his comment that "Romans 9–11 has long **A** been a test case in Pauline exegesis. Decisions made concerning the internal consistency or inconsistency of these chapters, or concerning the place of the thoughts expressed in them in Paul's theology at large, will deeply influence — or quickly reveal — one's understanding of many central issues of New Testament interpretation" (1988, 178). Some scholars, such as Dodd, have expressed surprise that Paul did not conclude his theological argument with the high point reached at Rom. 8:39. This is partly because 12:1ff. seems to be a theological sequel to 8:39 rather than the somewhat self-contained and compact argument of 9–11 that "can be read quite satisfactorily without reference to the rest of the epistle." This section was possibly in existence as "a separate treatise which Paul had by him, and which he used for his present purpose" (1932, 148).

Dodd is aware, of course, that the inclusion of Romans 9–11 has been **H** hinted at or envisaged at earlier points in the letter and admits that it is likely that Paul already knew that he was going to use his sermon on the rejection of Israel when he briefly discussed the difficulties raised in 3:1–9. The surprise presented by the inclusion of chs. 9–11 is, according to Dodd, that Paul has apparently already spoken of the abrogation of the privilege of Israel, in a dispensation in which no distinctions are drawn (1932, 151). As Dodd understands Paul's argument, the promise is not broken even if the *entire nation* is rejected (155; cf. Räisänen 1988, 184; Watson 1986, 162–63).

Few scholars would favor Dodd's reading here. Schlatter sees the con- **A** nection between the two sections of the letter very differently. "The **H** question, for what purpose did God make Israel and what does he make of them now, was precipitated by all of the following: The designation of the message of Jesus for the Jew first (1:16); the rejection of any favouritism for Israel on God's part." Schlatter gives seven more reasons from Romans 1–8 why the new topic rises with compelling urgency

---

A Inconsistency of Paul's argument.

H Discontinuity: Israel rejected but the promise kept.

A Consistency of Paul's argument.

H Continuity between old and new.

from the concluding sentence of ch. 8. He then goes on to note, "How woefully limited the interests of the Reformation's interpretation of Romans remained is demonstrated with unusual force in Calvin. He was completely surprised by the new section and saw no connection between it and the first section" (1995, 200).

Those for whom the inclusion of Romans 9–11 are a surprise are obviously missing something that was implicit if not explicit in Paul's reasoning in chs. 1–8. Whether or not the implicit logic of Paul's argument would permit the rejection of "all Israel," Paul himself could not entertain such a scandalous notion — "God forbid!" was his response. Schlatter is probably correct in claiming that "only the one who grieves over Israel's fall speaks correctly about it." To Christ Paul attributes the fact that he does not take pleasure in gloating over Israel's misery and that he does not merely stand before them as the angry messenger of judgment (1995, 200).

H Implicit in Paul's argument is that the faith of the Gentiles in Christ is the outcome of God's promises to Abraham (cf. Rom. 4:17ff.), and that Abraham is not merely a fine example of a man who believed as a Gentile, but rather the first of the faithful to whom all subsequent believers are deeply indebted. Gentile believers in Christ are deeply indebted also in that they are grafted into the stem of Abraham, as 11:13ff. will make plain. The Gentile branches are dependent on the stem of Abraham, and if this ceased to exist, or if they were separated from it, they too would fall.[8] Implicit here is the assumption that God is faithful to his covenant and that he will preserve his people to such an extent that his purposes for them will not fail. The latter is made explicit only in chs. 9–11. The righteous "remnant" concept, to be developed gradually from 9:6ff. through to ch. 11, assumes that God always maintains by his grace a faithful minority, and moreover that he will never cease to do so. The implicit thinking behind this appears to be that it is in and through this

C remnant that God's long-term goals for Israel will be attained. In Paul's thought, Gentiles can share in Israel's inheritance only with and through this righteous remnant. So the salvation of the Gentiles assumes the prior realization of the promise for Israel, and therefore excludes the possibility of a salvation for Gentiles alongside the *complete failure* of the promise to Israel, that is, even the concept of a Gentile "new Israel" is ruled out by this.[9] For Paul, the option of salvation "also for the Greek" presupposed that it is enjoyed by "the Jew first." For Paul, if not for his interpreters, it was meaningless to consider the election of Gentiles apart from the election of Israel; it is this that constitutes the priority of Israel.

H Continuity: God's faithfulness to the covenant.

C Paul's self-understanding among Jews and Gentiles.

In fairness to those interpreters whose readings perceive Romans 9–11 as somewhat of a surprise, it has to be acknowledged that it is only in these chapters that Paul spells out what seems to have been until now only implicit. The problem for these, as for the first interpreters to whom the letter was addressed, is that we all bring to these chapters preformulated views of the apostle and his thought that may need to be somewhat revised in the light of their content.

Paul appears to be insisting that it is not enough that individual Jews find faith in Christ; he wants the salvation of Israel, but not simply as a small remnant attached to a predominantly Gentile church. Thus, although his arguments in Romans may be read in light of the principle "there is no distinction" (Rom. 3:22; 10:12), and this might imply that since there can be no favoritism for Israel, then the elect may indeed be a purely Gentile phenomenon, this does not appear to be what Paul had in mind. It is here that we must stress again Paul's formula "to the Jew first and also to the Greek," which indicates that what he intends to argue for is an extension of Israel's privileges to Gentiles (rather than a transfer of them away from Israel). Paul's formula is thus an affirmation of Israel's status as the covenant people rather than an annulment.[10] But what has not always been realized is that the two elements — affirmation   **H** of Israel's covenant and its extension to Gentiles — belong together in Paul and are certainly not mutually exclusive, as might have been anticipated. Paul's theme in Romans, therefore, is *not* that the goal of the divine purpose is the salvation of the Gentiles; it is rather the salvation of Jews and Gentiles both.

This is where unconscious assumptions may color interpretation and lead to very divergent readings of the same text. This is clearest in the interpretation of Romans 9. Watson objects to the content of ch. 11, which seems to suggest that the ultimate purpose of Paul's Gentile mission is not the salvation of Gentiles, but the salvation of Jews, whereas "elsewhere the salvation of the Gentiles, together with the Jewish remnant, is itself seen as the ultimate goal of God's purposes" (1986, 169). The passages that Watson cites in support of his reading are 4:16ff. and 9:24ff. I want to question whether these are in fact supportive, because, as already noted, these are verses that repeat the formula, "not only/but also," which I have argued stresses the inclusion of Gentiles alongside Israel, as an extension of Israel's covenant. We need to look more closely at 9:24, as this is crucial to our discussion.

The dominant theme in Romans 9–11 is the people of Israel, and only indirectly and in relation to this, the inclusion of Gentiles. In ch. 9 Gentiles are introduced only at two points, 9:24 and 9:30. In 9:30 the reference to Gentiles enters merely as a foil to contrast their success with

---

H Continuity: extension of Israel's privileges to Gentiles.

Jewish failure, so we will concentrate on 9:24 to see whether there is
any basis here for the view that this chapter sets out a charter for God's
election of a new people (as Watson reads).

A Watson notes that whereas in Rom. 11:1ff. "his people" (*ton laon
autou*) refers to the present generation of Jews, in 9:25, in diametrical
opposition, "my people" (*laon mou*) refers to Gentile Christians (1986,
168). We need to look more closely at the text. Paul cites from Hos.
2:23, "Those who were not my people I will call 'my people,' and her
who was not beloved I will call 'my beloved.'" Dodd voices the senti-
ments of many commentators when he states, "It is rather strange that
Paul has not observed that this prophecy referred to Israel, rejected for
its sins, but destined to be restored." But it was Dodd's further comment
that aroused my curiosity and caused me to look more closely — "strange
because it would have fitted so admirably the doctrine of the restoration
of Israel which he is to expound in ch. 11" (1932, 160). Further evidence
for the strangeness of Paul's application of Hosea's words to Gentiles is
demonstrated in the two further citations that succeed this one. Fitzmyer
points out that "whereas Paul quoted Hosea's promise apropos the Gentiles, he will next quote Isaiah's admonition apropos of Israel" (1993,
573). Surely, Paul himself must have been aware of the arbitrariness of
his application of Scripture in the space of a few chapters. And of course,
it seems foolish that he would not avail himself of the benefit of a scriptural text that offered apparent support for the restoration of Israel, a
desired outcome toward which his own argument is tending.

An alternative reading of Romans 9 may be required in order to clarify
Paul's consistency. According to this reading, the chapter is not a further
argument for the inclusion of Gentiles — as if 9:24 were the point toward
which all of Paul's argument is tending, as if the inclusion of Gentiles were
in and of itself the goal of God's purpose, the thing in need of justification.
But neither the starting point of the chapter, Paul's grief over Israel, nor
its contents, such as the emphasis that God can have mercy on whomever
he wills, adequately supports this notion. As Räisänen rightly notes, "It is
the negative traits in God's dealings that according to Romans 9 cry for an
explanation; the salvation of Gentiles is not a sufficient one" (1988, 184).

A That Rom. 9:21–22 reaches some sort of a conclusion is clear; it sums
up the argument about the divine freedom in relation to Israel: "Has the
potter no right over the clay, to make out of the same lump one vessel
for beauty and another for menial use?" (9:21). That 9:22 continues this
emphasis is not so clear, because here Paul introduces what is apparently
a hypothetical statement, "What if God...?" In succession to this in
9:23, he adds a purpose clause but fails to conclude the condition he

A Inconsistency of argument in Romans 9–11; strange use of Hosea.
A Consistency: allowing for surprises.

began in 9:22, thus creating an anacoluthon (Bornkamm 1952, 76–92). So we are left with the unexpected hypothesis "What if God, because he wished to display his wrath and to make known his power, endured with much long-suffering vessels ripe for destruction?" Where Paul could have argued that God had cast off Israel, having first of all established the divine right of freedom, he surprisingly argues for God's right to be patient with Israel. It is only after this proposition that Paul, after a fuller elaboration and explanation of what has already been established in describing the purpose of the divine patience as being "to make known the riches of his glory," proceeds to further elaborate on the identity of its recipients in 9:24.

If we were to proceed into Rom. 9:24 without a break, it might give **H** the impression that Gentiles are equally if not primarily the object of the divine purpose. With Fitzmyer and others, it is advisable to put 9:24–29 in a new subsection, which Räisänen entitles, "the inclusion of Gentiles" (1988, 183). But as he himself notes, the inclusion of Gentiles is not the primary emphasis of the chapter. Fitzmyer's heading is therefore more appropriate: "God does not act arbitrarily: Israel's call, infidelity and remnant as foreseen in what God announced in the Old Testament" (1993, 571). This heading makes clear what I think is the case, that the topic under discussion is still primarily Israel or, more precisely, God's activity, but particularly in relation to Israel.

I conclude from this that it would be most unlikely for Paul to use the **A** Hosea citation with reference to Gentiles when this was not its original purpose and especially since it is immediately followed by two other Scripture citations that clearly apply to Israel. I would maintain that the Hosea citation is taken by Paul to apply *primarily* to Israel and thus the three citations all have the same point of reference, Israel. Rejected Israel, like the northern tribes, will be restored. This is Paul's primary thesis, but in and with the restoration, another "non-people," the Gentiles, will also be blessed. Paul does apply the Hosea citation in a secondary sense, typologically, to Gentiles also, but only after he has first used it to refer to Israel.[11] Like Hosea, he envisages the reuniting of the twelve tribes into one people, that is, the hardened and the remnant parts of Israel will one day be reunited.

When we see how minimal are the references to Gentiles in Romans 9 and recognize that all the discussion about God's selection in 9:6ff. is not about the choice of Gentiles at all but only about selection *within* the people of Israel in their *past* history,[12] then it is plain that another reading is possible; the chapter may now be read as not being about God's choice of a new people, but as being still specifically focused on

H Continuity: God's faithfulness to Israel.

A Consistency: Hosea refers to Israel.

the people of Israel. Where the Gentiles are included at 9:24 and at 9:30, it is either in a secondary reference after Israel, or in 9:30 to contrast the outcome of the Gentile mission with the Jewish response to Jesus, as if the two were causally related (as they seem to be in relation to the concept of hardening). The beginning of ch. 10 supports this reading because it refers to bearing witness to "them," where it is clear that the referents can only be the people of Israel.

A   The most surprising factor in Romans 9 is the somewhat unexpected twist with which Paul makes use of his powerful argument about the divine freedom. Instead of arguing that God is free and therefore can cast off Israel, Paul turns this around and asks, What if, as is the case, God patiently endures his people Israel (Barrett 1961, 189). When we follow closely the manner and sequence of Paul's argument in ch. 9, and recognize that the primary interest is in God's activity with Israel, then ch. 11 and its ending are not such a surprise after all, because the "surprise" has already been tentatively introduced in 9:22ff.

Recontextualizing Paul's Statements in Romans 9

H   No other passage in Paul's letters or perhaps even in the entire New Testament suffers so severely from the Augustinian[13] and Reformation

C   readings as does Romans 9. Despite the valiant efforts of Karl Barth (though his own reading has led to further problems), Johannes Munck, Franz Leenhardt, and Krister Stendahl, among others, there is an inherent tendency to regard Paul's words in this chapter as referring to the timeless election of individuals by an arbitrary act of a mysterious and omnipotent deity.

A   Although there is now general agreement that the purpose of the argument of Romans 9–11 as a whole is to maintain or defend the trustworthiness of God regarding his promises to Israel, there are diverse opinions as to how ch. 9 serves this purpose. Watson sees ch. 9 as offering a different definition of the chosen people from ch. 11: "[Rom.] 9:6–29 offers a clear and coherent argument for the view that the salvation of Gentiles and the rejection of Jews was entirely consistent with God's purpose of election as revealed in scripture. Yet in 11:1ff., and indeed throughout this chapter, Paul reverts to the old view of the people of God which he had previously rejected" (Watson 1986, 168).

A Consistency: allowing for surprise.

H Augustinian and Reformation readings.

C Empathetic response to Augustinian and Reformation readings.

A Inconsistency between Romans 9 and 11.

Räisänen also, in his reading, finds problems with the content of Romans. Is Paul thinking theologically or historically? "Paul's argument is curious. It implies that empirical Israel — the unbelieving majority — should be identified with Ishmael and Esau. But what seems bewildering in terms of common sense is possible in Pauline theology" (1988, 182–83). Räisänen feels that interpreters eventually have to make a choice between the negative view of Israel in ch. 9 and the positive view in ch. 11. Romans 9:6–13 shows that the majority of Israel never belonged to the elect (and therefore God's promise is not affected by the unbelief of empirical Israel). In fact, "v. 22 implies predestination in damnation" (1988, 182–83).

We can see that Räisänen seems to be dealing here with what he con- **H** siders to be an abstract doctrine of predestination very similar to that of Augustine or Calvin. But scholarship has progressed radically on this topic since the Reformation. Barth correctly argued that if we start where Calvin started and if we are as consistent as he was, we will inevitably end up at the same point of conclusion (1957, 35ff.). So Barth moved the discussion forward by arguing not for the election of individuals as such but for election in Christ.[14] Munck, Leenhardt,[15] and Stendahl, all in differing ways, have stressed the need to see Romans 9–11 as a text of the missionary outreach of the first century, which as such should not be interpreted in the Augustinian and Calvinist manner of dealing with it as abstract and timeless theology.

What is lamentable, however, is that the insights of these interpreters from Barth to Stendahl seem to have been forgotten or overlooked even in some of the most recent studies of Romans 9–11.[16] I am not suggesting that there is no basis for discussing some of these issues (election and predestination) in relation to ch. 9. Paul himself applies these theological categories to his own day: "So too at the present time there is a remnant chosen by grace" (11:5).

Nevertheless, it is legitimate to read Romans 9 as a discussion of God's dealings with Israel in its *past,* as distinct from its present to which Paul specifically refers in 11:5. It is also clear that ch. 9 is not even about the number of the elect in Israel in the past. The categories of "the rest" and "the remnant" are implicit throughout the entire discussion, but these represent categories rather than a specific number of individuals. It is gratuitous to add, as in the RSV translation, "only" before the reference to a remnant in 9:27. In point of fact, the emphasis in ch. 9 is not upon individuals *as such* but on chosen leaders and a righteous remnant to secure the future of the people. On this reading, it is an argument to show *how* God has maintained his purpose for this people throughout their history, sometimes through a minority, even by using Pharaoh.

H Discontinuity of timeless theology or continuity as missionary outreach.

Paul does make general theological statements about the "children of
the promise" in distinction from the "children of the flesh." But he is not
discussing God's election outside of or beyond Israel; the entire discussion
up to Rom. 9:24 is about God's elective purpose *within* Israel. It is not
until 9:24, and then, as already noted, almost as an aside, that Gentiles
are mentioned. Thus, it *cannot* be argued that the interest here lies in the
ingathering of Gentiles. Paul's primary aim is to demonstrate that God is

H not tied to Israel in any specific way. Despite the covenant, God remains
free even in relation to Israel — free, that is, within his compassion to
do as he wills (9:18).[17] Though it is also part of the divine method of
working in the history of his people, Paul's primary interest is not in
hardening either. The point Paul makes in both the hardening and having
compassion is that God is free in his choice of individuals or groups to
use them as he wills for the divine purpose for his people in history.

A   Read from this perspective, Pharaoh's future salvation (Rom. 9:17–
18) is not the issue, but rather the future of Israel as perceived from
the perspective of Paul's contemporary mission. The choice of people
to serve, whether positively or negatively, God's purpose for Israel in
its *past* prior to the coming of the gospel era is by no means the same
issue as God's choice of people for eternal life, whatever parallels may
legitimately be drawn between them.

If Romans 9 is read as not being primarily concerned with those whom
God elects, but rather about his manner of acting in history, then it would
be inconsistent to view it as a charter for the election of Gentiles as the
new people of God. Again, if ch. 9 is primarily about establishing God's
freedom in relation to Israel, whether then or in the present and the
future, the fact that *only* a remnant was elect *in the past* does not necessarily prevent all Israel, in whatever sense, being within God's purpose
of election *in the future*. It appears from this that it is because Paul's
use of election terminology is anachronistically interpreted in the light of
post-Augustinian categories that a conflict is perceived between the fate
of Israel in ch. 9 and a posited future in ch. 11. Theologically speaking,
there cannot actually be a contradiction between the content of chs. 9
and 11 as we now have them. The basis for the salvation of Israel in both
chapters is the same: God remains free to be compassionate with Israel
as he wills. But when this is interpreted as we have already argued in

H relation to 9:22, God's freedom means that he is not obligated to discard
Israel, however unworthy an object of his mercy it may actually be at any
particular point in history. The freedom of God in relation to Israel is not

----

H Image of God as being free.
A Consistency about the historical future of Israel.
H God's radical freedom and Israel's fluctuating loyalty.

a threat to Israel, because God's action toward Israel must then be based solely upon divine steadfastness and compassion rather than on Israel's fluctuating loyalty.[18] Since neither Israel nor the Gentiles can constrain God to accept them, because he is free, so too he is not compelled by their failures to cast them off. A salvation determined by works cannot be denied on the one hand and reaffirmed on the other.

My conclusion on this point is that the perceived contradictions within Romans 9, or in its relation to ch. 11, or in its relation to the letter as a whole, have been at least partly due to interpreting "a missionary's contribution to a discussion" (Munck 1959, 200; cf. Dahl 1977, 70–71) as if it were a timeless theological treatise seeking to solve questions that Paul, at this juncture at least, had no interest in asking. It is, moreover, inconsistent and anachronistic to read most sections of this letter in the light of the contemporary interpretation of Paul's letters as a whole, and yet read this particular section as if we were living in the seventeenth century.

Divergent Understandings of the Significance of Paul's Gentile Mission as a Factor in the Roman Context

In my reading, I have argued, with Munck, that Romans 9 ought to be interpreted as "a missionary's contribution to a discussion" rather than in abstract theological or philosophical categories. A sociological approach might lead us to regard, with Räisänen and Watson, this chapter as addressed to those who, like Paul, felt the plight of Israel to be a calamity, that is, to Roman Jewish Christians for whom Paul's predestination language would function as consolation for their lack of success among their own people.[19] But 11:17ff. makes it clear that the addressees of Paul's argument are Gentile Christians for whom the fate of Israel was of little concern.

A possible scenario is that Paul addresses Gentile Christians throughout Romans 9–11, and that Paul, in ch. 9, using himself as exemplar, thus demonstrates what their proper attitude to Israel ought to be. At the same time, this would also provide comfort and reassurance to those who wished to continue to follow a Jewish lifestyle. But why, then, should Paul need to protest so solemnly that he indeed does care for Israel? He appears to be refuting rumors to the contrary.[20]

A Consistency as a missionary text.

A Sociological approach to the text.

H The text as contribution to a concrete social situation versus abstract theology.

H Paul's personal experience as paradigm.

What alternative images of Paul and his mission may have been current at Rome? It had been anticipated that Paul would pay a visit. He protests that despite wanting to come and remembering them continually in his prayers, he has hitherto not been able to do so (cf. Rom. 1:9–13; 15:22). It is not until 15:25 that he admits that he is actually not going to visit them even now, but is going instead to Jerusalem with the collection. From Paul's obvious embarrassment here, we can be sure that some of the Roman Christians expected Paul to visit them, and he recognizes that they reside within the sphere of his Gentile mission (1:13).

C   If Paul's reputation depicted him as a champion of the Gentiles, it would then probably be Gentile Christians who legitimately expected a visit from him, especially if there was conflict between rival groups at Rome. The reason Paul gives for not visiting the Romans is significant: he is a pioneer missionary unwilling to build on another's foundation (Rom. 15:20–22). But now that this kind of work has been completed in the east, he is heading for Spain to continue in a similar vein. He does not come to evangelize in Rome, but for mutual edification in each other's company (1:11–13), and hopefully to receive support for a new outreach in Spain (15:24).

The crucial issue is this: did Paul delay a visit to Rome because Rome was regarded by Paul as already founded, that is, because in coming there he would in fact not be going to those who had never heard (15:21)? The best explanation is that Rome differed from Paul's normal pioneering areas in that it already possessed Christian communities, most of whom were formerly, and continued to be, in association with the city's synagogue communities. In this context, Gentile Christians may have felt, particularly in the earlier days of their communal existence, a need of Paul's support to champion their cause and maintain their rights.

C   As Paul writes, however, to the Romans, we do not get the impression that they are either weak or dominated by Jews or Judaizers. They are self-confident enough to interpret the world from their own conceited perspective. Paul seeks to prevent this by helping them to understand "the mystery of Israel" (Rom. 11:25ff.). We can be reasonably sure of that. Therefore, they are deficient in their understanding of God's purposes for Israel, and this deficiency is a cause for boasting (11:13ff.). There is an additional factor not sufficiently noted. In 11:13ff. Paul not only warns the Gentile Christians against boasting over Jews, but he somewhat surprisingly introduces his own mission as an element in the discussion. Paul, while addressing them as Gentiles, wants them to realize that his ministry to Gentiles has direct relevance not only to the salva-

---

C View of Paul as missionary to Gentiles by Gentile Christians.

C The Romans' self-understanding and the pro-Gentile Paul.

tion of his fellow Jews, but also that the salvation of them relates to their own salvation (11:13ff.).

Taking these two factors together, it seems beyond reasonable doubt that a misunderstanding of the significance of Paul's mission on the part of the Roman Gentile Christians had contributed to their inflated self-esteem (cf. Rom. 12:3ff.) and to their corresponding denigration of Israel,[21] which was manifesting itself in their intolerance of those conscientiously committed to living a Jewish lifestyle.[22]

Paul is implicated in the situation at Rome, in fact, doubly implicated. 🇨 As apostle to the Gentiles, the churches there come within his remit, but beyond this, it is clear that reports of his own gospel and mission have probably been a catalyst in the situation. Based on the knowledge that Paul viewed himself as apostle to Gentiles and that he set up congregations that did not force their adherents to observe the Jewish law, it would have been easy for a one-sided, Gentile-sided, image of Paul to develop. This, coupled with the frequent hostility of Jewish opponents who regarded him as a disloyal apostate, could soon have assisted the development of an image of the "partisan Paul." By the very location of his work — predominantly Gentile territory — it would also be unlikely that Paul would have often needed to discuss the future or even the evangelization of his own people. It would have been very easy for an image of a pro-Gentile Paul to gain credibility. His opposition to Judaizers in Galatians in defense of his Gentile converts must have had some such outcome. His "face to face" with Cephas in the encounter at Antioch was no doubt perceived in this way and thus served as a pivotal event in the creation of the image of the partisan, pro-Gentile Paul.

This was the Paul the Roman Gentiles were expecting to visit them. Even allowing for the normal exaggeration of hearsay reporting, it must be recognized that before the letter was sent to them, the Roman Christians could have expected a somewhat pro-Gentile apostle — in my view, one very similar to the Paul of Paulinism.[23] But there were new elements in the situation at Rome as well as possibly in Paul's own mission that were to combine to bring to light a rather different apostle.

However Romans is read, it is beyond dispute that Jewishness in one form or another was an issue among the Roman Christians. If Nanos and others are correct in their reading that there were some Jews there who were at least open to the Christian message, if not already fully committed, then Paul had to take these into account, particularly if, as seems to be the case, they were a minority. Since Paul did not found the 🇨 churches in Rome, he faces a problem, because he has to accept what already exists there or run the risk of destroying the weak "for whom

🇨 The Romans' image of the partisan Paul.

🇨 Paul's image is beyond his control.

Christ died" (Rom. 14:15). Moreover, if he simply supports the arrogant Gentiles in their mistaken conceit, such support will have repercussions throughout the church, not least in Jerusalem, where Paul now heads with fear for his own safety. But more serious still, as Stendahl notes, "Paul may have found something unnerving in the missionary zeal of his bragging Gentile converts over against the Jewish people" (1976b, 53).

H Perhaps Paul encountered here for the first time a supersessionist form of Christianity that his own mission, at least as it was reported, had helped to produce.

The Inclusive Paul: The Purpose of God for Jews and Also for Gentiles

A As Paul writes Romans, he is apparently faced with a dilemma. Not only is he not coming now to Rome, but worse still, he is heading for Jerusalem with a collection from his Gentile communities, something in itself open to great misunderstanding. If he alienates the Gentile Christians, not only will this help to accentuate their errors but he may also lose their much-needed support for his mission in Spain. This combination of factors resulted not only in the creation of the content of Romans,[24] but also helps to explain the manner of its presentation. Paul is forced to start with the images of himself and his mission that the Gentiles actually hold and then to seek discreetly to lead them in the direction he wants them to proceed; hence his employment of the dialogical style of the diatribe (Campbell 1991, 136ff.). It is this point of departure that helps to explain why the earlier parts of Romans can be read in such a way that Romans 11, with its *apparently* pro-Jewish conclusion, is not even envisaged, and why many scholars see such similarities between these chapters and Galatians (Sanders 1977, 487–88). Paul stealthily prepares throughout the letter for the disclosures concerning his attitude toward and his hope for his own people. If, as Sanders claims, Paul works from solution back to problem (Sanders 1977, 443ff., 499), then Romans as we now have it perhaps ought to be read in reverse! In this approach, the content of chs. 9–11 would not be seen so much as a surprise.

H For Paul, the entire argument of Romans presupposes the faithfulness of God to his people, and this is made clear at many significant points. See, for instance, Rom. 1:16, the gospel is the power of God "to the Jew first and also to the Greek"; 3:26, "it was to prove at the present time that he himself is righteous"; 4:16, "in order that the promise may rest on

---

H Risk of Christian supersessionism.

A Consistent argument as an attempt to reorient Paul's image.

H Continuity through God's faithfulness.

grace and be guaranteed to all his descendants, not only to the adherents of the law but also to those who share the faith of Abraham." Paul was certain that the faithlessness of Israel could not destroy the faithfulness of God, and he gives only a hint about this in 3:1–8 in order to alert the observant reader that this is a presupposition throughout the letter. For Paul, in contrast to his interpreters, to insist on faith in Jesus Christ while also maintaining God's promises to Israel is not irreconcilable.

It should be acknowledged, however, that despite the many indications already given in Romans 1–8, even a superb exegete such as Ernst Käsemann could still find problems with the Paul of ch. 11. Admittedly, this was in the different intellectual climate of 1961, when the significance **C** of the Holocaust for interpretation was not yet fully recognized. Käsemann holds that Israel has exemplary significance for Paul — "in and with Israel he strikes at the hidden Jew in all of us" — and he finds it fortuitous that "Romans 9–11 repeats the argument of the whole letter." He continues, "Is the apostle contradicting himself when he nevertheless ends ch. 11 with the promise of salvation for the whole people of Israel?" Despite Käsemann's recognition that Paul concedes to Israel "the rights of the first-born," he eventually concludes, "Thus the justification of the ungodly, which is also the resurrection from the dead, is the only hope both of the world in general and also of Israel" (1969, 182–87).

Our conclusion from all this must be that different readings of Romans, especially from chs. 9–11, arise chiefly from those presuppositions we bring with us to this point. Included in these, and of primary importance, is our image of Paul himself and his mission. Also of some significance is our larger understanding of how Christianity, particularly in its origins, relates to Judaism.[25] In Käsemann's reading it is clear that he interprets chs. 9–11 out of chs. 1–8, and Israel becomes an exemplar or symbol for the justification of the ungodly. There may be a parallel here to what happens when Paul commences to write his letter to the Romans. He is faced with the fact that they are already in possession of an image of the apostle to the Gentiles and that they therefore think they know how he will respond to their situation. So Paul has to present as discreetly as possible another image of himself, this time one that includes his own understanding of how the Gentile mission relates to God's purposes for Jews and Gentiles *both*. The image of the "partisan Paul" — the apostle for the Gentiles — is thus revised and updated to become the image of the "inclusive Paul" of "not only the Jew but also the Greek," of Paul among Jews and Gentiles.

Despite dedicated attempts to get behind the overlay of centuries of **A** readings of Romans, scholars will never be able fully to comprehend its

---

C The Holocaust as a bridge-category?

A Full comprehension of the text's message when priority is given to the text?

message as it was first delivered to the Romans. But we must give the text its due weight and not interpret it on the basis of Galatians,[26] of an already known gospel, or of a familiar portrait of the apostle at an earlier stage in his career. As far as is humanly possible, we must interpret Paul's mission and Paul himself as they are presented in this specific text before we resort to harmonization or revision from any other sources, however significant. Within the letter, the same principle applies: we must allow, as we are able, each section of the letter to reveal its own peculiar content before we seek to relate it to a coherent view of the whole.

Notes

1. Dahl, in a review of Bultmann's *Theology of the New Testament,* noted that although Bultmann had much to say about Romans 1–8, he had relatively little to say about chs. 9–11 (1954, 21–40).

2. Munck's study of Romans 9–11, *Christ and Israel,* was completed in Danish in 1952 (English translation by Ingeborg Nixon, 1967) as a prelude to his better-known *Paul and the Salvation of Mankind* (1959).

3. See, for example, Malherbe 1976.

4. See D. J. S. Chae's *Paul as Apostle to the Gentiles* (1997). If there were no intrinsic connection between Christian anti-Judaism and the Holocaust, Chae's thesis that post-Holocaust guilt has contributed to a revised reading of Paul would be more convincing.

5. Leenhardt rightly criticizes Michel's view (probably based on Rom. 4:11) that for Paul Abraham is the father of the uncircumcised much more than of the circumcised (Leenhardt 1961, 119). Michel, however, correctly emphasizes that the discussion in Romans 4 is not about the faith of individuals but rather about Abraham's "house" (*Abrahamskindschaft*) (1976, 167–71).

6. So Dunn (1988, 216), who also correctly notes that the inverted order — uncircumcised followed by circumcised — is due simply to following the sequence of events in Abraham's case, and does not contradict the "not only/but also" pattern that we have noted (211). Nor does it indicate a complete rejection of Jewish salvation history, as Klein asserts (1963, 434ff.).

7. That this is so should have been evident from the very different understanding of *sperma* in Gal. 3:16ff. and Rom. 4:13ff.; in the former it is interpreted in relation to the one seed, Jesus Christ, but in the latter specifically with reference to two peoples (cf. J. C. Beker 1991, 327–32).

8. Schlatter develops this further: "The existence of a people of God is not due to those in the church who believe in Christ; rather, because there is a people of God, they are its members" (1995, 223; cf. 107).

9. As Beker notes, "Such a rejection of Israel by God would simply cut the connection of the gospel to its foundation in the Hebrew scriptures and degrade the God of Jesus Christ into the God of Marcion — a 'new God' who has no relation either to creation or to Israel's salvation history'" (1991, 330).

10. The occurrence of *bebaios* in Rom. 4:16 (as also *bebaiōsai* in 15:8 in a final construction) denotes "legally guaranteed security" (Dunn 1988, 216).

The latter verse with its reference to Christ indicates the intertwined relation of the salvation of Jews and Gentiles in Paul's thought; as Fitzmyer renders it, "Christ became a servant to the circumcised to show God's fidelity, to confirm the promises made to the patriarchs, and Gentiles have glorified God for his mercy" (1993, 704).

11. There is some support for this proposal from Karl Barth, who interprets somewhat differently: "To whom did these words originally apply? To the Israel of the kings of Samaria, which had been rejected by God and which had yet been granted such a promise. And because these words have now been fulfilled in the calling of the Gentiles to the church of Jesus Christ, they obviously also speak with renewed force in their original sense; they also speak of the rejected, disobedient Israel. Now that he has fulfilled it superabundantly among the rejected without, how could God's promise not apply also to the rejected within, to whom he had once addressed it?" (1959, 122–23).

12. Cf. Campbell 1991, 43–49. There I describe Romans as "a reinterpretation of covenant righteousness in the light of the Christ-event." From a theological perspective, a distorted view of Paul's mission reveals a mistaken view of covenant (173).

13. See Stowers 1991.

14. This recognition of Barth's contribution does not overlook its weaknesses. Goppelt, for example, complains, "He understands election too much as predestination outside of history" (1964, 163).

15. Leenhardt realized that the theme here was not the personal salvation of those who were called, but rather their utilization as instruments in a saving process, and that the interest is not so much in named individuals as much as in peoples who are thus named after their eponymous ancestors according to Old Testament practice (1961, 249–50).

16. Despite being aware of the problems surrounding these approaches to Romans 9–11, Cosgrove frequently reverts to them as if they still had some validity (1997, 26ff.); see also Räisänen 1988.

17. Cf. Barth's assertion: "God remains free as regards the disobedient, just as he remains free as regards the obedient" (1959, 143).

18. This is clearly recognized by Leenhardt: "If his reaction had depended on 'man's will or exertion,' ... then Yahweh could only have punished with the greatest severity. Instead of that he gave to this rebellious people a new revelation of his grace and at the same time displayed its basic principle: my mercy is utterly free" (1961, 252–53).

19. Räisänen rightly focuses on the social function of the doctrine of predestination (1988, 186). However, it seems to point to Jewish Christians as the addressees (181). On this view, Paul's real concern seems to be with Jewish Christian queries (195). Watson's sociological approach likewise seems to target Jewish Christians, especially their social reorientation away from the synagogue (1986, 97–98; cf. 151–53, 163–64, 172).

20. "Paul had to dispel suspicions that he is hostile or indifferent to Israel" (Watson 1986, 180). Räisänen notes that besides Rom. 9:1, *ou pseudomai* occurs in Paul only in 2 Cor. 11:31 and Gal. 1:20 (assuming that 1 Timothy is non-Pauline), and that in both cases Paul is refuting rumors (1988, 198), whereas

Käsemann sees this as resulting from Paul's often being accused of hostility to Israel (1969, 257).

21. For further emphasis on the deficiency of the Gentile Christians see Romans 11 (Campbell 1991, 170–77). Schlatter claims, "For those who were Greeks by birth, it was easy to assume that Paul had separated himself completely from the Jews. In this case they also argued...that they were under no obligation to the Jews" (1995, 221). Theologically speaking, they had misinterpreted the covenant and hence the divine purpose for the world, that is, for Jews and Gentiles *both*.

22. See Jewett 1982. It is not possible to deal adequately here with the vast literature on the *Sitz im Leben* of the Roman Christians, but see also Nanos 1996, 75ff.

23. Against Watson's thesis that Paul wants to convert the Roman Jewish congregation to Paulinism (1986, 98).

24. On the combination of Rome, Jerusalem, and Spain, see Käsemann 1969, 405–6.

25. As long as Judaism and the Hebrew Scriptures are regarded as simply preparatory to Christianity, then it is inevitable that the Gentile mission will be viewed as the climax of God's work, and the Christian church will continue to be confused with the kingdom of God (Soulen 1996, 19).

26. Against Cosgrove's proposal: "As part of the Christian canon, Galatians 2 now supplies part of the canonical story of the Gentile mission. In a constructive canonical interpretation, it is therefore appropriate to interpret Rom. 11:19 within the context of this canonical story" (1997, 88).

References

Barrett, C. K. 1961. *A Commentary on the Epistle to the Romans.* London: Black.

Barth, K. 1957. *The Doctrine of God.* Vol. 2 of *Church Dogmatics.* Edinburgh: T. & T. Clark.

———. 1959. *A Shorter Commentary on Romans.* London: SCM.

Beker, J. C. 1991. "The Faithfulness of God and the Priority of Israel in Paul's Letter to the Romans." Pp. 327–32 in *The Romans Debate,* ed. K. Donfried. Peabody, Mass.: Hendrickson.

Bornkamm, G. 1952. *Das Ende des Gesetzes: Paulusstudien.* Munich: Kaiser.

Campbell, W. 1991. *Paul's Gospel in an Intercultural Context: Jew and Gentile in Paul's Letter to the Romans.* Frankfurt and New York: Peter Lang.

Chae, D. J. S. 1997. *Paul as Apostle to the Gentiles.* Carlisle: Paternoster.

Cosgrove, C. 1997. *Elusive Israel: The Puzzle of Election in Romans.* Louisville, Ky.: Westminster John Knox.

Dahl, N. A. 1954. Review of *Theologie des Neuen Testaments,* by Rudolf Bultmann. *Theologische Rundschau* 22:21–40.

———. 1969. "The Atonement: An Adequate Reward for the Akedah?" Pp. 27–28 in *Neotestamentica et Semitica,* ed. E. E. Ellis and M. Wilcox. Edinburgh: T. & T. Clark.

———. 1977. *Studies in Paul: Theology for the Early Christian Mission.* Minneapolis: Augsburg.

Dodd, C. H. 1932. *The Epistle to the Romans*. London: Hodder and Stoughton.

Dunn, J. D. G. 1983. "The New Perspective on Paul." *Bulletin of the John Rylands Library* 65:95–122.

———. 1988. *Romans*. 2 vols. Word Biblical Commentary 38A, 38B. Dallas: Word.

Fitzmyer, J. 1993. *Romans: A New Translation with Introduction and Commentary*. Anchor Bible 33. New York: Doubleday.

Goppelt, L. 1964. *Jesus, Paul, and Judaism: An Introduction to New Testament Theology*. New York: Nelson.

Jewett, R. 1982. *Christian Tolerance: Paul's Message for the Modern Church*. Philadelphia: Westminster.

Käsemann, E. 1969. *New Testament Questions of Today*. Trans. W. J. Montague. New Testament Library. London: SCM.

Klein, G. 1963. "Römer iv und die Idee der Heilsgeschichte." *Evangelische Theologie* 23:424–47.

Leenhardt, F. J. 1961. *The Epistle to the Romans*. London: Lutterworth.

Malherbe, A. 1976. *Social Aspects of Early Christianity*. Baton Rouge: Louisiana State University.

Michel, O. 1976. *Der Brief an die Römer*. Kritisch-exegetischer Kommentar über das Neue Testament. Gottingen: Vanderhoeck and Ruprecht.

Munck, J. [1952] 1967. *Christ and Israel*. Trans. I. Nixon. Philadelphia: Fortress.

———. 1959. *Paul and the Salvation of Mankind*. London: SCM.

Nanos, Mark. 1996. *The Mystery of Romans: The Jewish Context of Paul's Letter*. Minneapolis: Fortress.

Noack, B. 1965. "Current and Backwater in the Epistle to the Romans." *Studia Theologica* 19:155–65

Räisänen, H. 1988. "Paul, God, and Israel: Romans 9–11 in Recent Research." Pp. 178–206 in *The Social World of Formative Christianity and Judaism: Essays in Tribute to Howard Clark Kee*, ed. J. Neusner et al. Philadelphia: Fortress.

Sanders, E. P. 1977. *Paul and Palestinian Judaism*. London: SCM.

———. 1983. *Paul, The Law, and The Jewish People*. Philadelphia: Fortress.

Schlatter, Adolf von. 1995. *Romans: The Righteousness of God*. Trans. S. S. Schatzmann. Peabody, Mass.: Hendrickson.

Soulen, R. K. 1996. *The God of Israel and Christian Theology*. Minneapolis: Fortress.

Stendahl, K. 1976a. *Paul among Jews and Gentiles, and Other Essays*. Philadelphia: Fortress.

———. 1976b. "In No Other Name." Pp. 48–63 in *Christian Witness and the Jewish People: The Report of a Consultation Held under the Auspices of the Lutheran World Federation, Department of Studies, Oslo, August 1975*, ed. A. Sovik. Geneva: Lutheran World Federation.

Stowers, S. K. *A Rereading of Romans: Justice, Jews, and the Gentiles*. New Haven: Yale University Press.

Watson, F. 1986. *Paul, Judaism, and the Gentiles: A Sociological Approach*. Cambridge: Cambridge University Press.

–EIGHT–

Challenging the Limits
That Continue to Define Paul's
Perspective on Jews and Judaism

Mark D. Nanos

——— ◆ ———

A Response to Günter Wasserberg's Essay

C In his essay in this volume, "Romans 9–11 and Jewish-Christian Dialogue: Prospects and Provisos," Günter Wasserberg has taken a contextual stance as a post-Holocaust German Lutheran to respect Jewish people and religion as equal before God independent of faith in Christ. Since his reading of Paul will not provide for a similar viewpoint, and since he is unconvinced by the attempts of others to modify Paul's voice in this direction (for example, in Romans 11) — especially those he calls "a two-scheme salvation" — he concludes that the Paul of the historical **H** text must, for himself, be dismissed on this matter. He notes — rightly, on my understanding of the traditional reading too — that when taken to indicate the future conversion of all Jewish people, Romans 9–11 does not hold as much promise for mutual respect as many may think. I applaud **I** and welcome this ideological decision, not least as a Jewish person. If I read Paul in the same way, I would likewise find it necessary to dismiss the voice of Paul on this and other matters. But I do not believe that one must read Paul as Wasserberg or those he cites have read him, and therefore I question the need for this conclusion. **A** Wasserberg's view of Paul is based upon at least two major premises:

C Dismissing Paul in order to respect Jewish people and religion.

H No future conversion of Jewish people.

I Nanos interpreting as a Jewish person.

A Conclusions about Paul's belief that Christ is the Messiah of Israel and that synagogue Judaism is obsolete and inferior.

the interpretation of Paul. One might expect, then, that his conclusions regarding Paul's usefulness would be rewoven not from these threadbare remnants, but with the various new fabrics available to the exegete in view of recent insights into the period and Paul. But as I see it, this has not occurred. Take the unqualified appeal to the traditional interpretation of the Antioch meeting of Galatians 2 to establish the certainty of Paul's abandonment of Judaism. Yet this reading is no longer a given. I have argued, along with some other interpreters, that this example may be read in another way in which Paul is shown not to be against Jewish identity and behavior, but rather a champion thereof (Nanos 1996a, 337–71).

To illustrate my concern, consider the exegetical limitations Wasserberg finds himself constrained by when deducing the possible value of Paul's voice. He resists the conclusion of interpreters where he believes that it necessitates the premise that Paul was schizophrenic in dividing his understanding of God's salvation into two parts.

This premise about Paul is based, as Wasserberg states it, upon the following logic: "To perceive Paul as, on the one hand, remaining a faithful Jew while, on the other hand, proclaiming Jesus as Messiah for the Gentiles without the law seems to posit a certain schizophrenia in Paul." This is, of course, based upon a premise unstated here, which may, however, be observed at work throughout his essay, and which is elsewhere made explicit. On one hand, Wasserberg asserts, "Paul was a Jew and continued to perceive himself as a Jew, one who believed in Christ." But on the other hand, he denies discussion of the problem that this logically adumbrates, as though unconnected: "Whether [Paul] was aware that his understanding of Judaism in light of the Christ event in effect abrogated Judaism by denying to the law the position it occupied in much of Judaism in his day is a different question." However, that this is not a different question may be observed in his own deduction when he states, "Paul's theology breaks with Torah Judaism inasmuch as he claims that the Torah has lost its binding authority."

It seems to me that this is the interpretive bedrock upon which Wasserberg rightly concludes the need to dismiss Paul, for this position attributes to Paul an ideological dismissal of Jewish identity or behavior that stands in the way of his post-Holocaust sensibilities and my own. Moreover, while it is an ideology of which he is willing to consider that Paul remains unaware, it is nevertheless one he appears to believe is logically

---

🅰 Paul does not speak of Jewish legalism and works of self-righteousness, and does not abandon Judaism.

🅰 Did Paul see a contradiction between belief in Jesus as the Messiah for Gentiles without the law and remaining a faithful Jew?

🅰 Paul's dismissal of Judaism.

🅷 Ideological dismissal of Judaism as logically compelling.

(1) Paul believed in Christ as the Messiah of Israel and thus tha **A**
Jewish people must necessarily believe in Christ as well; (2) Paul b
and taught that Jewish identity and behavior were necessarily o
for himself and other Jewish believers in Christ and thus logically i
for other Jewish people as well.

But I question whether the reading of Paul that has led to this c
sion is necessary, or the only alternative. First, in view of Wasser
commitment to the insights of the so-called new perspective on Pa
Judaism, I find his argument internally inconsistent, being based
traditional exegetical insights that must now be challenged. Seco
view of the historical contextual divide separating Paul and us, I si **A**
that setting Paul's language in his context as differentiated from ou
fers more flexibility for incorporating Paul's voice than Wasserber
considered.

I agree with the first premise of Wasserberg's view. Paul did b
in Christ and thought that all humankind, Jew and Gentile, shou
likewise. But I disagree with the conclusion that this means Paul v
reject a Jewish (or other) position or person not sharing this fa
believe that Paul's view may be contextualized differently than W
berg has done, and thus subordinated to Paul's larger understandi
the Creator God drawn from his confession of the *Shema,* that
is the One God of Jews (particularistic) and the One God of Ge
(universalistic) (Nanos 1996a, 1996b).

I disagree entirely with the second premise of Wasserberg's view. I
my perspective and exegesis, Paul did not believe or teach that
ish identity or behavior had been made obsolete for the Jewish pe
whether they believed in Jesus Christ or not. And this is the cru
the problem for recontextualizing Paul in regard to the first p
ise. Here I find Wasserberg's exegetical observations inconsistent
"new perspective" observations and unnecessary as the grounds for
conclusions drawn.

I would like to elaborate briefly. Wasserberg admits that the traditi **A**
view of Paul has been undermined by the advances of the so-called
perspective.[1] He observes that this view had relied upon material
in important ways has been discredited as eisegesis, with its worn- **F**
assertion of Jewish legalism or works of self-righteousness as a foil

---

A It is inconsistent to use insights from both new and traditional exegesis; it is cleare
focus on Paul's language in its historical context.

A Paul's language about both particularism and universalism.

A Conclusion that Paul does not hold Judaism to be obsolete or inferior.

H Jewish legalism and works of self-righteousness as inadequate theological categorie compelling for the Christ-believer on Paul's terms. The juxtaposition of statements illustrates how it is precisely the simultaneous retention of the traditional interpretive premise that prohibits Paul's participation in the dialogue, since "this Paul" does not share Wasserberg's sensibilities or **C** respect for Jewish people and behavior. I suggest that this is the matter that we should turn to in order to render a decision on the place of Paul.

A solution may be noted in the midst of Wasserberg's own argument, for he recognizes that among other Jewish believers in Jesus it is not apparently necessary to conclude that there can be no mixing of Jewish Torah observance and faith in Christ. Wasserberg grants that the Jeru- **A** salem Christ-believing communities remained "within the boundaries of Judaism"; therefore, they exist as an alternative Jewish coalition or Judaism, but not the only one. Thus, for these Jewish people faith in Christ **H** did not go necessarily hand in hand with the rejection of Torah identity or behavior; they may remain faithful Jews yet proclaim faith in Jesus for Gentiles without suffering a kind of schizophrenia. For them it is not an ideological necessity, and the kind of disrespect of Jewish identity and behavior that Wasserberg rejects is not inherent. Yet for Paul, somehow, his faith in Christ logically "marks a decisive break with Jewish self-identity and lifestyle," so that his Judaism is "a Gentile movement." (Admittedly, "Christianity," when *later* founded, did become one. But I believe this later development is in spite of Paul, not because of him, even if his writings were and continue to be construed in such a way that this may not appear to be the case.)

The view attributed to Paul cannot then be grounded on an ideological **I** premise that is not necessarily deduced for other Jewish believers in Jesus without cause. For example, it would have to be grounded in Paul's own statements. That is, it would have to be based upon exegesis. And this Wasserberg recognizes as well. However, while in his essay Wasserberg grants that the traditional portrait of Paul is flawed on the matter of Paul's view of "Torah Judaism," he nevertheless draws deeply from this well for the exegetical basis of his argument. In this light, I submit that the prior logical and exegetical conclusions Wasserberg has accepted about Paul needlessly constrain the possibilities for Paul's voice.

I propose that Paul's historical framework may be contextualized in **C** such a way that we find his even greater conviction, that the One God of Israel is the One God of all humankind, provides a guiding voice for

---

C Sensibilities and respect for Jewish people in Paul's time and in a post-Holocaust setting.

A Jerusalem Christ-believing communities and Paul are in a similar situation, and should be approached in the same way.

H Possibility of remaining faithful Jews while proclaiming faith in Jesus for Gentiles.

I Analytical frames constrain hermeneutical conclusions.

C Paul's historical context and our context are radically different.

our own context today. To accomplish this, I suggest the following three steps.

H   First, we recognize that Paul's viewpoint was that of a Jewish reformer, so that his beliefs were framed within the Judaisms of his day. His beliefs represent a view of Jewish identity and behavior that was Torah driven and observant, although informed by the "revelation" of Christ.

Second, we note that Paul's conviction in the One God of Jews and Gentiles provides a framework for reconsideration of the context of his statements about, for example, Jewish identity or Torah observance, instead of universalizing them (i.e., applying statements in the same manner to Jews and Gentiles both). For this Paul, the differences remained, but the discrimination did not. That is, his views of Torah for Jewish or Gen-

A   tile people were not the same. In this way, we keep in front of ourselves the view that Paul's writings represent his perspective on an inter- and intra-Jewish matter of his own time (Nanos 1998, 1999). This offers a different way to cast the question Wasserberg asks today as a Christian, and a different premise for conceiving of Paul's response.

H   Third, we consider that Paul's plan for mission and his statements about the restoration of Israel or of all humankind are limited to their historical context, that is, within the framework of his own ministry. Developments since then would need to be reconsidered in later times

A   for appropriate application — for example, of principles and patterns of thought. When considered in this way, the cross is no longer only a symbol of a Jewish martyr of the Roman Empire, but also of harmful

C   Christian policies toward Jewish people. So, too, the context of arguments against the adoption of Jewish identity by Gentile believers in Christ is worlds apart. This has so changed that the priority of the concern and even the grounds of the argument are obscured if not entirely lost on the modern Gentile Christian reader of Paul. Most would hardly consider such a course of interest to be a logical extension of their faith in this Jewish person, Jesus Christ; however, in the context of Paul's life and message, this was sensible and desired. One need but consider the context of Galatians! In fact, recognizing this lack of resonance with the historical situation may go a long way toward explaining the common interpretive recontextualization so that it appears to be Jewish identity and behavior for Jewish people as well as Gentile people in view in these Pauline texts. Perhaps it is inconceivable for the later interpreter that

---

H Paul as Jewish reformer with Jewish conviction about the One God of Jews and Gentiles.

A Text reflects intra-Jewish debate.

H Paul's plan for mission and restoration of Israel.

A Principles and patterns of thought are most significant.

C Argument against adoption of Jewish identity by Gentile Christians in Paul's time and today.

Pauline law-free gospel-believing Gentile people could be so engaged by the desire for Jewish identity and behavior that after their faith in Christ these people could really imagine becoming Jewish proselytes was an advantage for themselves.

These considerations will permit us to reframe the question. We may seek to understand how Paul's larger view of God's intentions for his creatures, because of his conviction of God's oneness, would effect what might be said in our context now. In other words, that Wasserberg has chosen to let an ideological conviction shape the context of his faith in Christ in view of historical developments since Paul's time, need not require a conclusion that Paul would not share this sensibility. Rather, I imagine that Paul would. I believe that since Paul's faith in Christ was set within a particular historical context shaped by an understanding of who God is and what God is doing that was driven, for example, by the Scriptures of Israel, the confession of the *Shema,* and trust in the irrevocable calling and gifts of God, we might responsibly undertake the task of reassessing his voice guided by a hermeneutic rooted in his respect for the convictions of Jewish people who did not share his belief in Christ. But this is a perspective that can arise only in a time after Paul, a time after this Jewish coalition and the other Judaisms took different directions than he had foreseen, a time after the foundation of Christianity and its history checkered with the failure to respect Jewish people and behavior, or worse.

In Romans 11 Paul was occupied with challenging the growing arrogance among Gentiles toward Jewish people who did not share their faith in Christ. He reveals a surprising mystery of God's present dealings with an unforeseen outcome for Israel: although there is vicarious suffering on behalf of these Gentiles now, ultimate restoration is certain (Nanos 1996a, 239–88). I do not read this as an outline for some distant triumphalism, when all Jews will be converted to Christianity, which would be against the rhetorical intent to confront Christian gentile conceit. Nor do I read it as the "two-scheme salvation" that Wasserberg finds too modern for Paul.

Rather, I read this as an expression of the process Paul expects to unfold as he proclaims the gospel: when he turns successfully to the

---

H Paul's and present-day Christians' respect for the convictions of Jews not sharing belief in Christ.

A Development of Judaism and Christianity.

I Hermeneutical conclusions about respect for the convictions of the Jews as guide for historical analysis.

A Romans 11 neither an outline of triumphalism nor a "two-scheme salvation."

A Romans 11 about the process of Israel's restoration through the proclamation of Israel's Lord as the One God of humankind begun in Jesus Christ.

Gentiles with the message of Israel's Lord as the One God of humankind, it will provoke other Jewish people to emulative jealousy "of his
ministry" (Nanos 1999). They too will want to participate in the ministry that Israel has long awaited, once they see the Gentiles coming in,
turning to the worship of the One God with renewed minds. He hopes
that they will recognize that this means Israel's restoration has begun in
Jesus Christ, and thus those who have not yet believed will reconsider.

C   But Paul's conception of how things would turn out has not come to
pass. And so his view must be read within its historical context, and not
directly transferred to our own.

A   Paul's recognition of this as a mystery only now revealed, that is, as
a process unrealized before in the contexts of his own time, implicitly
admits of the limits of human understanding, without revelation, to dis-
tinguish the way things are from how they may appear. Paul provides a
context for this mystery resonating with echoes of the *Shema*. For Paul
explicitly admits that there is much he still does not comprehend, an
insight that may point the way toward a mutually respectful hermeneu-

C   tic for those who seek to bring Paul's voice to bear upon the topic of
Jewish-Christian relations in the later context of our own time:

> O the depth of the riches and wisdom and knowledge of God!
> How unsearchable are his judgments and how inscrutable his ways!
> "For who has known the mind of the Lord, or who has been his
> counselor?" "Or who has given a gift to him that he might be
> repaid?" For from him and through him and to him are all things.
> To him be the glory for ever. Amen. (Rom. 11:33–36)

A Response to William S. Campbell's Essay

A   William S. Campbell's essay, "Divergent Images of Paul and His Mission," highlights the tension perceived in the received view of Paul
between Romans 11 and elsewhere, including a text as close as ch. 9.
Campbell discusses the various solutions in modern scholarship, which
suggest that Paul was going one way in his earlier work, and in this letter
too, but then changed course suddenly in ch. 11. This is seen as inconsistent, an anomaly that needs to be set in its subordinate role and explained
on the basis of some flaw on Paul's part, or at least in his argument. In

---

C Factual course of history.

A The process of proclamation of the gospel and its effect upon Israel is an actual mystery
for Paul.

C The process of gospel proclamation and its effect on Israel through the centuries is
revealed today.

A The text is inconsistent because it reflects three inconsistent images of Paul.

the various proposals considered, the priority given to Israel in ch. 11 is regarded as a compromise of Paul's principal new insight of God's impartiality argued in chapter 9, which is due to his failure to divest himself fully of his former ideological particularism as a Jewish person. The critique of such positions and their presuppositions is excellent.

But Campbell accepts the appearance of Paul's inconsistency, and thus **H** advances another way to reduce the resulting dissonance this creates for the interpreter seeking coherence. He proposes that the most powerful case against Paul's consistency may come from Paul's own three different voices: one found in his other letters, one from his missionary activity to the Gentiles, and the third, which seems to arise suddenly in ch. 11 in contrast to the preceding chapters. Thus, Campbell divides the possible approaches along the line of, Was "the apostle facing a changed situation, or the outcome of a development in his thought"?[2] This may prove helpful for the traditional exegete, but I suggest that the problem really vexing a "new perspective" interpreter like Campbell, or a Jewish interpreter like myself, lies elsewhere, namely, in the portrait of Paul that sets up this inconsistency.

In other words, I question whether Paul's approach in Romans 11 **A** needs to show him to be inconsistent in any of the ways suggested. Ironically, I find the foundational conviction that Campbell shares with these other interpreters of Paul to be inconsistent with the spectrum of Paul's voices as I hear them. Consider briefly each of the three discussed from another perspective.

First, in a (presumably) earlier letter such as Galatians, for example, Paul's mission to the Gentiles is set within a prophetic call by the God of Israel, and his letter ends with a blessing upon the Israel of God. The struggle may be interpreted *within Israel* regarding the proper means for including gentiles as full children of Abraham since the coming of Christ. That is, the struggle is between the former conclusion maintained by the guardians of the traditions of the fathers (i.e., proselyte conversion) and a new development (claiming to be consistent with the Scriptures) that has now been revealed by Israel's God in Christ to Paul and the other apostles of this movement. Thus, Paul understands the tension created by the good news of Christ (which now includes Gentiles without proselyte conversion as equal participants among the people of God with Jewish people) to set this Judaism apart from the other Judaisms, including those of which he had been formerly a most zealous and outstanding member.

Second, as I read Galatians 2, this mission is in unity with that of the Jerusalem apostles (Nanos 1996a, 337–71; 1997; 1998; so too Koptak 1990). When we look for evidence from outside of Paul, the only picture

---

H Dissonance versus coherence.

A Neither the texts nor the images of Paul are inconsistent.

available with any time proximity is that of Luke, with which this would agree. This suggests that Paul's mission to the nations has always been set within the framework of Israel's restoration.

And third, the letter to the Romans is full of positive comments about Jewish identity and the value of Torah *prior* to arriving at ch. 11:

- Paul opens by locating his good news of Christ within Israel's history ("the good news of God, which he promised beforehand through his prophets in the holy scriptures . . . concerning his Son, who was descended from David according to the flesh" [1:1–3]);

- he continues with such affirmations as Jewish diachronical priority ("to the Jew first" [1:16; 2:10]);

- and notes the advantage of Jewish identity demonstrated in the possession of "the oracles of God" (3:1–2);

- he explains the powerful unification derived from exegesis of the *Shema,* along with the confirmation of the Torah by faith (3:29–31);

- and clarifies the fatherhood of Abraham, who "received circumcision as a sign or seal of the righteousness that he had by faith" (4:11);

- he emphasizes the positive nature of Torah as "holy and just and good" (7:12), not to mention "spiritual" (7:14), while the very aim of walking in the Spirit is the fulfillment of "the just requirement of the Torah" (8:4);

- moreover, he powerfully affirms the eternal value of Jewish identity and privilege at the beginning of ch. 9 (9:4–5).

In sum, I do not find Paul's "other voices" raised against the pro-Jewish Paul of Romans 11, but rather consistent with it, and, interestingly enough, Campbell goes on to point out some of these references as well. For example, it seems that Campbell's recognition of the role of Abraham as father equally and inclusively of Jews and Gentiles in the argument of ch. 4 is consistent with the "earlier Paul," if you will. It is certainly central in Galatians, and to the same purpose: non-Jewish people may step up to equal status with Jewish people as children of Abraham and thus of God, a step that had usually been understood to be reserved for Gentiles who became Jewish proselytes. In fact, Paul begins ch. 9 with the assertion of Israel's special and eternal place and his own willingness to suffer vicariously for Israel, noting that "God who is over *all* be blessed for ever" (9:5). And this is echoed in the final verse of ch. 11, from which the "therefore" of 12:1, which sets up the balance of the letter's message, emanates: "For from him and through him and to him are *all* things. To him be the glory forever" (11:36).

This dynamic may be helpfully clarified in terms of social identity theory.[3] The way in which we understand ourselves to be identified socially, for example, within group A rather than group B, is instrumental in our self- as well as group-identity and differentiation, and thus, discrimination. Social identity theorists have demonstrated that it does not take a value judgment beyond group identification to account for discrimination: group A people will discriminate against group B people (and vice versa) merely by the fact of group membership.

As long as the choice for the interpreter is to understand Paul socially defined as pro-Jewish *or* pro-Gentile, he or she must locate Paul along only one side of the spectrum of social self-interest (within either group A or group B). It seems that interpreters draw the line between Jews and Christ-believers, or more recently, Jewish Christ-believers and Gentile ones. But I suggest that another way to read the text indicates that Paul has drawn the line in keeping with the understanding often expressed in the Scriptures of Israel, that is, around all of the created order, with Israel in service of the other nations. In this sense, Abraham is the father of *all* who trust in the One Creator God, who is Lord of Israel *and* the nations. Paul understands even what might be regarded as socially embedded self-interest as an Israelite (group A) to be in the service of God when the focus is on reaching out to the Gentiles (group B), and thus in no way associated with turning away from Israel. They all are his children (group C), all one family. The social identity is inclusive of both people equally, of all of creation (A plus B within C).[4]

At points, Campbell avoids the usual category bifurcation, noting that the argument of Romans is pro-Jewish *and* pro-Gentile, because it is set within the particular role of Israel on behalf of the universal good of all humankind. Building on the suggestion of Fitzmyer and others regarding Paul's usage of Hosea and Isaiah in Rom. 9:24–29, he observes that the topic under discussion is God's activity with relation to Israel, and not a switch to the Gentiles. Rather, Israel will be restored and the Gentiles' blessing, which is the minor focus of the section, develops in this light. In this way, a foreshadowing of the discussion of Israel's hardening and restoration in ch. 11 is provided, and the element of "surprise" exclaimed by many commentators is instead anticipated.

Campbell notes that what Paul "intends to argue for is an extension of Israel's privileges to Gentiles (rather than a transfer of them away

---

◼ Social identity theory.

◼ Paul is neither pro-Jewish nor pro-Gentile, but sees one group inclusive of both.

◼ Israel's privileges and those available to Gentiles are equal.

from Israel)." I would qualify this slightly. It is not that Gentiles get
Israel's privileges, but that Israel's privileges and those now available to
the nations by the service of Israel are equal, as they were given equally
to all of creation, to all of Abraham's children, even if by necessity to one
of the children (that is, Israel) first, it then being that child's privileged
responsibility to bring this news to all of the other nations. It is not
a zero-sum situation of the present evil age, but a conviction that the
awaited one has dawned. This would help Campbell to avoid the trap he
seeks to overcome because of his sensitivities toward Jewish people, but
that logically follows in the received view: the notion of a transfer from
Israel to the Gentiles, meaning in effect the Gentile church; moreover,
it avoids the problem of considering Gentiles who believe in Jesus as
thereby becoming Jewish people or members of a "spiritual Israel" or
"true Israel." Thus, Campbell's notice of distinction is maintained, that
Jews in Christ remain Jews, while Gentiles remain Gentiles. I have tried
to put this simply, in stating that the difference (A or B) remains, but the
discrimination does not (all are C) (Nanos 1996a, 1996b).

In further discussion of Romans 9, Campbell notes that the consensus
has largely moved away from the earlier systematic treatments of predestination toward a recognition that the intention is to show how God has
maintained his purpose for his people, even through unexpected figures
such as a Pharaoh. I think that this can be pushed further in the light
of the foreshadowing Campbell has recognized, so that the real surprise
is that God may be up to something with Israel and the Gentiles that
is different than it may appear presently to the addressees in Rome —
Paul's message meaning, "Do not be fooled, God is faithful to Israel and
all who call upon him, and faithful too to prevent Israel harm, such as
may result from Gentile conceit against Israel."

I understand the mystery in Romans 11 to set out Paul's view that in
some unexpected way the pro-Gentile aspects of the development, and
the current lack of participation in this scheme by some Israelites, is not
to be taken to mean that the line has been redrawn so as to exclude
these Jewish people. But they are rather "surprisingly" served by these
fortunate Gentiles. And this is to confront a social identity boundary
among the Roman Gentiles that is beginning to be drawn mistakenly, so
as to preclude the continued participation of Jewish people who were
not part of this coalition. Paul's message undermines this Gentilecentric
viewpoint by asserting this to the Gentiles: the Jewish people's good has
been on behalf of you, so now your good as Gentiles is on behalf of

---

H Jews and Gentiles viewed from the perspective of creation rather than election-salvation.

A The real surprise is that God's dealings with Israel and Gentiles are different from the
perceptions of addressees in Rome, undermining Gentilecentric views.

H The mystery of Israel in Romans 11.

them (ch. 11); "therefore," have your viewpoint altered (to see things from God's vantage point) so that you are dedicated to their service, not destruction (chs. 12–16). It is in this light that the jealousy motif may be taken to redirect the Gentiles' misunderstanding of their current role, for even Paul's mission to the Gentiles is in the service of Israel first (11:11–15). And it is arguably the purpose of the remaining chapters, wherein the appropriate halakhic behavior for the Roman Gentiles in Christ is spelled out.

In the end, I do not see that the proposed different voices of Paul demonstrate inconsistency within or between the Paul(s) of Romans 11 and elsewhere. That is, the problem of Pauline inconsistency — to the degree ◧ that one considers this a problem — appears to lie with the interpreter's fashioning of a Paul and Paulinism that bifurcates his pro-Gentile and pro-Jewish stances. I suggest that these texts may be read so that Paul's ◨ pro-Gentile concern derives from a corresponding, indeed, a prior one that is pro-Jewish. I submit that this comes from his guiding Israelite conviction: God is One.

Notes

1. The phrase was coined by James D. G. Dunn in an article now reprinted (Dunn 1990), with reference to the groundbreaking work of E. P. Sanders (1977). It should be noted that one of the features of this article was a challenge to the internal inconsistency in Sanders's argument that is not dissimilar to my challenge of Wasserberg herein, and such problems of internal inconsistency may also be observed among the many otherwise welcome advances made by "new perspective" proponents, including Dunn; see, for example, discussion of "Luther's trap" (Nanos 1996a, 88–95, 115–19).

2. It may be noted that both are, of course, natural, but I think that "changed situation" may imply that it is a continuum in a location, rather than emphasizing the case that it is a *different* situation in each location, although each situation certainly changes as well. This distinction can be important in that we ought not to look for the kind of development likely to be explainable within an evolving situation when we are dealing with an entirely different one, with different people, set in a different location, as is obviously the case, for example, between Galatians and Romans.

3. This school of social psychology traces many of its fundamental insights to the work of Henri Tajfel (e.g., 1978; see also Hogg and Abrams 1988; Robinson 1996). Groundbreaking application of this theory to Pauline material is available in Esler 1998; and also for Matthew in Saldarini 1994.

◧ On an analytical level, Paul's inconsistency or consistency is according to the interpreter's hermeneutical frame.

◨ Pro-Jewish and pro-Gentile stances either in discontinuity or continuity.

4. I take this formation of a unified community to be the principle expressed in Paul's "new creation" language (e.g., Gal. 6:15; 2 Cor. 5:16–19; cf. Rom. 12:1–5; 1 Cor. 7:17–24; Gal. 3:28).

References

Dunn, J. D. G. 1990. "The New Perspective on Paul." Pp. 183–214 in *Jesus, Paul and the Law: Studies in Mark and Galatians*. Louisville: Westminster/John Knox.

Esler, Philip F. 1998. *Galatians*. New Testament Readings. London and New York: Routledge.

Hogg, Michael A., and Dominic Abrams. 1988. *Social Identifications: A Social Psychology of Intergroup Relations and Group Processes*. London and New York: Routledge.

Kotpak, Paul E. 1990. "Rhetorical Identification in Paul's Autobiographical Narrative: Galatians 1:13–2:14." *Journal for the Study of the New Testament* 40:97–115.

Nanos, Mark D. 1996a. *The Mystery of Romans: The Jewish Context of Paul's Letter*. Minneapolis: Fortress.

———. 1996b. "Why Was Gentile Circumcision So Unacceptable to Paul? The Role of the *Shema* in Paul's Gospel." Paper presented at the Central States regional meeting of the Society of Biblical Literature, St. Louis, March 23–24.

———. 1997. "Intruding 'Spies' and 'Pseudo' Brethren: The Intra-Jewish Context of 'Those of Repute' in Jerusalem (Gal. 2:1–10)." Paper presented at the International Research Consultation: Ideology, Power and Interpretation. Birmingham, England, August 1–3.

———. 1998. "The Inter- and Intra-Jewish Political Contexts of Paul and the Galatians." Paper presented at the session, Paul and Politics. Annual meeting of the Society of Biblical Literature, Orlando, Florida, November 21–24.

———. 1999. "The Jewish Context of the Gentile Audience Addressed in Paul's Letter to the Romans." *Catholic Biblical Quarterly* 61:283–304.

Robinson, W. Peter, ed. 1996. *Social Groups and Identities: Developing the Legacy of Henri Tajfel*. Oxford and Boston: Butterworth-Heinemann.

Saldarini, Anthony J. 1994. *Matthew's Christian-Jewish Community*. Chicago and London: University of Chicago Press.

Sanders, E. P. 1977. *Paul and Palestinian Judaism: A Comparison of Patterns of Religion*. Philadelphia: Fortress.

Tajfel, Henri, ed. 1978. *Differentiation between Social Groups: Studies in the Social Psychology of Intergroup Relations*. London and New York: Academic Press.

NINE

A Post-Holocaust Biblical Critic Responds

Daniel Patte

Know what happened here. Do not forget it. And yet, you will
never know.　　　　　　　　— Anonymous voice from Auschwitz

The truly remarkable transformation is not from
unbelief to belief
nor from
despair to hope.
The truly remarkable (and frightening) transformation is from
dogma to wonder
from
belief to awe.
　　　　　　　　　　　— Renita Weems, *Listening for God*

The essays by Joseph Sievers, Günter Wasserberg, William S. Campbell,
and Mark Nanos should be *read together* rather than independently of
each other. It is possible and legitimate to do so because they are parts of
an ongoing discussion about the relationship between the receptions of
Romans through history and cultures and critical studies of Romans. Together they form a collective discourse, which can be read as a whole. By
being in dialogue with each other these essays posit multiple analytical,
hermeneutical, and contextual frames, as the marginalia show. Together
they exemplify ways in which the text is interpreted in terms of certain
life-contexts and certain religious perceptions of life. Together they initiate a responsible interpretive practice — scriptural criticism — which the
overture presents in general terms.

　　Adding my voice to this discussion, I want now to prolong it in directions suggested by the overture, by underscoring that the text interprets
the interpreters, their life-contexts, and their religious perceptions of life.

My starting point should be clear. I read Romans 9–11 as open to multiple interpretations. Charles Cosgrove has made this point in *Elusive Israel: The Puzzle of Election in Romans*. The four preceding essays do the same thing, when they are read together. Their respective arguments in favor of one of these interpretations represent interpretive choices, which, as Cosgrove notes, need to be assessed in the present situation from a post-Holocaust perspective (1997, 26) — a perspective found among the contextual frames of each of the papers. Furthermore, I take the fact that Romans 9–11 is so blatantly open to multiple interpretations as a sign of Paul's incertitude regarding the way in which God deals with Israel and what is its relationship to the Gentile Christians. Yet, I do not construe this incertitude in a negative way. I view it as Paul's contemplation of an actual "mystery" (11:25, 33–36) — the mystery of Israel, with its rejection of the gospel and its irrevocable calling by a faithful God.

From this perspective, Romans 9–11 is an invitation for us to meditate on the mystery of Israel in our present context and on the place of Israel in our religious perception of life. This involves allowing the *tremendum* of the abyss, the Holocaust, to silence us and to transform our individualistic perceptions of our task into a collective one. Then the significance of the hermeneutical frames of the interpretations by Sievers, Wasserberg, Campbell, and Nanos appears. There is something beyond the reach of the interpretations. Each interpretation points toward it by its hermeneutical frames. Together, a series of interpretations delimits the space of this mystery, their respective hermeneutical frames marking its boundaries.

Resisting a Collective Reading of These Essays

My first inclination was to read the essays by Sievers, Wasserberg, Campbell, and Nanos independently of each other. It is, of course, possible and legitimate to do so. In our consumerist, individualistic Western way of reading (Griffiths 1999, 40–54), this is how we have been trained to read and how we commonly read. We want to know what each author has to say, here, about Romans 9–11 and its receptions. We resist reading these essays as a single collective discourse.

It is appropriate to read these essays as self-contained pieces. Each scholar wrote by himself in the isolated space of a study or of a library. According to the norms of Western scholarship in which each has been trained, each wrote with the intention that his essay would make sense in and of itself. Each strove to convey his interpretation of Romans 9–11 or of some parts of these chapters and argued why, for one reason or another, this is in his view "the best" interpretation. The scholarly genre of these essays justifies such a reading. This is how Daniel Boyarin read them (see chapter 10), as he was called to do in preparing his response to essays that, without the marginalia, appeared to be only loosely related. I can even say that each author expects his essay to be read as a self-contained piece. I know. This is how I usually write my studies of biblical texts. We biblical critics resist conceiving our studies as parts of a collective discourse that encompasses our debates with colleagues.

From this individualistic perspective, each essay tends to be totally framed by the unipolar analytical goal of elucidating "what the text really says," because this textual evidence is the only legitimate basis for subsequent hermeneutical applications — the bipolar interpretive process in the tradition of Gabler's gap. Each paper advocates a particular reading of Romans 9–11 or one of its parts, as many exegetical studies have done before it. In so doing, each paper suggests that it should be assessed for its contribution to the advancement of our knowledge of the text. Does it clarify features of the text that heretofore remained obscure? Each does, in its own way. And these results are not to be neglected.

Problems with Reading These Essays as Self-Contained Entities

In the give-and-take of the collective discourse in which these essays were developed, a primary focus on the independent contribution of each is problematic. From this perspective, each essay appears to make exclusive claims for its analytical conclusions. Of course, each author would vehemently deny making such a claim. Who, in a discussion, would want to claim that he or she has the only true interpretation and that all other interpretations are inept? And yet, this is what these essays convey when they are read as self-contained pieces.

Thus, when Sievers's essay is read independently of the others, its point is that the only legitimate reading is his rigorous analytical interpretation of Rom. 11:29 in terms of the appropriate literary context, Romans 9–11 (and not Hebrews). Accordingly, taken alone, this reading of Rom. 11:29 allows us to acknowledge the mystery of God's faithfulness to the Jewish people apart from faith in Jesus Christ — a much welcomed message in a post-Holocaust context. Does this mean that Sievers proposes his reading as the only true one? Does he intend to say that because of its special rigor, his analytical study of the text addresses issues regarding reading Israel in Romans that all other interpreters failed to address? Of course not.

Similarly, in their respective essays, Wasserberg, Campbell, and Nanos propose results of their critical studies of "what the text really says." In so doing, they address issues left open or inappropriately resolved by other interpretations, including those of their colleagues in the group. But, does each intend to say that his study offers definitive answers to the interpretive questions left open for twenty centuries, and that all interpreters should adopt his specific interpretation if they really want to be true to the text? Of course not. In our discussions, Sievers, Wasserberg, Campbell, and Nanos have vehemently denied that they make such a claim through their essays. Their essays are contributions to an ongoing discussion. Reading them as self-contained pieces would have as problematic an effect as reading a pericope from Romans out of its context.

Thus, we receive ambivalent signals. On the one hand, the scholarly style of these essays suggests that they should be read independently of each other. On the other hand, their authors' vehement denial of the problematic implications of such a reading strongly signals that it is appropriate to read them as a collective discourse. It soon appears that it makes a significant difference to read these essays together, as I now propose to show.

Entering an Ongoing Discussion among Four Scholars: Scriptural Criticism as Collective Endeavor

Sievers's essay was originally written to initiate the discussion about the relationship between the receptions of Romans through history and critical studies of Romans. Sievers did so by presenting the broad range of receptions of Rom. 11:29 through the centuries up to present-day debates related to post-Holocaust receptions. Then he rewrote it to reflect the first fruits of this discussion, namely, the recognition that distinguishing analytical, contextual, and hermeneutical frames is helpful for comparing receptions of a text. The question is raised, How does each of these receptions read Israel and its relationship to the (Gentile) Christian church? The ambivalence of the verse, especially in Latin translation, but also when read in terms of one literary context or another in Romans and the New Testament, provides textual grounding for a diversity of analytical frames through which Israel is read. Furthermore, theological and ethical concerns also frame Israel, and God's gifts and calling of Israel. The harrowing question is, Is it possible to read Israel in Romans in such a way that the reading be appropriately grounded in textual evidence (analytical frame) and also be theologically acceptable (hermeneutical frame) and ethically responsible (contextual frame)?

Wasserberg, in an essay developed to help the group to pursue this discussion, gives a negative answer to that question. For him, this is the pressing issue of the appropriation in post-Holocaust Germany of Romans 9–11 as Scripture by Christians who want to engage in Jewish-Christian dialogues. Through his own excruciating reception of this text, he illustrates fundamental aspects of the last stage of Sievers's history of receptions, concerning receptions of Romans 9–11 after the Holocaust. In the process, Wasserberg raises the issue of the relationship between the analytical frame and both the contextual and hermeneutical frames, and thus between the results of analytical critical studies that establish "what the text says" and theological and ethical concerns that Christians bring to the text read as Scripture. Wasserberg's theological concerns are related to basic Christian convictions regarding the faithfulness of God, God's relationship with Israel, and the nature of the good news of salvation through faith in Jesus Christ. His ethical concerns are no less weighty, since they are about anti-Judaism and anti-Semitism, which are too often (always, according to Ruether [1974]) latent in proclamations of Jesus as Christ.

Campbell makes a quite different contribution to the discussion by addressing the issue of the plurality of interpretations. Is this plurality due to polyvalence in the text of Romans that results from inconsistencies in Paul's argument? Or from different "images of Paul" in terms of which readers might read the letter? In the process, Campbell exposes a variety of analytical frames through which Romans 9–11 are read as inconsistent or as consistent. He also shows the correlation of these analytical frames with hermeneutical frames through which the interpreters perceive either discontinuity or continuity between Israel and the (Gentile) Christian community.

Nanos continues this collective discourse by responding to Wasserberg and Campbell. Since Nanos proposes alternative analytical interpretations, neither Wasserberg's nor Campbell's analytical conclusions can be the immutable basis for addressing hermeneutical and contextual concerns. Israel in Romans can be read in other ways. The text offers other possibilities for addressing the issues raised by Paul's teaching regarding the relationship between Jews and Christians.

We biblical critics — here, Campbell, Nanos, Wasserberg, and I — are primarily concerned with establishing as rigorously as possible "what the text says." The centripetal pull toward unipolar interpretation is hard to resist by ourselves. Yet, we can do so with the help of our colleagues. We cannot ignore that theologians and church historians readily point out that our analytical conclusions about the text and about what it says have hermeneutical and ethical implications; they are framed by theological and ideological categories, as well as by pragmatic contextual concerns. Our interpretations, even though they are primarily analytical, are also receptions of the text in terms of certain religious perceptions of life in specific contexts. Although the theologians' and church historians' comments often have a critical edge — "You biblical critics are not as objective as you might claim!" — in the perspective of our collective endeavor these comments are heard as the description of a normal state of affairs that ensues when one interprets a scriptural text, even if one does not view it as Scripture.

Conversely, theologians and church historians — here, Sievers —

cannot ignore that biblical critics readily point out that the believers' receptions that they present are highly selective in their choices of particularly significant textual features upon which they ground their interpretations. Though at first biblical critics might be disparaging when formulating such observations — "Look at all the textual features ignored by the believers' receptions!" — in the perspective of our collective endeavor these comments are heard as calling biblical critics to acknowledge that even the most sophisticated scholarly interpretation is highly selective in its choice of textual evidence. When we allow one critical method or another to focus our reading, as is necessary for the sake of scholarly rigor, we also focus our attention on certain textual features. We also posit that these particular features are more significant than others, and thus we are highly selective in our choices of significant textual features.

Through the marginalia, Cristina Grenholm and I have already made explicit the diverse ways in which Sievers, Wasserberg, Campbell, and Nanos have framed their interpretations of (parts of) Romans 9–11. Yet, questions raised by this collective discourse linger. Is it legitimate to frame one's reading of the text in terms of a specific critical category, and thus in terms of certain textual features viewed as particularly significant, while ignoring other critical categories and other textual features (analytical frame)? Is it appropriate to bring to the text certain theological categories and to frame one's reading in terms of these? Is it ethically responsible to relate the text to life in terms of certain bridge-categories, which might have nothing to do with the bridge-categories used in the original context?

For me, as can be expected, each of these questions is to be answered by a resounding yes! But this positive answer does not dispel, in itself, the twinges of skepticism from all parties involved. Biblical critics ask, Is this not betraying the text? Theologians ask, Is this not caving in to political or other pressures? Believers and practical theologians ask, Is this not undermining the authority of Scripture? All of us, at least in the European-American academic world, fear that "engagement," through which we bring to the text our hermeneutical and contextual concerns in the interpretive process, will somehow distort and invalidate the interpretation. Thus, even though we know it to be an illusory goal, we instinctively strive to make our interpretation as "disengaged" as possible.

The best way to dispel these doubts and to overcome this instinctive resistance is to make explicit what is at stake in acknowledging that the critical study of a scriptural text is a tripolar collective endeavor. For this, on the basis of Sievers's, Wasserberg's, Campbell's, and Nanos's critical studies of Romans 9–11 — in which the text is analytically read and reread in terms of hermeneutical and contextual concerns both — I propose to consider how the *interpreters' situations* (their life-contexts and their religious perceptions both) are reinterpreted in terms of the text.

At the dawn of a new millennium, we Christian biblical critics and church historians read Israel in Romans 9–11 in terms of hermeneutical and contextual concerns arising out of the dreadful events of the recent past — the Holocaust. As Wasserberg makes explicit, we must reexamine our conclusions regarding the teaching of this text about the relationship between Israel and the (Gentile) Christian community. Such a teaching has far-reaching religious implications regarding salvation, its conditions — does it require faith in Jesus Christ or not? — God's faithfulness (see Sievers), continuity or lack of continuity between Israel and the church (see Campbell and Nanos), and the mystery of God's dealings with human beings. It also has far-reaching ethical implications, with the flames of the Holocaust exposing triumphalism, supersessionism, and their claim that salvation depends on faith in Jesus as Christ as potential bases for anti-Judaism and latent anti-Semitism. Against this background, the importance of the diversity of potential analytical, hermeneutical, and contextual frames discussed by Sievers, Wasserberg, Campbell, and Nanos becomes apparent. We have an actual choice of interpretations. Consequently, even if we accept Paul's letter as Scripture, we Christian believers are no longer condemned to adopt those tragic interpretations that, in one way or another, condone the Holocaust. Yet, this choice of interpretation is not a private or personal matter, as we European-Americans have been trained to think in our Western cultures. It is a choice that we need to learn to make in a responsible and disciplined way through an ongoing dialogue with others in a community of discourse.

Scriptural criticism, as a collective scholarly endeavor, prepares us to make such a choice. Beyond helping us to recognize that we made choices as we interpreted the text from specific hermeneutical and contextual perspectives, scriptural criticism makes us aware of the fact that, conversely, we interpret our situation in terms of the text. Here also, we need to learn to do so in a responsible and disciplined way with others in a community of discourse.

Our task as biblical critics in a post-Holocaust context is an important aspect of the concrete situation that we interpret from the perspective of Romans 9–11. The question is, How does Paul's struggle with the mystery of the relationship between Israel and the (Gentile) Christians call us to rethink the task of biblical criticism that we pursue in a post-Holocaust context? For me, Rom. 11:25 encapsulates the perspective from which the text calls us to look at our situation. Οὐ γὰρ θέλω ὑμᾶς ἀγνοεῖν, ἀδελφοί, τὸ μυστήριον τοῦτο does not mean, in my interpretation, that Paul wants to explain the mystery to his readers, as the NRSV suggests: "brothers and sisters, I want you to understand this mystery." If that were the case, there is no mystery left. Rather, as the AV expresses — "For I

would not, brethren, that ye should be ignorant of this mystery" — Paul
wants his readers to be aware of the presence of this mystery so that
they might contemplate it. Similarly, in order to avoid being arrogant —
ἵνα μὴ ἦτε [παρ'] ἑαυτοῖς φρόνιμοι, "So that you may not claim to be
wiser than you are" (NRSV) (always a good exhortation for scholars) —
we biblical critics have to be aware that there is a mystery we should
contemplate, namely, the mystery of Israel, of its situation, and of its
relationship to (Gentile) Christians. For us today, this means that we
should rethink our practice of biblical criticism even as we contemplate
the dreadful mystery of the Holocaust.

Contemplating Biblical Criticism and the Holocaust

As I silently contemplate the Holocaust, it becomes plainer to me, as it
is to Wasserberg, that Christian biblical interpretations are laced with
anti-Judaism and share responsibility for the lethal anti-Semitism that
engendered the death camps.

In this silent contemplation, I begin to see that through our work, we
Christian biblical scholars have contributed and continue to contribute
to make of the Crucified One the center of the cataclysm that engulfed
European Jewry,[1] as is poignantly represented by Marc Chagall's *White
Crucifixion*.[2]

The silence of biblical critics during the entire period of the rise of
Nazism and during the Holocaust cries out for explanation. Their interpretation of the text reflects their interpretation of their situation.
Splendid scientific detachment made critical biblical studies more and
more respected and influential, because of their *Wissenschaft*. But biblical scholars remained silent regarding the burning predicament of
European Jewry.

The sorrow and the pity[3] experienced in presence of "the desolation"
of the *Shoah* teach us that detachment — be it for the sake of objectivity,
for the pursuit of other duties, or because of indifference — is never neutral. Whenever and wherever anti-Judaism and anti-Semitism are fueled
by Christian biblical interpretations — unfortunately, almost always and
everywhere in Western cultures — detachment in critical biblical studies
becomes an accomplice in this unthinkable crime.

Sorrow and pity permeate the hermeneutic of suspicion that we must
adopt as we examine our practices as European-American biblical scholars, because, at least in our contexts, critical biblical studies and the
Holocaust are closely intertwined. Our noblest endeavors contribute to
generate what we execrate (cf. Rom. 7:15–19).

Unfortunately, this tragic vision of our work as critical biblical scholars is not a nightmare from which we could wake up to a more pleasant
reality. The unthinkable reality of the killing of six million men, women,

and children (see Phillips 1999), each with his or her personal anguished face,[4] clings to Western critical biblical studies. The stench of death[5] seems to emanate not only from the New Testament texts, their Christologies (Ruether 1974, 246 and passim), and their theologies (Burnett 1992), but also from the very core of critical biblical scholarship, namely, disengaged reading practices that condone the complicity of silence.

And yet, scholars as sensitive to the Holocaust as are Sievers, Wasserberg, Campbell, and Nanos are reluctant to give up disengaged reading practices, by keeping them separate from engagement. Each, in his own way, seeks to establish as objectively as possible "what the text says." Collectively, they warn us that our contemplation of the Holocaust should not become a denial of reality, be it the reality of the text and what it says or the reality of the Holocaust itself.

Biblical Criticism as Both Disengaged and Engaged

The radical implications of the Holocaust for biblical criticism begin to appear as soon as one remembers the broken glass of its beginning. *Kristallnacht* "testifies to a deeper breaking of basic human continuities" (Plank 1994, 141). When they are suspect of condoning the Holocaust, our unipolar interpretations and their smooth continuity between interpreters and biblical texts as objects break apart. We scholars who use such approaches born in Europe must reexamine all aspects of our critical practice. But this does not mean completely rejecting them.

Most generally, the Holocaust demands both disengagement and engagement in scholarship. Against neo-Nazis who would deny that the Holocaust took place, a disengaged critical study that establishes its factuality is ever necessary. Yet, engagement is also necessary, since lack of engagement was the complicity that empowered the perpetrators. In the aftermath of the Holocaust, neither disengagement nor engagement can be excluded from critical biblical studies. Then, both detached critical analysis and engaged hermeneutics are transformed. They are no longer polar opposites; they are complementary processes in each interpretation; as disengagement and engagement, they engender each other.[6]

Disengagement is necessary to recognize that anti-Jewish and anti-Semitic interpretations of New Testament texts do accurately reflect something found in the texts. For instance, Wasserberg's interpretation of Romans 9–11 appropriately underscores anti-Jewish features in these texts. But this does not mean that such texts are unambiguous. As Boyarin underscores regarding Gal. 3:10–4:7, these texts are not simply anti-Jewish; they are both anti-Jewish and not anti-Jewish (1994, 136–57).[7] The juxtaposition of Nanos's interpretation with that of Wasserberg makes this point regarding Romans 9–11. Because of their ambiguity, such texts give rise to both anti-Jewish and not anti-Jewish interpretations.

Disengagement requires us to affirm the reality of the textual evidence, as that which has the power to affect readers, especially believers for whom the text is Scripture. But after *Kristallnacht,* disengagement also requires from us to question our perception of the textual evidence and the continuity we perceive in it. Some might fear that pointing out the necessary bias of any description of the Holocaust amounts to denying it happened. But as Haas shows, elucidating the constructed character of these historical descriptions contributes to establish the factuality of the event they describe (1995, 6–12).[8] Similarly, disengaging ourselves from our own interpretations by acknowledging the analytical frames through which we construct the text (what the text is) and its subject matter (what the text says) does not deny the reality of textual evidence. It reveals that the text-object studied with disengagement is itself a construct, without denying that it is an actual object that can be analyzed. As Campbell illustrates regarding several interpretations of Romans 9–11, and as the marginalia express regarding his own interpretation, recognizing the constructed character of the continuity (and discontinuity) we perceive in the text helps us to make explicit actual features of the text that became most significant for the interpreters.

Then it appears that disengagement presupposes engagement and calls for further engagement. The *Kristallnacht* breaking of the unified text-object studied with disengagement reveals that it is constructed by choosing certain features in a polyvalent text — it presupposes a choice and thus engagement. Since there are several potential text-objects, any interpretation reflects an engagement. In each case, we interpreters choose one constructed text-object among several potential ones because it makes sense in our cultural and religious milieu (hermeneutical frame) and because in a given situation it is particularly valuable for us (contextual frame).

Meditating before the Holocaust reveals both the significance and implications of the denials involved in a "detached" unipolar practice of biblical criticism that exclusively defines its task in terms of disengagement. Denying that disengagement is necessarily intertwined with engagement, description with contextualization, analytical frames with hermeneutical and contextual frames is not merely the denial of parts of the interpretive process but also the denial of a reality that demands engagement, a denial of a part of what critical thought should account for.

Denial, suppression, and repression transform the denied reality into a monster that destroys self and society. This is especially true when the denied reality is close to the core of existence, as pointed out in the post-Freudian tradition.[9] It comes back and haunts us as a devouring monster, such as the dragon spitting fire toward the little girl it will devour — the self-portrait that one of the fifteen thousand children from the Prague ghetto drew at the Theresienstadt camp in the days preceding their deportation to a death-*Lager*. Then we have to wonder, Is this what happens to our well-intentioned critical biblical interpretations when they become dangerous, hellish? Did they deny a reality close to the core of existence? As the overture argues, from the perspective of the Holocaust the denial of engagement in critical interpretation is the denial of two basic modes of existence, relationality and heteronomy. This twofold denial, fueled by an obsession for the unipolar "security" of a detached, single, universally true interpretation, disavows our place in the interpretation, the transforming power of the scriptural text upon believers. It is therefore a denial of that which transcends us in the text and in the interpretation, that is, the heteronomous mode of existence. Yet, in order to acknowledge this denial and recognize our responsibility for it, we need to continue our meditation before the monster it engendered.

Meditating before the Holocaust as Outsiders — Patterns of Relationship Being Transformed

From the outset, meditating before the Holocaust reveals to us our status as Christian European-American biblical scholars. We are outsiders, on the other side of the fence.[10] The enormity of the monstrous suffering of the Holocaust prevents us from facile identification with the insiders, for whom it is the *Shoah,* the desolation. Suggesting, "We know how you feel," would be insulting, to say the least. Pointless suffering commands respectful silence, contemplation, before saying anything.

Meditating before the Holocaust transforms the pattern of relationship that we Christian biblical critics had with the text and with other readers in our common practice of biblical criticism. Acknowledging our position of outsiders, listening to insiders, affirming and respecting their otherness, then speaking with them from our otherness as outsiders is a pattern of relationality born out of heteronomy. This pattern of relationship arises out of the contemplation of a mystery to which we abandon ourselves.

In our unipolar practices we follow the pattern that Spivak finds in European-American colonialist discourse (1988, 295). It includes listening to others, but as a preparation for speaking about them as objects and for speaking for them as subalterns who have value only insofar as they conform to us. The otherness of the other is indeed recognized and described, but is not allowed to speak in its own voice, and therefore is neither respected nor affirmed. Thus, we listen to a biblical text in order to speak about it and to speak for it. As we do so, we deny, suppress, or repress essential characteristics of biblical texts as words of a person to be respected in his or her mysterious otherness. Furthermore, this implies that we exclude the religious dimension of the texts as religious speech-acts pointing to experiences of the Holy Other and as Word of God for present-day believers.

Meditating before the Holocaust transforms our relationship to other interpreters, as we acknowledge and respect their otherness. Priority is no longer given to speaking for them with a condescending tone — "I know what you mean." Rather, we listen to the anonymous voice from Auschwitz: "Know what happened here. Do not forget it. And yet, you will never know." Consequently, we can no longer adopt a polemic tone, speaking about them and their interpretations after reducing them to the status of objects to be analyzed and then to be either co-opted or rejected. (We find this tendency in the essays by Sievers, Wasserberg, Campbell, and Nanos when read as self-contained pieces rather than as parts of a collective discourse.) By contrast, we are now invited to ponder the mystery of the otherness of other interpreters and of their interpretations.

Meditating before the Holocaust helps us to recognize that our unipolar scholarly studies dismiss as childish the interpretations by most readers of the Bible, and in particular, by those reader-believers who have the audacity to think that these texts have a word for their lives. But at what cost? What are we suppressing? Nothing less than the voices of others who also read the text, as well as the mystery of the relationship of the scriptural text to its reader-believers, and the religious character of the text.

From the outset, meditating before the Holocaust questions our suppression of all relationship to otherness and to the Holy as manifested in different parts of the interpretive process.

Thinking the Unthinkable and Accounting for the Holy: The Task of Biblical Criticism

As Christians listen to the meditation before the *Shoah* of an insider, Arthur Cohen,[11] the places and roles of scriptural texts, of their traditional interpretations, of critical biblical studies, and of theological language are clarified.

Meditating before the *Shoah*, Cohen first notes that it reveals the limits of a theological language that cannot encompass it, because it gives us, in this secular age, an experience of the Holy. "We of the modern age [who] are no longer able to deal with the Holy, cannot perceive it, or authenticate it" (1981, 18) can once again perceive, authenticate, and deal with the Holy, and be shaken to our foundations by it, even though it is an inverted *tremendum*.[12]

Because "the *tremendum* marks an end" that "augurs a beginning" (Cohen 1981, 59), it calls into question the continuity with past and future. "The challenge of the *tremendum* to Judaism is not that traditional reality cannot survive the scrutiny of its teaching... but rather that its view of its own depths will be found shallow, insufficiently deep and flexible enough to compass and contain the *tremendum*" (82). Thus, all that can be done is to build a bridge above the abyss. Thus, the traditions are not excluded; they are transfigured, becoming building material for this bridge after close examination against the background of the *tremendum*. Then this bridge of traditions makes the abyss ever visible, and the ever-present mysterious abyss exposes the inadequacy of these traditions, their shallowness and their lack of flexibility. The *Shoah* brings to light that it is fundamentally wrong to claim that any tradition — and thus also any biblical text and *a fortiori* any given interpretation of it — could encompass and master the *tremendum*. This is true whether it is the "transcending" *tremendum* of divine mystery or the "subscending" *tremendum* of the abysmal mystery (Tracy's vocabulary in Cohen 1981, vii). Before the awful mystery of the *Shoah*, the Jewish philosopher is freed from the temptation to absolutize either traditions or thinking and reason — their limitations are plain. Similarly, before the awful mystery of the Holocaust, we outsiders are freed from the temptation to absolutize either the scriptural texts or their scholarly interpretations.

What is this temptation to absolutize to which we easily succumb as long as we are not confronted by the presence of the *tremendum* in either of its forms? We can recognize it when the *Shoah* painfully reveals to us that the abyss, "meaningless inversion of life," occurs and is perpetuated when the human is infinitized; when death is denied by "build[ing] a mountain of corpses to the divinity of the dead, to placate death by the magic of endless murder" (Cohen 1981, 19). The abyss also occurs, for instance, when the ultimate is confused with the final; when the *tremendum* is viewed as final, something it is not, although "it is ultimate because it comprehends and articulates all negativity and contradiction" (49); when "what is taken as God's speech" (in the Bible) is viewed as final, although it "is really always [hu]man's hearing," thus ultimate; when God is taken as the final "strategist of our historical condition," although God as ultimate is "the mystery of our futurity" (97; cf. Vahanian 1966, 1992).[13]

These brief quotations and selected reflections by Cohen, an insider, are but a few of the many insights that his work offers to us outsiders who seek to forge a meaningful connection to the Holocaust without trivializing and reducing its scandal (Plank 1994, 2). Yet, these are enough to reveal the glaring gap in the practice of biblical criticism by Christian European-American scholars: our critical interpretations

do not account for the Holy as *tremendum*. This is the reality of
the core of human experience that our interpretations deny with dire
consequences.

As people "of the modern age [who] are no longer able to deal with
the Holy, cannot perceive it, or authenticate it" (Cohen 1981, 18), by
ourselves we have no clue regarding how a practice of biblical criticism
could account for the Holy. When this issue is raised, we revert to the
debate regarding disengagement and engagement, as we ponder how to
deal with the Holy as *mysterium tremendum et fascinans* that we relegate
to the general domain of "feelings" (Otto 1923, 41–49).[14] How could
we account for something beyond our grasp and merely felt? But Cohen
resolves our confusion. Accounting for the Holy does not mean encompassing it. This is why one can think the unthinkable. Accounting for the
Holy involves acknowledging the inadequacy of language, and thus the
inadequacy of all interpretations.

Thus, the first lesson from Cohen is that we European-American biblical scholars must acknowledge that we are commonly driven by the false
confidence that there is nothing beyond the reach of critical thought.
Following Cohen, we can denounce the triumphalism of critical thought
in biblical studies that posits as its task "mastering its object, dissolving
the difficulties, containing and elucidating the conundrum." The entire
unipolar quest implied in this view of critical thinking breaks into pieces
against the Holocaust.

Scriptural Criticism
Acknowledging the Limitations
of the Interpretive Process

Renouncing a triumphalist practice of biblical criticism is not a loss, but
a gain. This means, of course, that we cannot trust that biblical criticism will overcome all obstacles and master the biblical texts and their
significance. But this is simply recognizing the reality of the interpretive
process. Mastering a text is a very limited and reductionist form of interpretation. Positively, such a renunciation puts us in a position to perceive
the dimensions of the text and of the interpretive process that transcend
us, namely, religious perceptions of life, heteronomous experiences of
human otherness and of divine Otherness, the Holy, mysteries.

Acknowledging the inability of biblical criticism to encompass the
Holy is not a matter of abandoning positivistic illusions. We have con-
fessed for a long time that our critical interpretations have nothing more
than a relative legitimacy, since they "must be seen as claiming only a
greater or a lesser degree of probability and as always open to revision"

(Harvey 1966, 14). Yet, we have not abandoned the false confidence that there is nothing beyond the reach of this nonpositivist critical thought.

Similarly, it is not a matter of denying any usefulness to biblical criticism on the grounds that all interpretations are inadequate, unable to establish with certainty the significance of biblical texts, and thus on the grounds that with its subjective relativism none can be viewed as more authoritative than another. For Cohen, as for Fackenheim, giving up the possibility of meaningful thinking and becoming nihilist would be "to hand Hitler yet another, posthumous victory" (Fackenheim 1987, 159). The Holocaust does not call us to deny the value of biblical criticism, which it has shown to be unable to master the biblical text, any more than it calls us to deny the value of the Jewish traditions, which it has shown to be unable to encompass the Holy.

Rather, when our critical interpretations acknowledge their inadequacy and their limitations, at last they fully perform their task by making explicit the presence of the Holy. Indeed, by making explicit that they are totally unable to get hold of and encompass the *tremendum,* our interpretations also take note of, and thus account for, the presence of the *tremendum,* instead of ignoring it, denying it, suppressing it. It is by such an acknowledgment that Cohen thoughtfully accounts for the unthinkable as unthinkable, as *tremendum.*

What this means for the practice of biblical criticism by Christian European-Americans has been spelled out in the overture. Accounting for the presence of the *tremendum,* that is, also, accounting for the heteronomous mode of experience and for its religious perceptions of life requires a collective tripolar interpretive practice that Cristina Grenholm and I called scriptural criticism. The terrified and resigned face of a little girl before a fiery dragon at Theresienstadt demands from us Christian European-American scholars a practice of critical biblical interpretation of New Testament texts that accounts for the Holy, the religious, the experiences of the *tremendum,* the ideologies of these texts. Otherwise, our interpretations risk, again and again, becoming oppressive. The face of the little girl demands from us an accounting for all that elicits from Christian believers the confession that these texts are Scripture, Word of God. The face of the little girl also demands from us an accounting for the religious perception of life as a pole of the interpretive process.

How should we do this? Precisely, in the same way as one accounts for any experience of the Holy. It involves acknowledging that we have reached the limits of language; that we are beyond words. For each of us, it means making explicit the point where our interpretation loses its grip, where it can no longer stay in control, where it encounters issues that it cannot resolve or elucidate. Then, as a collective, we can survey the boundaries around the sacred space of the Holy marked by the places where we lost our grip (see Cohen 1981, 58).

Collective Mapping Out of Boundaries of the Holy
in Interpretations of Romans 9–11:
The Hermeneutical Frames

Using the marginalia to indicate the hermeneutical frames, Cristina Grenholm and I have already mapped out the boundaries of the Holy that
the authors of the essays have collectively marked. In these essays as
final products of biblical interpretations, hermeneutical frames reflect religious perceptions of life related both to the text and the interpreters'
heteronomous experience. As such, hermeneutical frames point toward
the Holy, the mystery of the Other. A brief review of the marginalia in
the essays by Sievers, Wasserberg, Campbell, and Nanos is enough to
recognize the sacred space of the Holy in these interpretations.

For Sievers, the interpretations of Rom. 11:29 through the centuries
lose their grip on four issues that begin to mark boundaries for the
mystery that interpreters encounter in this text (and its literary context): Christian views of Judaism; the relationship between Israel and the
church; the character of God; and salvation. Regarding each of these issues, Sievers notes much ambivalence in the interpretations through the
centuries. Wasserberg, Campbell, and Nanos bring additional ambivalence to these issues by formulating them in their own ways, and they
add five other markers of the boundaries for this mystery: Jesus Christ as
the Messiah; the meaning of Torah; Paul's Jewish identity; Paul's primary
role as author of Romans; and the shame and sense of responsibility
Christians have after the Holocaust.

Each of these issues points toward something that transcends the interpretations, as is signaled by the diversity of hermeneutical frames in
which it is formulated. This mystery of the text for the interpreters as a
collective is best represented by a series of questions for which no definite
answers are given by the collective of interpreters.

1. *Christian views of Judaism.* Regarding these views we can ask, from
a Christian perspective and according to Romans, Is Judaism a sign of
God's judgment and condemnation? Or, is there a continuing theological significance for Judaism, which has a permanent vocation (Sievers)?
Is Judaism the self-sufficient religious system of God's chosen people?
Or, for a Christianity with an anti-Jewish "left hand," is Judaism a legalistic faith that is the paradigm of deficient religions (Wasserberg)? Is
there continuity and discontinuity between the old and the new? Is the
continuity the extension of Israel's benefits to Gentiles and the discontinuity due to the rejection of Israel (whether or not the promise is kept)
(Campbell)?

2. *The relationship between Israel and the church.* Regarding this relationship we can ask, Is the role of Israel superseded by the Church
or not (Sievers, Campbell)? Is there neither superiority nor inferiority

between Jews and Christians? Or, do Christians have the gospel of grace, with a redefinition of the election that supersedes Jewish legalistic faith (Wasserberg)? Is an ideological dismissal of Judaism involved (Nanos)?

3. *The character of God.* Here we can ask, Is God's faithfulness unconditional or conditional (Sievers)? Is God called into question by the Jewish refusal of Christ (Wasserberg)? Is God impartial or favoring Israel? Is God's faithful toward Israel? Is God free and Israel fluctuating in loyalty (Campbell)? Is God the One God of Jews and Gentiles (Nanos)?

4. *Salvation.* Here we can ask, Is salvation universal or limited to those who confess that Jesus is the Christ (Sievers, Wasserberg)? Is conversion of Jewish people required or not for their salvation (Nanos)?

Beyond these four common points, several other issues point toward the mystery of Romans 9–11. There is mystery about Jesus Christ as the Messiah. Is he the Messiah of both Jews and Gentiles (Wasserberg)? There is mystery about the meaning and function of Torah (Wasserberg). There is mystery about Paul's identity and role in relation to Judaism. Can he be a faithful Jew and proclaim Jesus as Messiah (Wasserberg, Nanos)? What is the role of Paul's own experience (Campbell)? Was he a Jewish reformer (Nanos)? There is mystery about the role of contemporary Christians in anti-Jewish interpretations of Romans (the shame and sense of responsibility of Christians) (Wasserberg). Finally, pondering this mystery needs to account for its shape. Does this mystery concern Paul's timeless, abstract theology or Paul's missionary program (Wasserberg, Campbell, and Nanos)?

The mystery surrounded by these boundaries concerns Israel, its relationship to God, its salvation, its relationship to the Christian faith in Jesus as the Messiah, its Torah, and therefore how Israel should be construed by Christians in their missionary activities as well as in their theologies. As a collective of interpreters of Romans, we can only stop and ponder the great variety of ways in which we can construct Israel as we are "reading Israel in Romans." Our traditional interpretations then become a bridge above the mystery (both the transcending *tremendum* of divine mystery and the subscending *tremendum* of the abyss [again using Tracy's vocabulary in Cohen 1981, vii]). Thus, traditional interpretations are not excluded; they are transfigured, becoming building material for this bridge after close examination against the background of the mystery. Then this bridge of traditional interpretations makes the mystery ever visible and the ever-present mystery exposes the inadequacy of these traditional interpretations, their shallowness, and their inflexibility.

Then, knowing that we are on sacred ground, we have to proceed with awe and wonder, and with a deep sense of the tremendous responsibility we have as we construct Israel in our interpretations. And throughout, we must remain humbly cognizant of the fact that we will never know this mystery that is before us. This is what the note hidden near the ovens of Auschwitz by one of the millions of victims expressed in a poignant way about the dreadful mystery of the *Shoah:* "Know what happened here. Do not forget it. And yet, you will never know."[15]

Notes

1. This comment applies also to scholars who in Germany resisted the rise of Nazism in their private lives, and today to those who deny the Christian character of their own interpretations.

2. Located in the Art Institute of Chicago. Karl A. Plank describes this 1938 painting in terms of the Holocaust (1994, 141–44).

3. Marcel Ophuls has illustrated this in his motion picture *Le chagrin et la pitié (The Sorrow and the Pity)* by presenting ordinary, well-intentioned people progressively condoning the deportation of their Jewish neighbors.

4. It is true that in the death camps, the killing was highly depersonalized in the gas chambers. But as Browning (1992) has documented, about half of the six millions Jews were killed in a more personal way: they were gunned down with revolvers as well as machine guns; they were left to die of deprivation in ghettos or of exhaustion in labor camps. While the depersonalized, systemic character of evil in the Holocaust should not be forgotten, its personalized character must also be accounted for. Then the unthinkable horror of the Holocaust can be more directly perceived, when comparing it to horrible tragedy occurring in our present — such as the Oklahoma City bombing and its 168 victims, whose stories fill the newspapers at the time I write (during the trial of the accused perpetrator). A few personal faces of victims of the Holocaust are the subject matter of Karl A. Plank's *Mother of the Wire Fence* (see the faces in the title-page photograph on which this book meditates). See also Phillips 1999.

5. As I continue to meditate on Chagall's *White Crucifixion* — the Crucified One as center of the Holocaust cataclysm — the ambivalence of our reading practices in critical biblical studies as applied to christological texts reminds me of Paul's observation that his Christian testimony was "read" in opposite ways by different people: "For we are the aroma of Christ.... To the one a fragrance from death to death, to the other a fragrance from life to life" (2 Cor. 2:15–16).

6. I use "disengagement" rather than "detachment," because the latter could be a process independent of "engagement."

7. Boyarin's detailed discussion can be summarized by these concluding sentences: "Paul's hermeneutic of the Jews as signifier of the faithful body of Christians, of the Jews as the literal κατὰ σάρκα of which Christians are the allegorical signified, κατὰ πνεῦμα, even if not the 'origin of anti-Semitism,' certainly has effects in the world until this day. In other words, I argue that while Galatians is not an anti-Judaic text, its theory of the Jews nevertheless is one that is inimical to Jewish difference, indeed to all difference as such" (1994, 156). Note that I use "anti-Jewish" in the sense of Boyarin's "anti-Judaic" to designate a rejection of the Jews as Jewish believers, and thus a rejection of Judaism.

8. Haas surveys these histories from the monolithic descriptions of "the banality of evil" in an anonymous machinery of destruction (the bureaucratic evil of Adolph Eichmann and of the death camps, with a focus on the perpetrators' perspective; e.g., see Arendt 1963) to the presentation of the *Shoah* as the result of a myriad of individual decisions (with a focus on the diverse experiences of the victims).

9. From Paul (Rom. 1:18–32) to the neo-Marxist reinterpretations of Freud (see Patte 1983:256–77, 382), we have learned this is what happens when one denies a reality close to the core of human existence.

10. As Plank writes, "On the one hand, the fence must be overcome, for its perpetuity grants 'posthumous victory' to Hitler and continually segregates the surviving Jew.... On the other hand, the fence must not be overcome in such a way that robs the Holocaust's victims and survivors of their particular identity, for doing so would only replicate, in another way, the Holocaust's basic condition" (1994, 4).

11. Arthur Cohen, as a Jewish scholar, is an insider who, as a Jew, cannot but face the *Shoah*. He deliberately espouses the title and task of "Jewish theologian" by thinking theologically about the Holocaust through "a revisionary retrieval of Rudolph Otto's language for the holy as the uncanny *mysterium tremendum*" (David Tracy's words in the foreword to Cohen 1981, vii). As such, Cohen seeks to develop "a theological language out of the calamity of Jewish historical existence which is not only relevant to the Jew but to any other monotheist" (1981, xvi).

12. The death camps are the *tremendum* despite this inversion, as Cohen insists: "I call the death camps the *tremendum*, for it is the monument of a meaningless inversion of life to an orgiastic celebration of death, to a psychosexual and pathological degeneracy unparalleled and unfathomable to any person bonded to life" (1981, 19; cf. 98). The *tremendum* is a caesura, a rupture in Jewish history that, unlike the Christian caesura, "emerge[s] from below, a verticality as infernal as incarnation may be divine" (52–53).

13. In sum, from the inside, Cohen underscores that the *tremendum* of the abyss is rooted in the thoughtlessness that fails to account for the constructed character of all that we perceive as significant. Thus, he opens his theological reflections by observing that the Holocaust belongs together with "confounded" thinking, since it is unthinkable. "Thinking and the death camps are incommensurable. The procedures of thought and the ways of knowing are confounded. It is to think the unthinkable — an enterprise that is not alone contradictory but hopeless — for thought entails as much a moral hope (that it may be triumphant, mastering its object, dissolving the difficulties, containing and elucidating the conundrum) as it is the investment of skill and dispassion in a methodic procedure" (1981, 1)

14. This is true, however one might translate Otto's *Gefühle*. For a sophisticated mapping out of this domain of "feelings," see Blumenthal 1993, 23–31.

15. As quoted in Levinas 1991, 115; my translation from the French, "Sachez ce qui s'est passé, n'oubliez pas, et, en même temps, jamais vous ne saurez." I could not find the original.

References

Althusser, Louis. 1984. *Essays on Ideology.* London: Verso.

Arendt, Hannah. 1963. *Eichmann in Jerusalem: A Report on the Banality of Evil.* New York: Viking.

Blumenthal, David R. 1993. *Facing the Abusing God: A Theology of Protest.* Louisville: Westminster/John Knox.

Boyarin, Daniel. 1994. *A Radical Jew: Paul and the Politics of Identity.* Berkeley: University of California Press.

Browing, Christopher R. 1992. *The Path to Genocide: Essays on Launching the Final Solution.* Cambridge and New York: Cambridge University Press.

Burnett, Fred W. 1992. "Exposing the Anti-Jewish Ideology of Matthew's Implied Author: The Characterization of God as Father." Pp. 55–191 in *Ideological Criticism of Biblical Texts,* ed. David Jobling and Tina Pippin. *Semeia* 59. Atlanta: Society of Biblical Literature.

Cohen, Arthur A. 1981. *The Tremendum: A Theological Interpretation of the Holocaust.* New York: Crossroad.

Cosgrove, Charles H. 1997. *Elusive Israel: The Puzzle of Election in Romans.* Louisville: Westminster/John Knox.

Fackenheim, Emil. 1970. *God's Presence in History: Jewish Affirmations and Philosophical Reflections.* New York: New York University Press.

———. 1987. *The Jewish Thought of Emil Fackenheim: A reader.* Ed. Michael L. Morgan. Detroit: Wayne State University Press.

Griffiths, Paul J. 1999. *Religious Reading: The Place of Reading in the Practice of Religion.* New York: Oxford University Press.

Haas, Peter J. 1995. "What We Know Today That We Didn't Know Fifty Years Ago: Fifty Years of Holocaust Scholarship." *CCAR Journal: A Reform Jewish Quarterly* (summer/(fall): 1–15.

———. 1988. *Morality after Auschwitz: The Radical Challenge of the Nazi Ethic.* Philadelphia: Fortress.

Harvey, Van A. 1966. *The Historian and the Believer: The Morality of Historical Knowledge and Christian Belief.* New York: Macmillan.

Levinas, Emmanuel. [1961] 1969. *Totality and Infinity: An Essay on Exteriority.* Trans. Alphonso Lingis. Dusquesne Studies Philosophical Series 24. Pittsburgh: Dusquesne University Press.

———. [1982] 1985. *Ethics and Infinity.* Trans. Richard A. Cohen. Pittsburgh: Dusquesne University Press.

———. [1968, 1977] 1990. *Nine Talmudic Readings.* Trans. Annette Aronowicz. Bloomington: Indiana University Press. (French, 1968 & 1977)

———. 1991. *Entre nous: Essais sur le penser-à-l'autre.* Paris: Bernard Grasset.

Otto, Rudolf. 1923. *The Idea of the Holy: An Inquiry into the Non-rational Factor in the Idea of the Divine and Its Relation to the Rational.* Trans. John W. Harvey. New York: Oxford University Press (quotations taken from the 1958 Galaxy Book edition).

Patte, Daniel. 1983. *Paul's Faith and the Power of the Gospel.* Philadelphia: Fortress.

———. 1987. *The Gospel according to Matthew: A Structural Commentary on Matthew's Faith*. Philadelphia: Fortress. Reprint, Valley Forge, Pa: Trinity Press International.

———. 1988. "Anti-Semitism in the New Testament: Confronting the Dark Side of Paul's and Matthew's Teaching." *Chicago Theological Seminary Register* 78:31–52.

———. 1995. *Ethics of Biblical Interpretation: A Reevaluation*. Louisville: Westminster/John Knox.

Phillips, Gary A. 1999. "The Killing Fields of Matthew's Narrative." Pp. 249–65 in *The Labour of Reading: Desire, Alienation, and Biblical Interpretation*. Ed. Fiona Black, Roland Boer, and Erin Runions. Semeia Studies 36. Atlanta: Scholars Press.

Plank, Karl A. 1994. *Mother of the Wire Fence: Inside and Outside the Holocaust*. Louisville: Westminster/John Knox.

Ruether, Rosemary. 1974. *Faith and Fratricide: The Theological Roots of Anti-Semitism*. New York: Seabury.

Spivak, Gayatri C. 1988. "Can the Subaltern Speak? Pp. 277–313 in *Marxism and the Interpretation of Culture*, ed. G. Nelson and L. Grossberg. London: Macmillan.

Traverso, Enzo. 1996. *L'histoire déchirée. Essai sur Auschwitz et les intellectuels*. Paris: Cerf.

Vahanian, Gabriel. 1966. *No Other God*. New York: Braziller.

———. 1992. *L'utopie chrétienne*. Paris: Desclée de Brouwer.

Weems, Renita. 1999. *Listening for God: A Minister's Journey through Silence and Doubt*. New York: Simon and Schuster.

West, Gerald, and Musa W. Dube, eds. 1996. *"Reading With": An Exploration of the Interface between Critical and Ordinary Readings of the Bible: African Overtures*. *Semeia* 73. Atlanta: Scholars Press.

Israel Reading in "Reading Israel"

Daniel Boyarin

———— ◆ ————

The series for which this book is an opening salvo is a welcome entry into what would otherwise seem to be a rather crowded field, that of Pauline studies. The editors of this series are interested in proposing a dialogue between Pauline scholarship and biblical theology/church history that has not been attempted before in such a systematic and sustained fashion. They are beginning this enterprise with the most theologically crucial of Pauline texts, the Epistle to the Romans, and, moreover, with one of the most vital of questions for all Christian theology (if I may be so bold) and surely for theological readers of Romans, namely, the place of the Jews in the Christian theological (and often enough, physical) world — thus, *Reading Israel in Romans*.

This is, I daresay, theory at its best. Questions of hermeneutics are here put to their ultimate test. How do we read a text when that text is normative and weighty with consequence for our own lives, those of our intimates, and those of others? Or, as a colleague once said to me in the Talmud department at Bar-Ilan University, "Our department is the most important one in the university, for our students go out to kill with volumes of the Talmud under their arms." (And this was a decade before the murder of Yitzhaq Rabin by one of those very students.) People go out to murder and to perform lesser crimes and also acts of love with the Epistle to the Romans tucked under their arms; the ground zero of reading, of theory, is how many dead bodies are left at the other end of the hermeneutical process, how many bodies well fed and well clothed, how many spirits impoverished and how many filled. As the editors of the present volume state right out, "Interpretation of the Bible always matters."

And since interpretation of the Bible always matters, it is obviously correct that all interpretation of the scholarly and "scientific" variety is also conditioned by the mattering that it will do, even when it hardly recognizes that in itself: "To what extent was this theological or critical focus [a certain religious perception of life] chosen by an ordinary believer (or nonbeliever), hidden in the scholarship?" Reflection on the interaction between biblical scholarship and biblical theology/hermeneutics is a task for which it is difficult to find a competitor in importance in the field of humanistic endeavor.

What is important to emphasize in this project is that by setting it up as they do, the editors (and the conveners of the discursive situations in which the text was generated) have implicitly challenged the very binary opposition that they seemingly enshrine, the one between scholars and believers. Through the confrontation with those who declare themselves believers, those who declare themselves scholarly readers (bracketing belief or nonbelief) are challenged to perceive the difference within themselves, the believer (and for this purpose, nonbeliever does just as well, as the editors explicitly remark above) *en kryptō*, who can be disavowed but not denied.

The metaphor "Auschwitz" in this text, while surely retaining all of its concrete specificity — the specificity of bodies of Israel burned there (but if that, then why "Auschwitz," the always/already metaphorical, rather than, less rhetorically, "Nazi genocide"?) — also must surely open up to the body of Matthew Shephard as well, perhaps one of the most recent of victims of a certain reading of "Israel" in Romans; and after all, "Auschwitz" was also a site for the burning of other queer bodies. Numbers here is not the issue; Romans is.

The editors/authors of the overture raise the critical question for this task when they write,

> The role of religious perceptions...has a critical edge. It is not an automatic endorsement of religious perceptions and of their role in scriptural readings. For both the feminist theologian and the biblical critic, there are many scriptural readings that, in our view, are both ethically and academically irresponsible, because the religious perceptions and the particular heteronomous experiences out of which they arise construct the relationship among the analytical/autonomous, the pragmatic/relational, and the hermeneutical/heteronomous in ways that we strongly feel are unacceptable both ethically and academically. Nevertheless, for both of us there are many scriptural readings that are both ethically and academically responsible.

Which obviously raises the question, What is the ground for this value judgment? Indeed, one could say that the formulation given above by the editors/authors not only raises the question but begs the question (in the classical rhetorical and not the modern debased sense). I leave it to readers to decide whether the editors/authors' answer provides a way out of the hermeneutical circle that they draw around themselves and us. Obviously, I feel a certain skepticism, which is not to say that I believe that there are better answers, just that I would adopt a certain necessary — *meiner Meinung nach* — tone of despair. That said, I find the authors bordering on the brilliant in suggesting that three moments of reading (analytical, pragmatic, and hermeneutical) correspond to three states of human existence (autonomy, relationality, and heteronomy). The notion that responsible preaching is the model for responsible scholarship and not its stepchild is startling, rich, and, I think, most productive.

One thing that strikes me is that in their lucent articulation of ways of constructing scriptural authority, as located in the text as Word of God or words about God, these Christian authors seem not to take into their field of cognizance the Logos (incarnate) as authoritative interpreter of the Word of God or of the words about God, or, perhaps better put, the fundamental theological notion that the Word of God in the text or the words about God in the text have been interpreted by many Christians historically as having an authoritative hermeneutical structure alongside of them — the Word of God revealed in the incarnation in Jesus, Messiah. As Robert Brawley will write later in the volume, "God's 'son' is theoretically either the source of the gospel or its content" — or, of course, both, which is what gives Christian reading a certain particular theoretical fascination and structural complexity from the very beginning.

There is no need for me to comment further on the overture, for its text is as lucid as one could desire. Therefore, as the Talmud says, "Go and read the rest"; and I will do so also, providing now some responses, more occasional than systematic, to the actual products of the tripolar reading practice that is envisioned in this volume.

If there is anything that Karl Barth has written with which I can heartily agree, it is surely, "Our problems are the problems of Paul." I part company with him, however, at, "If we be enlightened by the brightness of his answers, those answers must be ours." In general, I find that Thomas Parker's reproduction of Barth on Romans 4 hardly advances any independent theological or hermeneutical project, because precisely, if I have not misunderstood, the tension between the three poles of a tripolar reading of the analytical, contextual, and hermeneutical has been lost. Paul and Paul's text disappear in such a heavily theological practice of reading (which is not to delegitimate the practice within its own ecclesial framework, but precisely to mark the irony that the Barth who, according to Parker, is less oriented toward the ecclesial and more toward the existential than Luther or Calvin, provides less for the non-Christian than either of those); the ecclesial is universal and the universal proves ecclesial. I do not want to be included in Barth's "us," and find his readings consistently excluding, while those readings that focus on the specificity, even the particularity of Paul's claims for a universal "church" allow me some room to listen to them and him. Barth leaves me room only to protest with Tonto: What do you mean "we"?

Indeed, in his identification of "Judaism" as, among other things, the bourgeois Christianity that all people are called upon to renounce, Barth offends every bit as much as does Käsemann in his identification of the "inner Jew" that is in everyone in Romans 2 (and out of the same broad tradition). Why should I have to listen to such talk? I would rather listen to Paul (and to Luther, let alone Calvin).

I am on happier ground from the beginning of Robert Brawley's essay, which marks that Romans speaks with multiple voices from the beginnings of its history of reception. Brawley, unlike most biblical scholars, seems to have a clear sense of what "intertextuality" means (in some essays for a recent issue of *Semeia,* one finds the term being used as a synonym for allusion and utilized to anchor meanings). Brawley has done his homework and really understands the literary theory that he invokes, and to good effect. He moves us forward in reading Romans. Brawley writes clearly, "[Romans'] language and rhetoric [like that of all other texts] derive from an indeterminate intertextuality that already represents a host of voices." In an important (if not unique) move, Brawley accordingly refuses to make certain exegetical choices that have animated the work of many critics, choosing rather to leave the ambiguity between various interpretive possibilities in place and in play — notably the (no longer) vexed question of the "faith of Jesus Christ." However, he does not merely leave ambiguity alone; he explores its determination through the multiple scriptural and cultural voices that are incorporated in the multilayered text of Romans 1–4. We are not, accordingly, thrown into a (largely imaginary) postmodern world of nihilistic anarchy in interpretation, but rather, a very precise account of ambiguity in the text, generated through its multiple registers and voices, as the reservoir of disagreement among interpreters — disagreement that can, itself, now not be read as a problem but as a resource. The possibilities of appropriation of this readerly perspective for a faithful community are palpable.

The essay of Joseph Sievers is the first one to adopt the categories that emerged in the collective work of the group and were further developed in the overture to the volume, namely, the interaction between the theological and the philological in the interpretation of Romans. However, it seems to do so in a way explicitly counter to the program of the editors of the volume, namely, by announcing a procedure that places the philological as autonomous of and preceding the theological. That said, the essay is a highly useful survey of the history of exegesis of Rom. 11:29, showing, among other things, how an early, ambiguous translation in the Latin versions produced strange theological notions (or perhaps, strange theological notions provoked a particular acceptance of an equivocal term in the Latin — and here is where perhaps we can detect a glimmering of the theoretical position outlined by the editors).

Wasserberg's essay is perhaps a caution of the limits of theology as one of the philological disciplines (*sic*). Nanos disagrees. I too find the whole enterprise misguided. Paul certainly argued as a Jew for a fundamentally new interpretation of Judaism. There is nothing problematic in that. What Christians have to repent is not Paul but the *Wirkungsgeschichte,* for which Paul is not (directly) responsible. Christians may hold any theology they wish, including supersession. (Why not? After all, biblical theology is supersessionist with respect to polytheists!) They just have to learn to let Jews live. There is nothing in Paul, however understood, that precludes that. I suspect that what I am saying is, in fact, not all that different from Nanos, but on exegetical grounds (which I have defended at length in my own book on Paul), I find hard to credit the notion that Paul's strictures against the law after Christ are directed only at Gentile Christians, or for that matter, only at Christians altogether.

Campbell's helpful essay is interesting in precisely the same way that Brawley's is, that is, it provides resources for hermeneutics from the insights of literary exegetics, suggesting, like Brawley, that the divergent readings of Romans through the history of reception are already encoded in the text in its own intertexuality: "[It] is not just that there are divergent readings of the letter itself, but rather that there were already in existence, whether implicitly or explicitly, divergent understandings of the significance of Paul's gospel and mission." He then sets out to explore some of that intertextual dimension, but unfortunately, at that point his essay evolves into an interesting but preintertextuality theory exegetical exercise. In other words, once more we have a Paul, who can be consistent or inconsistent, but not a language or set of languages, communities, ideologies speaking through the textuality of Paul's letters. This, in turn, enables Nanos's text understandably to miss the radical force of Campbell's theoretical proposal, since the latter's interpretative practice does not quite live up to the declared promise. Nanos's essay does make some beginning in inscribing the two-way relays of exegetical and theological vectors, including implicitly the vector of experience, if not, strictly speaking, of religious experience as well.

In short, I find here a promising direction for new ways of reading Paul, well worth pursuing, and I look forward to the future installments of the project.

Contributors

——— ◆ ———

DANIEL BOYARIN teaches Talmudic culture at the University of California, Berkeley. He is the author of *Intertextuality and the Reading of Midrash* (1990); *Carnal Israel: Reading Sex in Talmudic Culture* (1993); *A Radical Jew: Paul and the Politics of Identity* (1994); *Unheroic Conduct: The Rise of Heterosexuality and the Invention of the Jewish Man* (1997); and *Dying for God: Martyrdom and the Making of Christianity and Judaism* (1999).

ROBERT L. BRAWLEY teaches New Testament at McCormick Theological Seminary, Chicago. He is the author of *Luke-Acts and the Jews: Conflict, Apology, and Conciliation* (1987); *Centering on God: Method and Message in Luke-Acts* (1990); *Text to Text Pours Forth Speech: Voices of Scripture in Luke-Acts* (1995); and the editor of *Biblical Ethics and Homosexuality: Listening to Scripture* (1996).

WILLIAM S. CAMPBELL teaches New Testament at the University of Wales, Lampeter. He is the author of *Paul's Gospel in an Intercultural Context: Jew and Gentile in the Letter to the Romans* (1991); important essays on Romans, including "Romans 3 as a Key to the Structure and Thought of the Letter" (1991, in K. P. Donfried, ed., *The Romans Debate*) and "The Rule of Faith in Romans 12:1–15:13" (1995, in D. M. Hay and E. Johnson, eds., *Pauline Theology*, vol. 3); and the editor of the *Journal of Beliefs and Values: Studies in Religion and Education*.

CRISTINA GRENHOLM teaches in theology and gender studies at Karlstad University, Sweden, from where she directs a long-term research project on "Subordination in Theology: Fundamental Principle or Heavy Deadweight?" She is the author of *Romans Interpreted: A Comparative Analysis of the Commentaries of Barth, Nygren, Cranfield and Wilckens on Paul's Epistle to the Romans* (1990); *The Old Testament, Christianity and Pluralism* (1996); and *Merciful and Vulnerable: Contemporary Christian Faith in Jesus* (in Swedish, 1999).

MARK D. NANOS pursues research in Pauline studies at the University of St. Andrews from his Jewish perspective. He is the author of *The Mystery of Romans: The Jewish Context of Paul's Letter* (1996, National Jewish Book Award for Jewish-Christian Relations); *Galatians, An Ironic Rebuke* (forthcoming); and several articles, including "The Jewish Context of the Gentile Audience Addressed in Paul's Letter to the Romans" (1999) and "The Inter- and Intra-Jewish Political Contexts of Paul and the Galatians" (2000).

THOMAS D. PARKER is professor emeritus of McCormick Theological Seminary, Chicago, where he taught systematic theology. A specialist in Karl Barth, he is a coeditor of *Christian Theology: A Case Method Approach* (1976) and *Peace, War and God's Justice: Essays Prepared for the Theological Committee of the Caribbean and North American Area Council of the World Alliance of Reformed Churches* (1989).

DANIEL PATTE teaches New Testament at Vanderbilt University. He is the author of *Early Jewish Hermeneutic in Palestine* (1975); *Paul's Faith and the Power of the Gospel* (1983); *Preaching Paul* (1984); *The Religious Dimensions of Biblical Texts* (1990); *Ethics of Biblical Interpretation* (1995); *Discipleship According to the Sermon on the Mount: Four Legitimate Readings, Four Plausible Views of Discipleship, and Their Relative Values* (1996); and *The Challenge of Discipleship: A Critical Study of the Sermon on the Mount as Scripture* (1999).

JOSEPH SIEVERS teaches Jewish history and literature of the Hellenistic period at the Pontifical Biblical Institute, Rome. He is the author of *The Hasmoneans and Their Supporters: From Mattathias to the Death of John Hyrcanus I* (1990); and coeditor of *Josephus and the History of the Greco-Roman Period: Essays in Memory of Morton Smith* (1994). Besides his many essays on Josephus and Judaism in late antiquity and his other editorial work, he is a coeditor of *Good and Evil after Auschwitz: Ethical Implications for Today* (2000).

GÜNTER WASSERBERG teaches New Testament at Christian Albrechts University, Kiel, and is a pastor of the Evangelical-Lutheran Church, Nordelbien (Germany). He is the author of *Aus Israels Mitte — Heil für die Welt: Eine narrativ-exegetische Studie zur Theologie des Lukas* (1998); of several essays, including "Theologie nach Auschwitz — Stunde Null und weiter wie gehabt?"; and a coauthor of *Preaching Luke-Acts* (forthcoming).

Index of Scriptural References

————— ◆ —————

Index of Names

——— ◆ ———

Index of Subjects

———— ◆ ————

ANALYTICAL FRAMES

(Critical categories: "textual dimensions" viewed as most significant and analytical methods)

Analytical frame
  definition of, 7, 13, 36f, 41f
  in tripolar interpretive process, 18, 20–34, 228–35, 247f

Ambivalence of the text, 157f
Authorial audience, 75f

Consistency of the text, 188–89, 194, 198, 199, 200, 202f, 206, 229

Diatribe in the text, 75, 99

Existential exegesis, 57, 109–10

Form criticism
  of doxology, 181
  of fixed religious axiom, 135
Function of the text, 182

Gabler's gap, 21–27
Grammatical and syntactical construction, 83

Historical-critical exegesis, 58, 98

Inconsistencies of the text, 187f, 190, 194, 198, 200, 218ff, 229
Intertextuality, 74, 84
Intratextual relations, 128, 135, 158, 184, 194, 207f, 227

Literal (or historical) sense, 58

Narrative in and beyond the text
  Jesus as centerpoint, 70
  narrator, 75
  plot, 88

Patriarchy in the text, 107, 115ff
Pattern of thought, 216
Philology, 130ff
Reference to biblical texts, 199
Rhetoric of conversation, 60

Scriptural criticism
  believers' reading as model, 8–12
  vs. bipolar practice, 21–30
  definition, 3, 19ff
  preachers' interpretive practice as model, 12ff, 248
  as tripolar practice, 14–19, 30–34, 248
  vs. unipolar practice, 20
Scriptural criticism accounting for
  autonomy, 9, 35
  heteronomy, 9–12, 35
  readers'/believers' concrete life situations, 3, 7, 35
  readers'/believers' religious perceptions of life, 3, 7, 35
  relationality, 9, 35
  text and its religious dimensions, 3, 35
  three frames of scriptural interpretation, 36–42
Social identity, 221
Sociological approach, 192, 203
Subject matter of the text, 57, 59, 99

Text as multivocal
  authorial voice, 75
  voice of Abraham, 85
  voice of Abraham's descendants, 86
  voice of God, 78f, 87, 100f, 113f
  voice of narrator, 75
  voice of Paul, 189
  voice of Scripture, 81f, 84, 97

CONTEXTUAL FRAMES

*(Bridge-Categories Interrelating
Text and Life, Contexts, and
Contextual Approaches)*

HERMENEUTICAL FRAMES

(Theological categories interrelating text and religious perception of life)